Eric Hobsbawm was born in Alexandria in 1917 and educated in Austria, Germany and England. He was a Fellow of the British Academy and the American Academy of Arts and Sciences, and a Foreign Member of the Japan Academy, with honorary degrees from universities in several countries. He taught until retirement at Birkbeck College, University of London, and then at the New School for Social Research in New York. In addition to *The Age of Revolution 1789–1848*, *The Age of Capital 1848–1875*, *The Age of Empire 1875–1914* and *The Age of Extremes 1914–1991*, his books include *Bandits*, *Revolutionaries*, *Uncommon People*, *How to Change the World: Tales of Marx and Marxism* and his memoir, *Interesting Times*. All have been translated into several languages.

Eric Hobsbawm died in London in October 2012, aged 95.

Interesting Times

A Twentieth-Century Life

ERIC HOBSBAWM

ABACUS

ABACUS

First published in hardback in Great Britain by
Allen Lane, an imprint of Penguin Books, in 2002
This paperback edition published by Abacus in 2003.
Reprinted 2005, 2006, 2008, 2009, 2010, 2012 (three times), 2013, 2014

The author and publishers are grateful to the following
for permission to reproduce copyright material:

R. S. Thomas, 'Song at the Year's Turning', from *The Border Country*, published
by Rupert Hart Davis, reproduced by permission of HarperCollins;

A. E. Housman, 'Epitaph on an Army of Mercenaries', from *Last Poems*,
published by Harrap UK and Henry Holt USA, reproduced by permission
of the Society of Authors, Literary Representative of the Estate of
A. E. Housman, and the publishers;

Bertolt Brecht, translated by John Willett, from *Poems 1923–1956*, published by
Suhrkamp Verlag in German and Methuen Publishing Ltd in English, reproduced
by permission of the publishers;

Pablo Neruda translated by Eric Hobsbawm, from *Canto General*, published by
Editorial Losada, Buenos Aires, reproduced by permission of the publishers.

A CIP catalogue record for this book is available from the British Library.

ISBN 978-0-349-11353-1

Typeset in Times Roman by
Rowland Phototypesetting Ltd, Bury St Edmunds, Suffolk
Printed and bound in Great Britain by Clays Ltd, St Ives plc

Papers used by Abacus are from well-managed forests
and other responsible sources.

MIX
Paper from
responsible sources
FSC
www.fsc.org   FSC® C104740

Abacus
An imprint of
Little, Brown Book Group
100 Victoria Embankment
London EC4Y 0DY

An Hachette UK Company
www.hachette.co.uk

www.littlebrown.co.uk

To my grandchildren

Contents

CONTENTS

List of Illustrations

Photographic acknowledgements appear in parentheses.

List of Illustrations

completely from sight, like my parents' grave stone in the Vienna Central Cemetery, for which I vainly searched one January so, there would be an discernible gap in the narrative of the past, Japanese in twentieth-century history and of British intellectual life.

Preface

Writers of autobiographies have also to be readers of autobiographies. In the course of writing this book I have been surprised to find how many of the men and women I have known have gone into print about their own lives, not to mention the (usually) more eminent or scandalous ones who have had them written by other people. And I am not even counting the considerable number of autobiographical writings by contemporaries disguised as fiction. Perhaps the surprise is unjustified. People whose profession implies writing and communicating tend to move around among other people who do so. Still, there they are, articles, interviews, print, tapes, even videotapes, and volumes such as this, a surprisingly large number of them by men and women who have spent their careers in universities. I am not alone.

Nevertheless, the question arises why someone like myself should write an autobiography and, more to the point, why others who have no particular connections with me, or may not even have known of my existence before seeing the jacket in a bookshop, should find it worth reading. I do not belong to the people who appear to be classified as a special sub-species in the biography section of at least one London bookshop chain as 'Personalities', or, as the jargon of today has it, 'celebrities', that is to say people sufficiently widely known, for whatever reason, for their very name to arouse curiosity about their lives. I do not belong to the class whose public lives entitle them to call their autobiographies 'Memoirs', generally men and women who have actions on a wider public stage to record or defend, or who have lived close to great events and those who took decisions affecting them. I have not been among them. Probably my name will figure in the histories of one or two specialized fields, such as twentieth-century Marxism and historiography, and perhaps it will crop up in some books on twentieth-century British intellectual culture. Beyond that, if my name were somehow to disappear completely from sight, like my parents' gravestone in the Vienna Central Cemetery, for which I vainly searched five years ago, there would be no discernible gap in the narrative of what happened in twentieth-century history, in Britain or elsewhere.

Again, this book is not written in the now very saleable confessional mode, partly because the only justification for such an ego-trip is genius – I am neither a St Augustine nor a Rousseau – partly because no living autobiographer could tell the private truth about matters involving other living people without unjustifiably hurting the feelings of some of them. I have no good reason for doing so. That field belongs to posthumous biography and not to autobiography. In any case, however curious we are about these matters, historians are not gossip columnists. The military merits of generals are not to be judged by what they do, or fail to do, in bed. All attempts to derive Keynes's or Schumpeter's economics from their rather full but different sex lives are doomed. Besides, I suspect that readers with a taste for biographies that lift bedclothes would find my own life disappointing.

Nor is it written as an apologia for the author's life. If you do *not* want to understand the twentieth century, read the autobiographies of the self-justifiers, the counsels for their own defence, and of their obverse, the repentant sinners. All of these are post-mortem inquests in which the corpse pretends to be the coroner. The autobiography of an intellectual is necessarily also about his ideas, attitudes and actions, but it should not be a piece of advocacy. I think this book contains answers to the questions that I have been most often asked by journalists and others interested in the somewhat unusual case of a lifelong but anomalous communist and 'Hobsbawm the Marxist historian', but answering them has not been my object. History may judge my politics – in fact it has substantially judged them – readers may judge my books. Historical understanding is what I am after, not agreement, approval or sympathy.

Nevertheless, there are some reasons why it may be worth reading, apart from the curiosity of human beings about other human beings. I have lived through almost all of the most extraordinary and terrible century in human history. I have lived in a few countries and seen something of several others in three continents. I may not have left an observable mark on the world in the course of this long life, although I have left a good quantity of printed marks on paper, but since I became conscious of being a historian at the age of sixteen I have watched and listened for most of it and tried to understand the history of my lifetime.

When, having written the history of the world between the late eighteenth century and 1914, I finally tried my hand at the history of what I called *The Age of Extremes: The Short Twentieth Century*, I think it benefited from the fact that I wrote about it not only as a scholar but as what the anthropologists call a 'participant observer'. It did so in two ways. Clearly my personal memories of events remote in time and space brought the history of the twentieth century closer to younger readers, while it reawakened their own memories in older ones. And, more even than my other books, however compelling the obligations of historical scholarship, this one was written with the passion that belongs to the age of extremes. Both kinds of readers have told me so. But beyond this there is a more profound way in which the interweaving of one person's life and times, and the observation of both, helped to shape a historical analysis which, I hope, makes itself independent of both.

That is what an autobiography can do. In one sense this book is the flip side of *The Age of Extremes*: not world history illustrated by the experiences of an individual, but world history shaping that experience, or rather offering a shifting but always limited set of choices from which, to adapt Karl Marx's phrase, 'men make [their lives], but they do not make [them] just as they please, they do not make [them] under circumstances chosen by themselves, but under circumstances directly encountered, given and transmitted from the past' and, one might add, by the world around them.

In another sense the autobiography of a historian is an important part of the construction of his or her work. Next to a belief in reason and the difference between fact and fiction, self-awareness, that is to say standing both in one's body and outside it, is a necessary skill for players of the game in both history and the social sciences, particularly for a historian who, like myself, has chosen his subjects intuitively and accidentally, but ended by bringing them together into a coherent whole. Other historians may pay attention to these more professional aspects of my book. However, I hope others will read it as an introduction to the most extraordinary century in the world's history through the itinerary of one human being whose life could not possibly have occurred in any other.

History, as my colleague the philosopher Agnes Heller put it, 'is about what happens seen from outside, memoirs about what happens seen from within'. This is not a book for scholarly acknowledgements, but only for thanks and apologies. The thanks go above all to my wife Marlene who has lived through half my life, read and criticized all chapters to good purpose and who tolerated the years when an often distracted, bad-tempered and sometimes discouraged husband lived less in the present than in a past he struggled to put on paper. I also thank Stuart Proffitt, a prince among editors. The number of people whom I have consulted over the years on questions relevant to this autobiography is too large for acknowledgement, even though several of them have died since I began. They know why I thank them.

My apologies also go to Marlene and the family. This is not the autobiography they might have preferred, for, though they are constantly present, at least from the moment when they entered my life and I theirs, this book is more about the public than the private man. I should also apologize to those friends, colleagues, students and others absent from these pages, who might have expected to find themselves remembered here, or recalled at greater length.

Finally, I have organized the book in three parts. After a brief overture, the personal–political chapters 1–16, roughly in chronological order, cover the period from when memory begins – in the early 1920s – to the early 1990s. However, they are not intended as a straightforward chronicle. Chapters 17 and 18 are about my career as a professional historian. Chapters 19–22 are about countries or regions (other than my native Mitteleuropa and England) with which I have had associations for long periods of my life: France, Spain and Italy, Latin America and other parts of the Third World and the USA. Since they cover the entire range of my dealings with these countries, they do not fit easily into the main chronological narrative, though they overlap with it. I have therefore thought it best to keep them separate.

Eric Hobsbawm
London, April 2002

1

Overture

lived. And aunt Nancy photographed them. I had thought she was the only one two still shared a connection of the Seutter Villa. Now it quite alive again.

I have that photo too, in my own family photos, which have ended up with me, the last survivor of my parents' and siblings, the snapshots on the terrace of the Seutter Villa form the record contigue, the record of the existence and the brief of my sister Nancy

One day in the autumn of 1994, my wife Marlene, who kept track of the London correspondence while I was teaching my course at the New School in New York, phoned me to say there was a letter from Hamburg she could not read, as it was in German. It came from a person who signed herself Melitta. Was it worth sending on? I knew no one in Hamburg, but without a moment's hesitation I knew who had written it, even though something like three quarters of a century had passed since I had last seen the signatory. It could only be little Litta – actually she was my senior by a year or so – from the Seutter Villa in Vienna. I was right. She had, she wrote, seen my name in some connection in *Die Zeit*, the German liberal-intellectual weekly. She had immediately concluded that I must be the Eric with whom she and her sisters had played long, long ago. She had rummaged through her albums and come up with a photo which she enclosed.

On it five small children posed on the summery terrace of the villa with our respective Fräuleins, the little girls – perhaps even myself – garlanded with flowers. Litta was there with her younger sisters Ruth and Eva (Susie, always known as Peter, was not yet born), I with my sister Nancy. Her father had marked the date on the back: 1922. And how was Nancy, Litta asked. How could she know that Nancy, three-and-a-half years my junior, had died a couple of years earlier? On my last visit to Vienna I had gone to the houses in which we had

1

lived, and sent Nancy photographs of them. I had thought she was the only one who still shared a memory of the Seutter Villa. Now it came alive again.

I have that photo too. In the album of family photos which has ended up with me, the last survivor of my parents and siblings, the snapshots on the terrace of the Seutter Villa form the second iconographic record of my existence and the first of my sister Nancy, born in Vienna in 1920. My own first record appears to be a picture of a baby in a very large wicker pram, without adults or other context, which was, I assume, taken in Alexandria, where I was born in June 1917, to have my presence registered by a clerk at the British Consulate (incorrectly, for they got the date wrong and misspelled the surname). The diplomatic institutions of the United Kingdom presided over both my conception and my birth, for it was at another British Consulate, in Zurich, that my father and mother had been married, with the help of an official dispensation personally signed by Sir Edward Grey, Foreign Secretary, which allowed the subject of King George V, Leopold Percy Hobsbaum, to marry the subject of the Emperor Franz Josef, Nelly Grün, at a time when both empires were at war with one another, a conflict to which my future father reacted with residual British patriotism, but which my future mother repudiated. In 1915 there was no conscription in Britain, but if there were, she told him, he should register as a Conscientious Objector.[1] I would like to think that they were married by the consul who is the main figure in Tom Stoppard's play *Travesties*. I should also like to think that while they were waiting in Zurich for Sir Edward Grey to turn from more urgent matters to their wedding, they knew about their fellow-exiles in the city, Lenin, James Joyce and the Dadaists. However, they obviously did not, and almost certainly would not have been interested in them at such a time. They were plainly more concerned with their forthcoming honeymoon in Lugano.

What would have been my life if Fräulein Grün, aged eighteen, one of three daughters of a moderately prosperous Viennese jeweller, had not fallen in love with an older Englishman, fourth of eight children of an immigrant London Jewish cabinet-maker, in Alexandria in 1913? She would presumably have married a young man from the Jewish Mitteleuropean middle class, and her children would have grown up as Austrians. Since almost all young Austrian Jews ended up as emigrants or refugees, my subsequent life might not have looked very different – plenty of them came to England, studied here and became academics. But I would not have grown up or come to Britain with a native British passport.

Unable to live in either belligerent country, my parents returned via Rome and Naples to Alexandria, where they had originally met and got engaged before the war, and where both had relatives – my mother's uncle Albert, of whose emporium of *Nouveautés* plus staff I still have a photograph, and my father's brother Ernest, whose name I bear and who worked in the Egyptian Post and Telegraph Service. (Since all private lives are raw material for historians as for novelists, I have used the circumstances of their meeting to introduce my history of *The Age of Empires*.) They moved to Vienna with their two-year-old son as soon as the war ended. That is why Egypt, to which I am shackled by the lifetime chains of official documentation, is not part of my life. I remember absolutely nothing about it except, possibly, a cage of small birds in the zoo at Nouzha, and a corrupt fragment of a Greek children's song, presumably sung by a Greek nursemaid. Nor have I any curiosity about my place of birth, the district known as Sporting Club, along the tramline from the centre of Alexandria to Ramleh, but then, there is not much to be said about it, according to E. M. Forster, whose stay in Alexandria almost coincided with my parents'. All he says about the tram station Sporting Club in his *Alexandria, A History and a Guide* is: 'Close to the Grand Stand of the Race Course. Bathing beach on the left.'

Egypt thus does not belong in my life. I do not know when the life of memory begins, but not much of it goes back to the age of two. I have never gone there since the steamer *Helouan* left Alexandria for Trieste, then just transferred from Austria to Italy. I do not remember anything about our arrival in Trieste, meeting-point of languages and races, a place of opulent cafés, sea captains and the headquarters of the giant insurance company, Assicurazioni Generali, whose business empire probably defines the concept of 'Mitteleuropa' better than any other. Eighty years later I had occasion to discover it in the company of Triestine friends, and especially Claudio Magris, that marvellous memorializer of central Europe and the Adriatic corner where German, Italian, Slav and Hungarian cultures converge. My grandfather, who had come to meet us, accompanied us on the Southern Railway to Vienna. That is where my conscious life began. We lived with my grandparents for some months, while my parents looked for an apartment of their own.

My father, arriving with hard savings – nothing was harder than sterling in those days – in an impoverished country with a currency subsiding towards collapse, felt confident and relatively prosperous. The Seutter Villa seemed ideal. It was the first place in my life I thought of as 'ours'.

Anyone who comes to Vienna by rail from the west still passes it. If you look out of the right-hand window as the train comes into the western outskirts of Vienna, by the local station Hütteldorf-Hacking, it is impossible to miss that confident broad pile on the hillside with its four-sided dome on a squat tower, built by a successful industrialist in the later days of the Emperor Franz Josef (1848–1916). Its grounds reached down to the Auhofstrasse, which led to the west along the walls of the old imperial hunting ground, the Lainzer Tiergarten, and from which it was reached by a narrow uphill street (the Vinzenz-Hessgasse, now Seuttergasse) at the bottom of which there was then still a row of thatched cottages.

The Seutter Villa of my childhood memories is largely the part shared by the old and young of the Hobsbaums (for so, in spite of the Alexandrian consular clerk, the name was spelled), who rented a flat on the first floor of the villa, and the Golds, who rented the ground-floor apartment below us. Essentially this centred on the terrace at the side of the house, where so much of the social life of the generations of both these families was conducted. From this terrace a footpath – steep in retrospect – led down to the tennis courts at the bottom – they are now built over – past what seemed to a small boy a giant tree, but with branches low enough for climbing. I remember showing its secrets to a boy who had come to my school from a place called Recklinghausen in Germany. We had been asked to take care of him, because times were hard where he came from. I can remember nothing about him except the tree and his home-town in what is now the Land Nordrhein-Westfalen. He soon went back. Though I did not think of it as such, this must have been my first contact with the major events of twentieth-century history, namely the French occupation of the Ruhr in 1923, via one of the children temporarily sent out of harm's way to well-wishers in Austria. (All Austrians at that time saw themselves as Germans, and, but for a veto from the peacemakers after the First World War, would have voted to join Germany.) I also have a vivid memory of us playing in a barn full of hay somewhere in the grounds, but on my last visit to Vienna with Marlene we checked out the Villa and could find no place where it might have been. Curiously enough, I have no indoor memories of the place, though a vague impression that it was neither very light nor very comfortable. I cannot, for instance, recall anything about our own or the Golds' apartments, except perhaps high ceilings.

Five, later six, children of pre-school age, or at best in the first years of primary school, in the same garden, are great cementers of inter-family relations. The Hobsbaums and the Golds got on well, in spite of their very different backgrounds – for (notwithstanding their name) the Golds do not seem to have been Jewish. At all events they remained and flourished in Austria, that is to say in Hitler's Greater Germany, after the Anschluss. Both Mr and Mrs Gold came from Sieghartskirchen, a nowheresville in Lower Austria, he the son of the only local innkeeper–farmer, she the daughter of the only village shopkeeper (anything from socks to agricultural equipment). Both maintained strong family links there. They were sufficiently prosperous in the 1920s to have their portraits painted – a black-and-white copy of the two, sent by one of the two surviving Gold girls a year or so ago, is before me. The picture of a serious-looking gentleman in a dark lounge suit and a starched collar brings nothing back, and indeed I had no close contact with him as a small boy, although he once showed me his officer's cap from the days before the end of the empire, and was the first person I knew who had actually been to the USA, to which he had travelled on business. From there he brought a gramophone record, the tune of which I now recognize as 'The Peanut Vendor', and the information that they had a make of motor-car called 'Buick', a name I found, for some obscure reason, hard to credit. On the other hand the image of a handsome long-necked lady with short hair waved at the sides, looking at the world with a serious but not very self-confident gaze over her *décolleté* shoulder, immediately brings her to life in my mind. For mothers are a much more constant presence in the life of young children, and my mother, Nelly, intellectual, cosmopolitan, educated, and Anna ('Antschi') Gold, with little schooling, always conscious of the provincialism of her origins, soon became best friends and remained so to the end. Indeed, according to her daughter Melitta, Nelly was Anna's *only* intimate friend. This may explain why photos of unknown and unidentifiable Hobsbawms still keep turning up in family albums of the Gold grandchildren who remained in Vienna. One of the Gold girls recalls, almost as vividly as I do, going (with her mother) to see my mother in her last days. Weeping, Antschi told her: 'We will never see Nelly again.'

Two people, almost as old as the 'short twentieth century', thus began life together and then made their different ways through the extraordinary and terrible world of the past century. That is why I begin the present reflections on a long life with the unexpected reminder of a photo in the albums of two families which had nothing else in common except that their lives were briefly brought together in the Vienna of the 1920s. For memories of a few years of early childhood shared by a retired university professor and peripatetic historian with a retired former actress, television presenter and occasional translator ('like your mother!') are of little more than private interest for the people concerned. Even for them, they are no more than the thinnest of threads of spider silk bridging the enormous space between some seventy years of entirely separate, unconnected lives conducted without knowledge or even without a moment's conscious thought of one another. It is the extraordinary experience of Europeans living through the twentieth century that binds these lives together. A rediscovered common childhood, a renewal of contact in old age, dramatize the image of our times: absurd, ironic, surrealist and monstrous. They do not create them. Ten years after the five infants looked at the camera, my parents were dead, and Mr Gold, victim of the economic cataclysm – virtually all the banks of central Europe were technically insolvent in 1931 – was on his way with his family to serve the banking system in Persia, whose Shah preferred his bankers from remote and defeated empires rather than from neighbouring and dangerous ones. Fifteen years after, while I was at an English university, the Gold girls, returned from the palaces of Shiraz, were – all of them – beginning their careers as actresses in what was about to become part of Hitler's Greater

Germany. Twenty years after, I was in the uniform of a British soldier in England, my sister Nancy was censoring letters for the British authorities in Trinidad, while Litta was performing under our bombs in the Kabarett der Komiker in wartime Berlin to an audience, some of whom may well have rounded up my relatives who had probably patted the Gold girls' heads at the Seutter Villa, for transport to the camps. Five years later, as I began to teach in the bombed ruins of London, both the Gold parents were dead – he, probably from hunger, in the immediate aftermath of defeat and occupation, she, evacuated into the western Alps before the end, of disease.

The past is another country, but it has left its mark on those who once lived there. But it has also left its mark on those too young to have known it, except by hearsay, or even, in an a-historically structured civilization, to treat it, in the words of a game briefly popular towards the end of the twentieth century, as a 'Trivial Pursuit'. However, it is the autobiographical historian's business not simply to revisit it, but to map it. For without such a map, how can we track the paths of a lifetime through its changing landscapes, or understand why and when we hesitated and stumbled, or how we lived among those with whom our lives were intertwined and on whom they depended? For these things throw light not only on single lives but on the world.

So this may serve as the starting-point for one historian's attempt to retrace a path through the craggy terrain of the twentieth century: five small children posed eighty years ago by adults on a terrace in Vienna, unaware (unlike their parents) that they are surrounded by the debris of defeat, ruined empires and economic collapse, unaware (like their parents) that they would have to make their way through the most murderous as well as the most revolutionary era in history.

2

A Child in Vienna

I spent my childhood in the impoverished capital of a great empire, attached, after the empire's collapse, to a smallish provincial republic of great beauty, which did not believe it ought to exist. With few exceptions, Austrians after 1918 thought they should be part of Germany, and were prevented from doing so only by the powers that had imposed the peace settlement on central Europe. The economic troubles of the years of my childhood did nothing to increase their belief in the viability of the first Austrian Federal Republic. It had just passed through a revolution, and had settled down temporarily under a government of clerical reactionaries headed by a Monsignor, based on the votes of a pious, or at least strongly conservative, countryside, which was confronted by a hated opposition of revolutionary Marxist socialists, massively supported in Vienna (not only the capital but an autonomous state of the Federal Republic) and almost unanimously by all who identified themselves as 'workers'. In addition to police and army, which were under government control, both sides were associated with paramilitary groups, for whom the civil war had been only suspended. Austria was not only a state which did not want to exist, but a predicament which could not last.

It did not last. But the final convulsions of the first Austrian Republic – the destruction of the social democrats after a brief civil war, the assassination of the Catholic prime minister by Nazi rebels, Hitler's triumphant and applauded entry into Vienna – happened after I left Vienna in 1931. I was not to return there until 1960, when the very same country, under the very same two-party system of Catholics and Socialists, had become a stable, enormously prosperous and neutral little republic, perfectly satisfied – some might say too satisfied – with its identity.

But this is a historian's retrospect. What was a middle-class childhood like in the Vienna of the 1920s? The problem is how to distinguish what one has learned since from what contemporaries knew or thought, and the experiences and reactions of adults from those who were children at that time. What children born in 1917 knew of the events of the still young twentieth century which were so alive in the minds of parents and grandparents – war, breakdown, revolution, inflation – was what adults told us or, more likely, what we overheard them talking about. The only direct evidence we had of them were the changing images on postage stamps. Stamp collecting in the 1920s, though it was far from self-explanatory, was a good introduction to the political history of Europe since 1914. For an expatriate British boy it dramatized the contrast between the unchanging continuity of George V's head on British stamps and the chaos of overprints, new names and new currencies elsewhere. The only other direct line to history came through the changing coins and banknotes of an era of economic disruption. I was old enough to be conscious of the change from Kronen to Schillings and Groschen, from multi-zeroed notes to notes and coins, and I knew that before Kronen there had been Gulden.

Though the Habsburg Empire had gone, we still lived on its infrastructure and, to a surprising extent, by pre-1914 central European assumptions. The husband of one of my mother's great friends, Dr Alexander Szana, lived in Vienna and, unhappily for his wife's peace of mind, worked on a German-language newspaper thirty miles down the Danube in what we called Pressburg and the Hungarians called Pozsony, and what had then become Bratislava, the chief Slovak city in the new Czechoslovak Republic. (It is now the capital of an internationally sovereign Slovakia.) Except for the expulsion of former Hungarian officials, between the wars it had not yet been ethnically cleansed of its polyglot and polycultural population of Germans, Hungarians, Czechs and Slovaks, assimilated westernized and pious Carpathian Jews, gypsies and the rest. It had not yet *really* become a Slovak city of 'Bratislavaks' from which those with memories of what it had remained until the Second World War still distinguish themselves as 'Pressburaks'. He went there and returned by the Pressburger Bahn, a tram which ran from a street in the centre of Vienna to a loop on the central streets of Pressburg. It had been inaugurated in the spring of 1914 when both cities were part of the same empire, a triumph of modern technology, and simply carried on; as did the famous 'opera train' by which the cultured of Brünn/Brno in Moravia went for a night at the Vienna Opera, a couple of hours' distant. My uncle Richard lived both in Vienna and in Marienbad, where he had a fancy goods shop. The frontiers were not yet impenetrable, as they became after the war destroyed the Pressburg tram's bridge across the Danube. The ruins of the bridge could still be seen in 1996, when I helped to make a television programme about it.

The world of the Viennese middle class, and certainly of the Jews who formed so large a proportion of it, was still that of the vast polyglot region whose migrants had, in the past 80 years, turned its capital into a city of two million – except for Berlin by far the largest city on the European continent between Paris and Leningrad. Our relatives had come from, or were still living in, places like Bielitz (now in Poland), Kaschau (now in Czechoslovakia) or Grosswardein (now in Romania).[1] Our grocers and the porters of our apartment buildings were almost certainly Czech, our servant-girls or child-minders not native Viennese: I still remember the tales of were-wolves told me by one from Slovenia. None of them was or felt uprooted or cut adrift from 'the old country' unlike European emigrants to the United States, since for continental Europeans the sea was the great divider, whereas travel on rails, even over large distances, was something everyone was used to. Even my nervous grandmother thought nothing of taking short trips to visit her daughter in Berlin.

It was a multinational, but not a multicultural society. German (with a local intonation) was its language, German (with a local touch) its culture, and its access to world culture, ancient and modern. My relatives would have shared the passionate indignation of the great art historian Ernst Gombrich, when, to fit in with late twentieth-century fashions, he was asked to describe his native Viennese culture as Jewish. It was plain Viennese middle-class culture, unaffected by the fact that so many of its eminent practitioners were Jews and (faced with the endemic anti-Semitism of the region) knew themselves to be Jews, any more than by the fact that some of them came from Moravia (Freud and Mahler), some from Galicia or the Bukovina (Joseph Roth) or even from Russe on the Bulgarian Danube (Elias Canetti). It would be just as pointless to look for consciously Jewish elements in the songs of Irving Berlin or the Hollywood movies of the era of the great studios, all of which were run by immigrant Jews: their object, in which they succeeded, was precisely to make songs or films which found a specific expression for 100 per cent Americanness.

As speakers of the *Kultursprache* in a former imperial capital children instinctively shared the sense of cultural, if no longer political, superiority. The way Czechs spoke German (*böhmakeln*) struck us as inferior and therefore funny, and so did the incomprehensible Czech language with its apparent accumulation of consonants. Without knowing, or having any opinion about, Italians we referred to them with a touch of contempt as *Katzelmacher*. Emancipated and assimilated Viennese Jews talked about Eastern Jews as of some other species. (I distinctly remember asking an embarrassed older member of the family whether those Eastern Jews had surnames like ours, and if so what names, since they were obviously so different from us.) It seems to me that this explains much of the enthusiasm with which Austrians greeted their annexation by Hitler's Germany: it restored their sense of political superiority. At the time I only noticed that one or two of my classmates in secondary school were *Hakenkreuzler* (swastikers). Since I was an English boy, however culturally indistinguishable from the Austrians, this clearly did not concern me directly. But it brings me to the question of politics.

Because I was to be seized so young and so long by that typical twentieth-century passion, political commitment, it seems reasonable to ask how much of its roots can be found in a childhood in 1920s Vienna. That is difficult to reconstruct. We lived in an era steeped in politics, although the affairs of the wider world came to us, as I have said, mainly through overheard adult conversations, whose purport children did not fully grasp. I remember two of these, both probably around 1925 or so. One occurred in an alpine sanatorium where I had been sent to recover from some illness (we children appeared constantly to have some sickness or other) under the supervision of my aunt Gretl who was also convalescing there. 'Who is this Trotsky?' asked a woman, whom I vaguely recall or imagine as maternal and middle-aged, but not without a touch of satisfaction. 'Just a Jewish boy called Bronstein.' We knew about the Russian Revolution, but what exactly was it? Another happened at an athletics meeting to which my uncle (and presumably my father) had taken me, made memorable by my first experience of a black sprinter by the name of Cator. 'You say there's no war anywhere at the moment,' said someone, 'but surely, there's a revolt in Syria?' What did or could this mean to us? We knew there had been a world war, as any British boy born in 1944 would grow up knowing that there had been one. Two of my British uncles had been in it, our neighbour Mr Gold would show me his tall officer's cap, and my best friend was a war orphan – his mother kept her husband's sword on the wall. However, nobody I knew, English or Austrian, regarded the Great War as a heroic episode, and Austrian schools kept quiet about it, partly because it concerned another country at another time – the old Habsburg Empire – partly perhaps also because the Austrian armies had not covered themselves with much glory. It was not until I went to Berlin that I experienced the ex-officer schoolmaster proud of his front-line service. Before that, my most powerful image of the Great War came from Karl Kraus's wonderful documentary super-drama *The Last Days of Humanity*, which both my mother and my aunt Gretl had bought as soon as it came out in 1922. I still have my mother's copy, and still re-read it from time to time.

What else did we know about the times we lived in? Vienna schoolchildren took it for granted that people had the choice between two parties – the Christian socials and the social democrats or Reds. Our simple materialist assumption was that if you were a landlord you voted for the first, if you were a tenant for the second. Since most Viennese were tenants, this naturally made Vienna a Red city. Until after the civil war of 1934 communists were so unimportant that a number of the most enthusiastic ones chose to be active in other countries where there was more scope for them – mainly Germany, such as the famous Eislers: the composer Hanns, the Comintern agent Gerhart, and their sister, the formidable Elfriede, better known as Ruth Fischer, who briefly became leader of the German Communist Party – but also in Czechoslovakia, such as Egon Erwin Kisch. (Many years later the painter Georg Eisler, Hanns's son, became my best friend.) I cannot recall paying attention to the only communist in the circle of the former Grün sisters, who wrote under the pen-name Leo Lania, then a young man who declared Zola's *L'Oeuvre* to be his favourite book and Eugene Onegin and Spartacus his favourite heroes in literature and history. Our family was, of course, neither Black nor Red, since the Blacks were anti-Semites and the Reds were for workers and not people of our class. Besides, we were English, so the matter did not concern us.

And yet, moving from primary to secondary school, and from infancy towards puberty in the Vienna of the late 1920s, one acquired political consciousness as naturally as sexual awareness. In the summer of 1930 I made friends in Weyer, a village in Upper Austria where the doctors were vainly trying to deal with my mother's lungs, with Haller Peter, the boy of the family from whom we rented lodgings. (By the tradition of bureaucratic states, when names were called for, surnames came before given names.) We fished and went robbing orchards together, an exercise I thought my sister would also enjoy, but which, as she admitted to me many years later, had terrified her. Since his father was a railwayman, the family was Red: in Austria, and especially in the countryside, it would not have occurred to any non-agricultural worker in those days to be anything else. Though Peter – about my age – was not visibly interested in public affairs, he also took it for granted that he was Red; and somehow, between lobbing stones at trout and stealing apples, I also concluded that I wanted to be one.

Three years earlier I remember another summer holiday in a Lower Austrian village called Rettenegg, at a time situated vaguely in my private life, but firmly in history. As usual, my father did not join us, but remained at work in Vienna. But the summer of 1927 was the time when the workers of Vienna, outraged by the acquittal of rightwingers who had killed some socialists in an affray, went on to the streets en masse, and burned down the Palace of Justice on the Ringstrasse (the great circular boulevard which surrounds the old central city of Vienna), eighty-five of them being massacred in the process. My father had, it seems, been caught up in the riot, but got away safely. I have no doubt that the grown-ups must have discussed this intensively (not least, my mother), but I cannot say that it made the slightest impact on me, unlike the story that, once upon a time – namely in 1908, on a journey to Egypt, his ship had passed close to Sicily at the time of the great Messina earthquake.

What I actually remember from that holiday was watching the local craftsman build a boat outside our lodgings and the pine forests up the mountain which I explored alone, until I reached a woodcutters' site, where the men gave me some of their *Sterz*, the stiff cereal porridge on which they lived in the woods. On the way there I saw, for the first time in my life, the great black woodpecker, all one-and-a-half foot of it under the vivid red helmet, drumming against a stump in a clearing like a mad miniature hermit, alone under the stillness of the trees.

Still, it would be too much to say that the summer at Weyer made me political. It is only in retrospect that my childhood can be seen as a process of politicization. At the time playing and learning, family and school defined my life, as they defined the lives of most Viennese children in the 1920s. Virtually everything we experienced came to us in these ways or fitted into one or another of these frameworks.

Of the two networks which constituted most of my life, the family was by far the more permanent. It consisted of a larger Viennese clan, the relatives of my grandparents and a smaller Anglo-Austrian part, two Grün sisters, my mother and her younger sister Gretl, married to two Hobsbaum brothers, namely my father and the younger Sidney, who also lived in Vienna for much of the 1920s. As for school, one did not go there until the age of six. After that, as our addresses changed I passed through two primary schools and three *Gymnasia*, and my sister – who left Vienna before the age of ten – through two primary schools. In these circumstances school friendships tended to be temporary. Of all those I came to know at my five schools in Vienna, all but one were to disappear totally from my subsequent life.

The family, on the other hand, was an operational network, tied together not only by the emotional bonds between mothers, children and grandchildren, and between sisters and brothers, but by economic necessity. What there was of the modern welfare state in the 1920s hardly touched middle-class families, since few of their members were employed for wages. Whom else could one call on for help? How could one not help relatives in need, even if one did not particularly like them? I don't believe that this was specially characteristic of Jewish families, although my mother's Viennese family undoubtedly had a sense that the *mishpokhe*, or at least the kinsmen and kinswomen living in Vienna, constituted a group, which met from time to time – always, as I recall from long and spectacularly boring sessions round tables placed together in some open-air café – to take family decisions or just gossip. We were given ice-cream, but short pleasures do not compensate for lengthy tedium. If there was anything specifically Jewish about it, it was the assumption among all of them that the family was a network stretching across countries and oceans, that shifting between countries was a normal part of life, and that for people engaged in buying and selling – as so many members of Jewish families were – earning one's living was an uncertain and unpredictable matter, especially in the era of catastrophe which had engulfed central Europe since the collapse of civilization in August 1914. As it turned out, no part of the Hobsbaum–Grün family was to need the safety net of the family system more than my parents, especially after my father's death changed an economic situation of permanent crisis into one of catastrophe. But until then – in my case until the age of eleven plus – we children were barely aware of this.

We were still in the era when taking a taxi seemed an extravagance that required special justification, even for relatively well-off people. We – or at least I – seemed to have all the usual possessions our friends had and do all the things they did. I can recall only one occasion when I had an inkling of how tough things were. I had just entered secondary school (Bundesgymnasium XIII, Fichtnergasse). The professor in charge of the new form – all teachers at a *Gymnasium* were automatically *Herr Professor*, just as we automatically were now addressed like adults as *Sie* and not like children as *Du* – had given us the list of books we needed to buy. For geography we needed the *Kozenn-Atlas*, a large and evidently rather expensive volume. 'This is very dear. Is it absolutely necessary for you to have it?' my mother asked in a tone which must clearly have communicated to me a sense of crisis, if only because the answer to her question was so obvious. Of course it was. How could Mummy not see this? The book was bought, but the sense that on this occasion, at least, a major sacrifice had been made has remained with me. Perhaps this is a reason why I still have that atlas on my shelves, a bit tattered and full of the graffiti and marginalia of someone in the early forms of secondary school, but still a good atlas, to which I refer from time to time.

Perhaps other children of my age might have been more conscious of our material problems. As a boy I was not much aware of practical realities; and adults, insofar as their activities and interests did not overlap with my own, were not part of practical reality so far as I was concerned. In any case I lived for much of the time in a world without clear boundaries between reality, the discoveries of reading and the creations of imagination. Even a child with a more hard-headed sense of reality, such as my sister, had no clear idea of our situation. Such knowledge simply was not supposed to be part of the world of our childhood. For instance, I had no idea what work my father did. Nobody bothered to tell children about these things, and in any case the ways in which people like my father and uncle earned their living were far from clear. They were not men with firmly describable occupations, like the figures on 'Happy Families' cards: doctors, lawyers, architects, policemen, shopkeepers. When asked what my father did, I would vaguely say, or write, '*Kaufmann*' (merchant), knowing quite well that this meant nothing, and was almost certainly wrong. But what else was one to put?

To a large extent, our – or at least my – lack of awareness of our financial situation was due to the reluctance, no, the refusal, of my Viennese family to acknowledge it. It was not that they insisted on the last resort of the middle class fallen on bad times, 'keeping up appearances'. They were aware of how far they had fallen. 'It really lifts the heart to see this in our impoverished and proletarianized times,' my grandmother wrote to her daughter, marvelling at the smoothness and opulence of a nephew's wedding, noting bitterly that the bridegroom had given his bride 'a very beautiful and valuable ring, made by us' in better days. That is before Grandpa Grün, his savings reduced in value by the great inflation of the early twenties to the price of a coffee and cake at the Café Ilion, returned in old age to the occupation of his youth as a commercial traveller, selling trinkets in provincial towns and alpine villages. Large swathes of the Austrian middle class were in a similar position, impoverished by war and postwar, getting used to tightened belts and a far more modest lifestyle than 'in peacetime' – i.e. before 1914. (Nothing since 1918 counted as peace.) They found having no money hard –

harder, they thought, than the workers who were, after all, used to it. (Later, when I became an enthusiastic communist teenager my aunt Gretl shook her head over my refusal to accept what, to her, was this self-evident proposition.) Not that the English husbands of Grün daughters were better off. Two of them were spectacularly unfitted for the jungle of the market economy: my father and Wilfred Brown, a handsome wartime internee who married the oldest sister, Mimi. Even my uncle Sidney, the only Hobsbaum brother to earn a living in business, spent most of the decade extracting himself from the ruins of one failed project only to plunge into the next, equally doomed, enterprise.

At bottom my Viennese family found any other way of life than that before 1914 inconceivable, and carried on with it, against the odds. Thus my mother, even when unable to pay the grocery bills, let alone the rent and utilities, always employed servants. Nor were these old retainers, such as Helene Demuth, who is buried with the Karl Marxes in Highgate Cemetery. They were and remained the quintessential 'servant problem' of middle-class ladies, an endless succession of young women from agencies who stayed a month or two, ranging from the rare '*eine Perle*' (a pearl), to the clumsy arrival straight from the country, who had never seen a gas-stove, let alone a telephone. When my mother visited England for the first time in 1925, to take care of her sister Mimi who was then ill in Barrow-in-Furness, she wrote to her other sister, impressed not only with the efficiency, equanimity and lack of fuss with which households were run (so different from Vienna Jewish families . . .), but that it was done *without servants*. 'Here you find ladies who do everything themselves, and have children, and even do all the laundry themselves, and still remain ladies.'[2]

Even so, she never seriously considered the British option. 'As someone with years of experience of being broke,' she wrote to her sister who complained of money troubles in Berlin,

let me give you one major piece of advice, which I urge you to take seriously. Try not ever to admit that you could do without a maid!! In the long run you can't manage without one anyway, and so it is best to start with the assumption that a maid is just as much a necessity as food or a roof over your head. What you save is nothing compared to the loss in health, comfort, and above all the state of your nerves: and the worse things get, the more you need them. True, just lately I wondered whether to give Marianne notice – not that I could do it before Christmas, it's too late, and she was always so good – but the only reason I did was that I'm ashamed that she should see that I can't pay the grocer etc. And, deep down I know perfectly well it is best to grow a thick skin and to keep her.[3]

Of all this we knew or understood nothing except that the parents had rows, possibly with increasing frequency – but whose parents do not have rows? – and, in the central European winters, that the rooms were icy. (Had we lived in Britain in the era of coal-fired fireplaces, very nearly the most inefficient form of indoor heating invented, this would not necessarily have been due to lack of money to buy winter fuel.)

Firm and cohesive, partly because of the very precariousness of its material base, the family divided the world, and therefore my life, into two parts: inside and outside. In effect, so far as we children were concerned, the family and its close friends constituted, or determined, the world of adults that I knew as *people* and not merely as service providers or, as it were, stage extras on the filmset of our life. (It also determined which children would remain permanently part of our lives and we of theirs, like the Gold girls, or the daughter of the Szanas.) The adults I knew consisted almost entirely of relatives, or of the friends of parents and relatives. Thus I have no memory as a person, of the dentist my mother took me to, even though the experience of going there was only too unforgettable, for he was not someone she 'knew'. On the other hand I remember Doktor Strasser as a real person, presumably because the family knew him and his family. Curiously enough, teachers do not appear to have belonged to the world of individual adults until my last year in Vienna, and only became people with whom I had personal relations, in Berlin.

School was strictly outside. And 'outside', lacking adults as real persons, consisted essentially of other children. The world of children, whether 'inside' or 'outside', was one which the adults did not really understand, just as we did not really understand what they were about. At best, each side of the generation gap accepted what the other side did as 'how like children' or 'that's what grown-ups do'. Only puberty, arriving in my last year in Vienna, began to undermine the walls between these separate spheres.

Of course the two spheres overlapped. My reading, especially my English reading, was largely supplied by adults, although I found Arthur Mee's *Children's Newspaper* which well-meaning relatives sent from London both boring and incomprehensible. On the other hand from an early age I gobbled up the German books on birdlife and animals which I received as presents, and after primary school, plunged into the publications of *Kosmos, Gesellschaft der Natur-freunde*, a society for the popularization of the – mainly biological and evolutionary – natural sciences, to which they subscribed for me. We were taken to the theatre from an early age to plays we might enjoy, but which adults also admired – say, to Schiller's *William Tell* (but not to Goethe's *Faust*), and the works of the early nineteenth-century Viennese popular playwrights – the charming sentimental magic plays of Raimund, the savagely funny comedies of the great Johann Nestroy, whose bitter wit we did not yet understand. But we would be sent with other primary schoolchildren to the morning sessions of films at the local cinema, the long-gone Maxim-Bio, to see shorts of Chaplin and Jackie Coogan, and, more surprisingly, Fritz Lang's rather longer *Nibelungen* epic. In my Viennese experience adults and children did not go to the movies together. Again, intellectual children would naturally make their choice among the books on their parents' and relatives' shelves, perhaps influenced by what they heard at home, perhaps not. To this extent the generations shared some tastes. On the other hand, the reading material selected for children by our elders was not, in general, supposed to be of serious interest to adults. Conversely, of all adults with whom we had any dealings, only teachers (who disapproved) were even aware of the passionate interest of thirteen-year-olds in the pocket-sized adventures of detectives with invariably English names which circulated in our classes under such titles as *Sherlock Holmes the World Detective* – no connection with the original – Sexton Blake, *Frank Allen, the Avenger of the Disinherited* and the most popular of all, the Berlin detective Tom Shark, with his buddy Pitt Strong, who operated out of the

Motzstrasse, familiar to readers of Christopher Isherwood, but as remote to Viennese boys as Holmes's Baker Street.

Children in the Vienna of the mid-twenties still learned to write the old Gothic script by scratching letters on slates framed in wood, and wiping them with small sponges. Since most post-1918 school texts were in the new roman print, we obviously also learned to read and later write that way, but I cannot remember how. By the time one entered secondary education at the age of eleven one was obviously expected to have acquired the three Rs, but what else we learned in primary school is less clear. Plainly, I found it interesting, since I look back on my elementary schooldays with pleasure, recalling all manner of stories about Vienna and trips into the semi-rural neighbourhood to search for trees, plants and animals. I suppose all this came under the pedagogic heading 'Heimatkunde', which, since the German word Heimat notoriously has no exact English equivalent, can best be translated as 'knowledge of where we come from'. I can see now that it was not a bad preparation for a historian, since the great events of conventional history in and around Vienna were only an incidental part of what Viennese children learned about their habitat. Aspern was not only the name of the battle the Austrians won against Napoleon (neighbouring Wagram, which they decisively lost, was not in the collective memory), but a place in the remote zone beyond the Danube, not yet part of the city, where people went to swim in the lagoons left by the old course of the river, and explored wildernesses of martens and waterfowl. The Turkish sieges of Vienna were important because they had brought coffee into the city as part of the Turkish booty, and therefore our Kaffeehäuser. Of course we had the enormous advantage that the official history of the old imperial Austria had disappeared from sight, except as buildings and monuments, and the new Austria of 1918 had no history yet. It is political continuity that tends to reduce school history to the canonical succession of dates, monarchs and wars. The only historical event I recall celebrating at school in the Vienna of my childhood was the centenary of Beethoven's death. The teachers themselves knew that in the new era school also had to be different, but they were not yet clear just how. (As my school songbook put it at the time – 1925 – 'the new methods of teaching having not yet been entirely clarified'.)

I was to discover the '1066 and all that' type of history in the secondary *Gymnasium*, not yet emancipated from traditional pedagogy. Naturally this was unexciting. German, geography, Latin and eventually Greek (which I had to give up on coming to England) seemed much more to my taste, but not, alas, mathematics and the physical sciences.

And certainly not religious instruction. I do not think this arose at all in primary school, but in secondary school I seem to recall that the non-Catholics, Lutherans, Evangelicals, the odd Greek Orthodox, but mainly the Jews, were excused the periods presumably devoted to this subject in class. The minority alternative, an afternoon class for Jews conducted in another part of town by a Miss Miriam Morgenstern and her various successors, was uninspiring. We were repeatedly told and interrogated on the Bible stories in the Pentateuch. I recall the shock I caused when I answered yet another question on who was the most important of the sons of Jacob, unable to believe that they were, once again, going on about Joseph, 'Judah'. After all, I reasoned, had not all the Jews (*Juden*) been called after him? It was the wrong answer. I also acquired a knowledge of printed Hebrew characters which I have since lost, plus the essential invocation to the Jews, the 'Shema Yisroel' (the language was always pronounced in the Ashkenazi manner and not in the Sephardic pronunciation imposed by Zionism), and a fragment of the 'Manishtana', the ritual questions and answers supposed to be recited during Passover by the youngest male. Since nobody in the family celebrated Passover, took notice of the Sabbath or any of the other Jewish holidays, or kept any Jewish dietary rules, I had no occasion to use my knowledge. I knew that one was supposed to cover one's head in the Temple, but the only times I ever found myself in one were at weddings and funerals. I watched the one school friend who practised the full ritual when addressing the Lord – prayer-shawl, phylacteries and the rest – with an uninvolved curiosity. Moreover, if our family had practised these things, an hour a week at school would have been neither necessary nor sufficient to acquire them.

Though entirely unobservant, we nevertheless knew that we were, and could not get away from being, Jews. After all there were 200,000 of us in Vienna, 10 per cent of the city's population. Most Viennese Jews bore assimilated first names, but – unlike those in the Anglo-Saxon world – rarely changed their surnames, however recognizably Jewish. Certainly in my childhood nobody I knew had been converted. In principle, under the Habsburgs as under the Hohenzollerns, the abandonment of one form of religious service for another had been a price willingly paid by very successful Jewish families for social or official standing, but after the collapse of society, the advantages of conversion disappeared even for such families, and the Grüns had never aimed so high. Nor could Viennese Jews think of themselves simply as Germans worshipping (or not worshipping) in a particular way. They could not even dream of escaping their fate of being one ethnicity among many. Nobody gave them the option of belonging to 'the nation', because there was none. In the Austrian half of the Emperor Franz Josef's dominions, unlike in the Hungarian half, there was no single 'country' with a single 'people' theoretically identified with it. Under such circumstances for Jews to be 'German' was not a political or national but a cultural project. It meant leaving behind the backwardness and isolation of *shtetls* and *shuls* to join the modern world. The city fathers of the town of Brody in Galicia, 80 per cent of whose population was Jewish, had petitioned the emperor long ago to make German the language of school education, not because the emancipated citizens of Brody wanted to be like beer-drinking Teutons, but because they did not want to be like the Hasidim with their miracle-working hereditary *wunderrabbis* or the *yeshiva-bokhers* explicating the Talmud in Yiddish. And that is why middle-class Viennese Jews, whose parents or grandparents had migrated from the Polish, Czech and Hungarian hinterlands, demarcated themselves so decisively from the Eastern Jews.

It is no accident that modern Zionism was invented by a Viennese journalist. All Viennese Jews knew, at least since the 1890s, that they lived in a world of anti-Semites and even of potentially dangerous street anti-Semitism. '*Gottlob kein Jud*' (Thank God it wasn't a Jew) is the immediate reaction of a (Jewish) passer-by to the cries of newspaper vendors on the Vienna Ring, announcing the assassination of Archduke Franz Ferdinand, in the opening scene of Karl Kraus's wonderful *The Last Days of Humanity*. There was even less reason for optimism in the 1920s. There was no doubt in most people's minds that the governing Christian-Social Party remained as anti-Semitic as its founder, Vienna's celebrated mayor Karl Lueger. And I still recall the moment of shock when my elders – I was barely thirteen – received the news of the 1930 German Reichstag election, which made Hitler's National Socialists the second-largest party. They knew what it meant. In short, there was simply no way of forgetting that one was Jewish, even though I cannot recall any personal anti-Semitism, because my Englishness gave me, in school at least, an identity which drew attention away from my Jewishness. Britishness probably also immunized me, fortunately, against the temptations of a Jewish nationalism, even though Zionism among the central European young generally went together with moderate or revolutionary socialist views, except for the disciples of Jabotinsky, who were inspired by Mussolini and now govern Israel as the Likud party. Of course Zionism had a greater presence in Herzl's city than among indigenous Jews in, say, Germany where, until Hitler, it attracted only an untypical fringe. There was no way of overlooking the existence either of anti-Semites or of the blue-white football club Hakoah, which faced my father and Uncle Sidney with a problem of conflicting loyalties when it played the visiting British team Bolton Wanderers. However, the vast majority of emancipated or middle-class Viennese Jews before Hitler were not, and never became, Zionist.

We had no idea what dangers threatened the Jews. Nobody had, or could have. Even in the benighted pogrom-ridden corners of Carpathian Europe and the Polish–Ukrainian plains from which the first-generation immigrants came to Vienna, systematic genocide was inconceivable. In case of serious trouble, the old and experienced argued in favour of keeping a low profile, taking evasive action and staying on the right side of such authorities as were in a position to protect them, and might have an interest in doing so, or at least an interest in re-establishing law and order, however inequitable, on their domains. The young and revolutionary called for resistance and active self-defence. The old knew that, sooner or later, things would settle down again; the young might dream of total victory (e.g. world revolution) but how could they imagine total destruction? Neither actually expected a modern country permanently to get rid of all its Jews, something that had not happened since· Spain in 1492. Still less could one imagine their physical extirpation. Moreover, only the Zionists actually envisaged the systematic exodus of all Jews into a mono-ethnic nation-state, leaving their former homes, in the Nazi expression, '*judenrein*'. When people before, or even in the first years of, Hitler talked of the dangers of anti-Semitism, they meant an intensification of what Jews had always suffered: discrimination, injustice, victimization, the confident, contemptuous strong intimidating and sometimes brutalizing the minority of the inferior weak. It did not and could not yet mean Auschwitz. The word 'genocide' was not coined until 1942.

What exactly *could* 'being Jewish' mean in the 1920s to an intelligent Anglo-Viennese boy who suffered no anti-Semitism and was so remote from the practices and beliefs of traditional Judaism that, until after puberty, he was unaware even of being circumcised? Perhaps only this: that sometime around the age of ten I acquired a simple principle from my mother on a now forgotten occasion when I must have reported, or perhaps even repeated, some negative observation of an uncle's behaviour as 'typically Jewish'. She told me very firmly: 'You must never do anything, or seem to do anything that might suggest that you are ashamed of being a Jew.'

I have tried to observe it ever since, although the strain of doing so is sometimes almost intolerable, in the light of the behaviour of the government of Israel. My mother's principle was sufficient for me to abstain, with regret, from declaring myself *konfessionslos* (without religion) as one was entitled to do in Austria at the age of thirteen. It has landed me with the lifetime burden of an unpronounceable surname which seems spontaneously to call for the convenient slide into Hobson or Osborn. It has been enough to define my Judaism ever since, and left me free to live as what my friend the late Isaac Deutscher called a 'non-Jewish Jew', but not what the miscellaneous regiment of religious or nationalist publicists call a 'self-hating Jew'. I have no emotional obligation to the practices of an ancestral religion and even less to the small, militarist, culturally disappointing and politically aggressive nation-state which asks for my solidarity on racial grounds. I do not even have to fit in with the most fashionable posture of the turn of the new century, that of 'the victim', the Jew who, on the strength of the Shoah (and in the era of unique and unprecedented Jewish world achievement, success and public acceptance), asserts unique claims on the world's conscience as a victim of persecution. Right and wrong, justice and injustice, do not wear ethnic badges or wave national flags. And as a historian I observe that, if there is any justification for the claim that the 0.25 per cent of the global population in the year 2000 which constitute the tribe into which I was born are a 'chosen' or special people, it rests not on what it has done within the ghettos or special territories, self-chosen or imposed by others, past, present or future. It rests on its quite disproportionate and remarkable contribution to humanity in the wider world, mainly in the two centuries or so since the Jews were allowed to leave the ghettos, and chose to do so. We are, to quote the title of the book of my friend Richard Marienstras, Polish Jew, French Resistance fighter, defender of Yiddish culture and his country's chief expert on Shakespeare, '*un peuple en diaspora*'. We shall, in all probability, remain so. And if we make the thought experiment of supposing that Herzl's dream came true and all Jews ended up in a small independent territorial state which excluded from full citizenship all who were not the sons of Jewish mothers, it would be a bad day for the rest of humanity – and for the Jews themselves.

3

Hard Times

In the late evening of Friday 8 February 1929 my father returned from another of his increasingly desperate visits to town in search of money to earn or borrow, and collapsed outside the front door of our house. My mother heard his groans through the upstairs windows and, when she opened them on the freezing air of that spectacularly hard alpine winter, she heard him calling to her. Within a few minutes he was dead, I assume from a heart attack. He was forty-eight years old. In dying, he also condemned to death my mother, who could not forgive herself for the way she felt she had treated him in what turned out to be the last terrible months, indeed the very last days, of his life.

'Something has broken inside me,' she wrote to her sister in the first letter after his death.

> I can't write about it yet. You can imagine how every cross word and every unkind thought now cuts through me like a knife. That 'never again', Gretl! What wouldn't I do now, and what would I have done before, if I had known this would happen . . . If at least he had been ill for only one day, I could have nursed him and been loving to him again . . . At least I was there and he didn't have to die alone.

It was no consolation.

Within two and a half years she was dead also, at the age of thirty-six. I have always assumed that her many self-lacerating, underdressed visits to his grave in the harsh winter months after his death contributed to the lung disease which killed her.

It is not surprising that her self-control frayed and snapped in those appalling months – far less surprising than the fact that, by superhuman efforts, she managed to conceal the situation from her children. Times had never been good since the first years when the young couple had arrived from Egypt with a modest reserve of hard and stable pounds sterling in an Austria sliding into hyperinflation. I have no idea how my father expected or hoped to earn his living in a country whose language he never learned to speak well. Indeed, I have no idea how he had earned his living before he went to Egypt, where a presentable and well-spoken, intelligent but not too intellectual man in his twenties, with a rather impressive record as a sportsman, would have no trouble in finding a job in some shipping or trading office in the large colony of British expats. Perhaps he expected to find similar help as an Englishman in Vienna, although the expatriate colony here was small (even if it had given birth to several of Vienna's football teams). All I know for certain is that he ordered notepaper headed 'L. Percy Hobsbawn, Vienna. Tel. Ad. "Hobby". Tel. Nr. . . . . . .'. For a brief moment in 1920 my mother reported to her sister that she had servants in the plural: a cook and a maid (who disappeared almost immediately).

From then on it was downhill all the way. From the Seutter Villa we moved into a distinctly more modest flat in a neighbouring suburb, Ober St Veit. From the mid-twenties the family seems to have constantly lived from hand to mouth, barely knowing where the money for the daily expenses would come from. That, I suspect, is why my mother began seriously to try to earn money from her writing, working increasingly long hours with increasing intensity. Still, whatever her literary work contributed to the family income, in the course of 1928 the situation became increasingly catastrophic. By late 1928 the landlord had given us notice. We had to negotiate to avoid the gas being cut off. Two days before Christmas my mother wrote to her sister: 'It's Friday and I haven't bought a single present yet. If Percy doesn't bring any money tomorrow, I don't know what I shall do.'

The new year had brought no respite. Three days before my father's death she complained to her sister that things were getting worse by the day, the rent and phone bill were unpaid, and 'I usually don't even have a Schilling in the house' and she still had no idea where the family would live when the notice to quit expired. Such was the situation when my father went out for the last time. And now he was dead. He was buried a few days later in the Jewish section of the Central Cemetery of Vienna. All I can remember of his death was a dark night when my sister and I were moved, half asleep, from our room to our parents' bedroom to be vaguely told that something terrible had happened, and the icy wind sweeping over us at the open grave.

Perhaps this is the moment for a son to confront the difficult task of writing about his father.

The task is unusually difficult, because I have virtually no memories of him, that is to say I have clearly chosen to forget most of what I might have remembered. I know what he looked like, a medium-size sinewy man in rimless pince-nez, black hair parted in the middle, with a horizontally lined forehead, but even this impression may owe more to the camera than to my own memory. In my mental family photo album of childhood he is preserved in no more than a half-dozen or so images, all, I think, from the years at Ober St Veit: Daddy wearing a tweed suit – unusual in Vienna; Daddy taking me to an amateur football match; acting as his ball-boy at mixed-doubles tennis games somewhere on the road between our house and the Lainzer Tiergarten, the old imperial hunting ground; Daddy singing English music-hall songs; one short but radiant memory of going for a walk with Daddy on the nearby hills. Then one or two less agreeable images: Daddy trying – and evidently failing – to teach me boxing (he did not persist); and one much more specific image of Daddy in a towering rage in the garden of the Einsiedeleigasse. I must then have been in the last years of primary school, aged nine or ten. He had asked me to fetch a hammer to knock in some nail, possibly something that had come loose from a deck-chair. I was at that time passionately into prehistory, possibly because I was in the middle of reading the first volume of the trilogy *Die Höhlenkinder* (The Cave Children) by one Sonnleitner, in which a couple of (unrelated) Robinson Crusoe orphan children in an inaccessible alpine valley grow up to reproduce the stages of human prehistory, from palaeolithic to something like recognizable Austrian peasant life. As they were reliving the stone age, I had constructed a stone-age hammer, carefully lashed to its wooden handle in the proper manner. I brought it to him and was amazed at his furious reaction. I have since been told that he was often short-tempered with me, but if, as is likely, this was so, I have blotted it out. I have only one image of him in work. One day he brought home a device he was (as so often) unsuccessfully trying to sell, a shop-sign in which a luminous word – it might have been the name of a product or retailer – was visible on the street as reflected in a mirror. Perhaps he wanted to discuss its prospects with a visitor, which almost certainly meant his brother; for if he had any Viennese friends of his own, I cannot recall them.

Nor can I remember him by the memory of others. There were anecdotes about him in his London youth, and in Egypt, mostly to do with his physical prowess and his attraction for women (although I have never heard the faintest suggestion that he had been unfaithful to his wife). Every East End Jewish family needed at least one brother who could, as they used to say, 'handle himself' and stand up to the local Irish. In the Hobsbaum family this was my father's role; and, since the ring was an accepted option for poor young East Enders, including young Jews with good muscles and quick reflexes, he became a more than useful boxer. He remained an amateur, but the visible record of his success was the two cups which he won as amateur lightweight champion of Egypt in 1907 and 1908 or thereabouts, presumably mainly against competitors from the British occupying forces. They stood on a shelf in our home – Austrian rooms, lacking fireplaces also lacked mantelpieces – and my sister, who remembered him fondly even though she was only just eight when he died, later kept them in her house. He is said on one occasion to have saved his brother Ernest, who had got into trouble swimming. My mother's novel, which is about a young woman in pre-1914 Egypt, contains a portrait of an all-round athlete demi-god in action, which is almost certainly based on him.

However, he does not come into family anecdotes or jokes in the Vienna years. It seems clear that he did not get on well with his parents-in-law, certainly not with Grandmother Grün. Beyond this, there is very little indeed about him in my mother's very full letters to her sister – much less than about Sidney, her brother-in-law. Nothing about his plans, his activities, his failures. Nothing about what they did or where they went together. After our parents' death, he, or more precisely his Vienna years, were hardly talked about in Sidney and Gretl's household. He seems to disappear from sight.

The truth is that for him the years in Vienna were a disaster. In my mother's words: 'So much worry, so much misery, so many disappointments, and then for it to end like that.' With a regular salary from a regular, not too demanding, job he would have been a happy man, a charming companion, an asset in any milieu that appreciated sport, a little music and fun. Such things were available to men without means or professional qualifications in the formal or informal outposts of the British Empire but not in postwar Vienna. Perhaps, in the distant, irrecoverable world before 1914, he would have been found some job in or through the then prosperous network of the grandparents' families. After all, one has to do something for one's daughter's husband, even if he is a bit of a *schlemiel*. In the 1920s this was no longer possible. He was on his own. Few people I know have been as unsuited to earning their living in a pitiless world as my father. By the end there can have been very little confidence left in him, if only because nobody believed in him any more. After his death his wife took momentary comfort in the thought that 'it wouldn't have got better in the future, only worse. He has been spared that.'

He did not leave much behind except his boxing cups, his season ticket, with photo ID, for the Vienna transport system and a substantial collection of English books, mostly the paperbacks produced by the German firm of Tauchnitz for sale exclusively outside Britain, and therefore, I assume, acquired in Egypt. I cannot recall any new Tauchnitzes coming into the house in Vienna, but perhaps that was because there was no money for them. As I recall, they were mostly late Victorian and Edwardian titles, a lot of Kipling stories (but not *Kim*), which I read avidly but without understanding, some lesser pre-1918 authors and works on travel and adventure, among which I still remember a now forgotten epic of old-time whaling, *The Cruise of the Cachalot*. There were also some hardbacks, among which I recall Wells's *Mr Britling Sees It Through*. I never opened it. And there was a thick bound volume of Tennyson's poetry, which looked like a present or school prize. What my father gave to me came through those books, which presumably he (with or without my mother) had chosen or chosen to preserve. Did he himself read to me 'The Revenge' ('In Flores on the Azores Sir Richard Grenville lay') which, with 'The Charge of the Light Brigade', 'Sunset and Evening Star' and, of course, 'The Lady of Shalott' are the only poems I can retrace to that Tennyson volume? If so, it represents the only direct intellectual contact with him that I can remember.

However, I still have one of the few surviving documents of his life. It is a 1921 entry in one of his sister-in-law's confessional albums, those sets of answers to questions about oneself which were still popular, at least in central Europe. I reprint the questions and answers. They may serve as his epitaph.

FAVOURITE QUALITY IN MAN: Physical strength
FAVOURITE QUALITY IN WOMAN: Virtue
YOUR IDEA OF HAPPINESS: To have all wants fulfilled
YOUR IDEA OF UNHAPPINESS: Unluck
WHAT ARE YOU BEST AND WORST AT: Missing opportunities.
   Grasping them.
WHAT IS YOUR FAVOURITE SCIENCE: None
WHAT TENDENCY IN ART DO YOU LIKE: Modern
WHAT SOCIAL LIFE DO YOU PREFER? My family
WHAT DO YOU HATE MOST? Modern society
FAVOURITE WRITER/COMPOSER: —
FAVOURITE BOOK AND MUSICAL INSTRUMENT: Piano
FAVOURITE HERO IN FICTION OR HISTORY: Earl of Warwick
FAVOURITE COLOUR AND FLOWER: Rose
FAVOURITE FOOD AND DRINK: —
FAVOURITE NAME: —
FAVOURITE SPORT: Boxing
FAVOURITE GAME: Bridge
HOW DO YOU LIVE? Quietly
YOUR TEMPERAMENT AND CHIEF CHARACTERISTIC: False
   idealist. Tendency to dream.
MOTTO: Sufficient for the day and perhaps a little over.

He did not realize even this modest ambition.

My father's death left the family temporarily destitute. There seems to have been no insurance of substance. When, a few days later, I needed new footwear, because my existing shoes let in the icy cold of that terrible winter – I remember crying with the pain of it on the Ringstrasse – my mother had to get new ones for me from a Jewish charity. The family did what they could to help, but there was no money to spare. In any case, the only money she would accept as a cash gift was the £10 which Uncle Harry sent from London. This was a far from negligible sum. Together with what was left of a publisher's advance and a few book reviews she reckoned it would keep us for about two months.

In spite of my mother's justified apprehensions, we had to move into the grandparents' flat. There was nowhere else to go. The three of us slept in the small side room of the three-room apartment, and my mother had to set about earning her living. In the meantime some of her more prosperous friends saved her self-respect by disguising their help as payment for English lessons. (I am fairly sure that the first money I ever earned, which was during these months for lessons to help the daughter of one of her best friends through the entry exam for secondary school, was a tactful way of saving her the cost of my pocket money.) I do remember at least one genuine paying pupil who contributed to our income, a Miss Papazian, the daughter of an Armenian businessman.

Fortunately my mother had already built up her literary connections. Since 1924 she had relations with Rikola-Verlag (later Speidelsche Verlagsbuchhandlung), a small Viennese publishing house, which had already published what proved to be her only novel. The publisher, a Mr Scheuermann, did what he could to help. In any case he valued her as a translator. She had already translated one novel by a now forgotten mid-western Scandinavian-American writer and Scheuermann gave her a contract for another and offered to put her relations with his firm on a more permanent basis. I vaguely remember him as a tallish man with a stoop. She had also been selling short stories in the periodical market, her own or translated English ones, both in Britain and in Germany. They brought in something, though pretty certainly not a living income. (After her death my aunt Mimi, in one of her many spells of financial embarrassment, returned to trying to market my mother's material.)

In the end she had to take a job with the firm of Alexander Rosenberg, Vienna and Budapest, representing British textile producers, presumably on the strength of her knowledge of English. She enjoyed office life, after years of solitary labour at home – she got on well with people – and besides, it gave her the chance to get away from the constant nervous tension of living at close quarters with her mother in an overcrowded flat. Until then she would escape by going to the café for an hour, simply to have some time of her own. I remember being taken to the office and shown off to her colleagues.

Then, at the end of 1929, she began to spit blood. By early April the doctors had collapsed one lung. For the last year and a half of her life she died slowly in a succession of hospitals and sanatoria. The exact nature of her lung disease is not clear, for I understand that it does not entirely fit the diagnosis of tuberculosis, which in those days was both common and potentially lethal. Whatever it was, medical help could not do much to slow it down. As it happened, regular paid employment had put her into the social insurance system of 'Red Vienna', the benefits of which she now discovered. It is impossible to imagine how her medical care could otherwise have been paid for.

Her illness transformed our situation. There was no way in which she could henceforth look after a boy of twelve and a girl of nine. Fortunately for both her children, in the spring of 1929 Sidney had finally managed to strike it rich – at least by the undemanding standards of the Hobsbaum and Grün families in the 1920s. He landed a job, insecure, imprecise but with pay and scope, in Berlin with Universal Pictures. This not only satisfied his lifelong ambition to be associated with the world of artistic creation, but gave him and Gretl the means to take responsibility for the half-orphaned children of his brother and her sister. We thus owe the shape of our future lives to Carl Laemmle, founder of the Hollywood star system and Universal Pictures. We were now split. Nancy went to Berlin immediately. I stayed in Vienna until my mother's death in July 1931.

I do not know why. Perhaps Sidney and Gretl felt that they could not immediately cope with two additional children, or with the problem of finding at a moment's notice a Berlin school that would suit a boy halfway through his third year at a secondary school in Vienna. It is true that my mother was patently more attached to me than to my sister, but she had got used to the thought that, as it was unlikely that she would be able to cope permanently with two children, she would have to lose them. In any case her idea had long been that, if possible, I should eventually go to England to be educated there, and to make a career as a real Englishman. Most central European middle-class Jews tended to idealize Britain, so stable, strong, boring and lacking in neuroses, not least, evidently, the Grün girls all of whom had married Englishmen. Even so, leaving marriage aside, my mother was an exceptionally passionate Anglophile. As she wrote to her sister, the mere thought that the letter she drafted for Mr Rosenberg was going to Huddersfield made her feel sentimental about England. It was she who insisted that in our house only English should be spoken, not just with my father but with her. She corrected my English and tried to expand it from the basic vocabulary of domestic communication. She dreamed that I might one day find myself in the Indian Civil Service – or rather, since I was so obviously interested in birds, in the Indian Forestry Service, which would bring me (and her) even closer to the world of her admired *Jungle Book*.

Until my father's death, these were dreams for a remote future. Now a chance to send me to England arose immediately, for her sister Mimi offered to invite me to the boarding house she and her husband had just opened in Lancashire, on the edge of Southport, close by the Birkdale golf-links. I went there after the end of the 1928–9 school year. It was my first visit to Britain, and indeed my first journey alone. (Mimi's first action when I arrived was to take the money I carried on me, for, as so often, her cash-flow was in one of its periods of pause.) For a while my mother hoped I might be able to stay there permanently, asking me to find out when school started, and 'whether you will have to learn a lot in order to catch up with the boys of your age'. 'I am anxious to hear about your plans for the autumn – or rather Auntie Mimi's plans for you,' she wrote in another letter. 'I hope for your sake you can stay there, and I'm sure you hope so too.' It is impossible to know how seriously she took the possibility, and clearly there was no concrete planning. In any case there was never more than the ghost of a chance that the footloose and always cash-strapped Mimi, with or without her handsome but economically useless husband, could provide a permanent base for me. I returned to Vienna at the end of the school vacation.

Whether I wanted to stay in Britain, or what I thought of the idea, I can no longer remember. Visiting England, being shown round London and getting to know Uncle Harry and Aunt Bella, but especially my cousin Ronnie – my senior by five years – was exciting, although I found Southport a dead loss, and life among the paying guests at Wintersgarth uninspiring. Apart from the memory of endless streets of small yellowy-grey brick houses on the way into London, and the surprising discovery that Lancashire people pronounced English vowels quite differently from us, I brought back two main discoveries from England. The first was the weeklies read avidly by British working-class boys – *The Wizard*, *Adventure* and other such titles, very different from the *bien-pensant* material English relatives had sent us in Vienna from time to time. I read them hungrily and with unalloyed enjoyment, spent all my pocket money on them, and took a collection back to Vienna. (They did not cost much – 2d an issue, if I remember correctly.) I did not realize it then, but reading these dense grey columns of fantasy adventure and dreams made me, for the first time, a genuine Briton since, at least for a moment, they put me on the same wavelength as most British boys of my age group.

The second was the Boy Scouts. I was taken to a world jamboree of the movement, which took place at the time not far from Southport, and returned an enthusiastic convert, with a copy of Baden-Powell's *Scouting for Boys*, determined to join them. I did so the next year in Vienna, where the '*Pfadfinder*' (Scouts) competed with the blue-shirted Social-Democratic 'Red Falcons', which my mother dissuaded me from joining on the grounds that their campfires were admirable, but I was still too young to commit myself to the Marxism that went with them. I was thus to make my entry into public life at the age of fourteen not under revolutionary auspices, but at a Boy Scout parade, composed mainly of middle-class Viennese Jewish boys, formally inspected by the then President of Austria, an undistinguished and doubtless anti-Semitic Catholic politician by the name of Miklas.

I was a passionately enthusiastic Scout, even recruiting some of my classmates, though not much gifted either for fieldcraft or group life. It was among the Scouts that I found my best friend in the days between the deaths of my father and my mother. We maintained contact until his death, for he escaped to England after Hitler occupied Austria, found a job as a doorkeeper to the Afghan legation in London and remained to become a medical technician. (My troop leader ended up in Australia.) Had there been any Baden-Powell Scouts in Germany, I might well have joined them there too, after my mother's death, but there were none, any more than at that time – difficult though this may be to credit now – there were any German football teams that counted internationally. If there were the equivalent of the Austrian 'Red Falcons', they belonged to a very much less exciting and not at all revolutionary Social-Democratic Party. Marxism thus had no competitors.

For the two years after my return from England I lived a curiously provisional semi-independent life. To stay with a neurotic and semi-invalid grandmother after my mother went into hospital was clearly out of the question. For a few months I was taken over by Great-uncle Viktor Friedmann and Aunt Elsa, who had at least one child still in the house, my cousin Herta, several years my senior. (Her brother Otto had been boarding with Sidney and Gretl in Berlin, so there was some obligation of reciprocity.) For the rest of the school year I commuted daily from their flat in the Seventh District, the other side of the Old Town, to my *Gymnasium* in the Third District, opposite – though I did not then know it – the house built for himself by the philosopher Wittgenstein. In the summer of 1930 I joined Gretl, Nancy and Peter in an Upper Austrian alpine village, Weyer-an-der-Enns, to be near my mother, who had been sent to a hospital/sanatorium there. As all readers of Thomas Mann's *Magic Mountain* know, mountain air was prescribed for TB sufferers. But it did her no good.

I spent my last school year in Vienna alone, or rather as a sort of male au pair. Someone discovered a Mrs Effenberger, widow of a colonel and, like so many good Viennese, from southern Bohemia – she came from Pisek – whose son Bertl, two or three years younger than me, wanted English lessons. In return for these, and possibly a very modest subsidy, she was prepared to look after me. Since she lived in the outer suburb of Währing, I had to move school yet again and joined the Federal Gymnasium XVIII in the Klostergasse, my third secondary school in three years. By this time my mother had left Weyer and been transferred to a hospital not too far from Währing. I visited her there every week. Sidney and Gretl invited me to join them and my sister in Berlin over Christmas, but sitting by my mother's bed was my only regular physical contact with family. I, in turn, was all that was left of her life's work and hopes, within regular reach of her hand.

Sometime in the early summer of 1931 it became clear to the adults that the end was close. Gretl must have come to Vienna and stayed there. My mother was transferred to a garden sanatorium in Purkersdorf, just west of Vienna, where I saw her for the last time shortly before going to camp with the Scouts. I can remember nothing of the occasion except how emaciated she looked and that, not knowing what to say or do – there were others present – I glanced out of the window and saw a hawfinch, a small bird with a beak strong enough to crack cherry stones, that I had never seen before and for which I had long been on the lookout. So my last memory of her is not one of grief but of ornithological pleasure.

She died on 12 July 1931. I was fetched from camp. Shortly after the funeral she was buried in the summer heat in the same grave as my father. I left Vienna for good and went to Berlin. From then on Nancy and I were together again, and Sidney, Gretl and their son Peter (then just six) were our family. It was not to be the last death in the family in that decade.

Perhaps this is the moment for some reflections on my mother.

She was the smallest of the three Grün girls, the most intelligent, clearly the most gifted except in *joie de vivre*. Less pretty and spontaneous than her younger sister, the family beauty Gretl, less rebellious and adventurous than the older Mimi, she was in many ways perhaps the most conventional of the three. Engaged to Percy at the age of eighteen, married earlier than the other two – and according to her letters as a virgin – she returned to Vienna after the war a married woman with one child, and on the verge of expecting another. Her sisters and many of her friends had meanwhile passed through that pressure-cooker of change and emancipation, the war and the era of breakdown and revolution at the end of it, unmarried and unattached. Not that she missed all the war. For a few months, while waiting to go to Switzerland to marry at the British Consulate in Zurich, she worked as a volunteer nurse in a military hospital. There she learned that wounded men could not bear lying on any but the most smoothly laid bedsheets – she later taught me the trick of making such beds – and tried to communicate with a dying

Ruthenian soldier by selecting phrases from a volume of what she discovered to be translations of fairy tales from the Brothers Grimm, the German text of which she could easily refer to. Still, life in the colonial society of Alexandria was an exotic, but recognizable version of life in Europe before 1914. Not so life in the Vienna to which she returned after four years' absence.

In some ways she remained conventional in the pre-1914 Viennese middle-class sense. As I have already said, she found it almost inconceivable to live without servants, and was amazed to discover that in England ladies could both do their own cooking and house-work without them and stay ladies. She took it for granted that a married woman must put her interests second to those of husband and children, and was shocked and irritated by her sister Mimi who refused to do so. Not that this made her a particularly successful mother, but then, as my sister and I agreed many years later when comparing notes about our youth, none of the several people who were or acted as our parents was fitted for the job by talent or training. None was very good at it, nor was there any reason why one would expect them to have been. Their parents had not been either. She did not plunge headlong into the new ways of the world, though she eventually followed them. She did not cut her hair until 1924 or 1925, and was disappointed when nobody seemed to notice that she had.

Life in Vienna made few concessions to one who (in her album 'confession') claimed that her idea of happiness was 'to look into a glowing fireplace, having no further wishes' and who claimed that her favourite book was Andersen's *Fairy Tales*. I do not think she was an efficient or enthusiastic housewife or much of a manager, although she seems to have enjoyed dressmaking and even the endless adaptation and adjustment of old clothes to new uses or growing children, which tight budgets made necessary. There were times when she went on strike against the constant unceasing struggle to make ends meet. 'I just went into town and into the Café, and thought *"après moi"* . . .' she wrote one day when the laundry was due to return, there was not enough money in the house to pay for it, and the two friends to whom she had run to borrow it from were not in. Or she might simply decide to go to the movies alone to forget. Or else, increasingly, she buried herself in her writing, which had at least the material justification that it brought in money. Or in the handful of close friendships (including the one with her younger sister) from which, as time went on, she almost certainly received her main moral support. And who, in turn, relied on her friendship, loved and admired her.

Curiously enough, she was not a great reader of contemporary literature. In the mid-twenties, asked by her convalescent sister for books to read, she said she had read hardly anything lately other than Shakespeare, and had not been in a bookshop for ages.

When did she begin to think of herself as a writer, a far less common occupation for women in central Europe at that time than it would have been on the already heavily feminized scene of British fiction? When did she choose the pen-name of 'Nelly Holden'? By 1924 she had already sent manuscripts to Rikola-Verlag and written, or at least drafted, a novel – presumably the one based on her own experiences about a young girl in Alexandria which was published by Rikola as *Elisabeth Chrissanthis* in 1926. Another novel was written by the time my father died, but, to her dismay, the publisher was unenthusiastic, urged rewriting and in the end it was never published. Conceivably it might have been, if my mother had been able to go on working. The manuscript does not seem to have survived. There is no way of telling how seriously she took the short stories she wrote for the magazine market. On the other hand, she clearly took great and legitimate pride in the professionalism and literary quality of her translations.

How good a writer was she? I read her novel only many years later. When young I kept away from it, I don't know why. She wrote seriously with style in an elegant, lyrical, harmonious and carefully considered German, which was perhaps natural for a young Viennese intellectual who had once been a faithful attender at the recitals of the great Karl Kraus, but I cannot honestly claim that she looked like a writer of the first class. She also wrote poems which have disappeared. When I read them as a teenager, I shocked my aunt Gretl by telling her I did not think highly of them, believing even then that one should not delude oneself even about the people or things one cared about most in life.

These are the reconstructions of an old man, who still tries to be guided by this principle in his professional and private passions.

And in any case all this is quite irrelevant to my relations with the person who has had the most profound influence on my life. I am now old enough to be the grandfather of a woman who died at the age of thirty-six, and yet, it would seem absurd if somewhere across the Styx we were to meet and I would see her or treat her as a young woman. She would still be my mother. I would expect her to ask me what I had done with my life, and to tell her that I had managed to realize at least some of her hopes for me, that I had accepted at least some of the signs of public recognition because I believed they would have pleased her. And I think I would be no more honest or dishonest than Sir Isaiah Berlin who used to excuse taking his knighthood by saying that he had only done it to give pleasure to *his* mother. I have no doubt at all that the measurable proof that the boy she had made such efforts to turn into a proper Englishman had in the end become an accepted member of the official British cultural establishment would have given her greater happiness than anything in the last ten years of her short life.

I think her influence on me was above all moral, though in the days of her illness I was also moved by the desire not to hurt her or go against her wishes. I took notice of her even when she criticized my behaviour. I took her seriously. I think it was her honesty as well as her pride that carried conviction. She had no religious faith and no interest in being Jewish as such, although, to please her mother, she had gone through a religious marriage ceremony as well as a secular one. Yet, as I have already recalled, she gave me the lasting foundation for my own sense of being a Jew, to the irritation or puzzlement of those who cannot believe that a mere negative can be a sufficient basis for identity. She probably postponed my political commitment by suggesting that even very bright boys might need time for reflection and intellectual growth, just as she taught me that there were great writers who could be understood only when one got older. And, since she always levelled with me, she made me believe her.

Not that, even leaving age aside, we were on the same intellectual wavelength. Her enthusiasm for Pan-Europe, a somewhat conservative movement for a single European polity (but excluding Russia) propagated by an Austrian aristocrat, Count Coudenhove-Kalergi, never infected me. It was the one excursion of a liberal but basically non-political mind into the realm of politics. On the other hand she was frankly bored by the writings of her friend Grete Szana's husband, the peripatetic Alexander Szana, in which he reported on his politico-social travels to Russia (highly critical), to North Africa, and elsewhere. I listened to him avidly, no doubt encouraged by his generous gifts of the cosmopolitan stamps arriving in his newspaper office. Thanks to these memories I was later to choose to go to North Africa, when Cambridge offered me an undergraduate travel grant in 1938. I obviously derive my admiration for Karl Kraus from her, but her insistence on making me listen to a full performance of Saint-Saëns's *Samson and Delilah* on our grandparents' radio – I don't think we had one ourselves – put me off classical music for several years.

I still remember sitting by her bedside in the hospital, both of us listening to one another, as I prepared for growing up and she for death. She wanted to live. 'I wish I could believe it,' she told me, pointing to Mary Baker Eddy's *Christian Science Scriptures*, which a visitor had left her. 'Perhaps if I had that faith, it might do more for me than the doctors have done so far,' I remember her saying, 'but I can't believe it.' But shortly before her death she imagined she was getting better, she might even be cured. I am told this is always a reliable sign that the end is close at hand.

In retrospect the years between my parents' deaths appear a period of tragedy, trauma, loss and insecurity, which was bound to leave deep traces on the lives of two children who passed through it. This is certainly true, and it is clear that my sister took many years to recover from the loss of her father followed by an uncomprehending childhood and a resentful youth of constant disruption and emotional insecurity. I have no doubt at all that I must also bear the emotional scars of those sombre years somewhere on me. And yet I do not think I was conscious of them as such. That may be the illusion of someone who, like a computer, has a 'trash' facility for deleting unpleasant or unacceptable data, but one from which others may be able to recover them. However, I do not believe that this is the only explanation why, though not particularly happy, I did not experience these years as specially distressing. Perhaps the realities of the situation passed me by because I lived most of the time at some remove from the real world – not so much in a world of dreams, but of curiosity, enquiry, solitary reading, observation, comparison and experimentation – this was the only time in my life when I built myself a radio set (crystal-sets were easy to construct out of cigar boxes). Although in my year as a Boy Scout I developed at least one lasting friendship, I lived without intimacy. When I think about my own life in the last year before my mother's death, what comes into my mind are three memories: first, sitting alone on a swing in the garden of Mrs Effenberger, trying to learn by heart the song of the blackbirds, while noting the variations between them; second, receiving my mother's birthday present – a very cheap secondhand bike – with the sort of embarrassment that only teenagers suffer, since its frame was visibly both repainted and bent; and third, passing by a shop window framed by mirrors one afternoon and discovering what my face looked like in profile. Was I as unattractive as that? Even the fact (which I had learned from one of the fascinating popular science booklets of *Kosmos, Gesellschaft der Naturfreunde*) that I must clearly belong to the thin one of Kretzschmer's three psychosomatic types, and that, like Frederick the Great, I would therefore look better in old age, did not bring consolation. Like so much else, then and later, I kept my feelings to myself.

Nor, in later life, was I to think much about those times. After leaving Vienna in 1931 I never saw the grave again. In 1996 I went to look for it, as part of a television programme about interwar history as experienced by a central European child. But after more than sixty years of world history the grave, with the stone plate that my mother had ordered for it (at a cost of 400 Schillings), could no longer be found. The camera crew filmed me looking for the site. Only the electronic databank which the authorities of the Jewish section of the Vienna Central Cemetery, conscious of the American tourist trade, had had the foresight to compile, recorded that the grave contained the remains of Leopold Percy Hobsbaum, died 8 February 1929, Nelly Hobsbaum, died 12 July 1931 and – to my surprise – also Grandmother Ernestine Grün, died 1934.

4

Berlin: Weimar Dies

When I went back to Vienna in 1960 for the first time after almost thirty years, nothing appeared to have changed. The houses we had lived in and the schools we had attended were still there, even if they looked smaller now, the streets were recognizable, even the trams ran under their old numbers and letters, along the same routes. The past was physically present. Not so in Berlin. The first time I returned there, I stood outside what should have been the house we had all lived in, on the Aschaffenburgerstrasse in Wilmersdorf. On the map the street still ran from the Prager Platz to the Bayrischer Platz. The Barbarossastrasse should have opened just opposite the front door of our old apartment building, leading directly to my sister's school. But nothing was there any longer. There were houses, but I did not recognize them. As in one of those nightmares of disorientation and displacement, not only could I no longer identify anything about the place, but I did not even know in which direction to look to get my old bearings. The ruined building of my old school was still physically present on the Grunewaldstrasse, but the school itself had not survived the war. The location of my uncle's office in the city centre was not even identifiable on the map, since the whole area round Leipziger Platz and Potsdamer Platz, a bomb-destroyed no-man's land between East and West, had not been even notionally restored since the war. In Berlin the physical past had been wiped out by the bombs of the Second World War. On ideological grounds, neither the two Germanies of the Cold War nor the reunited Germany of the 1990s were interested in restoring it. The capital of the new 'Berlin Republic', like the West Berlin of the Cold War a subsidized showcase for the values of wealth and freedom, is an architectural artefact. The German Democratic Republic was not a great builder – its most ambitious construction, apart from the Stalinallee, was the Berlin Wall – neither was it much of a restorer, although it did its best with the architecturally very beautiful old Prussian centre of the city, which happened to lie in its territory. So the city in which I spent the two most decisive years of my life lives on only in memory.

Not that the Berlin of the last Weimar years was much to write home about architecturally. It was a boom city of the nineteenth century, that is to say essentially heavy late Victorian (in German terms: Wilhelmine), but lacking the imperial style and urban cohesion of the Vienna of the Ringstrasse, or the planning of Budapest. It had inherited a rather fine neo-classical stretch, but most of it consisted, in the heavily proletarian East – Berlin was a centre of industry – of the endless courtyards of giant 'rent-barracks' (*Mietskasernen*) on treeless streets, and in the greener and solidly middle-class West of more decorated and (obviously) more comfortable apartment blocks. Weimar Berlin was still essentially William II's Berlin which, except for its sheer size, was probably the least distinguished capital city of non-Balkan Europe, apart perhaps from Madrid. In any case, intellectual teenagers were unlikely to be impressed by the imperial efforts at memorability, such as the Reichstag and the adjoining Siegesallee, a ridiculous avenue of thirty-two Hohenzollern rulers immortalized in statues, all indicative of military glory and – this was a source of endless Berlin jokes – invariably with one foot behind and one in front. It was destroyed after the war by the victorious but humourless Allies, presumably as part of the elimination of Prussia, and all that might remind Germans of Prussia, from the post-1945 memory. It has left only one equally incongruous literary monument. Rudolf Herrnstadt, the former editor of the official daily of the East German government, purged from the Socialist Unity Party's leadership in 1953 and denounced as a supporter of Beria, the (executed) Soviet secret police chief, was exiled to the Prussian State Archives. (In fairness to a regime that has had a justifiably bad press, it must be said that no alleged traitor within its ranks was executed, even in the worst Stalinist years.) There he amused himself by writing a brilliantly funny squib, *Die Beine der Hohenzollern* (The Legs of the Hohenzollern) on the basis of a file he had discovered there. This was a collection of essays by secondary-school boys, set by some master desperate to extract pedagogic content from a class visit to the (then new) monument to Prussian patriotism. How far did the postures of the statues express the characters of their subjects? This was the topic on which the class wrote its compositions; evidently with such loyal success that the Kaiser himself asked to see the essays and commented on them in his own imperial hand. It was an exercise very much in the spirit of Weimar Berlin.

The Berlin in which the young of the middle class lived in 1931–3 was a place to move about in, not to stand and stare, of streets rather than buildings – the Motzstrasse and Kaiserallee of Isherwood and Erich Kästner and of my youth. But for most of us, the point of these streets was that so many led to the really memorable part of the city, the ring of lakes and woods that surrounded and still surrounds it: to the Grunewald, and its narrow tree- and bush-lined lakes, the Schlachtensee and the Krumme Lanke, along whose frozen surfaces we skated in winter – Berlin is a distinctly cold city – to Zehlendorf, gateway to the marvellous Wannsee system of lakes in the west. The eastern lakes were not such a regular part of our world. The west was where the rich and the very rich lived in grey stone mansions amid the trees. By a paradox not uncharacteristic of Berlin, the 'Grunewaldviertel' had been originally developed by a millionaire member of a local Jewish family that prided itself on a long left-wing tradition, going back to an avidly book-collecting ancestor converted to revolution in 1848 Paris – he had bought a first edition of Marx and Engels's *Communist Manifesto* there. It was represented in my lifetime by the sons and daughters of R. R. Kuczynski, a distinguished demographer who found refuge after 1933 at the LSE. All of them became lifelong communists, the two best known being Ruth, who, in a long and adventurous career in Soviet intelligence acted, among other things, as contact for Klaus Fuchs in Britain, and the charming and ever-hopeful economic historian Jürgen, an ingenious defender of what he took to be Marx's thesis on the pauperization of the proletariat, who took the gigantic family library back to East Berlin, where he died at the age of ninety-three, the doyen of his subject, having probably written more words than any other scholar of my acquaintance, even without counting the forty-two volumes of his *History of the Conditions of the Working Class*. He simply could not stop himself reading and writing. Since the family still owned the Grunewaldviertel, he was probably the richest citizen of East Berlin, which enabled him to extend the library and to offer an annual prize of 100,000 (Eastern)

Deutschmarks for promising work by young GDR scholars in economic history which, thanks to his support, flourished in East Germany. He survived the GDR, where he had expressed moderately dissenting opinions, which were tolerated because his ingenuous loyalty was so patent. And he had after all been in the Communist Party longer than the state's rulers.

For Berlin, like Manhattan (with which it liked to compare itself in the Weimar years), was politically a city left of centre. It lacked a historically rooted indigenous bourgeois patriciate, and was therefore more welcoming to the Jews. (The aristocratic tradition of Prussian court, army and state looked down on bourgeois of any description.) It was a bullshit-detecting city sceptical of claims to social superiority, nationalist rhetoric and sentimentality. In spite of Dr Goebbels, who made it his business to wrest it from the Reds on Hitler's behalf, it never became a Nazi city at heart. Unlike the dialect of Vienna, spoken in one way or another by everyone from emperor to dustman, the Berlin dialect, a speeded-up, wisecracking urban adaptation of the *plattdeutsch* language of the north German plain, was primarily a demotic idiom separating the people from the toffs, though well understood by all. The mere insistence on specific Berliner grammatical forms which, correct in dialect, were patently incorrect in school German, was enough to keep it separate from educated talk. Naturally the middle-class pupils of my classical *Gymnasium* took to it with enthusiasm, as the pupils of prestigious Paris *lycées* take to the plebeian argot of their city, and after the end of the GDR, inhabitants of the former East Berlin, resentful but proud, liked to distinguish themselves from the Western rulers of their part of Germany by insisting on 'berlinering', i.e. talking the broadest dialect. It was a confident, brash, in-your-face idiom, into which I also plunged with enthusiasm, even though to this day the native inflection of my German hints at Vienna. Even today the sound, now rare on the street, of pure Berlinerisch, brings back to me the historic moment that decided the shape both of the twentieth century and of my life.

I came to Berlin in the late summer of 1931, as the world economy collapsed. Within weeks of my arrival, Britain, its axis for the past century, abandoned both the gold standard and free trade. In central Europe catastrophe had been expected since the Americans called in their loans and it had occurred earlier that summer when two major banks had collapsed. Financial cataclysm did not have much direct impact on a displaced teenager, but unemployment, already rising steeply – it hit 44 per cent of the German labour force in 1932 – reached into our own family. My cousin Otto, who had lived with Sidney and Gretl and still visited them from time to time, had lost his job, and reacted by becoming a communist. He was not the only one: in 1932 85 per cent of the membership of the KPD (Communist Party of Germany) was unemployed. Younger than him, I was naturally impressed by someone so tall, handsome, successful with women, and now wearing a badge with the Russian initials of the Young Communist International. I suppose he was the first communist I had ever knowingly met: in Austria there were hardly any, and joining the Communist Party was therefore not something that would come to young men's minds until after the civil war of 1934 had discredited the social-democrat leaders.

The collapse of the world economy was up to a point something young persons of the middle class read about, rather than experienced directly. But the world economic crisis was like a volcano, generating political eruptions. That is what we could not escape, because it dominated our skyline, like the occasionally smoking cones of the real volcanoes which tower over their cities – Vesuvius, Etna, Mont Pelée. Eruption was in the air we breathed. Since 1930 its symbol was familiar: the black swastika in a white circle on red ground.

It is difficult for those who have not experienced the 'Age of Catastrophe' of the twentieth century in central Europe to see what it meant to live in a world that was simply not expected to last, in something that could not really even be described as a world, but merely as a provisional way-station between a dead past and a future not yet born, unless perhaps in the depth of revolutionary Russia. Nowhere was this more palpable than in the dying days of the Weimar Republic.

Nobody had really wanted Weimar in 1918, and even those who accepted, or even actively supported it, thought of it as at most a second-best compromise: better than social revolution, bolshevism or anarchy (if they were on the moderate right), better than the Prussian Empire (if they were on the moderate left). It was anybody's guess whether it would outlast the catastrophes of its first five years:

47

a penal peace treaty almost unanimously resented by Germans of all political stripes, failed military coups and terrorist assassins on the extreme right, failed local Soviet republics and insurrections on the extreme left, French armies occupying the heartland of German industry, and on top of all this, the (to most people) incomprehensible, and even to this day unparalleled, phenomenon of the galloping Great Inflation of 1923. For a few years in the middle 1920s it looked briefly as though Weimar might work. The Mark was stabilized – it remained stable until the war and again from 1948 until its demise – the most powerful economy of Europe, recovered from the war, had regained its dynamism, and for the first time political stability seemed in sight. It did not, it could not, survive the Wall Street Crash and the Great Slump. In 1928 the lunatic ultra-right had seemed virtually extinct. In the elections of that year Hitler's Nazi Party was reduced to 2.5 per cent and twelve seats in the Reichstag, actually less than the increasingly enfeebled Democrat Party, the most loyal supporters of Weimar. Two years later the Nazis came back with 107 seats, second only to the social democrats. What remained of Weimar was ruled by emergency decree. Between the summer of 1930 and February 1932 the Reichstag was in session for barely ten weeks, all told. And as unemployment rose, so, ineluctably, did the forces of some kind of radical-revolutionary solution: National Socialism on the right and communism on the left. These were the circumstances in which I came to Berlin in the summer of 1931.

I joined Nancy and seven-year-old Peter in Sidney and Gretl's flat in the Aschaffenburgerstrasse, rented from one of the many financially hard-pressed elderly widows of good family. I can remember very little about this apartment except that it was light and that the dinner conversation of the adults with their evening guests could be overheard from the room I slept in. Sidney and Gretl had a reasonably active social life, what with business acquaintances, relatives and Viennese friends visiting or living in Berlin, for little and impoverished interwar Austria was too small a scene for Viennese talent. We were too young to take much part in this. We took the *Vossische Zeitung*, a newspaper my aunt appreciated chiefly for the cultural pages, which she cut out. I have vivid memories of great cinemas and the elaborate luxury automobiles parked outside – Maybachs, Hispano-Suizas, Isotta-Fraschinis, Cords.

Within a few days of my arrival Uncle Sidney found a place for me within walking distance of the flat and Nancy's neighbouring Chamissoschule, at the Prinz-Heinrichs-Gymnasium in Schöneberg, in time to join the Obertertia (upper third form). Unlike Austrian and British secondary schools, German ones numbered downwards: one started in the Sexta (sixth form) and graduated with the leaving certificate (*Abitur*) from the Oberprima (upper first form). Of all the thirteen years I spent at seven educational establishments before going up to Cambridge, the nineteen or so months at the PHG have left the deepest impression on my life. It was the medium through which I experienced what I knew even then to be a decisive moment in the history of the twentieth century. Moreover, I experienced it, not as the child of Austria (even though I just reached puberty in my last year in Vienna), but at the Columbus-like moment of adolescence when passion and intelligence discover the world for the first time, and the very experience of living is unforgettable. Many years later an old friend brought me together with the then German ambassador to the UK, Günther von Hase, who, when my name had come up in conversation, immediately recalled me as having been in his form. And I, in turn, had immediately identified the name as that of a remembered face in the classroom in which both of us had sat – and that only for a few months in a long life, in which it is pretty certain neither of us had given any thought to the other since 1933. We were merely classmates, not in any sense friends. But we were there together at a time in our lives and in history which one does not forget. The very names revived it. In the low-lying landscape of my school years the PHG stands out like a sierra. For the first years after Berlin, life in England held no real interest.

Was my Berlin school really as important as it seems to me in retrospect? The artillery of Weimar bombarded an expectant fourteen-year-old from all sides. School did not teach me the songs which still mean 'Berlin' to me – those from the Brecht–Weill *Dreigroschenoper* to the bronze voice of Ernst Busch singing Erich Weinert's '*Stempellied*' ('Song of the Dole'). The great events of the times – the fall of the Brüning government, the three national elections of 1932, the Papen and Schleicher governments, Hitler taking power, the Reichstag fire – did not reach me through school, but through street posters, and via the daily paper and the periodicals at home (though, curiously, I have less memory of the radio news in Berlin than in Vienna). Those monuments of Weimar design and Weimar content, the books of the Malik Verlag, I remember them from the stands in the book department of the KaDeWe, the great department store on the Tauentzienstrasse, which is one of the few continuities with the Berlin of my youth: full of authors such as B. Traven, Ilya Ehrenburg, Arnold Zweig and, in a different mode, Thomas Mann and Lion Feuchtwanger.

Much of it, obviously, must have reached me through home. Uncle Sidney was enjoying one of his occasional spells of economic sunshine working for Universal Pictures, which as the producer of Lewis Milestone's *All Quiet on the Western Front*, the movie of Erich Remarque's celebrated antiwar novel, was at the epicentre of Weimar cultural politics. The Nazis had organized demonstrations against it and demanded that it should be banned. More than this: its boss, 'Uncle' Carl Laemmle, was the only Hollywood tycoon who came from Germany and had personal knowledge of what was going on there, because he returned for an annual visit to keep in touch. And he did. He was far from a highbrow, but to the informed eye the movies for which Universal was best known – *All Quiet* apart – the horror pictures such as *Frankenstein* and *Dracula*, clearly showed the influence of the German expressionist avant-garde.

Who knows how Sidney got into the movie business? Sometime in 1929 he had succeeded in talking himself into some kind of a job at Universal. It was uncertain and insecure. But while it lasted, it was recognized – if only by the personal gift by Uncle Carl himself of a signed copy of his biography, by the hand of an English litérateur and forgotten minor poet in the Georgian mode, John Drinkwater. (Laemmle had picked him after H. G. Wells had refused him because he was told that Drinkwater, of whom he had naturally not heard, had written a biography of Abraham Lincoln.) The book sold 164 bona fide copies in England.[1] Our copy has not survived the peripeties of the Hobsbawm family in the twentieth century.

What his *precise* functions in the company were, I never knew. A letter from my grandmother reports an offer to give him a job in the Paris office in the autumn of 1931, which he refused, because Gretl said the children (my sister and myself) had hardly had a chance to get used to the new schools in Berlin. Fate is determined by such short-term family decisions. What would our lives have been if we had gone to Paris in 1931? One of the jobs he certainly did was to fit out the expedition to shoot the film *S.O.S. Eisberg*, a polar adventure with Luis Trenker, a veteran of snow-and-rock pictures, and the air-ace Ernst Udet, who was earning his living as a stunt flyer until German rearmament gave him a distinguished place in Hitler's air force. Technical advice came from members of the Alfred Wegener expeditions, one of whom came to the house and told me about the theory of continental drift, and how he had all his toes frozen off in the Greenland winter. On at least one other occasion he promoted Hollywood products distributed in Europe – more specifically, *Frankenstein* in the Polish market. His campaign, of which he was proud, included the word-of-mouth rumour (for the benefit of the then very large Jewish public) that Boris Karloff, whose real name was an undramatic Pratt, was merely a lightly gentilized Boruch Karloff. He certainly had some connection with Poland, for at one time in the summer of 1932 there was some question of a permanent posting to Poland, and Sidney tried to prepare us for the very different life there. We would live in Warsaw. The Poles, he told me, were touchy people with a strong sense of honour, and a tendency to fight duels. I never had the chance to check out his information.

Nevertheless, on reflection, home was not anchored in Berlin as school was. As will be clear by now, the Hobsbawm household lived, not in Berlin, but in a transnational world, where people like us still – though the 1930s were to make it much more difficult – moved from country to country in search of a living. We might have roots in England or Vienna, but Berlin was merely one stop on the complicated route that might take us almost anywhere in Europe west of the USSR. Nor did home in Berlin – three addresses and two different forms of household in eighteen months – have the continuity of school. My window on the world at its moment of crisis was the Prinz-Heinrichs-Gymnasium.[2]

It was a perfectly conventional school in the conservative Prussian tradition, founded in 1890 to meet the needs of a rapidly growing middle-class area. Prince Henry, whose name it bore, a brother of Emperor William II, was a naval figure, which may explain why the school rightly prided itself on its boat club on the Little Wannsee (a model of its boat-house 'in the Spreewald style' had won a gold medal at the Brussels World Exposition of 1908). Rightly, because, while providing good training it was not, unlike its British equivalents, particularly interested in competitive races and it provided a wonderful opportunity for junior and senior boys to meet on equal terms. The club had somehow acquired a meadow, known as '*unser Gut*' (our estate) on the small fishery-protected Sakrower See, accessible only by special permission through a narrow waterway. Groups of friends made up crews to row there or meet there at weekends, to talk, look at the summer skies and swim across the green waters before returning to the evening city. For the first and only time in my life I could see the point of a sports club. An old boy of the school, Dr Wolfgang Unger, a physician at the Spandau hospital, kept an eye on the training of new recruits. I understand that, after being removed from his hospital post on racial grounds in 1934, he committed suicide, unwilling to leave his country, Germany.

A Prussian school with military connections was naturally Protestant in spirit, deeply patriotic and conservative. Those of us who did not fit this pattern – whether as Catholics, Jews, foreigners, pacifists or leftwingers, felt ourselves as a collective minority, even though in no measurable way an excluded minority.[3] Nevertheless it was not a Nazi school. (Few of the boys I knew showed much enthusiasm for Hitler and the Brownshirts, except Kube, the unusually dense son of a man who was Hitler's Gauleiter of Brandenburg, and who made it his business to get a literature teacher at the school fired on the grounds that he 'favoured' the surviving Jewish students and taught chiefly the degraded literature of the Weimar Republic. He was to become the notorious boss of occupied Belorussia during the war, until eventually assassinated by his patriotic local mistress.) On the contrary. Whatever sympathy the school might have had for the national revival promised by Hitler did not survive the forcible purging, not long after I left for England, of the highly respected and popular headmaster, *Oberstudiendirektor* Dr Walter Schönbrunn, a political undesirable under the new regime. He was replaced by an imposed and bitterly resented *Kommissarischer Leiter*. One can hardly call the PHG of the 1930s a centre of dissidence, but it is characteristic that Franz Marc's 'Tower of Blue

Horses' – I remember it well from the school hallway – banned as 'degenerate art' by the new authorities, was rescued from a store-room by one form and hung in its own classroom. Pupils protested against the dismissal of Professor 'Sally' Birnbaum, the popular mathematics and science teacher: signatures were collected all over the school for a petition to retain him. In the winter of 1936–7 the entire lower first form still made a collective visit to his home in the Rosenheimerstrasse. (He survived in Berlin until 1943 when he and his wife were loaded on to 36. Osttransport, destination, presumably, Auschwitz.) Indeed, there is some evidence that the school went out of its way to treat Jewish students and teachers well, at least while they remained. However politically unacceptable to a would-be teenage revolutionary, who would never have dreamed of wearing the peaked school cap (rather in the yachtsman's style with a soft top), it was a decent school.

This was undoubtedly due to what the Hitler regime recognized in Schönbrunn (generally known as 'der Chef' or 'the boss') as the anti-hierarchical and socially suspect spirit of Weimar. The boat club was one expression of it. The stress on student self-government and participation in disciplinary cases was another. The unforget-table camping and youth-hostelling class journeys through the Mark Brandenburg and Mecklenburg were a third. (Not for nothing had Dr Schönbrunn, equally qualified to teach German, Latin, Greek and mathematics, published a work with the title, whose tone is virtually untranslatable into non-German languages, *Jugendwandern als Reifung zur Kultur* (Youth Ripening into Culture by Hiking). I did not, personally, warm to this smallish man with sharp eyes behind rimless glasses and a receding hairline, who wore plus-fours when he joined his charges on a *Wandertag* or school journey. (But then, as every reader of the Tintin books knows, this was in Europe the era of plus-fours.) He dismissed my admiration for Karl Kraus and his journal *Die Fackel* with the phrase: '*Der Fackelkraus, ein eitler Schwätzer*' ('vain and garrulous'), which, in retrospect, is not 100 per cent off target. He criticized my prose style, which he regarded as excessively mannered.

Perhaps I would have forgiven him, had I known that he was an admirer of the architecture of the '*neue Sachlichkeit*' (new sobriety) and regarded both its uncluttered lines and 'the conscious austerity of modern creative writing ... as signs of a return to a new classicism', an apollonian spirit welcome to a teacher of ancient Greek. He chose the communist Ludwig Renn's novel *Krieg* (War) as an example of this new classicism. (He had of course, like most of our teachers, served in the 1914 war.) Still, if I did not exactly like him, I respected him. And I unquestionably benefited from his efforts, finally successful in the year before I came to the Grunewaldstrasse, 'finally to get truly modern works into the school library'.

Several of these works shaped my life. In a large encyclopedic guide to contemporary German writing I discovered the poems (as distinct from the songs and plays) of Bertolt Brecht. And it was to the school library that an exasperated master – his name was Willi Bodsch, and I remember nothing else about him – referred me when I announced my communist convictions. He told me firmly (and correctly): 'You clearly do not know what you are talking about. Go to the library and look up the subject.' I did so, and discovered the *Communist Manifesto* ...

What I learned in the formal schoolroom lessons is less clear. I can see that they were not a particularly central part of school experience, except as occasions for observing, manipulating and sometimes testing the nerves and authority of a group of ill-understood adults. Most of them seemed to me to be almost caricatures of German schoolmasters, square, with glasses and (when not bald) crew-cut, and to be rather old – they were mostly in their late forties or early fifties. All of them sounded like passionate conservative German patriots. No doubt those who were not kept a low profile, but most of them probably were. None more so than the George Groszian figure of Professor Emil Simon, whose Greek lessons we became expert at side-tracking, either by asking what Wilamowitz would have thought of the passage (good for at least ten minutes of panegyric about the greatest of German classical scholars) or, more reliably, stimulating his reminiscences of the world war. This would invariably lead us from construing Homer's *Odyssey* to a monologue about the experience of the frontline soldier, an officer's duty, the need for postwar order, Russian barbarism, the horrors of the October Revolution and the Cheka, Lenin's praetorian guard of Lettish riflemen and the like, plus a reminder that, contrary to what ignorant workers might think, Spartacus, far from of proletarian origins, had been a person of high social status before he was enslaved. It was, as I now recognize many decades later, an early version of the thesis used in the 1980s in mitigation of the Third Reich, namely that it had been necessary to defend an ordered society against bolshevism, and in any case the horrors of the Hitler era had been anticipated and were inspired by the horrors of Red Russia. So far as I know Emil Simon was not a Nazi, but merely a German conservative reminding himself of better days, such as might be heard in middle-class bars round the *Stammtisch* (the regulars' table). Irrespective of our politics, we made fun of him and pitied his son, a pale, fragile boy who sat in the front row of the class and carried the triple burden of being Emil's son, his pupil, and the witness to our ridicule of him.

In any case, life was too interesting to concentrate essentially on school work. I did not at this time have particularly brilliant school reports. The truth is, teachers and at least this pupil talked past one another. I learned absolutely nothing in the history lessons given by a small, fat old man, '*Tönnchen*' ('little barrel') Rubensohn, except the names and dates of all the German emperors, all of which I have since forgotten. He taught them by dashing round the form pointing a ruler at each of us with the words: 'Quick, Henry the Fowler – the dates.' I now know that he was as bored by this exercise as we were. He was, in fact, the most distinguished scholar in the school, author of a monograph on the mystery cults of Eleusis and Samothrace, a contributor to Pauly-Wissowa, the great encyclopedia of classical antiquity and a recognized classical archaeologist in the Aegean and papyrus expert long before the war. Perhaps I should have discovered this in the sixth form where education was no longer based on compulsory memorization. Until then the main effect of his teaching was, in effect, to turn at least one potential future historian off the subject. It is not surprising that in Berlin I learned by absorption rather than instruction. But, of course, I did learn.

The months in Berlin made me a lifelong communist, or at least a man whose life would lose its nature and its significance without the political project to which he committed himself as a schoolboy, even though that project has demonstrably failed, and, as I now know, was bound to fail. The dream of the October Revolution is still there somewhere inside me, as deleted texts are still waiting to be recovered by experts, somewhere on the hard disks of computers. I have abandoned, nay, rejected it, but it has not been obliterated. To this day I notice myself treating the memory and tradition of the USSR with an indulgence and tenderness which I do not feel towards Communist China, because I belong to the generation for whom the October Revolution represented the hope of the world, as China never did. The Soviet Union's hammer and sickle symbolized it. But what exactly made the Berlin schoolboy a communist?

To write an autobiography is to think of oneself as one has never really done before. In my case it is to strip the geological deposits of three quarters of a century away and to recover or to discover and reconstruct a buried stranger. As I look back and try to understand this remote and unfamiliar child, I come to the conclusion that, had he lived in other historical circumstances, nobody would have forecast for him a future of passionate commitment to politics, though almost every observer would have predicted a future as some kind of intellectual. Human beings did not appear to interest him much, either singly or collectively; certainly much less than birds. Indeed, he seems to have been unusually remote from the affairs of the world. He had no personal reasons for rejecting the social order and did not feel himself suffer even from the standard anti-Semitism of central Europe, since, fair-haired and blue-eyed, he was not identified as '*Der Jude*' but as '*Der Engländer*'. To be blamed for the Treaty of Versailles could be tough in a German school, but it was not demeaning. The activities to which I gravitated spontaneously at a school where I felt unquestionably happy had nothing to do with politics: the literary society, the boat club, natural history, the marvellous school journeys through the Mark Brandenburg and Mecklenburg, camping or staying the night in youth hostels on straw palliasses while, full of joy and passion, we talked half the night away. About what? About everything, from the nature of truth to who we were, from sex and more sex, to literature and art, from jokes to destiny. But not about the politics of the day. At least that is how I remember those unforgettable nights. Certainly I cannot recall political discussions, let alone disagreements, with my two closest friends, Ernst Wiemer and Hans-Heinz Schroeder, the class-room poet – he died in Russia during the war. What I had in common with them is unclear. I merely note that, on the graduation photograph of my class in 1936, they were among the only four of the twenty-three young men and two masters who had their *Abitur* recorded in open-necked shirts. Certainly it was not politics. While the one may not actually have been nationalist, our common subject was the nonsense poetry of Christian Morgenstern and the world in general. I did not disagree with the other's conventionally Prussian admiration for Frederick the Great, who may indeed also be admired on other grounds, but I certainly did not share the views that made him collect models of the soldiers of his armies.

In short, if I were to make the mental experiment of transposing the boy I was then into another time and/or place – say, into the England of the 1950s or the USA of the 1980s – I cannot easily see him plunging, as I did, into the passionate commitment to world revolution.

And yet, the mere fact of imagining this transposition demonstrates how unthinkable it was in the Berlin of 1931–3. It has indeed been imagined. Fred Uhlman, a few years older than me when he left Germany, a refugee lawyer who took to painting sad pictures of the bleak Welsh countryside, wrote a quasi-autobiographical novella later made into a film (*Reunion*) about the dramatic impact of the new Hitler regime on the school friendship of a Jewish boy, unconscious of impending cataclysm, and a young 'Aryan' aristocrat at a South German *Gymnasium* not unlike my own. Perhaps this was a possible scenario in Stuttgart, but in the crisis-saturated atmosphere of the Berlin of 1931–3, such a degree of political innocence was inconceivable. We were on the *Titanic*, and everyone knew it was hitting the iceberg. The only uncertainty was about what would happen when it did. Who would provide a new ship? It was impossible to remain outside politics. But how could one support the parties of the Weimar Republic who no longer even knew how to man the lifeboats? They were entirely absent from the presidential elections of 1932, which were fought between Hitler and the communist candidate Ernst Thälmann and old imperial Field Marshal Hindenburg, supported by all non-communists as the only way of holding up the rise of Hitler. (Within a few months he was to call Hitler to power.) But for someone like myself there was really only one choice. German nationalism, whether in the traditional form of the PHG or in the form of Hitler's National Socialism was not an option for an *Engländer* and a Jew, though I could understand why it appealed to those who were neither. What was there left but the communists, especially for a boy who arrived in Germany already emotionally drawn to the left?

As I entered the school year 1932–3, the sense that we were living in some sort of final crisis, or at least a crisis destined for some cataclysmic resolution, became overpowering. The presidential election of May 1932, the first of several in that ominous year, had already eliminated the parties of the Weimar Republic. The last of its governments, under Brüning, had fallen shortly after and given way to a clique of aristocratic reactionaries governing entirely by presidential decree, for the administration of Franz von Papen had virtually no support in the Reichstag, let alone even the makings of a majority. The new government immediately sent a small detail of soldiers to dismiss the government of the largest German state, Prussia, where a Social-Democratic–Centre Party coalition had maintained something like democratic rule. The ministers went like lambs, as Papen, trying to bring Hitler into his government, revoked a recent ban on the wearing of their uniforms by Nazi stormtroopers. Their deliberately provocative parades now became part of the normal street scene. Every day saw battles between the uniformed protection squads of the various parties. In July alone eighty-six were killed, mainly in clashes between Nazis and communists, and the number of those seriously injured ran into hundreds. Hitler, playing for higher stakes, forced a general election in July. The Nazis were returned with almost 14 million votes (37.5 per cent) and 230 seats – barely fewer than the combined strength of the Weimar parties (Social Democrats, Catholics and the now virtually invisible Democrats) and the communists with over 5 million and eighty-nine seats. For practical purposes the Weimar Republic was dead. Only the form of its funeral remained to be determined. But until there was agreement between the President, the army, the reactionaries and Hitler (who insisted on the Chancellorship or nothing), its corpse could not be buried.

This was the situation in which the school year began. If I remember my first year in Berlin in colour, my memories of the last six months are in darkening shades of grey with touches of red. The change was not only political but personal.

For as 1932 advanced, our prospects in Berlin dimmed. We became victims not of Hitler but of the 'Great Crisis' or, more specifically, of a new law vainly trying to stem the rising flood of unemployment by obliging foreign film companies (and no doubt other foreign enterprises) to employ a minimum of 75 per cent of German citizens. Sidney was dispensable. At least that is the most plausible explanation of what happened. Nothing came of the Polish proposal, but in the autumn of 1932, the Berlin job having evidently come to an end, Sidney took Gretl and Peter, then just seven, to Barcelona – whether on a mission for Universal, or with some local prospects in mind, I cannot say. I suspect that there were no firm prospects of permanence, for if there had been, the whole family would have moved. As it was, Nancy and I were left in Berlin for the time being to continue our schooling, until the outlook became clearer. It was the end of the new house and garden in Lichterfelde, an upmarket suburb to which we had moved from the Aschaffenburgerstrasse, next to someone in the music world who actually had the luxury of a small but genuinely private swimming-pool. Nancy and I moved in with the third of the Grün sisters, our peripatetic aunt Mimi, whose life had brought her, via various failed enterprises in English provincial towns ('we have too few debts to make bankruptcy worth while and just have to carry on'[4]) to a sublet apartment by the railway line in Halensee, a Berlin district by the far end of the Kurfürstendamm. There, as always, she took paying guests, offering the English ones German lessons. That is where we spent our last months in Berlin and saw in the Third Reich.

This was probably the only time in our lives that my sister Nancy and I lived together outside a family setting, for Mimi, living from hand to mouth as always and anyway unused to children – she never had any herself – hardly counted as such. I can only guess how the absence of any effective parental authority in these last months in Berlin affected Nancy, but I am fairly certain that my political activities would have been a good deal more constricted if Sidney and Gretl had stayed in Berlin. Being three and a half years older than my sister, I felt responsible for her. There was no one else now. I had never previously bothered about how she went to school, but only about the daily trauma of being forced to cycle from Lichterfelde to the *Gymnasium* on a machine of which I felt ashamed as only a teenager can, namely my dying mother's present, the black repainted secondhand bike with the bent frame. (I would arrive half an hour early at the bike-shed and sneak out late, afraid of being seen on it.) Now, however, we went to and came back from school together, for Halensee was a long way from Wilmersdorf (the PHG and the Barbarossaschule were virtually neighbours). Presumably we did so by tram, but I only recall the endless footslog during the dramatic four-day Berlin transport strike of early November. We were two youngsters alone. When she reached her twelfth birthday, I felt it was my duty to 'enlighten' her (as the German phrase went), namely to tell her about the facts of life, which she claimed she did not yet know. She may have been too polite to tell me she knew them already, or at any rate the part concerning women's periods, which were then the most immediately relevant to a girl reaching puberty. I cannot say that those months brought us closer together than two siblings who have gone through the same traumatic experiences are anyway. We had very little in common except these traumas, and my intellectualism and lack of interest in the world of people gave me a protection she lacked. I did not recognize this then. She did not share my interests or my life, increasingly dominated by politics. I did not even know what her life at school was, who were her friends or if she had any. I suppose we gossiped about Mimi and the paying guests, played cards in the evening, and sent letters to Spain. I elaborated stories for young Peter on the basis of a combination of Hugh Lofting's *Doctor Dolittle* and Christian Morgenstern's 'Nasobem', the animal that walks on its noses.

I seem to remember the Friedrichsruher Strasse only in grey or artificial light, presumably because in those months we were away from it for most of the day. In the evening we all met in the sitting room, which contained the original tenant's bookcase, which allowed me, for the first time, to read Thomas Mann (*Tristan*) and a short novel by Colette. Mimi, familiar with these situations, showed a genuine interest in the lives of her lodgers and went through her usual social repertoire, palmistry and other forms of character- and fortune-telling, and conversation about the reality of psychic phenomena with examples. She had – it is one of the few concrete details of life in Halensee that sticks in my mind – tried to save money by buying potatoes by the sackful for cooking, sending me down to the cellar from time to time to fetch up the necessary supply. As always, she lived on a financial knife-edge. As time went on they began to sprout, and had to be peeled with care to conceal this.

5

Berlin: Brown and Red

Meanwhile my revolutionary inclinations moved from theory to practice. The first person who attempted to give more precision to them was an older social-democratic boy, Gerhard Wittenberg. With him I passed the initiation ritual of the typical socialist intellectual of the twentieth century, namely the shortlived attempt to read and understand Karl Marx's *Capital*, starting on page one. It did not last long – at this stage of my life anyway – and, while we remained friends, I was attracted neither by German (as distinct from Austrian) social democracy nor by Gerhard's Zionism, which led him, after Hitler came to power, to emigrate to a kibbutz in Palestine, and eventually – so I understand – to be killed on a return trip to Germany on a mission to rescue Jews. (Zionist militants in those days were, of course, overwhelmingly socialists, mostly of various Marxist convictions.)

The person who recruited me to a communist organization was also older than me. How we got in touch I cannot remember, but it is not unlikely that there would have been talk about the Englishman in the Untersekunda (lower second form) who announced his red convictions. As I remember him, Rudolf (Rolf) Leder was dark, saturnine and with a taste for leather jackets, and clearly took the Party's idealized version of the Soviet bolshevik cadre as his model. He lived with his parents in Friedenau, and I can still visualize the two or three shelves on the narrow side of his small room on which he kept his books about communism and the Soviet Union. He must have lent me some – who else could I have borrowed them from – since I read several Soviet novels of the 1920s. None of them suggested a particularly utopian view of life in revolutionary Russia. In this they were like all Soviet fiction written before the Stalin era. Yet when I suggested to Rolf – I can still remember that conversation – that communism must run into problems because of Russia's backwardness, he bristled: the USSR was beyond criticism.

Through him I bought the special edition of a volume of documents and photographs celebrating the fifteenth anniversary of the October Revolution, *Fünfzehn Eiserne Schritte* (Fifteen Iron Steps). I have it still in its simple sand-coloured hardcover designed by John Heartfield, and on the flyleaf a quotation in my youthful hand (naturally in the German version) from Lenin's '*Left-Wing' Communism, an Infantile Disorder*. Together with the half-decayed paper booklet of *Unter roten Fahnen: Kampflieder* giving the texts of revolutionary songs, it is the oldest record of my political commitment.

Rolf Leder was a man who saw himself as out of place in the bourgeois environment of our school. He had, he claims in his autobiography, joined the Young Communists on the street not much more than a year before he recruited me, and was proud to have won acceptance in the streetwise milieu of young Berlin working-class reds by 'proving himself' in the 'time of latent civil war' when the comrades faced the cops and the brownshirt stormtroopers.[1] However, he did not suggest that I should join the KJV but a distinctly less proletarian organization, the Sozialistischer Schülerbund (SSB), designed specifically to hold secondary-school students. I did so, and he went his own way. I never saw him again after I left Berlin. He died in 1996.

Yet our lives remained curiously intertwined. Many years later, in a West German work on writers and communism, I discovered that a rather prominent member of the literary establishment in the German Republic, the poet Stephan Hermlin, was actually called Rudolf Leder. He had, I later discovered from his autobiography, stayed on illegally in Germany, refusing his family's offer to send him to Cambridge, suffering some months' imprisonment in a concentration camp. In 1935 he had been in France, he fought in Spain and later in the French Resistance, before returning to the Soviet-occupied zone in 1946 and a distinguished literary career in what was to become the GDR. From what I have read of his work, I think he was a good rather than an outstanding poet, probably better as a translator and adapter of other poets, and his brief, allusive memoir *Abendlicht* is widely admired. On the other hand, as a prominent figure on the cultural scene under a philistine and authoritarian regime he behaved well, protesting and protecting, and using his friendship with Honecker against the Stasi (secret police). This is an instance when the old German phrase '*Guter Mensch, schlechter Musikant*' ('good guy, bad musician') should be read not as a disparagement of the artist but as praise for the public man. I wrote him a letter, presumably care of the Writers' Union, to ask whether he was the Leder I had known, and received a brief answer, saying he was, but he could not remember me. Nor did he react later, when friends in Berlin mentioned me to him. However, the brief connection between two Berlin schoolboys in 1932, both of whom, in different ways and countries, became well-known figures on the cultural left, seems to fascinate both journalists and readers in post-1989 East Germany. At all events I have frequently found myself asked about it.

There is a curious coda to the episode of Rudolf Leder. Shortly before his death, Karl Corino, a West German literary bloodhound hostile to Stephan Hermlin, followed the trail of his public biography, and discovered that most of it was romance sometimes only tangentially connected with reality.[2] He had not abandoned a wealthy, cultured, art-collecting and music-loving household of the Anglo-German high bourgeoisie for the struggle of the workers. His father was a Romanian and later stateless businessman, married to a Galician immigrant to Britain (and therefore with a British passport), who had known a brief era of financial glory in the inflation years, followed by collapse. The father had not served in the First World War, nor died in a concentration camp, but in 1939 had reached safety in London. Hermlin himself had not been in a concentration camp, even briefly. He had not been to Spain. There was no evidence of work in the French Resistance. And so on. It was a highly effective and, in spite of the evident bias of the author and some of his sources, a convincing hatchet-job.

Of course Leder is not the only autobiographical writer who has cast himself (or herself) in a more romantic or important role in the affairs of the world, and modified the scenario of his life accordingly. Especially if we accept the investigator's evidence that much of his actual life before the return to Berlin in 1946, including his school career, had been disappointing. After all, for most of the time he did not so much invent as embellish or turn intention into reality. He had, indeed, left his job in Tel Aviv (the official Hermlin did not insist on the brief emigration to Palestine) declaring that he was going to join the Brigades in Spain, and he might well have gone there but for an operation whose consequences were almost fatal; and by the time he could leave Palestine, his wife was pregnant. His father had, after all, been a millionaire briefly, who did collect art, and had had his wife painted by Max Liebermann and himself by Lovis Corinth. Moreover, the career of any frontier-crossing German Jewish refugee in the 1930s and 1940s provides plenty of opportunities to improve reality on forms to be filled and questionnaires to be answered, and plenty of incentive to do so. And there is no question that, from sometime before I knew him in 1932, he had been a communist, and remained devoted to the Party until it ceased to exist with the end of the GDR, and that he had paid a price for his communism. Curiously, this brings our lives together again. For if Corino is right, Leder got himself formally expelled from his *Gymnasium* for writing an inflammatory article in the January 1932 issue of the paper published by the Sozialistischer Schülerbund, to which he was about to recruit me, the suitably named *Der Schulkampf* (Struggle in the School). If this had happened at the Prinz-Heinrichs-Gymnasium in the school years between 1931 and 1933, it is inconceivable that I would not have heard about it. Most likely he was expelled from another *Gymnasium*, and only joined the PHG in 1932–3 after that. Both of us were thus birds of passage in our school. How and why he left it, I cannot say.[3] He certainly did not graduate.

The organization I joined has only a shadowy place in the history of German or any other communism, unlike its inspirer, Olga Benario. This dynamic young woman, daughter of a prosperous bourgeois family in Munich, had been converted to revolution after the short-lived Munich Soviet republic of 1919, in which a young teacher, Otto Braun, with whom she was to be linked for some years, had taken part. In 1928, at the head of a team of young communists, she broke into the Berlin courtroom where Otto Braun was being tried for high treason and liberated him. Both were spirited away and, now permanently illegal, joined the Comintern and Red Army operational services. In Moscow Benario was to be attached as adviser to Luis Carlos Prestes, a Brazilian officer who had led a group of military rebels for some years in a celebrated long march through the backwoods of his country and was now about to join and lead the Brazilian Communist Party. She married him, helped to plan and took part with him in the disastrous insurrection of 1935, was captured and returned to Hitler's Germany by the Brazilian government. In 1942 she was killed in Ravensbruck concentration camp. Meanwhile Otto Braun had gone east rather than west to become the only European actually to take part (with a marked lack of enthusiasm for Mao Ze Dong) in the Long March of the Chinese Red Armies. Retired in East Berlin, he published his memoirs in the 1980s. When I joined the SSB to serve the world revolution, I was unaware of the historic bonds that would link the organization to some of its most dramatic battles, although I had no doubt that those who became communists in the Berlin of 1932 faced a future of danger, persecution and insurrection.

A less dramatic aspect of Benario's devotion to world revolution was the SSB itself.[4] This organization seems to have originated in Neukölln, one of the reddest districts of working-class Berlin, with politically organized social-democratic and communist working-class pupils in the so-called *Aufbauschulen* – the schools supported by the Prussian government, where selected children would make the transition to full secondary education and eventually the *Abitur*. Arriving in Neukölln as a dynamic new agit-prop cadre in 1926, Benario inspired school Young Communists to form a 'communist secondary fraction' (*Kopefra*)[5] in the *Aufbauschulen* on the analogy of the already existing 'student fractions' (*Kostufra*). Since these schools contained students from both working-class parties, it was decided to form a wider association covering both, the SSB. Inevitably, when social democrats became 'social fascists' for the Communist International, not much of this spirit of unity remained. The SSB had become a dependency of the Communist Party. By 1928 it had also extended outside the red areas of Berlin, with groups in Zentrum and Westen – that is to say in middle-class schools such as mine – and indeed into other parts of Germany. It also published the newly founded *Schulkampf*.

By the time I joined it in the autumn of 1932, the SSB was pretty well on its last legs, largely, it seems, because financial cuts during the economic crisis made life increasingly difficult for the *Aufbauschulen*, which were still its main support. Several groups ceased to exist in the second half of 1932, or met only irregularly. Co-ordinated action was no longer possible. Even in the strongholds of the cause, such as the Karl-Marx-Schule in Neukölln, the atmosphere at the end of 1932 was depressed and resigned. The *Schulkampf* is said to have ceased publication after May 1932, but I assume that this meant in printed form, since I still possess a later copy of it, patently duplicated by comrades who were not very skilled at handling duplicators. However, my small West Berlin cell of the association showed no signs of discouragement.

We met first in the apartment of the parents of one of our members, then fairly regularly in the backroom of a communist pub situated close to Halensee. The grassroots history of both the German and the French labour movements, neither of which had a strong temperance component, can be largely written in terms of the bars, in the front rooms of which comrades met to lift a glass of wine or (as in Berlin) beer, while more serious meetings were going on round the table in the back rooms. Of course drinks could be ordered in the front room and taken to the back, but the practice was discouraged. As a proper organization we had an *Orglei* (organizational leader), a boy called Wolfheim – first name Walter, I think – and a *Polei* (political leader or commissar), Bohrer, whom I recall as chubby. German and Russian communist organizations preferred syllabic abbreviations to initials, as in Komintern, Kolkhoz and Gulag and the use of second names gave meetings a certain formality. The only other member of the cell who has remained in my memory is a handsome and stylish Russian called Gennadi ('Goda') Bubrik, who came to meetings in a Russian shirt and whose father worked for one of the Russian agencies in Berlin. I assume we must have discussed the situation in our various schools and potential recruits or 'contacts', but by late 1932 national politics was incomparably more urgent than the problems with a reactionary master in, say, the Unterprima of the Bismarck Gymnasium. So the political situation undoubtedly dominated our agenda, Bohrer indicating 'the line' we were to follow.

What did we think? It is now generally accepted that the policy which the KPD pursued, following the Comintern line, in the years of Hitler's rise to power, was one of suicidal idiocy. It rested on the assumption that a new round of class confrontation and revolutions was approaching after the breakdown of the temporary stabilization of capitalism in the middle twenties, and that the chief obstacle to the necessary radicalization of the workers under communist leadership was the domination of most labour movements by the moderate social democrats. These assumptions were not in themselves implausible, but, especially after 1930, the view that social democracy was therefore a greater danger than the rise of Hitler, indeed, that it could be described as 'social fascism', bordered on political insanity.* Indeed, it went against the instincts, the common sense, as well as the socialist tradition of both socialist and communist workers (or schoolchildren), who knew perfectly well that they had more in common with one another than with Nazis. What is more, by the time I came to Berlin it was patent that the major political issue in Germany was how to stop Hitler's rise to power. Indeed, even the ultra-sectarian Party line made an, albeit empty, concession to reality. On our lapels we wore not the hammer and sickle, but the 'antifa' badge – a call for common action against fascism, though of course only with the workers, not with their power-corrupted and class-betraying leaders. Both socialists and communists knew, if only from the Italian example, that their destruction was the chief aim of a fascist regime. Conservatives, or even elements in the centre, might consider fitting Hitler into a coalition government, which, underestimating him, they hoped they might control. Socialists and communists knew perfectly well that compromise and coexistence with National Socialism were impossible both for it and for them. Our way of minimizing the Nazi danger – and, like all others, we also underestimated it grossly – was different. We thought that, if they got into power, they would soon be overthrown by a radicalized working class under the leadership of the KPD, already an army of three to four hundred thousand. Had not the communist vote increased almost as fast as the Nazi vote since 1928? Was it not continuing to rise sharply in the last months of 1932, as the Nazi vote fell? But we had no doubt that before then the wolves of a fascist regime would be loosed against

* How preposterous it was is indicated by the example of the Italian communist leader Palmiro Togliatti who *in 1933* had to undertake 'self-criticism' for having observed that, at least in Mussolini's Italy, it was not possible to say that social democracy was 'the main danger'.

us. And so they were: the original concentration camps of the Third Reich were designed primarily to hold communists.

Excuses for the lunacies of the Comintern line may no doubt be found, even though there were socialists and dissident or silenced communists who opposed it. Seventy-odd years later, and with the historian's professional hindsight, one is less sanguine about the possibility of stopping Hitler's rise to power by means of a union of all antifascists than we came to be later in the 1930s. In any case, by 1932 a parliamentary majority of the centre-left was no longer possible even in the doubly improbable case that the communists had been willing to join it, and that the social democrats, let alone the Catholic Centre Party, had accepted them. The Weimar Republic went with Brüning. Hitler could indeed have been stopped by the President, the Reichswehr and the assorted authoritarian reactionaries and businessmen who took over then, and who certainly did not want what they got after 30 January 1933. Indeed, Hitler and the momentum of the rise of the swastika was stopped by them after the Nazis' electoral triumph in the summer of 1932. There was nothing inevitable about the events which led to his appointment as Chancellor. But by this time there was nothing either social democrats or communists could have done about it.

Nevertheless, in retrospect the Comintern line made no sense. Were we in any sense critical of it? Almost certainly not. Radical, once-for-all change was what we wanted. Nazis and communists were parties of the young, if only because young men are far from repelled by the politics of action, loyalty and an extremism untained by the low, dishonest compromises of those who think of politics as the art of the possible. (National Socialism did not leave much public scope for women, and at this stage, alas, its passionate support for women's rights did not attract more than a minority of exceptional women to an overwhelmingly male communist movement.) Indeed, the militant Young Communist Leagues were the Comintern's chief catspaws in pushing the often reluctant adult leadership of the Parties into the extremes of the 'class against class' policy. The Nazis were certainly our enemies on the streets, but so were the police, and the chiefs of police of Berlin, whose men had killed some thirty men on May Day 1929, were social democrats. The KPD had made this incident into an emblem of social-democratic class betrayal. And who could respect the institutions of Weimar law and government, which were essentially those of the empire, without the Kaiser?

We were thus recognizably like the young ultras of 1968, but with four major differences. First, we were not a minority of radical dissidents in societies that had never been more prosperous and with political systems of unquestioned stability. In the economically storm-tossed and politically brittle Germany of 1932 those who radically rejected the status quo were the majority. Second, unlike the 1968 student radicals, we – right or left – were not protesters but engaged in an essentially revolutionary struggle for political power; more exactly, disciplined political mass parties seeking sole state power. Whatever was to come after, taking power was the first, indispensable step. Third, comparatively few of us on the ultra left were intellectuals, if only because even in a well-schooled country like Germany over 90 per cent of young people never got even a secondary education. And among the intellectual youth, we on the left were a modest minority. The bulk of secondary students were almost certainly on the right, though – as in my own school – not necessarily on the National Socialist right. Among the university students support for Hitler was notoriously strong.

The fourth difference was that the communist intellectuals were not cultural dissidents. Culturally the major divide was not, as in the era of rock music, between generations, but the basically political conflict between those who accepted and those who rejected what the Nazis called 'cultural bolshevism', that is to say almost everything that made the fourteen years of the Weimar Republic such an extraordinary era in the history of the arts and sciences. In Berlin, at least, we shared this culture with our seniors, for pre-Stalinist communism, while distinguishing sharply between writers and artists with the 'right' and those with the 'wrong' line, did not yet reject the men and women of the cultural avant-garde who had so patently hailed the October Revolution and shared the KPD's distaste for the Republic of Ebert and Hindenburg. 'Socialist Realism' was still below the horizon. An admiration for Brecht, the Bauhaus and George Grosz did not separate parents and children, but it did separate the right from a sort of cultural popular front that stretched from the social-democratic authorities of Prussia and Berlin to the furthest outskirts of anarchist bohemia. It also united liberals with the left. The chief reason why in its day the German Democratic Republic had a far more liberal legislation on birth control and abortion than the western Federal Republic was that, in the days of Weimar, legalizing abortion, prohibited by the German Civil Code, had been a major campaigning issue for the KPD. I look at my surviving copy of the *Schulkampf*, and there it is still, together with announcements of meetings by the medical men so long associated with sexual emancipation.

Reconstructing my experience of the last months of the Weimar Republic, how can I disentangle memory from what I now know as a historian, what I now think after a lifetime of political reflections and debates about what the German left should or should not have done? Then I knew no more of what was happening between the triumph of the Nazis at the elections of 30 July 1932 and Hitler's appointment as Chancellor on 30 January 1933 than I read in the *Vossische Zeitung*. In any case, I did not really react to the news politically or critically, but as a romantic partisan, or a football supporter. The Berlin transport strike, which took place shortly before the last democratic election of the Republic in early November 1932, was then, and has been ever since, the subject of bitter polemics. It was successfully called, against the official (social-democratic) unions by the communist RGO (Red Union Opposition) and, since the National Socialists were anxious not to lose contact with the workers, supported by the Nazi union organization. It is not surprising that this temporary common front between red and brown in the dying weeks of the Republic has had a bad press, and is still quoted against the Weimar communists. It certainly demonstrates the irrationality of a party which, knowing that the entry of Hitler into government might be imminent, continued to treat the social democrats as its main adversary. As it happened the principal immediate consequences of the strike were, probably, to help the communist vote to rise quite sharply in the election on 6 November, and to contribute to the dramatic decline of the Nazi vote in that election – but both were soon forgotten. And yet I cannot remember either discussing the issue with anyone during the strike, or being worried about it, or even thinking about it. It was 'our' strike. Hence we were for it. We knew that we were the main enemy of the Nazis and their main target. Hence the idea that we could be accused of lending a helping hand to Hitler was absurd. Where was the problem?

Nevertheless there was a problem. Even as youthful believers in the inevitability of world revolution we knew, or must have known in the last months of 1932, that it was not going to happen just then. We were certainly not aware that by 1932 the international communist movement had been reduced to almost its lowest point since the establishment of the Comintern, but we knew that defeat was what faced us in the short run. Not we but someone else was making a bid for power. Indeed, neither the rhetoric nor the practical strategy of the KPD envisaged anything like an imminent takeover. (On the contrary, the Party was making serious preparations for illegality, though, as it turned out, nowhere near serious enough: its leader Ernst Thälmann was caught in the first months of the new regime and imprisoned in one of the new concentration camps.) What is more, once Hitler was in power, there was no more room for illusion. So what exactly was in the mind of teenage would-be militants like me?

Certainly the knowledge that we were essentially a global movement comforted us. The triumphant USSR of the first Five-Year Plan stood behind us. Somewhere even further east, the Chinese revolution was on the march. That there was *Storm over Asia* (to quote the title of Pudovkin's great film) made communists at that time probably more acutely aware of Asia than anyone else. That was the time when China became, for Bertolt Brecht and André Malraux, the quintessential locale of revolution, and the test of what it meant to be a revolutionary. It is probably not fortuitous that the only specific newspaper headline which I recall from those days (apart from the obvious ones announcing Hitler's appointment as Chancellor and the Reichstag fire) is one reporting the mutiny of a Dutch warship, the *Seven Provinces*, off Java a few days after Hitler took power. It was not the drama of insurrection we expected to experience, but that of persecution. In our minds – at least in mine – the image before us was that of danger, capture, resistance to interrogation, defiance in defeat. Ideally we imagined ourselves in the role that would be played in real life within less than a year by Georgi Dimitrov, defying Göring at the Reichstag fire trial. But always with the confidence, derived from Marxism, that our victory was already inscribed in the text of the history books of the future.

So much for the image. What of the reality? Until a few days before Hitler's appointment I cannot recall undertaking any actual communist activity other than going to the meetings of the SSB cell. No doubt, like all of us, my spirits were lifted by the sharp setback for the Nazis at the elections of 6 November, and by our own impressive advance, but I am quite certain that I had no understanding of the meaning of the Papen government's fall, and the activities of the shortlived new government of General Schleicher, the last Chancellor before Hitler, or of the December crisis within the Nazi Party, when Hitler eliminated the second most important, or at least prominent, member of his party, Gregor Strasser. On the other hand, there was nothing problematic about the increasing aggressiveness and deliberately provocative tactics of the brownshirts, and their tacit toleration by the public authorities. On 25 January 1933 the KPD organized its last legal demonstration, a mass march through the dark hours of Berlin converging on the headquarters of the Party, the Karl Liebknechthaus on the Bülowplatz (now Rosa Luxemburg-Platz), in response to a provocative mass parade of the SA on the same square. I took part in this march, presumably with other comrades from the SSB, although I have no specific memory of them.

Next to sex, the activity combining bodily experience and intense emotion to the highest degree is the participation in a mass demonstration at a time of great public exaltation. Unlike sex, which is essentially individual, it is by its nature collective, and unlike the sexual climax, at any rate for men, it can be prolonged for hours. On the other hand, like sex it implies some physical action – marching, chanting slogans, singing – through which the merger of the individual in the mass, which is the essence of the collective experience, finds expression. The occasion has remained unforgettable, although I can recall no details of this demonstration. I can only remember endless hours of marching, or rather alternately shuffling and waiting, in the freezing cold – Berlin winters are hard – between shadowy buildings (and policemen?) along the dark wintry streets. I cannot remember red flags and slogans, but if there were any – and there must have been some – they were lost in the grey mass of the marchers. What I can remember is singing, with intervals of heavy silence. We sang – I still have the tattered pamphlet with the texts of the songs, ticks against my favourites: the 'Internationale', the peasant war song '*Des Geyers schwarzer Haufen*', the sentimental graveyard doggerel of '*Der kleine Trompeter*', which (I am told) the leader of the GDR, Erich Honecker, wanted played at his funeral, '*Dem Morgenrot entgegen*', the Soviet Red Airmen's Song, Hanns Eisler's '*Der rote Wedding*', and the slow, solemn, hieratic '*Brüder zur Sonne zur Freiheit*'. We belonged together. I returned home to Halensee as if in a trance. When, in British isolation two years later, I reflected on the basis of my communism, this sense of 'mass ecstasy' (*Massenekstase*, for I wrote my diary in German) was one of the five components of it – together with pity for the exploited, the aesthetic appeal of a perfect and comprehensive intellectual system, 'dialectical materialism', a little bit of the Blakean vision of the new Jerusalem and a good deal of intellectual anti-philistinism.[6] But in January 1933 I did not analyse my convictions.

Five days later Hitler was appointed Chancellor. I have already described the experience of reading the news headline somewhere on the way back from school with my sister. I can see it still, as in a dream. It is now known that he resisted the Conservatives' proposal to ban the Communist Party immediately, partly because this might provoke a desperate attempt at public resistance by the Party, mainly because it strengthened the Nazi argument that only its paramilitaries, the SA, preserved the country from bolshevism, and to lend a national rather than partisan character to the enormous Nazi demonstration on the day of the transfer of power. (It is impossible to imagine that anyone, including themselves, took seriously the call for a general strike which the KPD leadership claimed to have issued on 30 January, presumably to go on record as not having given in without a gesture.) Indeed the SA and SS (at that time much less prominent) were soon authorized to act as auxiliary police, and began to organize their own concentration camps – as yet without official state authorization.

The new government avoided giving the Reichstag, or anyone in it, even the faintest chance of expressing an opinion, by dissolving it immediately and calling for new elections at the soonest possible constitutional moment, 5 March. Within days a suitable Emergency Decree for the Protection of the German People restricted press freedom and gave cover to 'protective custody'. On 24 February the brownshirt and blackshirt paramilitary forces of the Nazi Party were enrolled as 'auxiliary police'. On that day the police raided the Party headquarters, claiming to find great quantities of treasonable materials, though actually nothing of significance was discovered. Such were the conditions under which the last nominally free multi-party elections of the Weimar Republic were to be held. And then, less than a week before the vote, an utterly unexpected joker was slipped into the cards already stacked against the opposition. On the night of 27 February the Reichstag building was burned down. Whoever did it, the Nazis immediately exploited the occasion to such spectacular effect that most antifascists came to believe that they must have planned the fire.* An emergency decree on the next day suspended freedom of speech, association and the press as well as privacy of post and telephone services. For good measure, the decree also allowed the autonomy of the Länder by the right of the Reich government to intervene to restore order. Göring had already begun to round up communists and other undesirables. They were dragged into improvised prisons, beaten up, tortured and in some cases even killed. By April 25,000 were in 'protective custody' in Prussia alone.

The immediate reaction of the SSB, or at least my part of it, was to bring the duplicating apparatus to my aunt's flat. I like to think it may have been the very one on which the last issues of the *Schulkampf* had been produced. The comrades concluded that, since I was a British subject, I would be less at risk; or perhaps that the police would be less likely to raid our flat. I kept it under my bed for some weeks, a largish brown wooden case of that now antediluvian type where specially typed stencils had to be placed on a permeable inked surface, and each leaf had to be printed singly. Then someone came to take it away. I don't think any printing was done on it while it was in my charge, for if there had been any, even

---

* At the time of writing the general opinion among historians is still that it was a young Dutch leftist making a spectacular protest in the hope of galvanizing the workers into action, and not a put-up job by the Nazis.

my undomestic aunt would have protested at the almost inevitable spreading of fatty ink in my bedroom. It was that sort of machine.

Presumably a more efficient printing press must have been used to produce the leaflets which we were supposed to use for the election campaign. I suppose taking part in that campaign was the first piece of genuinely political work I did. It was also my introduction to a characteristic experience of the communist movement: doing something hopeless and dangerous because the Party told us to. True, we might have wanted to help in the campaign in any case, but, given the situation, we did what we did as a gesture of our devotion to communism, that is to say to the Party. Much in the way that I, finding myself alone in a tram with two SA men, and justifiably scared, refused to conceal or take off my badge. We would go into the apartment buildings and, starting on the top floor, push the leaflets into each flat until we came out of the front door, panting with the effort and looking for signs of danger. There was an element of playing at the Wild West in this – we were the Indians rather than the US cavalry – but there was enough real danger to make us feel genuine fear as well as the thrill of risk-taking. A year or so later I described it in my diary as 'a light, dry feeling of contraction, as when you stand before a man ready to punch you, waiting for the blow'. What might happen if a door opened on a hostile face, if a brown uniform came down the stairs, if our exits to the street were blocked? Distributing election appeals for the KPD was no laughing matter, especially in the days after the Reichstag fire. Nor was voting for it, although over 13 per cent of the electorate still did so on 5 March. We had a right to be scared, for we were risking not only our own skins, but our parents'.

The Party was officially banned. The unofficial concentration camps became official. Dachau, the first, was set up on the same day that the new Reichstag (now minus the banned communists) passed an Enabling Act which handed total control to the Hitler regime and abolished itself. Then, in late March, my sister and I heard that we were to go to England. Whatever plans Uncle Sidney had in Barcelona had not come off. Hitler had just announced a boycott of Jewish businesses in early April, and as I said good-bye to my friends, I arranged for one of them – probably Gerhard Wittenberg – to send me news of it. (He gave me the address of the kibbutz organization he would join on emigrating to Palestine.) Then we left. Aunt Mimi had also decided on yet another migration. Her Berlin venture had not been more successful than usual, and my sister's and my going removed a vital element in her income. I have a vague memory that Nancy was supposed to join Gretl and little Peter – could it have been in Barcelona? – from where they would follow Sidney and me to England. It was another disorientating move in the uprooted life of a displaced child. Sidney came for me. Political as my primary passion was by then, I still arranged that the old bike with the bent frame, the present from my mother that had caused me so much embarrassed teenage anguish, should be lost when the Hobsbaum effects were packed for storage.

I was not to return to Berlin for some thirty years, but I never forgot it and never will.

6

On the Island

I

The most unexpected thing about coming to Britain was the sheer size of London, then still by far the largest city in the western world, a vast shapeless polyp of streets and buildings stretching its tentacles into the countryside. Even after seventy years of metropolitan-based life, the size and incoherence of this city still astonishes me. In my first years in Britain I never ceased to marvel at the distances I traversed in it as a matter of course: by bike, north and south, to school in Marylebone from the heights of Crystal Palace, and later from Edgware; by car east and west, driving my uncle between Ilford and Isleworth, never out of sight of rows of buildings.

Somewhere among these 'twenty-thousand streets beneath the sky' (as the gifted but alcoholic communist writer Patrick Hamilton called his London novel of the 1930s) the Hobsbaum family had to find a footing. We were subjects of King George V, and therefore – as I still have to remind interviewers and other enquirers – not in any sense refugees or victims of National Socialism. However, in every other respect we were immigrants from central Europe, even provisional immigrants – for we did not reclaim our Berlin possessions from storage until 1935 – in a country unknown to all of us except Uncle Sidney, and even he had not lived in it since the Great War. Apart from relatives we did not know a soul. We were not even former emigrants returning to their native country, for the future situation of the Hobsbaums remained as cloudy as it had been until 1933. The first place after Berlin where all the family came together in the spring of 1933 was in one of Mimi's multiple ventures into the world of guest-houses, this time in Folkestone. It could have stood for any of so many temporary staging-posts on the endless migrations of the twentieth-century uprooted. A German refugee lady expressed incidental appreciation of the charm and physique of a Swiss teenage boy, evidently about to go to school somewhere in England. A German refugee of my age, on the way to a Zionist agricultural training camp, tried to teach me a little judo. A grey figure from Carpathian Europe, one Salo Flohr, stranded by Alekhine's refusal to accept his challenge for the world chess title, played chess with Uncle Sidney, while waiting to travel to Moscow to confront the Soviets' Mikhail Botvinnik. Flohr never made it to the top, but was to become a well-known figure in the Soviet chess world and, presumably, one of the few people for whom emigration to Stalin's Russia in the 1930s was not a disaster. There, on sunny mornings on the lawn, I discovered English lyric poetry through the *Golden Treasury* and read Lewis Carroll's *Through the Looking Glass* for the first time. For, already at school in London, I joined all of them in Folkestone for a few weeks, while I prepared to sit the examination of the London Matriculation in unknown or strange subjects, conducted in a language I had hardly used outside the household.

In fact, except for me, and for my indomitable aunt Mimi, coming to England in 1933 turned out to be yet another of many failed attempts by the Hobsbaum–Grüns to find a landfall in the stormy seas of the interwar world. Gretl died in 1936, a little older than my mother but still in her thirties. In 1939, after a few years of variable success, Sidney, aged fifty, abandoned the struggle to make a living in England and emigrated to Chile, taking Nancy and Peter with him. Santiago, where he remarried, remained his home. Nancy, whose life really began in South America with the war, returned to Britain with her husband, Victor Marchesi, in 1946, but as a naval officer's wife continued the peripatetic life for some years and ended it as a retired British settler in Menorca. Peter, qualified as a chemical engineer in Canada, spent most of his life as an expatriate oil company executive and ended it in Spain. Only my future was decided for good in 1935 by the decision to sit the Cambridge scholarship exam, and my aunt Mimi's, not much later, when she fell in love with an available site in an enchanting and protected corner of a South Downs valley a short bus ride from Brighton, on which she realized her life's ambition, a place of her own, namely the collection of sheds and stalls she built into the Old Vienna Café. There she died herself, defiantly red-haired, in 1975 at the age of eighty-two, leaving the modest proceeds of the sale of her property to Nancy and myself. It was the only money either of us ever inherited from Grüns or Hobsbaums.

Not that I felt like someone preparing for what turned out to be the long life of a British academic, although I hoped, even at the age of seventeen, that 'my future will lie in Marxism, in teaching or in both' (I knew well enough that it did not lie in poetry, although 'with practice I could develop quite an acceptable prose style').[1] Spiritually, I still lived in Berlin: a newly isolated teenager uprooted from an environment in which he had felt happy and at home, both culturally and politically. My diary keeps referring back to the friends and comrades, the opinions of my old headmaster, the dramatic political experiences I had left behind. That, no doubt, was the chief reason why I began to keep my diary in German. I did not want to forget. In mid-1935 the visit of a recent German socialist émigré who tried to involve me in the activities of her group – I suspect it was the one called *Neubeginnen* ('a new start') – reminded me of how isolated my life really was. She ('in short "the modern woman" of my dreams') was 'part of a world to which I once belonged for a few months and whose existence, living behind the stage settings of my ideas, I have almost forgotten'.[2]

After the excitements of Berlin, Britain was inevitably a comedown. Nothing in London had the emotional charge of those days, except – in a very different form – the music to which my viola-studying cousin Denis introduced me, and which we played on a hand-wound gramophone in the attic room of his mother's house in Sydenham, where the family first found shelter in London, and discussed with the intensity of teenage passion over tins of heavily sugared condensed milk ('Unfit for Babies') and cups of tea: hot jazz. Not much of it was as yet available, and certainly, given our cash limits, not much at any one moment. The sort of teenagers who were most likely to be captured by jazz in 1933 were rarely in a position to buy more than a few records, let alone build a collection.[3] Still, enough was already being issued in Britain for the local market: Armstrong, Ellington, Fletcher Henderson and John Hammond's last recordings of Bessie Smith. What is more, shortly before a trade dispute stopped American jazz-players from coming to Britain for some twenty years, the greatest of all the bands – I can still recite its then line-up from memory – came to London: Duke Ellington's. It was the season when Ivy Anderson sang 'Stormy Weather'. Denis and I, presumably financed by the family, went to the all-night session ('breakfast dance') they played at a Palais de Danse in the wilds of Streatham, nursing single beers in the gallery as we despised the slowly heaving mass of South London dancers below, who were concentrating on their partners and not on the wonderful noises. Our last coins spent, we walked home in dark and daybreak, mentally floating above the hard pavement, captured for ever. Like the Czech writer Josef Skvorecky, who has written better about it than most,[4] I experienced this musical revelation at the age of first love, sixteen or seventeen. But in my case it virtually replaced first love, for, ashamed of my looks and therefore convinced of being physically unattractive, I deliberately repressed my physical sensuality and sexual impulses. Jazz brought the dimension of wordless, unquestioning physical emotion into a life otherwise almost monopolized by words and the exercises of the intellect.

I did not then guess that in adult life my reputation as a jazz-lover would serve me well in unexpected ways. Then and for most of my lifetime a passion for jazz marked off a small and usually embattled group even among the cultural minority tastes. For two-thirds of my life this passion bonded together the minority who shared it, into a sort of quasi-underground international freemasonry ready to introduce their country to those who came to them with the right codesign. Jazz was to be the key that opened the door to most of what I know about the realities of the USA, and to a lesser extent of what was once Czechoslovakia, Italy, Japan, postwar Austria and, not least, hitherto unknown parts of Britain.

What contributed to the ultra-intellectualization of my next years was the fact that I lived constantly with an effective pair of parents, who flatly refused to allow their impassioned sixteen-year-old to plunge into the life of political militancy which filled his mind. No doubt they took the view that concentrating on getting into a university under his own steam was the first priority for an obviously bright boy who could not rely on family cash. They were of the firm opinion that I was too young to join the Communist Party.[5] For the same reason, and in spite of family solidarity with Uncle Harry, they were equally opposed to my joining the Labour Party, which I proposed to do in order to subvert it – what later political generations of Trotskyists knew as 'entryism'. I now know how they must have felt, confronted with my combination of priggishness and immaturity. I cringe as I reread the desperate entries in my diary for 1934 during this episode of family crisis. So, though the ban was slowly relaxed, for the following two and a half years I lived a life of suspended political animation, and correspondingly concentrated on intense intellectual activity and an amount of reading that in retrospect still amazes me. Not that the British revolution seemed to be making much progress with or without me.

Since for the next three years we lived so closely together, let me recall the two people who had become my sister's and my new parents. Both Nancy and I agreed that they were fairly useless at this job, but, looking back at my diary of 1934–5, I think we underestimated both the problems of adults forced to face a series of migrations in several countries, and the extraordinary strains of dealing with two difficult orphans whose disrupted lives had had no real chance to settle, not to mention a peripatetic small boy of eight who was always falling ill. Bringing up the two of us must have been a nightmare. Anyway, they made as much of a mess of their own son's upbringing as of ours, although it did me less harm than my sister, who developed a settled determination to live an adult life which had nothing whatever in common with the continental, emotional, argumentative, intellectual households of her teenage years. Indeed, I can recall her most fondly as a demonstrably conventional Anglican country matron and Conservative Party activist in Worcestershire in the 1960s.

Unlike her, I had no real reason for blaming them. On the contrary, they struck me not as tyrannical but, as I wrote shortly before my eighteenth birthday, as 'tragic'. I saw them, especially Gretl, as the victims of the decline and disintegration of the old conventions that had determined the relations between the generations. The Victorian rules about bringing up children were dead. They had been tough on the children – though probably not unacceptable to most – but a great prop for parents. Now nothing filled this gap. Paradoxically I came to analogous conclusions as my sister from the opposite point of view. The future should not bring a society without accepted rules and a firm structure of expectations. 'The socialist state,' I told my diary, 'must and will create a new socialist convention which will get rid of the disadvantages of the old conventions while maintaining their advantages.' One might even say that I developed the instincts of a Tory communist, unlike the rebels and revolutionaries drawn to their cause by the dream of total freedom for the individual, a society without rules.

I liked my aunt Gretl enormously, and developed a deep respect for her common sense. What is less usual between parents and touchy teenagers, I liked to talk to her about the problems of life, and parts of my reading. Furthermore, I took her opinions seriously, even on such subjects as sex and love, of which I knew nothing. However, obviously, she could not replace my mother.[6] As I passed people in the street, I would sometimes stare, shut my eyes for a moment and say to myself, 'he or she has eyes like Mama'.[7] The youngest, prettiest and socially the most successful of the Grün girls, cherished by both her sisters, and the only one never to have had to earn a living, Gretl faced the slings and arrows of the outrageous fortune of her life and family – and there were plenty – armed with charm, sympathy, an inborn sensibleness and a notable lack of self-pity. 'Sidney won't believe it, he is always the optimist,' she wrote in a brief note to her sister, as she waited for the operation to remove from her stomach a suddenly discovered tumour 'as big as a fist', a few months before I was due to go up to Cambridge. She was neither an optimist nor a pessimist. She took things as they came, and she knew, in this instance correctly, that what might come tomorrow was death. Sidney took me to see her corpse in bed in the old Hampstead General Hospital. I pass the site, now the car park of the Royal Free Hospital, most days on my way to and from Belsize Park. Hers was the first dead body I had ever seen.

I am not sure that I *respected* Sidney. I did not want to be like him. Indeed I was embarrassed by, and contemptuous of, his self-pity, his temperamental instability, those characteristic swings from outbursts of rage to effusive sentimentality and back again, the one an expression of impotence, the other a cry for help. As we both had the well-developed sense of confrontation (i.e. contrariness) so often found within Jewish families, our conversations at home tended to be loud, dramatic and often absurd. I think he was absolute hell for Nancy, especially after Gretl's death deprived him of ballast.

Fortunately I was by then that much older, and knew myself to be on the verge of independence. And yet, I remember him intensely and with pleasure. We talked, especially in Paris, and on the long journeys when I acted as his chauffeur – for after a year we were prosperous enough to buy a car, which I learned to drive, just in time to pass the newly introduced driving test. He knew about the ways of the world, and what he said about them I took seriously, not least the observation that men should keep quiet about the women they slept with. His tips on what was good in the French cinema of the 1930s came from the horse's mouth. He gave me what I clearly had not had from my biological father. And he, in turn, hoped that I would compensate for the repeatedly disappointed hopes of his own life.

For though Solomon Sidney Berkwood Hobsbaum, short, wearing pince-nez below a forehead that (unlike my father's) folded vertically, was the only one of Grandfather David's sons to become a full-time businessman, making money was not his dream. He had the salesman's ability to believe passionately in the product of the moment, the body armour protecting him against the blows of the unreturned phone call and the cancelled order. Years later I recognized much of him in Arthur Miller's wonderful *Death of a Salesman*, as must the intellectual sons of so many Jewish fathers. But though he had ambitions – Napoleon was his favourite character in history, Rawdon Crawley of Thackeray's *Vanity Fair* in fiction – money was not what inspired him.

What had his ambitions been in his East End youth? Had he been born much later, when there came to be money in the game and the British took to it, he might have made something of his natural talent for chess, which was evidently considerable. Putting up his hand somewhere in France when chess players were asked for had got him from the western front into intelligence (i.e. codebreaking) in the First World War. He seemed to know something about such matters, but then anyone in his position knocking around central Europe in 1919–33 was quite likely to have come across people involved in secret services. He kept out of politics.

In other respects he was not creative, but he had the self-educated poor Jew's passion for culture and loved being in the milieu of creative people – musicians, theatre actors and above all movie people. On his and Gretl's phonograph in Vienna I heard for the first time and many times after that, a still somewhat Victorian selection of the great vocal classics of the first recorded generation – Caruso, Melba, Tetrazzini – and the repertoire of the great, mainly Italian and French, arias: Verdi, Meyerbeer, Gounod. In practice his musical contacts were more modern: Rose Pauly-Dreesen, the most famous Elektra of her day, with whose career he was associated in the late twenties, was the leading dramatic soprano in Klemperer's Berlin Krolloper, very much at the cutting edge of Weimar music. He tried to mobilize on her behalf Dame Ethel Smyth (1858–1944), Edwardian feminist and the most celebrated female composer of her day, with whom he had somehow established a relationship as a young man. But it was the cinema that captured his heart for good. Not so much the atmosphere of bigshots, wheeler-dealers, the entrepreneurial adventurers and confidence-tricksters, though he had got to know them in his time with Universal. It was the milieu of the studio floor – the large world-creating hangars, small emigrant Jews around big stages, cameras, lights, make-up and scenery, all drenched in the atmosphere of technique, gossip, bohemian informality and scandal. I drove him there on his visits to Isleworth and Elstree. For him it was where man was in touch with creation. He succeeded in fighting his way back into it in England by convincing a British photographic firm that his contacts in the movie world made him the man to sell their film-stock in competition with Kodak and Agfa. After a few years of losing battle armed with an uncompetitive product ('Uncle Sidney goes to Budapest tomorrow. Furious telegram from Joe Pasternak. Selofilm apparently poor quality') he gave up the struggle, emigrated again and, presumably introduced by his brother Berk, invested his small capital in a share of a modest Chilean enterprise producing kitchenware. At the end of the war he left an unexciting but safe business on little more than the hint from an old contact that there might be a place for him on some new film operation to be launched in connection with the new United Nations. Nothing happened. The dream of the creative life was over. He had thrown up a reasonable livelihood in his mid-fifties for a dream. He never succeeded in getting another.

Still, for a few years in the 1930s he managed to live his fantasy on the edge of the European tragedy and I received some of the benefit. For who else would give him a chance but those on the margins of the film world – the refugees and the radicals? So he found himself involved in political movies financed by the French left in the Popular Front days, notably Jean Renoir's *La Marseillaise*, and in the political newsreels which enabled me to see the great Bastille Day of 1936 from the Socialist Party's camera truck with a Socialist Party steward's badge. During the Civil War he took up his Spanish, or rather Catalan, contacts again. He returned from visits to Barcelona in 1937 with stories of conversations with the Catalan leader, Luis Companys (later executed by Franco) and with an upper-class Englishman called Eric Blair. These were losing causes. My uncle, though his sympathies were with the left like the great majority of Jews from poor working-class families, wanted nothing better than to keep out of party politics. The logic of history pushed him into earning his living from and with the battling antifascists, while he and they still could. It was not to be for long.

II

The Britain I came to in 1933 was utterly different in almost every way from the country in which I write this at the start of the new century. The history of the island in the twentieth century divides sharply into two halves – to put it in a phrase, before and after the simultaneous shocks of Suez and rock and roll. Almost every generalization about the country to which I came in 1933 ceases to apply after 1956, even the notorious inefficiency of the British system of domestic heating and – one of its consequences – the impenetrable Dickensian fog which, until 1953, still occasionally forced London to a standstill. Britain was no longer a major empire or a world power, and after Suez nobody believed that it was. Popular culture compensated by creating sagas of British heroism and eventual victory against the Germans in the Second World War. In 1933 people thought about the Great War not as a heroic memory, but as a graveyard. However, everyone knew that a larger area of the world map than ever before was coloured pink, and that we were the only global empire, even if intelligent imperialists recognized that our grasp was already much more restricted than our reach. But British skins were still white. In 1933 black and brown faces were far easier to find on the streets of Paris than London and, except for Veeraswamy's in the West End, the Indian restaurant was still virtually absent. Indeed, foreigners of any kind were rare, since Britain was not a centre of international tourism, which was in any case still tiny by present standards.

Only Hitler and the war were to bring into Britain a modest number of the sort of middle-class continentals whose reactions the Hungarian George Mikes has described fondly in the little book *How to be an Alien*. Contrary to the native myth, the country did its best to exclude refugees but, unlike Mikes, the next generation of Hungarian immigrants, the refugees of 1956–7, would no longer have thought of describing Britain as a country where hot-water bottles took the place of sex. It was the 1950s that revolutionized the sexual and social mores of the British young. In the 1930s the idea of London as the international city of style, fun and promiscuity (as in the 'Swinging London' of the 1960s) was inconceivable. For heterosexual males the action was in Paris or the French Riviera, for homosexual ones – at least until Hitler came – in Berlin. For women the public scope was more limited either way.

Britain in 1933 was still a self-contained island where life was lived by unwritten but compelling rules, rituals and invented traditions: mostly class rules or gender rules, but also virtually universal ones, usually linked to royalty. The national anthem was played at the end of every performance in theatres and cinemas and people stood for it before they went home. Wherever you were, you did not talk during the two minutes' silence on Armistice Day, 11 November. The 'right' kind of accent bonded together the upper classes (but not parvenus who could thus be recognized) and ensured deferential behaviour from the lower orders, class-conscious or not, at least in public.

In the 1930s these things were obvious. But, of course, they were not expected to apply on the other side of the seas which separated us from the foreigners. Britain was insular in every sense. When an upper-middle-class Jewish refugee doctor applied for admission to Britain as a potential domestic servant (the only option available) and offered to work as a butler, the British Passport Control officer in Paris refused him without a moment's hesitation, humanitarian or otherwise. 'This is absurd,' he wrote, 'as butlering requires a lifelong experience.'[8] He could not imagine a non-British Jeeves.

Nevertheless, by continental European standards, Britain was still a rich, technically and economically advanced and well-equipped country, even if for a cash-strapped teenager Paris was unquestionably more enjoyable. Its train and underground seats were upholstered, even in third-class carriages, bumpy paving-stones were not frequent in its city streets and even rural by-roads had tarmac surfaces. Bathrooms and water-closets could be expected in the new, small family homes, each with its own garden, multiplying in their tens of thousands on the outskirts of the big cities in what few as yet recognized as a major building boom. Not only the rich had motor-cars and even most of the poor had radios. On the other hand, material expectations were low and most Britons had not yet poked their heads far outside the realm where income is still spent chiefly on the modest necessities of life, as I discovered when we briefly came to live among the car-owning and cocktail-drinking middle class of Canons Park, Edgware. Britain was a long way from a modern consumer society, especially for its teenagers. Not until the middle fifties and full employment did working teenagers have money to spend, and their parents could dispense with their contributions to the family budget. Fortunately the most readily available luxuries for budding intellectuals were also cheap: the films, performed in increasingly vast palaces and preceded by organs rising from the depths to changing lights, and books, second-hand, paperback – the new sixpenny Penguins – and even given away free by mass circulation newspapers competing to pass the two-million mark. I still have the copy of Bernard Shaw's *Collected Plays* acquired by buying six issues of the Labour Party's *Daily Herald*, which briefly won this race (and, in the later course of British twentieth-century history, turned into the tabloid *Sun*, which is unlikely to do its circulation-building by offering its readers classic literature). Even the form of transport that set us free was cheap, for we, or our parents, heeded the advertisements on the back of the London double-deckers: 'Get off that bus. It will never be yours. Twopence a day will buy you a bicycle.' And indeed, not many weekly instalments would purchase a bike – in my case a new shiny Rudge-Whitworth for something like five or six pounds. If physical mobility is an essential condition of freedom, the bicycle has probably been the greatest single device for achieving what Marx called the full realization of the possibilities of being human invented since Gutenberg, and the only one without obvious drawbacks. Since cyclists travel at the speed of human reactions and are not insulated behind plate glass from nature's light, air, sound and smells there was no better way in the 1930s – before the explosion of motor traffic – to explore a middle-sized country with an astonishingly lovely and varied landscape. With bike, tent, Primus stove and the newly invented Mars bar my cousin Ronnie (who pronounced it 'Marr', as though it had been French) and I explored large parts of the civilized beauties of southern England and, on one memorable but wintry tour, the more savage ones of North Wales. (Almost sixty years later the memory of those distant Mars-eating cycle rides was revived by the surprising proposal which reached me from the man himself in Las Vegas, Forrest B. Mars, then in his eighties and owner of the largest purely private company in the world, to assist him in explaining his ideas about the world to a wider public. I refused politely. It seems a studious young woman of his acquaintance had suggested this unique collaboration between a textbook example of unreconstructed rock-ribbed private enterprise and a Marxist historian.)

How was an immigrant teenager to come to terms in 1933 with this strange country, which was also his own? In some ways I came to it like Lewis Carroll's Alice to Wonderland, through a few narrow doors and passages opened by the family, and especially the cousins who were also my best, and indeed my only close, friends.

By then the English family was reduced. David and Rose Obstbaum, who first landed in London in the 1870s and doubtless acquired the initial H of their name from a Cockney immigration officer, were dead. So were three of their eight children: Lou, a provincial actor, Phil, who followed the family woodworking trade, and my father. (A daughter of David's first marriage, my aunt Millie Goldberg, had long since moved to America, matriarch of a clan now distributed through the USA and Israel.) A fourth, my uncle Ernest (Aron), who had originally persuaded my father to join him in Egypt where he worked in the Post and Telegraph Service, died not long after our arrival, amid the brass ornaments and anecdotes recalling life in the Orient. He left behind a Catholic Belgian widow, better at earning a living than he, and two attractive girls who were of some interest to the male cousins. Uncle Berkwood (Ike), with a Welsh wife and five children, had long since settled in Chile, though he remained in contact. That left Aunt Cissie (Sarah), a schoolteacher with a husband permanently absent 'on business' and Uncle Harry, the unshakeable pillar of the family – if only because he was the only member to earn a steady if modest salary of perhaps £4 a week as a telegraphist in the Post Office, where he remained all his life except for the Great War. He served on the Ypres salient and then, luckily for survival, on the Italian front. A Labour councillor in the London borough of Paddington, he eventually became its first Labour mayor. The Hobsbaums had arrived as a family of poor artisans. The family had advanced beyond its first recorded addresses in Whitechapel, Spitalfields and Shoreditch, but not very far. In England they stubbornly remained on the lower slopes of the mountains of society.

Nevertheless, the social universe in which they operated covered a large and representative part of England. It ranged from the classes run by my cousin Rosalie, Cissie's daughter, in dance and 'elocution', that is to say learning to speak with the bourgeois accent, for the daughters of aspiring suburban mothers in Sydenham, to the Labour milieu of councillor Harry Hobsbaum in North Paddington, and the world of self-shaping plebeian intellectuals and would-be artists in which my cousins moved, the world of meetings in Lyons or ABC tea shops, discussion groups, evening classes and that marvellous institution, the free public library and reading room. This was the world for which in 1936 Allen Lane created the first great self-educational paperback series, Penguin, or rather its intellectual section, Pelican Books, and Victor Gollancz his Left Book Club, in which my cousin Ruby (Philip's son) published the family's first contribution to left-wing literature, Reuben Osborn's *Freud and Marx*.

My introduction to the British scene outside family and school came through this world. It came in part through Cissie's son Denis, a dark and – within his financial limits – dandyish figure who bit his nails, dropped out of education and from the middle 1930s somehow got by without a clear job in the lower reaches of the worlds of music, theatre and popular entertainment. But chiefly it came through Harry's son Ronnie, small, physically wiry and very Jewish-looking, who was then still living with his parents in Maida Vale nursing a lifelong passion for the sea, which he satisfied in the navy during the war and as a sailor of small boats on the Blackwater estuary ever since. When I came to England he was working as a dogsbody somewhere in the entrails of the Natural History Museum, home at that time to a varied assortment of grassroots thinkers and quiet bohemians, while he studied nights at the Regent Street Polytechnic to pass the secondary-school examinations. He went on to take a First in economics at the London School of Economics that would allow him the slow climb up the steps of the civil service – clerical, executive – to the heights of the administrative grade in the Ministry of Labour.

I refused all contact with the suburban petty-bourgeoisie, which I naturally regarded with contempt. Since it was in the hands of reformist social democrats, I naturally also found the labour movement as represented by my uncle Harry, and even his somewhat more left-wing son, disappointing, but also puzzling. Unlike the German social democrats, it could not simply be condemned to the flames. For, though Harry was a Labour loyalist who defended the Party against the bitter attacks of the British CP, he shared the general assumption in the British labour movement (other than, perhaps, among those under the direct influence of the Catholic Church) that, say what you like, Soviet Russia was after all a workers' state. Like most Labour and union activists, he shook his head about communists, but saw them in basically the same game as Labour people. Moreover, I could not deny that, unlike in German social democracy, only a few Labour leaders had sold out to the bourgeoisie in 1931, when the Prime Minister of the 1929 Labour administration, Ramsay Macdonald, and two colleagues, had joined the Tories in a so-called 'National Government', which went on to govern the country until the fall of Neville Chamberlain in 1940. How could one regard the passionately anti-Macdonald bulk of the party, reduced to a rump of some fifty in the House of Commons, as class traitors in the same sense?

On the other hand, and in view of the 1926 General Strike, the labour movement simply did not correspond to my ideal vision of 'the (revolutionary) proletariat'. It was puzzling, for in some ways the British scene was recognizably like the German, shaken by the tremors of the global economic and political earthquake of the world crisis of 1929. Britain's politics had also been convulsed. There was radicalization on both right and left, including a blackshirted fascist movement which seemed to be a serious national threat for a moment. Nevertheless, though the structure shook a little, it did not seem, and indeed was not, on the verge of collapse. To judge by Britain, the world revolution would clearly take a lot longer than one supposed. Since, according to my diary, I did not expect to reach the age of forty years (at the age of seventeen even this seemed quite far away), perhaps I might not see it. But by this time the Comintern itself was about to discover that there would be no revolution unless the fight against fascism and world war was won first.

III

It may seem strange that I have said hardly anything so far about the institution I attended from the moment I arrived in England until I left it for Cambridge three years later, longer than any of my other schools in any country, namely St Marylebone Grammar School, on the corner of the Marylebone Road and Lisson Grove in central London. It had been my cousin Ronnie's old school (I followed him by winning its Debating Cup). Like the Prinz-Heinrichs-Gymnasium, it no longer exists, though it was destroyed not by enemy bombing, but by the ideology of the 1970s, a bad era for secondary education. It refused the choice it was given – to turn itself into a non-selective 'comprehensive' school for all comers or to go private – and was consequently shut down. It gave me as good an education as any available in England in the 1930s and I owe its teachers an incalculable debt of gratitude. But, for reasons that still puzzle me, it contributed surprisingly little to my understanding of England, except the discovery that, unlike the *Herren Professoren* of Berlin, *all* teachers at St Marylebone had a sense of humour. (I made a special note of this.) What did not strike me at the time is that in Britain secondary-school masters might have belonged *socially* but not *intellectually* to the world of the university. Unlike those who would have taught me in the top forms of German, French or Italian schools, they were only in the rarest of cases researchers, scholars and future academics. They had their being in the separate sphere of schoolmastering.

More surprisingly, I established no serious friendships in my three years there. Almost certainly the historic gap between my old and new countries was too wide. By 1932 Berlin standards London seemed a relapse into immaturity. There was no way to continue the conversations of the Prinz-Heinrichs-Gymnasium of 1931–3 on the Marylebone Road of 1933–6. Except with my cousin Ronnie, already a university student, I resumed them only when I arrived in Cambridge. That may also be one reason why for the first two years I underestimated the modest, but real, political radicalization of several of my fellow-pupils. To judge by my diary, another reason was plain conceit. I thought of myself as intellectually on the masters' level and superior to the rest. Nor did I take to the social aspirations of the school, a caricature version of the (non-boarding) bourgeois 'public school' – compulsory uniforms and school caps, prefects, rival 'houses', moral rhetoric and the rest, and did my best to indicate dissent. The school, in turn, was not quite sure what to make of the incompletely disciplined arrival from central Europe, ignorant of the rules of both cricket and rugby football and uninterested in both games, but too senior not to be made a prefect sooner or later and too intellectual not to be made editor of the school magazine, *The Philologian*. There, between reports of sports fixtures, my first printed writings appeared, all of which I have forgotten except a long review of the London Surrealist Exhibition of 1936, with one of whose exhibitors I spent some social nights in Paris later that year. Still, it was soon evident to the school that I took to examinations as to ice-cream, and might stand a good chance of a university scholarship.

What reconciled me to these pretensions of the school was the quality, and above all the devotion to their calling, of the masters, starting with the headmaster Philip Wayne (later the translator of Goethe's *Faust* for the Penguin Classics), who, in our first interview, regretted that the school could continue to teach me only Latin but not Greek, and pressed a volume of the philosopher Immanuel Kant and a selection of the essays of William Hazlitt into my hands instead.

The Philological School had been founded in the 1790s for the sons of the modest but aspiring parents of Marylebone, and continued, eventually taken over by the London County Council, as a grammar school providing the sort of instruction needed by London's lower middle class, who never expected to get beyond secondary education or to make much of a mark on the world. Fortunately for the generation of their sons who began to go to university from the 1930s, this was in no sense a second-best education, even though it sometimes seemed to come to us as a voluntary gift from those firmly established at the top to deserving social inferiors.

Harold Llewellyn-Smith, a handsome, well-connected, never-married pillar of the Liberal Party, son of the architect of the Labour policy of Edwardian and Georgian Britain and of a good part of the welfare state, who taught me history, steered me into Oxbridge, and eventually became headmaster of the school himself, knew that he came out of the top drawer – Winchester and New College, Oxford, war in the Scots Guards. If he had chosen to teach in an undistinguished state secondary school, the only one of whose Old Boys known to the outside world was that singer of London lower-middle-class adventure, Jerome K. Jerome, author of *Three Men in a Boat*, it was almost certainly for the same reason that he worked in a South London slum settlement. Leaving aside the attraction of working with boys, it was the desire to do good works among the unprivileged. He lent me his books, mobilized his connections on my behalf, told me (correctly) how to handle the Oxbridge scholarship examinations, which colleges were the right ones for me (Balliol in Oxford, King's in Cambridge), and warned me that I would there have to live like the rich, among gentlemen. He clearly never regarded me even as potentially belonging to his world.

A similar social gap divided us from the most interesting of the masters, a young English literature graduate, who came to Marylebone from Cambridge bringing to those who wanted to listen – certainly to me – the great gospel of I. A. Richards's *Practical Criticism* and F. R. Leavis. I gulped down *New Bearings in English Poetry* which he lent me, together with the editions of his most admired poets which he owned in private press editions, and moved me to name Leavis's college, Downing, as my third choice in the scholarship exam (after King's, and, because of the presence of Maurice Dobb, Trinity). Leavis's reputation as a great literary critic has not survived the twentieth century very well, and by the time I came to Cambridge my own Leavisite passion had cooled, but no don in his century had a greater impact on the teaching of literature. He had an awesome capacity to inspire generations of future school-teachers who, in turn, inspired their bright pupils. English, for Mr Maclean, was a crusade that had to be taken to the people. I am sure that he would have remained a teacher, had he not been killed during the war. Certainly his teaching inspired me. I felt he had much in common with me – if only because he also had an ugly, large-nosed, incompletely shaped face with brown eyes ill at ease under his horn-rims, a big, clumsy body which did not quite know what to do with its arms and legs, and a sensitive soul. Alas, I doubted whether he would make a Marxist.

For three years Marylebone was my intellectual centre – not only the school, but also, a few yards away, the splendid Public Library in the Town Hall of what was then a London borough, where I spent most of my mid-day breaks in omnivorous reading and borrowing. (Though I have never used the library since, this is the building which contains the Register Office where many years later, in 1962, I was to be married to Marlene.) I certainly did not get my education only at school. Indeed, in my last year there (1935–6) it was little more than a study where I did my own reading. But my debt to St Marylebone Grammar School is crucial, and not only because it introduced me to the astonishing marvels of English poetry and prose. Without its teaching and direction, I do not see how a boy who had never had any kind of English schooling, arriving in this country at the age of almost sixteen, could, in little more than two years, have got to the stage of winning a major scholarship at Cambridge and, once arrived there, have the choice of reading for a degree in at least three subjects. It was St Marylebone also who helped me to move from the no-man's land in which (but for the family) I had lived since leaving Berlin, once again into the essential territory of youth: of friendship, comradeship, of collective and private intimacy.

IV

What had actually happened to that young man's intellectual development in those three years? First, I had read more widely and *generally* during that time, particularly in literature, than in any period before or since. Since secondary-school examinations required far less in the way of specialized knowledge than universities, let alone research, they left adventurous pupils with relatively more time for their own explorations – and at that age almost everything is there to be discovered. Moreover, an English sixth form demanded less effort than a continental one, if only because one had to choose between the arts and the sciences, and therefore dropped half the continental syllabus. After arriving at a university nobody who takes the degree seriously has anything like the enterprising teenager's time to read about everything, rapidly, voraciously, and with endless curiosity. But what did I do with all this reading?

The short answer is: I tried to give it a Marxist, that is to say an essentially historical, interpretation. There was not much else to do for an impassioned but unorganized and necessarily inactive communist teenage intellectual. Since I had not read much more than the *Communist Manifesto* when I left Berlin – action came before words – I therefore had to acquire some knowledge of Marxism. My Marxism was, and still to some extent remains, that acquired from the only texts then easily available outside university libraries, the systematically distributed works and selections of 'the classics' published (and translated in heavily subsidized local editions) under the auspices of the Marx–Engels Institute in Moscow. Curiously, until Stalin's notorious *Short History of the Communist Party of the Soviet Union* (1939), which contained a central section on 'Dialectical and Historical Materialism', there was no formal compendium of Soviet communist orthodoxy in these matters. When this section appeared, I read it with enthusiasm, allowing for its pedagogic simplifications. It corresponded pretty much to what I, and perhaps most of the British intellectual reds of the 1930s, understood by Marxism. We liked to think of it as 'scientific' in a rather nineteenth-century sense. Since, unlike in continental *lycées* and *Gymnasia*, philosophy was not a central part of higher secondary education, we did not approach Marx with the philosophical interests of our continental contemporaries, let alone with their knowledge of philosophy. This helped to anglicize my way of thinking quite rapidly. What Perry Anderson has called 'western Marxism', the Marxism of Lukács, the Frankfurt School and Korsch, never crossed the Channel until the 1950s. We were content to know that Marx and Engels had turned Hegel the right way up, without bothering to find out just what it was they had stood on its feet. What made Marxism so irresistible was its comprehensiveness. 'Dialectical materialism' provided, if not a 'theory of everything', then at least a 'framework of everything', linking inorganic and organic nature with human affairs, collective and individual, and providing a guide to the nature of all interactions in a world in constant flux.

As I read my diary of 1934–5, it is perfectly clear that its writer was getting ready to be a historian. What I was trying to do above all else was to elaborate Marxist historical interpretations of my reading. And yet I was doing so in a way I almost certainly would not have done, had I continued my education on the continent. The 'materialist conception of history' was, of course, central to Marxism. However, Britain in the 1930s was one of the rare countries in which a school of Marxist *historians* developed, and I think this was partly due to the fact that on the arts side of British sixth forms literature took the space left vacant by the absence of philosophy. British Marxist historians began, more often than not, as young intellectuals who moved to historical analysis from, or with, a passion for *literature*: Christopher Hill, Victor Kiernan, Leslie Morton, E. P. Thompson, Raymond Williams and indeed myself. This may help to explain the otherwise surprising influence of the anti-Marxist F. R. Leavis on many who became communists. Cambridge communists who read English swore by him.

My own Marxism developed as an attempt to understand the arts. What filled my mind then was not the classic macro-historical problems of Marxist historical debate about historical development – the succession of 'modes of production'. It was the place and nature of the artist and the arts (in fact, literature) in society or, in Marxist terms, 'How is the superstructure connected to the base?' Sometime in the autumn of 1934 I began to recognize this as 'the problem', and to worry at it, like a small dog at an excessively large bone, with the help of a lot of unsystematic reading in psychology and anthropology and echoes from the continental days of my biological, ecological and evolutionary readings in the publications of *Kosmos, Gesellschaft der Naturfreunde.* The theory was ambitious. 'Marx could predict the socialist system on the basis of a precise analysis of the capitalist system. A precise analysis of capitalist literature, which takes into consideration all circumstances, all connections and relations, must allow us to draw similar conclusions about the proletarian culture of the future.' I soon thought no more about such global predictions, but the historical question I asked myself at the age of seventeen has permanently shaped my work as a historian. I am still trying to 'analyse the (social) influences which determine the form and content of poetry [and more generally of ideas] at different times'. But I had learned little more history than what was necessary, together with a little gamesmanship (a word that had not yet been invented) to get through the Cambridge scholarship exam.

V

At the start of 1936 I decided, cautiously – for 'I live in the twentieth century and . . . in any case I am not given to optimism' – to end the diary I had kept for almost two years. 'I just don't need it any more,' I wrote in the last entry.

> God knows why. Maybe because I've won my Cambridge scholar-ship, and, if all goes well, at least three years of independence lie ahead. Maybe because S. [whom I had got to know during the scholarship exam, and who became a lifelong friend] is the first acquaintance I have made myself, and not drawn parasitically from the pockets of other people . . . Maybe because I now have a year of nothing but my own work ahead of me? [i.e. until going up to Cambridge] Because things just look rosier for me? Because, perhaps, just maybe, I shall live a less 'second-hand' life?

It seemed the moment to balance the accounts, I hoped without sentimentality and self-delusion. I did so as follows:

Eric John Ernest Hobsbaum, a tall, angular, dangly, ugly, fair-haired fellow of eighteen and a half, quick on the uptake, with a considerable if superficial stock of general knowledge and a lot of original ideas, general and theoretical. An incorrigible striker of attitudes, which is all the more dangerous and at times effective, as he talks himself into believing in them himself. Not in love and apparently quite successful in sublimating his passions, which – not often – find expression in the ecstatic enjoyment of nature and art. Has no sense of morality, thoroughly selfish. Some people find him extremely disagreeable, others likeable, yet others (the majority) just ridiculous. He wants to be a revolutionary but, so far, shows no talent for organization. He wants to be a writer, but without energy and the ability to shape the material. He hasn't got the faith that will move the necessary mountains, only hope. He is vain and conceited. He is a coward. He loves nature deeply. And he forgets the German language.

In this spirit I faced the year 1936 and Cambridge University.

7

Cambridge

In a society like that of England in the first half of the last century, moving from the milieu of one class to that of another was a form of emigration. So winning a scholarship to Cambridge in 1935 meant moving into a strange new country – stranger because more unfamiliar than the ones I had settled in before. Except in one respect: after a break of three years I now returned to the politics and the conversations I had been forced to abandon when we left Berlin. I arrived in Cambridge quite determined to join the Communist Party at last and plunge into politics. As it turned out, I was not alone. Mine was the reddest and most radical generation in the history of the university, and I was in the thick of it. It happened that I also arrived in the middle of what, even allowing for a past that contained the names of Newton, Darwin and Clerk Maxwell, was probably the most distinguished era in the history of a university that was for some decades virtually synonymous with British scientific achievement. The two were not entirely separated: the 1930s was one of the few periods when an unusual proportion of eminent natural scientists was also politically radicalized. I am bound to add that the achievements of Cambridge science in the 1930s have survived better than those of the political radicalism of Cambridge students. Few of these have left much trace, even on public memory, except for one minor spin-off from 1930s communism, the 'Cambridge spies'.

Since I was one of the leading Cambridge undergraduate communists in the second half of the 1930s, most readers of this book who belong to the Cold War generations will certainly ask what I knew about them. I might as well answer this question at the outset. Yes, I knew some of them. No, I did not know they were or had been working for Soviet intelligence until after this became public knowledge. The 'big five' (Blunt, Burgess, Cairncross, Maclean and Philby) belonged to an earlier student generation than mine, and my contemporaries associated none of them with the Party except Burgess, whom we regarded as a traitor, because he took care to advertise his alleged conversion to right-wing views as soon as he had gone down. I knew none of them personally before the war, and only Blunt and Burgess casually after 1945. What I know about them came not from politics but via the Apostles (for which see chapter 11) or from homosexual friends or from survivors of the interwar Oxbridge establishment such as Isaiah Berlin, whose passion for gossiping about the people he had known was irrepressible. I recall Burgess only from two annual dinners of the Apostles – the one he presided over in 1948 at the Royal Automobile Club (a suitably bizarre location), recorded in the memoirs of Michael Straight whom Blunt tried to recruit for the Soviets,[1] and the one I organized in the late 1950s in a shortlived Portuguese restaurant in Frith Street, Soho, and to which, knowing his nostalgia for England, I sent him an invitation addressed to 'Guy Burgess, Moscow'. I remember the first occasion because Burgess asked us to agree that Roman Catholics were not suitable for membership of the Apostles, because their commitment to the Church's dogma precluded the intellectual frankness so essential to the society. I remember the second because he woke me with an early morning phone call from Moscow to Bloomsbury, regretting his inability to be at the dinner, and, I assume, making absolutely certain that my phone would thenceforth be bugged. His message helped to make the dinner a great success. If I had known Anthony Blunt at all well, I would not have committed a heartless gaffe, for which I am still sorry. When I found myself standing next to him at the bar at yet another Apostles dinner in Soho, shortly after the flight of Burgess and Maclean, and made some fairly cynical wisecrack, I had no idea of the close emotional ties between him and Guy Burgess. My words must have hurt him, but how could one tell? That elongated, elegant, slightly supercilious face showed no emotions it did not want to. According to his Soviet handler, he was the toughest of the bunch. He was a man of such ruthless self-control that he spent the day of his public exposure, besieged by the hacks and the paparazzi in the house of a friend, quietly correcting proofs.

I knew those of my contemporaries who became Soviet agents as militant members of the student Party, which makes it 99 per cent certain that they were not yet recruited for work which, by general convention, was quite separate from the open activities of a legal political party and, if discovered, might be regarded as discrediting these. We knew such work was going on, we knew we were not supposed to ask questions about it, we respected those who did it, and most of us – certainly I – would have taken it on ourselves, if asked. The lines of loyalty in the 1930s ran not between but across countries.*

After this brief intermezzo, let me return to Cambridge in the 1930s. It is first necessary to grasp, in spite of all apparent continuities, how different the place was then from what it is today.

I have had an association with Cambridge ever since I first went up for the scholarship exam in 1935, or rather with King's, for (apart from arranging to examine me for a BA and a Ph.D.) the university has firmly kept me at a distance. On the other hand, my links with King's College are unbroken. There is no time of day or night, no season of the year, and no phase of my life since 1935, when I have not looked from the humpbacked bridge over the river Cam, across the unbroken expanse of the great back lawn, to the extraordinary combination of the bleak Gothic rear of the chapel, giving no hint of the marvels inside, and the equally spare eighteenth-century elegance of the Gibbs Building: and always with the same astonished intake of breath as the first time. Not many people have been so lucky.

For young men who, like scholars of King's, passed all their undergraduate terms within college, Cambridge was like enjoying the constant and envied public company of a universally admired woman – you might say it was like going to all one's parties with Botticelli's *Primavera*. (The domestic side of college life in the

* 'The lines between the pro- and anti-fascist forces ran through each society. Never has there been a period when patriotism, in the sense of automatic loyalty to a citizen's national government, counted for less. When the Second World War ended, the governments of at least ten old European countries were headed by men who at its beginning (or, in the case of Spain, at the start of the Civil War) had been rebels, political exiles or, at the very least, who had regarded their own governments as immoral and illegitimate.' Eric Hobsbawm, *The Age of Extremes* (London, paperback, 1995), p. 144.

1930s – peeing into the sink in the gyp room since the nearest bathroom and toilet might be three flights of stairs, a courtyard and a basement away – could be less inspiring.) However, even the majority of undergraduates who spent at least part of their years in some remote bedsit in a Victorian terrace could not escape the sheer force of seven centuries of Cambridge teaching and learning. Everything was designed to make us into pillars of a tradition reaching back to the thirteenth century, though some of the most apparently ancient expressions of it, such as the Festival of Lessons and Carols on Christmas Eve in King's College Chapel, had in fact been invented only a few years before I came to the college. (Many years later this was to inspire a conference and book on *The Invention of Tradition*.)[2] Undergraduates wore their short black gowns to go to lectures and supervisions, into the obligatory collective dinner in college halls and (with caps) whenever out in the streets after dark, policed by more amply gowned and capped Proctors, assisted by their 'bulldogs'. Dons entered lecture rooms with their long gowns billowing and the squares planted with precision on their heads.[3] Scholars read the Latin grace to the standing multitude before dinner and lessons in ancient chapels. (With tongue in cheek, the chapel dean of King's made me read a piece of the book of Amos, the closest thing to a militant bolshevik preacher in the Old Testament.) The Cambridge past, like the ceremonial fancy-dress past of British public life, was not, of course, a chronological succession of time, but a synchronic jumble of its surviving relics. The glory and continuity of seven centuries were supposed to inspire us, to assure us of our superiority and to warn us against the temptations of ill-considered change. (In the 1930s they spectacularly failed to do so.) The main contribution of Cambridge to political theory and practice, as described brilliantly by the classicist F. M. Cornford in his little squib *Microcosmographia Academica* (1908), was 'the principle of unripe time'. Whatever anyone proposed, the time for doing it was not yet ripe. It was powerfully reinforced by the principle of 'the entering wedge'. Of course our undergraduate lives were lived at a level far below that of the master-operators of these principles, but those of us who became dons soon discovered their force.

Cambridge has changed so profoundly since the 1950s that it is difficult to grasp just how isolated and parochial the place was in the 1930s even academically – apart from the incomparable national and international distinction of its natural sciences. With the exception of its world-class economics, it refused to recognize the social sciences. Its arts subjects were, at best, patchy. However implausible it seems, outside the natural sciences most of the university took little interest in research, and none in higher degrees such as Ph.D.s which were regarded at best as a German peculiarity and, more likely, as a lower-middle-class affectation. Even on the eve of the war Cambridge contained fewer than 400 research students.[4] It remained essentially a finishing school for young men and a much smaller number of young women, operating a double standard. Getting a Cambridge First, or the rarer 'starred' First, was, indeed, extremely hard, but it was even more difficult *not* to get a degree *at all*, because 'passes', or even the bottom layer of Third class honours, were virtually given away. I recall a discussion at an examiners' meeting for the Economics Tripos in the early 1950s – I examined the economic history papers for some years – when we decided, not entirely with tongue in cheek, that anyone who knew the difference between production and consumption should pass the line. It was typical of this dichotomy that such degrees were known (among dons) as 'Trinity Thirds', for Trinity, Isaac Newton's own college, contained plenty of young men of this description as well as, at this period, probably more Nobel Prize winners and aspirants than any other educational institution of its size on the globe. At the time I arrived in Cambridge one future Nobel laureate (R. L. M. Synge) was already a research student in biochemistry, another (J. C. Kendrew) was just about to start his first year.

The university and college authorities would certainly have been amazed and appalled by the Cambridge of 2000, filled with 'science parks', business negotiations with global entrepreneurs and 'Cambridge's spires (that) dream not of academe but of profit'.[5] Theirs was a modest, introverted country town on the edge of East Anglia. Lacking industry it was not so much overshadowed as blotted out by the university, on which it largely depended in an antique way, by providing the colleges with porters, servants and landladies for the majority of the university's young men for whom there was no room in the actual college buildings, and multiple incentives for

5,000 undergraduates, assumed to be fairly well heeled, to spend more than their allowances. By later standards it had surprisingly few places for eating meals out, although the Arts Theatre, one of Maynard Keynes's many initiatives, had just opened, and included what set out to be a fashionable restaurant. It had ten cinemas. (Filmgoing was sufficiently familiar at the High Tables for an essay *De Fratribus Marx* (On the Marx Brothers) to be set in 1938 for one of the Classics prizes.)

What made Cambridge parochialism worse was that the place circumscribed within college walls the lives of the dons who lived there all the time – unlike undergraduates who spent only twenty-four weeks a year there – many of them bachelor scholars, then still so common. The Second World War, which sent so many of them into the wider world – if sometimes no further than the codebreaking centre at Bletchley – was still in the future. Some of them, one felt, knew about the world beyond Royston, ten miles south of Cambridge, only by hearsay. Indeed, compared to Oxford, Cambridge University was surprisingly remote from the centres of national life, which may explain why, unlike Oxford, none of its twentieth-century alumni became prime minister. Norfolk, where dons went on holiday, not to mention Newmarket, the famous racecourse, seemed a good deal closer than London.

Such was the place I came to, from a family no member of which had ever been to a university and a school which had never sent anyone to Cambridge. It was not like the university I had imagined. (In the vacations I soon discovered and frequented one that conformed to my idea of a 'real' university, namely the London School of Economics.) Cambridge was exciting, it was wonderful, but it took some getting used to for a stranger who knew nobody while, it seemed to me, everybody else knew somebody – a brother, a cousin or certainly earlier arrivals from their schools. The dons had even taught their fathers and uncles. I did not know that Cambridge was the centre of what my lifetime friend from King's, Noel Annan, called the 'intellectual aristocracy', a network of intermarrying professional families which has played so central a role in Britain, although anyone in King's soon discovered it. There were still plenty of Ricardos and Darwins, Huxleys, Stracheys and Trevelyans, both among undergraduates and dons. On the other hand, nothing was more obvious than that Cambridge was penetrated by the tribal customs of the British boarding schools, from which most arts undergraduates still came, and which were familiar to the likes of me only from boys' magazines designed for those who did not go to such establishments. For instance, to my amazement, academic life came to a stop for two or three hours every afternoon, when it was assumed that the young men would be practising games and sports. I now found myself surrounded by Etonians (they still had a special connection with King's, since in 1440 King Henry VI had founded both establishments together), Rugbeians, Carthusians, Stoics and crowds of people from major and sometimes virtually indistinguishable minor public schools. Ready to supply such a public, the firm of Ryder and Amies, still present on King's Parade opposite the University Church of Great St Mary's and the Senate House, stocked 656 old school, college, club and other institutional ties, where necessary designed in-house, as well as top hats, blazers and the other accoutrements of the traditional Cambridge under-graduate.[6] There were no prefects, but the undergraduate weekly *Granta* published regular profiles of persons regarded as important, such as presidents of major sports clubs and societies, under the heading 'In Authority'. (Those of its own retiring editors came under the modest heading 'In Obscurity'.)

For practical purposes, for the new undergraduates the university meant their college. Being at King's made things easier. The scholars, having as such the right to live in college, were decanted en masse into a gloomy slum generally known as 'The Drain', and thus had the chance to get to know each other, and the local mores of King's favoured informality in the relations between teachers and students, seniors and juniors. I cannot say that I was a very characteristic Kingsman – the college was at its social high noon and the centre of Cambridge theatre and music – or that I was of any great interest to its establishment. For instance, I never had occasion to meet its most famous fellow, Maynard Keynes. However, King's was liberal and tolerant, even of enthusiasts for team games, religious believers, conservatives, revolutionaries and heterosexuals, even of the less than good-looking young from grammar schools.

Fortunately, in spite of its Provost, it also respected the intellect and had a sense of its duty to bright students. After the war I got a post as a university lecturer within a year of leaving the army, entirely on the strength of the reference written about my under-graduate record by my pre-war supervisor, Christopher Morris, admittedly a master at this genre of literary composition. Since he had also originally interviewed me for my scholarship, I suspect that it was his recommendation that got me into King's. A few years older than me and – uncharacteristically for the college – a family man, he was typical of the don of the old school, who was primarily a teacher, or rather a personal tutor. His calling was to get average young men from a public school a decent Second in the Tripos. Beyond this he concentrated on asking what he called 'Socratic questions', i.e. forcing his pupils to discover what it was they had written or meant to write in their weekly essay. This worked extremely well in my case, even when I did not accept his critical remarks about my prose style. I did not much respect him, and we dealt with one another at arm's length, but I owe him a considerable debt.

I had less contact with the college's three serious historians. As professors, two no longer supervised undergraduates: the tiny, witty, eminent and unbelievably conservative F. A. Adcock, Professor of ancient history, and the impressive and craggy John Clapham, just retired from the chair of economic history, author of that rarest of products of history in interwar Cambridge, a major work on a major topic, namely the three volumes of his *Economic History of Modern Britain* (1926–38). He was a mountaineer, which fitted in with the ethos of King's; but was also both a solidly married man and firmly attached to the North of England nonconformity from which he sprang, which did not. (Nobody would have guessed that both Provost Sheppard and Maynard Keynes came from provincial Baptist stock.) I wish I had learned more from the third, John Saltmarsh, who did supervise me, for he published hardly anything, but poured his enormous learning into the lectures I did not attend.

The man who from 1933 to 1954 presided over the college's fortunes (which, though we did not know it, were growing rather satisfactorily thanks to the financial acumen of his backer, fellow-gambler and fellow-Apostle Maynard Keynes) was Provost Shep-pard. He was then in his mid-fifties, but since his full head of hair had gone white during the First World War, he had adopted the character of an old gentleman, doddering round the college in dark suits of stiffish cloth and a stiff wing-collar, saying 'bless you, dear boy' to (preferably good-looking) undergraduates encountered on his way. He kept open house at the Provost's Lodge every Sunday evening, and would sit on the floor among the young men pretending, or possibly actually trying, to light his pipe, to encourage conversation. It was on one of these occasions that I encountered my first Cabinet minister, a man of platitudes and pompous body language whom Neville Chamberlain had just appointed to co-ordinate British defence. Not unexpectedly, he confirmed all my prejudices against the government of appeasers.

Undergraduates enjoyed the Provost as a star music-hall turn, on and off the boards and in the lecture hall, which he treated as a stage.[7] He was not respected, but quite often sentimentalized, and he certainly sentimentalized himself. In fact, he was a lifelong spoiled child of quite appalling character, which, as he grew older, was no longer mitigated by the charm, sense of fun and liberalism of his younger days. As he grew older he became more passionately royalist. A classicist, he had long given up research himself, and was no longer taken seriously by others. A failure as a scholar and as the head of a college – he never had his brief stint as Vice-Chancellor, the usual reward for even moderately competent heads of houses – he became an active enemy to the pursuit of knowledge. King's may have been the centre of the Cambridge *beau monde* in the 1930s, but it was not an academically distinguished college (except in economics, over which he had no control). He was against science. 'King's College, Cambridge?' said the President of Harvard. 'Isn't that the place where the natural sciences are denounced from the chair?' As undergraduates we had little idea of the malice and bitchiness behind the mask of camp senile benevolence. Still, though he is one of the few people in my life for whom I came to feel genuine hate, I cannot bring myself not to feel pity for his miserable last years, when, no longer Provost and unable to conceive of a King's that was not an extension of his own personality, in visible mental decline, he chose the last of his roles on the college stage, that of a dishevelled King Lear standing by the college gates, silently denouncing the injustices done to him.

The only other fellows with whom I had contact were the Tutor and Dean, and the history teachers. The Tutor, Donald Beves, was a large, peaceful, broad-beamed man whose passions were amateur dramatics – he was a celebrated Falstaff – and collecting Stuart and Georgian glass, which he displayed in his comfortable set of rooms, from which he surveyed the disciplinary problems of the young with an intermittent attention to administrative detail. His field was French, and he kept in regular touch with that country by touring its restaurants during vacations with friends in his Rolls-Bentley. He is not known to have published anything on its language or literature. Many years later, since his surname had five letters and began with a B like Anthony Blunt's, some journalist, misinterpreting a leak, suggested that he might be the notorious 'third' or 'fourth' of the Cambridge spies for whom every editor was then looking. The idea of Donald Beves as a Soviet agent struck everybody who had ever met him as even more absurd than the suggestion, which was also floated for a moment at the peak of the espionage mania, that another closet bolshevik was the genuinely distinguished Professor A. C. Pigou, fellow of King's for fifty-seven years, the founder of welfare economics, and reputed (with the great physicist J. J. Thompson) to be the worst-dressed man in Cambridge. Still, Pigou, another lifelong bachelor, was at least a pacifist, when not reflecting on economic matters and inviting intelligent, athletic and handsome young scholars to climb the crags from his cottage in the Lake District.

Actually, with one alleged exception, the links of King's dons with intelligence were with the British rather than the Soviet secret services. Kingsmen, headed by the small, roly-poly later professor of ancient history, F. E. Adcock, had set up the British codebreaking establishment in the First World War, and at least seventeen King's dons were recruited by Adcock for the much more famous establishment at Bletchley during the Second World War, including probably the only genius at King's in my undergraduate years, the mathematical logician Alan Turing, whom I recall as a clumsy-looking, pale-faced young fellow given to what would today be called jogging. The person generally understood to be the local talent-spotter for the secret services – most Oxbridge colleges had at least one – was the Dean, Patrick Wilkinson, an exceptionally courteous and agreeable classical scholar with a constant half-smile and a tall head with very little hair that put me in mind, I don't know why, of Long

John Silver in *Treasure Island*. To everyone's surprise he returned after the war from Bletchley a married man. Unlike the Provost, he was genuinely, deeply and unselfishly devoted to the college and its members. For many years he was responsible for the annual college report which provided full, if sometimes not completely explicit, obituaries of *all* Kingsmen without exception, however obscure: a document as elegantly written as it was (and continues to be) sociologically invaluable.

Cambridge in the 1930s no longer paid much attention to the object of medieval universities, instruction for the professions requiring special forms of knowledge – the clergy, the law and medicine – although it made provision for the early stages of training for them. Its purpose, at least in the arts, was not to train experts, but to form members of a ruling class. In the past this had been done on the basis of an education in the classics of ancient Greece and, above all, Rome, largely achieved by instructing the young in such esoteric practices as writing Greek and Latin verse. This tradition was far from dead. Something like seventy-five people (as against about fifty each in history and natural sciences) won scholarships or exhibitions in classics in the 1935 scholarship examination, most of them, of course, from the public schools, since not many grammar schools like my own taught Greek. But increasingly since the late nineteenth century history (centred on the political and constitutional development of England) had become the vehicle for all-purpose 'general education' at Cambridge. It was therefore taken by undergraduates in their hundreds, almost none of whom envisaged using it to earn their living, except perhaps as schoolmasters. It was not an intellectually very demanding subject.

The essential elements in a Cambridge education outside the natural sciences were the weekly essay written for a private session with a 'supervisor', and the Tripos, the degree examination in two parts, at the end of a one-year and a two-year course. Lectures were less important. They were mainly aimed at those who relied on the notes taken in the so-called 'bread-and-butter courses' to get them through the Tripos. Good students soon discovered that they could get more out of an hour's reading in the magnificent libraries of college, faculty and university than an hour's listening to undemanding public speech. Except for the 'Special Subject' taken in one's last year, I doubt whether I went to any lecture course consistently after my first term, other than M. M. Postan's economic history lectures, lectures so intellectually exciting – at the time I wrote about 'that air of revivalism that pervaded' them[8] – that they brought the brightest of my generation of history students out at nine a.m. Good students might end by hardly going to lectures at all, but nobody seemed to mind. We learned more from reading and talking to other good students.

Not that getting a degree, let alone a good degree, was the only thing in the minds of young men and young women who found themselves in a place as full of interesting things to do as Cambridge, and with more leisure to do them than most other adults. I myself found no difficulty in combining enough academic work to do well at exams, with active undergraduate journalism and pretty full-time activity in the Socialist Club and the Communist Party. And that without counting such time spent on extra-curricular talking, social life, punting on the Cam, the pursuit of friendship and love, etc. There seemed to be time for almost everything. Perhaps the only two activities I started but gave up were taking the university course in Russian from the formidable Elizabeth Hill – which has confined me to remaining a purely western cosmopolitan – and the Cambridge Union, whose debates were commonly regarded as the training ground for future politicians. I cannot remember why I decided to give up the Union, although my early efforts had been encouraged by the then President, whom I discovered later to be a non-public Party member. It certainly saved money.

As soon as I arrived, my politics had been discovered and I was immediately invited to join the Cambridge Student Branch of the Communist Party. I eventually became a member of its 'Secretariat' of three, the highest political function I have ever occupied. The memoirs of a contemporary are mistaken in saying I became its Secretary in 1938, but correct in observing that I was not a natural leader figure.[9] Still, its two most prestigious leaders had gone: the dark and handsome John Cornford, whose photograph was on all progressive Cambridge mantelpieces, to fight and die in Spain; James Klugmann (see below) to Paris. Its most obvious nursery of revolution was the set of rooms, bursting with posters and leaflets, in Whewell's Court, Trinity, just below Ludwig Wittgenstein, shared by the American Michael Whitney Straight and the biochemist Hugh Gordon. However, Trinity was the centre of graduate rather than undergraduate communism. That was, somewhat unexpectedly, Pembroke College, which, in addition to one of the rare communist dons (the superb Germanist Roy Pascal), sheltered a number of comrades, including two of the main organizers, David Spencer and Ephraim Alfred ('Ram') Nahum, a squat, dark natural scientist with a big nose, radiating physical strength, energy and authority. He was the son of a prosperous Sephardic textile merchant from Manchester and, by general consent, the ablest of all communist student leaders of my generation. As a graduate physicist he stayed in Cambridge during the war, and was killed in 1941 by the only German bomb to fall on the city. Unlike Ram Nahum (who was known only on the left), Pieter Keunemann, a dashing, witty and remarkably handsome Ceylonese (the island was not yet Sri Lanka) who lived in Pembroke in some style, was a great figure in university society – President of the Union, among other things – not to mention the lucky partner of the ravishing Hedi Simon from Vienna (and Newnham), with whom I vainly fell in love. (After we graduated Pieter and I rented a tiny house together in the now no longer extant Round Church Street a few yards from the house where Ram was to die.) Although both were devoted Party members, I do not think anyone would have predicted that this debonair socialite, who first introduced me to the poems of John Betjeman, would spend most of his later life as the General Secretary of the Communist Party of Sri Lanka.

On the other hand, we all expected that the elegant charmer Mohan Kumaramangalam, of Madras, Eton and King's, also President of the Union, the admired friend of so many of us, would become an important figure in his native India, as indeed he did. As an Indian, Mohan was not, of course, officially in the Party. Nor were the other 'colonial students' – overwhelmingly from the Indian subcontinent. I soon found myself working with their special 'colonial group', headed, in a sort of local inheritance, by a succession of Trinity historians with a bent for 'Third World' history. Unlike their mentors, the young 'colonial communists' did not envisage academic life, although that is where one or two ended up. They looked forward to liberation and social revolution in their countries. The two Kingsmen among them did best, for Mohan's younger contemporary, the modest and selfless Indrajit ('Sonny') Gupta, after a succession of jobs as trade union and political leader ended up, in old age, as the General Secretary of the Communist Party of India and, for a short spell, as Interior Minister of his country.

The Party was, of course, my primary passion. But even for a 100 per cent communist there was simply too much to do in Cambridge to remain entirely confined to agitation, propaganda and organization, which in any case were not my forte. (In the end I reluctantly realized that the only really desirable career, that of the 'professional revolutionary', i.e. the Party functionary, was not for me, and I resigned myself to earning my living in a less uncompromising way.) Of course, everything was political in a sense, though not in the post-1968 sense for which 'the personal is political'. We felt that what we wanted *personally* was not of interest to the Party, so long as it did not conflict with the Party line. But it was our duty not only to get good degrees but to bring Marxism into our work, just as politics entered the activities of those who went for acting or undergraduate journalism. Nevertheless, I cannot honestly say that I wrote for, and eventually edited, the student weekly *Granta* primarily for political reasons; nor that it was ever a journal that had much place for politics. Looking at old numbers today, I must sadly acknowledge that it was not much good as a journal, though my predecessor as editor, Charles Wintour, successfully used it to join Lord Beaverbrook's stable, eventually editing the London *Evening Standard*. It was in fact pretty terrible, but we had a marvellous time in its office on Market Square over tea, gossip and jokes, and it gave us a golden opportunity to get free tickets for films: second to editing *Granta*, being its film editor was the potential contributor's chief ambition. The film reviews even provided a neutral territory for friends of different politics, such as the young Arthur Schlesinger Jr, whom I met there, then as later a consistent anti-communist New Dealer.

8

Against Fascism and War

Whatever happened in Cambridge in those years was coloured by the knowledge that we lived in a time of crisis. Before Hitler came to power, the modest student radicalization of the time was almost certainly precipitated by the world economic crisis, the miserable collapse of the 1929–31 Labour government, and such dramatic demonstrations of what mass unemployment and poverty meant as the Hunger Marches from the smokeless and silent industrial areas. After 1933 it was increasingly a movement to resist the advance of fascist dictatorships and the next world war their advance would certainly bring; that is to say a movement directed against craven, as well as capitalist and imperialist, British governments that did nothing to stop the drift to fascism and war. In the second half of the 1930s, and especially after the outbreak of the Spanish Civil War, this was certainly the main force behind the remarkable growth of the Socialist Club: the effect of Munich in Cambridge was that the Cambridge University Socialist Club (CUSC) recruited 300 new members in a week.[1]

Throughout the decade the black cloud of the coming world war dominated our horizons. Could it be avoided? If not, how should we act? Would we fight 'for King and Country' as the Oxford Union had notoriously refused to do in 1933? Certainly not, but should we fight at all? Pacifism divided the Cambridge left, or rather the awkwardly combined anti-fascist and anti-war movement, for pacifism extended far beyond those interested in the politics of parties and movements, and even beyond the range of organized religion. As most of this apolitical pacifism disappeared after the fall of France in 1940, its strength in the 1930s is often forgotten. Indeed, pacifism was the only important issue that divided the Cambridge left, for within the Socialist Club the CP's line of broad anti-fascist unity had virtually unanimous support. Only one prominent member,

Sammy Silkin of Trinity Hall, supported the official position of the Labour Party and was consequently cherished as proof of the ideological comprehensiveness of the Club (as distinct from the Labour Party itself which banned any organization with communists in it).

For most purposes the CUSC meant the 'Red Cambridge' of the 1930s. This was not true literally, since even at the peak of its strength, in early 1939, it had no more than 1,000 members out of fewer than 5,000 undergraduates, and when I went up in the autumn of 1936 only about 450.[2] The Party never had much more than 100 members. Nevertheless, given the family origins, socio-political milieu and traditional customs of undergraduates at the ancient universities, as well as the overwhelmingly right-wing political inclinations of west and central European university students between the wars, the domination of the left in both Oxford and Cambridge during the 1930s was quite astonishing. All the more so as, with the exception of the London School of Economics, the left was not particularly strong in any of the other British centres of higher education.*

What is more to the point, the political transformation of Cambridge came from below. The typical politics of Cambridge dons were no doubt in the moderate centre rather than (as in Oxford) strongly Conservative, but prominent supporters of the Labour Party were rare, and communist dons could be counted on the fingers of one hand. Even so uncontroversial a campaign as that nominally organized by the Cambridge Peace Council, which succeeded in raising the then enormous sum of £1,000 for food for the women and children of Republican Spain in the autumn of 1938, was officially supported by only two heads of houses (St John's and King's), six

---

* And the LSE needed less explanation. Founded by the great Fabians Sidney and Beatrice Webb, devoted exclusively to the political and social sciences, led by the later architect of the British social security system, William Beveridge, with a faculty whose most prominent and charismatic teachers were nationally known socialists – Harold Laski, R. H. Tawney – it stood on some kind of left almost *ex officio*. That is what attracted foreigners from inside and outside the empire. If that was not what necessarily attracted its British students, overwhelmingly an elite of first-generation scholarship-winning boys and girls from London families on the borderline between working and lower middle classes, it was likely to influence them once they had arrived.

professors – only one (M. M. Postan) in history – an eminent pacifist clerical don and Maynard Keynes.[3] In the natural sciences, what turned Cambridge red were junior physicists and biochemists from the two intellectual powerhouses, the Cavendish and the Biochem Lab. But Cambridge science went its own political ways, building its campaigns round the Cambridge Scientists' Antiwar Group, which entered wider consciousness mainly by demonstrating the inadequacy of the government's defences against air-raids and poison gas, in the next war. A scientists' faculty group of the Socialist Club was not established until late in 1938. Outside the natural sciences it was unquestionably the conversion of undergraduates that turned Cambridge red.

Who were the Cambridge reds? The question is easier to answer for the less numerous communists than for the CUSC. Before the era of anti-fascism and the Popular Front there were occasional aristocrats, such as the splendidly named A. R. Hovell-Thurlow-Cumming-Bruce, later a kind-hearted judge, who as a small child had played at Chatsworth, where he broke one of the Duke's massive oriental vases, but mostly they came from the prosperous professional, or more rarely business, upper middle class – the Schlegels rather than the Wilcoxes (to use the convenient distinction in E. M. Forster's novel *Howards End*). Noel Annan's 'intellectual aristocracy' was represented, not least by the charismatic John Cornford, a great-grandson of Charles Darwin, but not dominant. The proportion of members from public schools was distinctly smaller in my time, that is after the outbreak of the Spanish Civil War, when the numbers both of the Party and the CUSC shot up. The grammar schools of England and Wales (though not their equivalents in Scotland) were almost certainly better represented in the Party, and certainly in its leadership, than in the general body of Cambridge undergraduates. The student Party's chief local commissar at the time was a lean-and-hungry-looking mathematician from a working-class family, George Barnard of St John's, who ended his career as President of the Royal Statistical Society and in a chair at Essex University and whose younger sister, Dorothy (Wedderburn), whom I got to know after the war, was to become and remain an intimate friend of Marlene and myself. Equally prominent, a little later, was Ralph Russell, a working-class classics student of steely bolshevik demeanour – we called him 'Georgi' after Georgi Dimitrov, the Secretary of the Comintern. The products of 'progressive schools' (Bedales, Dartington, etc.) were also likely to move left, as were the young of Quaker families. It has been suggested that Jews were slightly over-represented, but that is not my memory. Communism – irreligious and anti-Zionist – attracted very few in the small body of Jewish students at Cambridge, sympathetic to Liberals and Labour though these tended to be. If anyone in my time was regarded as a prominent Jewish leftist student, it was the South African Aubrey Eban (Abba Eban), destined for political eminence in Israel, whose Zionism kept him safe from communist temptation. Nor did the few Party members who were Jews think about their Judaism until, I think in 1937, King Street decided we should, and formed a 'Jewish group' or committee in London which 'Ram' Nahum and I reluctantly attended a few times before concluding that it had little reference to what we were doing. I remember the committee for my first encounter with the sort of East End communists who could not stop telling (extremely funny) Jewish jokes, a practice not characteristic of Party meetings in Cambridge.

No doubt this type of socio-cultural analysis throws some light on the distinction between Cambridge right and left, but it is less illuminating than another phenomenon, which still needs explanation. More than one observer might agree with Henry Ferns, that 'the only element common to all the Communists I encountered (in Cambridge) was high intelligence'.[4] In the 1930s the left attracted the intellectually brightest members of the student generation in the country's elite universities.

Much larger though their numbers were, the members of the CUSČ were also characteristically people of intellectual interests, although the club was sufficiently aware of the social dimension of life to organize a dancing class. It had the substantial advantage, not enjoyed by many undergraduate societies, of a large membership in both Girton and Newnham, whose idea of political activism, though just as serious as the men's, was often less heavy. (The first Valentine I ever received was collectively from the Newnham group of the Communist Party of which I was the political instructor.) They were serious about studying. 'The Committee wishes all CUSC members success in their Trips (Triposes)' the Bulletin recorded before the

1937 exams. 'Let us be as much to the fore on the academic front as on the political.'[5] Starting with the modern linguists and historians, the club set up 'faculty' groups to debate problems of their subjects, and by late 1938 had twelve of them, including even such politically unpromising territories as agriculture, engineering and law.[6] On the other hand, contempt for organized sports (but not, of course, for such traditional pursuits of progressive Cambridge as long hikes and mountaineering) was part of CUSC political consciousness. The CUSC gloried in the (frequent) success of socialists or communists at the Union, in drama and journalism – at one moment the presidents of the Union and the ADC (the main dramatic society) and the editor of *Granta* were all in the Party – but I am not aware that it took much interest in converting any of the university's celebrated sports stars – admittedly an uphill task – or in the sporting or mountaineering achievements of its own members.

Whatever else the CUSC did, it campaigned: constantly, passionately, and in a spirit of hopeful confidence that surprises me as I look back in old age on my undergraduate years in Cambridge, the years when Europe (but not yet the world) slid into catastrophe.

The briefest headline summary of the politics of Europe in the 1930s shows that, from the point of view of the left, they were a virtually unbroken succession of disasters. Admittedly, as the song '*Gaudeamus igitur*' tells us, student days are not a time for depression, but should we not have been a little more desperate? We were not. Unlike the post-1945 anti-nuclear movement, we did not feel ourselves fighting a probably doomed rearguard action against enemies far beyond our reach. We lived from crisis to crisis, organizing like football teams living from match to match, each calling for the best efforts. As far as Cambridge was concerned, we were winning our matches. Each season was better than the last. In a way, the student left shared the university's remoteness from the national centre, not to mention its traditional self-absorption. In everyday practice, for Cambridge comrades 'the Party' and the International meant the Cambridge student Party, for our only regular pre-war contact with the national leadership came through the notably unauthoritarian student organizer Jack Cohen, whose political command we naturally accepted without question, but who was aware that a worker without much formal schooling and who came to the students from Party work in the industrial Northeast, had much to learn about universities.

And yet, could we really forget that our greatest triumph, Spain Week, was won at a time when the Spanish Republic was visibly on its last legs and virtually beyond hope? Moreover, though we constructed scenarios about how war could be avoided by firm collective resistance to Hitler, we did not really believe them. We knew in our bones that a Second World War was coming, and we did not expect to survive it. I remember one bad night in a hotel room, possibly in Lyon, in the middle of the Munich crisis of 1938 – I was returning from a long vac study trip to French North Africa – when the thought that war might break out within days suddenly hit me. The nightmares of mass aerial bombardments and clouds of poison gas, against which, as we had so often warned, there was no protection, would become reality. There was no comparable hysteria in September 1939. The year from Munich to the invasion of Poland had allowed us to get used to the prospect of war.

I think we kept cheerful for three reasons. First, we had only one set of enemies – fascism and those who (like the British government) did not want to resist it. Second, there was an actual battlefield – Spain – and we were on it. Our own hero, the charismatic John Cornford, fell on the Córdoba front on his twenty-first birthday. True, he and one or two others who had gone out during the summer of 1936 were to be our only direct participants in the war, for curiously – the fact has not been much noticed – a Party decision at the highest level actually discouraged recruiting students for the International Brigades, unless they had special military qualifications, on the grounds that their primary Party duty was to get a good degree first, so they would, presumably, be of greater usefulness to the Party. Finally, we thought we knew what the new world would be like after the old world had come to an end. In this, like all generations, we were mistaken.

Hence the 1930s were for us very far from the 'low and dishonest decade' of the disenchanted poet Auden. For us it was a time when the good cause confronted its enemies. We enjoyed it, even when, as for most of radical Cambridge, it did not occupy the bulk of our time, and we did a certain amount of world-saving as a matter of course, because it was the thing to do. 'On the other hand we avoided that strain of unhappiness which today frustrates people whose instinct it is to feel about world affairs exactly as we did then, but who find it impossible to translate their feelings into action, as we did.'[7]

In doing so we 'distributed our emotions and energies evenly over the public and private sectors of the landscape', or rather we made no sharp distinction between these two sectors. It is true that we sang, to a Cole Porter-like tune:

> Let's liquidate love
> Let's say from now on
> That all our affection's
> For the workers alone.
> Let's liquidate love
> Till the revolution
> Until then love is
> An un-bolshevik thing.

Nevertheless, since close comradeship between emancipated men and women was part of the cause, we did not live up to this aspiration, even though Cambridge communists' private lives, at least among the more specialized politicians, seem to have been less highly coloured than contemporary Oxford ones. The ethos of the CUSC and the Party was, of course, overwhelmingly heterosexual as, indeed, outside theatrical circles and King's College, it was among the undergraduates generally. In the 1930s even the Apostles had left the era of the Edwardian 'higher sodomy' behind. No doubt some of us were not as naïve as Henry Ferns, who claims that 'I never once encountered a Communist in Cambridge who was a homosexual', but it is true that inside the Comintern (and still less in the CUSC) one did not advertise membership of the Homintern. It was treated on both sides as a private matter. I can think of at least two friends I first knew in the pre-war Party of whose lifelong homosexuality I was simply not aware until after the war.

There was no sharp division between term and vacation. Students did not do much paid vacation work yet, other than tour-guiding for linguists. The odd grant was available – one of these paid for my study trip to Tunisia and Algeria in 1938 – and I financed the long vacation of 1939 with my share of the profits of editing *Granta*, which amounted to some £50. (Thanks to the May Week number, summer term was the time to be editor. At the end of each term the editor pocketed what was left after the technical owners, the printing firm of Messrs Foister and Jagg had been paid for production and distribution.)

My own vacations, broadly speaking, were divided between the London School of Economics and France. The LSE, or at least its main building in Houghton Street, Aldwych, is still recognizably what it was some sixty years ago, even down to the survival of a small snack-bar immediately to the left of the main entrance, which in those days was known as Marie's café, where the student activists used to discuss politics or try to win converts, usually observed by a silent lone central European rather older than ourselves, apparently one of those 'eternal students' who hang around inner-city campuses, but who was in fact the totally unknown and unconsidered Norbert Elias, just about to publish his great work on *The Process of Civilization* in Switzerland. Academic Britain in the 1930s was extraordinarily blind to the brilliance of the central European Jewish and anti-fascist refugee intellectuals unless they operated in conventionally recognized fields such as classics and physics. The LSE was probably the only place where they would be given house-room. Even after the war, Elias's academic career in this country was marginal, and the worth of scholars such as Karl Polanyi was not recognized until after they crossed the Atlantic.

I found the atmosphere of the LSE congenial, and its library, then still in the main building, a good place to work. It was full of central Europeans and colonials, and therefore markedly less provincial than Cambridge, if only by its commitment to social sciences such as demography, sociology and social anthropology, which were of no interest on the Cam. Curiously enough, the subject that gave its name to the school was at that time – and indeed had always been – both less distinguished and less enterprising than at Cambridge, though it attracted some very brilliant junior talent, which alas found no lasting posts in Houghton Street.

I must in some ways have felt more at ease in the LSE student atmosphere, and certainly with its women students, for I established a lifetime friendship with two of the girls I met there, and later married another, though less permanently. Three of my LSE communist student contemporaries became lifetime friends: the historian John Saville (then still known as Stamatopoulos or 'Stam'), his companion and later wife, Constance Saunders, and the impressive James B. Jefferys, who made the transition from a Ph.D. in economic history to wartime convenor of shop stewards at Dunlops, and – less successfully – back again to research, for he became a victim of the Cold War ban on communist academics. It was through another LSE contemporary that I maintained, or rather re-established, links with Austria: the sporting, bushy-haired charmer Tedy Prager, who later got his economics Ph.D. under Joan Robinson in Cambridge, more in tune with his ideas than the LSE's Robbins and Hayek. Sent by his family out of harm's way from Vienna, having got into trouble resisting the Austrofascist regime after the civil war of 1934, he abandoned promising careers in Britain and in the ruins of postwar Vienna, to which, like almost all Austrian communists, he returned from British exile.

In the summer vacations the Cambridge student Party militants went to France to work with James Klugmann. With Margot Heinemann, James was my link with the heroic era of Cambridge communism before my time. (Both remained communists to the end of their lives.) Margot, one of the most remarkable people I have ever known, had been John Cornford's last love, to whom he wrote one of his last poems from Spain, which has since become an anthology piece, and later partnered J. D. Bernal. Through a lifetime of comradeship, example and advice, she probably had more influence on me than any other person I have known.

James had been the Party's acknowledged co-leader with John. For most of the Cambridge student militants he was and long remained a person of enormous prestige, even a sort of guru. I assume that, of all the student communists of his time, he was the one in closest touch with the International, for after graduation, abandoning an academic future for which he was admirably suited, he moved to Paris as Secretary of the Rassemblement Mondial des Etudiants (RME) (World Student Assembly) a broad, but Party-controlled international student organization. On my way to see him there once I recall crossing the path of one Raymond Guyot, a French heavyweight and for several years the Secretary-General of the Communist Youth International. It operated out of one of those small dusty Balzacian backstairs offices so characteristic of unofficial pre-war politics, in the ill-named Cité Paradis, a gloomy dead-end in the 10th *arrondissement*, and later in a more ambitious locale on the Left Bank. Its most obvious public activities were to organize periodic world congresses, which Cambridge and other student volunteers helped to prepare. I acted as translator at the 1937 Congress, which coincided with the great Paris World Exposition, the last before the Second World War, in a marvellous series that began with Prince Albert's Great Exhibition of 1851. I can recall no major spell under James in 1938 – much of that summer I travelled in North Africa – nor can I confirm the report that I was mobilized for a meeting with Arab and Jewish students organized by James in the Easter vacation of 1939, to form a joint front against fascism, Mussolini having just occupied the largely Muslim country of Albania.[8] I spent all the summer of 1939 working on the technical preparations for what would be the largest of these congresses, which ended a few days before Hitler invaded Poland.

In almost every way except intelligence and political devotion James Klugmann was the opposite of the romantic, heroic, highly colourful image of his partner in leadership, John Cornford. Bespectacled, soft-voiced, with a demure wit, always looking as though he was about to smile, he lived alone in a hotel room just by the Odéon theatre. As far as I know he continued a monastic existence as an unattached man for the rest of his life, surrounded, when the occasion arose, by admiring juniors. I am told he made sexual jokes in the company of intimates – of whom I was never one – and, since he had been at Gresham's School, the nursery of more than one eminent homosexual of his day, he may very well have been queer, but one never associated him with any kind of sexual activity. His only obvious passion, at least in his postwar British life, when I saw more of him, was book-collecting. His personal remoteness added to the respect in which we, and indeed most of those who had anything to do with him, held him. What did one know about him? He gave nothing away. The only obvious thing about him was his capacity for remarkably lucid and simple exposition, and the air of authority he exuded – until he was ruined by the break between Stalin and Tito. Not that I can recall much political conversation with James in pre-war Paris in the intervals between work, when we sat in cafés playing chess – he was good at explaining why he beat us – or otherwise taking a break from meetings and the duplicating machine in bars playing table football, Jews playing Asians.

Almost certainly it was the RME that laid the foundations for James's extraordinary wartime career as the key figure in British relations with Tito's Partisans. Left-wing student movements of significance were rare enough in continental Europe, where the typical political stance of students (but not necessarily of university teachers) in the 1930s was a right-wing nationalism shading over into fascism. The great exception were the communist students of Yugoslavia, and especially the university of Belgrade, one of whose leaders, Ivo (Lolo) Ribar, a central figure in what would become the Partisan movement, was a familiar figure at the RME. Probably no man west of Moscow, and certainly no man in Cairo, knew more about who was who in Yugoslav communism and how to make contact with them.

After Stalin's break with Tito, James was forced, almost certainly by direct pressure from Moscow, to make his own irreparable break by writing an utterly implausible and insincere book, *From Trotsky to Tito*. His reputation as the only first-rate intellectual (other than Palme Dutt) to reach the Party leadership, never recovered. From then on he took no risks or initiatives and said nothing, and ceased to be a serious force even within the small CPGB. The Party put him in charge of Education (assisted by our old student organizer Jack Cohen), a job he did brilliantly well, for he was a born teacher. He was far too intelligent and perceptive not to feel the disappointment, indeed the pity of his admirers from the 1930s for a man from whom so much had been expected. He had had the stuffing knocked out of him. Only in 1975 was there a last flash of the old James Klugmann. British intelligence, which had periodically got at him ever since Burgess and Maclean left for Moscow in 1951 suggested that he might at last be prepared to help the British spooks as others had done. Perhaps inducements were offered.[9] The idea that British intelligence, which he knew well – he had after all been in it during the war – should have thought him capable of disloyalty to his cause, hurt him. He refused. He died not long after in a nondescript South London house filled with books.

My last term, May–June 1939, was pretty good. I edited *Granta*, was elected to the Apostles and got a starred First in the Tripos, which also gave me a Studentship at King's. There was only one downside. In the spring of 1939 Uncle Sidney, too old for any kind of war service, gave up the long struggle to make a living in Britain and decided to emigrate to Chile with Nancy, Peter and the few hundred pounds he had been able to raise to start a new life. There was never any question of my going a few weeks before Tripos, and in any case I was not going to leave the country with a war coming. In those days Chile was still a very long way from Europe. I saw them on to the boat in Liverpool, and took the train back to Edgware, to sleep one last night on the floor of the now totally empty house in Handel Close, where I had left my rucksack. The bottle of good Tokay, which I had saved from the old home, had somehow disappeared in my absence. Then I went back to Cambridge.

I spent the summer living in a grim but well-placed Paris hotel in the rue Cujas on the editorial profits of *Granta*, working on James's great Congress. A photograph from the Congress is before me: a mixture of whites (mostly from Cambridge) with Indians, Indonesians, the odd Middle and Far Easterner and a solitary African. I recognize that well-meaning girl from Amsterdam – she was later killed in the Dutch Resistance. There, among the crowd of forgotten youthful faces, is the handsome Javanese Satjadjit Soegono, who became a major trade union leader in Indonesia after the war until he was killed in the 1948 communist insurrection in Madiun. There, next to James, is Pieter Keunemann, the future General Secretary of the CP of Sri Lanka and P. N. Haksar, the future chief-of-staff of Mrs Gandhi. There are the Spanish refugees – little Miggy Robles, who worked so hard at the duplicator with Pablo Azcarate of the Spanish Communist Party. There is the small, intense, Bengali face of Arun Bose. It was a successful Congress except for one thing: the Second World War began less than two weeks later.

I needed a rest and hitchhiked for a few days to Concarneau in Brittany. I returned on 1 September. A well-dressed but somewhat preoccupied Frenchwoman in a sports car gave me a lift somewhere past Angers. Had I heard? Hitler had marched into Poland. We drove to Paris, stopping to discover the latest from the radio somewhere, with random conversation about the coming war. As this was France, it is inconceivable that we did not stop for lunch, but on such a day that does not stay in the memory. Some Parisians were already going the other way in loaded cars. We wished one another good luck as she dropped me off. I made for the Westminster Bank on the Place Vendôme and queued with the rest of the Brits. A bad-tempered man with a notably retreating chin was ahead of me, whose passport made him out to be the writer and painter Wyndham Lewis. There was not much to pack before going to St Lazare to get tickets, if I could, for the night train to London. It was full of tall, long-legged blondes: the English dancers from the Folies Bergère and the Casino de Paris were returning to their homes in Morecambe or Nottingham. If I remember it right, I came out of Victoria Station on the last morning of peace having underslept, but into a sunny London. I no longer had a home there, but I think I spent the last night of peace in the flat of, or shared by, Lorna Hay, a Scottish graduate from Newnham about to look for a career in London journalism. She had just been told by Mohan Kumaramangalam, returning to India, that his future as a professional revolutionary made it impossible to take her with him.

That is how the 1930s ended for me.

9

Being Communist

I

I became a communist in 1932, though I did not actually join the Party until I went up to Cambridge in the autumn of 1936. I remained in it for some fifty years. The question why I stayed so long obviously belongs in an autobiography, but it is not of general historical interest. On the other hand, the question why communism attracted so many of the best men and women of my generation, and what being communists meant to us, has to be a central theme in the history of the twentieth century. For nothing is more characteristic of that century than what my friend Antonio Polito calls 'one of the great demons of the twentieth century: political passion'. And the quintessential expression of this was communism.

Communism is now dead. The USSR and most of the states and societies built on its model, children of the October Revolution of 1917 which inspired us, have collapsed so completely, leaving behind a landscape of material and moral ruin, that it must now be obvious that failure was built into this enterprise from the start. Yet the achievements of those inspired by this conviction, and the associated belief that 'there are no fortresses that Bolsheviks cannot conquer', were indeed quite extraordinary. Within little more than thirty years of Lenin's arrival at the Finland Station, one third of the human race and all governments between the Elbe and the China Seas lived under the rule of Communist Parties. The Soviet Union itself, defeating the most formidable war machine of the twentieth century, which had pulverized Tsarist Russia, emerged from the Second World War as one of the world's two superpowers. There had been no comparable triumph of an ideology since the (slower and less global) conquests of Islam in the seventh and eighth centuries of our era.

This was achieved by small, often by relatively or absolutely tiny, self-selected 'vanguard parties' for, unlike the working-class parties which emerged at the end of the nineteenth century, also mostly inspired and encouraged by the ideas of Karl Marx, communism was not designed as a mass movement, and became one only by historical accident, as it were. In this respect it contrasted with, and indeed rejected, the classic approach of Marxist social democracy, which expected everyone who recognized themselves as a 'worker' to identify with parties whose essence, often expressed in their very name – Labour Party – was that they were parties of workers. To support the party of labour seemed to them not so much an individual political choice as the discovery of a person's social existence, which necessarily had certain public implications. Conversely, their least political activities were imbued with the sense of what defined a person's social existence, so that the clubs which met in the back rooms of pubs in 'Red Vienna' – I recall seeing such notices there as late as the 1970s – practised their hobbies not as stamp collectors but as Worker Philatelists, or as Worker Pigeon Fanciers. Such parties were sometimes also to be found in the communist movement, as notably in postwar Italy. There the Party, rooted in family and local community, combined the tradition of the old socialist movement with the organizational efficiency of Leninism and the moral authority of a secular Catholic Church. (As Palmiro Togliatti put it in 1945: 'in every household a picture of Marx next to the one of Jesus Christ'). It was the kind of Party in which a young woman from Modena could quite naturally ask her Party Federazione to make enquiries to the Padova Federazione, to discover whether the young *carabiniere* from that city who courted her was 'serious' (Alas, he turned out to be already married in Padova.)[1] Here public and private, becoming a better person and building a better world, were considered indivisible.

The Communist Parties of the Comintern era were of an entirely different kind, even when they claimed, sometimes correctly, to be rooted in the working class and to express its interests and aspirations. They were Lenin's 'professional revolutionaries', that is to say necessarily a relatively or absolutely small selected group. To join such an organization was essentially an individual decision, and was recognized as life-changing both by those who invited a 'contact' to join the Party and by the man or woman who joined it. It was a double decision, for remaining in the Party (at least outside countries of communist rule) implied the continuous choice not to leave it, which was possible easily and at any time. For most of those who joined, membership of the Party was a temporary episode in their political life. Nevertheless, unlike the 1968 generation, few interwar communists went into the revolution as into a political Club Med (which, by the way, was founded as a holiday mini-utopia by a young Communist Party ex-resister after the Second World War).

Giorgio Amendola, one of the pre-war generation of Italian communist leaders, called the first volume of his beautifully written autobiography *Una scelta di vita*, 'A Chosen Life'. For those of us who became communists before the war, and especially before 1935, the cause of communism was indeed something to which we intended to dedicate our lives, and some did so. The crucial difference turned out to be between communists who spent their lives in opposition and those whose Parties took power, and who therefore became directly or indirectly responsible for what was done in their regimes. Power does not necessarily corrupt people as individuals, though its corruptions are not easy to resist. What power does, especially in times of crisis and war, is to make us do and seek to justify things unacceptable when done by private persons. Communists like myself, whose Parties were never in power, or engaged in situations which call for decisions on other people's life or death (resistance, concentration camps), had it easier.

Membership in these Leninist 'vanguard parties' was thus a profound personal choice, but not an abstract one. For most interwar communists joining the Party was a further step on this road for someone who was already 'on the left' or, in the parts of the world where this was appropriate, 'anti-imperialist'. It was, of course, easier for those who came from politically homogeneous environments of the right kind – say, in New York, where, as I once overheard one contributor to *The New Yorker* say reflectively to another, 'One actually never meets any Republicans,' rather than in Dallas, Texas. It was even easier for those who came from communities, generally marginal to the larger society, whose situation placed them outside the national political consensus. Conversely, vast as is the number of ex-communists of my generation, it is uncommon to encounter among them people who have swung to the extreme political right. The exit-route of the politically disillusioned communist usually led either, if young enough, to some other branch of the political left, or, generally by stages, mainly to a militant anti-communist Cold War liberalism. Even in the USA a generation had to pass before the (anti-Stalinist) intellectuals of the New York left abandoned the old family loyalties and frankly declared themselves 'neo-conservatives'.

This is particularly clear among intellectuals, for the prevailing conventions of rational thinking about society are rooted in the rationalist eighteenth-century European Enlightenment. As the political right has never ceased complaining, this has made intellectuals inclined to sympathize with such causes as liberty, equality and fraternity. Even my friend Isaiah Berlin, with his visceral commitment to a non-negotiable Jewish identity, which made him defend, or at least try to understand, the critics of the Enlightenment, found it impossible not to behave like an Enlightenment liberal. Outside Germany a secular intellectual tradition suitable to the right hardly existed. In the first half of the past century, the left visibly attracted far more intellectuals than the right. Even in the major creative arts, where rational thinking is less relevant, anti-fascism prevailed. On this question the last word has been said with admirable brevity by 'Simon Leys', the pseudonym of an eminent Belgian sinologue with an unparalleled record as a deconstructor of the myths of Maoism: 'All of us in the intellectual world know people who have been communists who have changed their minds. How many of us have come across ex-Fascists?' The truth is, whether they changed their minds or not after the war, there simply were never that many.

This does not mean that communism attracted a particular type or types of personality open to extremism, authoritarianism and other 'undemocratic' traits, although in the Cold War era this was argued by authors anxious to demonstrate the similarity of communism and fascism, but politically angled social psychology need not detain us. In any case there is little base for the liberal belief in a fundamental affinity between 'extremisms' of right and left, which made it easy to pass from one extreme to the other. Since the British CP was small, communist workers and students, at least in the late 1930s, were exceptional but they were not untypical. I can detect no common personality traits among my Cambridge contemporaries who joined the CP that distinguished them from those who did not join, except perhaps a greater intellectual liveliness. Indeed, in later years, as I met some former comrade again in his post-communist existence as a respectable – though rarely Conservative – middle-class professional, I would sometimes say to myself: 'To think that I once recruited him and fellows like him into the Party!' It is less surprising that the workers who joined the Party were, in Britain at least, young, livelier than most, but otherwise typical of their class and trades – mainly engineering, building and in some regions mining. Between the 1930s and 1950s, before A-levels and higher education came within reach of their class, the way in which bright young apprentices or the dynamic young workshop activists would get their political and intellectual education was through the Party. It formed the future national leaders of British trade unionism, and, of course, provided the Party itself with capable working-class cadres, which a consciously 'proletarian' party insisted on. Contrary to common opinion, intellectuals as such played no significant part in the Party leadership, until the educational revolution removed the potential exam-passing youth from workshop to college, which therefore became the way into politics or better jobs – and not only in Communist Parties.

Communism was therefore not a way of picking out 'extremists' from 'non-extremist' personalities, although both poles of the political spectrum may sometimes attract the same clientele, namely persons, usually young, who have a natural taste for adventurous operations or political violence, the sort of people to whom terrorism or direct action appeal. Perhaps Rambo-types have been more attracted to the extreme left since the rise of street confrontation and small-scale armed groups in the aftermath of the student revolt of 1968, with its rhetoric of 'streetfighting men'. Nevertheless, a life devoted to making revolution is not the same as a life that gets its thrills from irregular warfare or adventure.

Given the tradition and importance of clandestine activities in the Communist Parties, which, with the rarest exceptions (such as Great Britain) were illegal for at least some of their history, there was obviously scope for the life of adventure in the international communist movement of my times, but bolshevism, whose motto was ruthless efficiency rather than romance, did not favour the culture of the bank-robber or commando-raid. It invented the supremacy of the 'political commissar' (i.e. the civilian) because it distrusted the impulses of the soldier. It was hostile in theory to individual terrorism. Lenin's own reaction to such gestures was utterly typical. He could not understand why in 1916 the social democrat Friedrich Adler had publicly shot dead the Prime Minister of the Habsburg Empire as a protest against the First World War. Would it not have been more effective for him, as secretary of the Party, to circulate the branches with a call for a strike?

I have known several communists whose career would interest, and in some cases has interested, the writers of thrillers, but on the whole their ideal of clandestinity, however dangerous, was not buccaneering or self-dramatization. Let me compare the character of Alexander Rado, the head of the extremely important Soviet spy network in wartime Switzerland and the only master spy with whom I have ever spent a somewhat bizarre Christmas in Budapest, and that of his radio operator Alexander Foote, apparently a British double agent, as described in the literature. Foote 'had not become a secret agent in the first place for ideology, money or patriotism. He made very little money out of spying, abstract political ideas bored him, and MI5 did not regard him as a patriot when he eventually returned to Britain. But he was a born adventurer . . .'[2] Rado did not look like a man thirsting for action, but like a comfortable middle-aged businessman whose natural leisure habitat was a central European café table. When I met him in 1960, returned to a chair at the Karl Marx University of Economics in Budapest after several years in Stalin's camps, he was what he had always wanted to be, a geographer and cartographer. He had spent his entire political life since 1918 in and out of clandestine or unavowable activities, always returning to this vocation. Neither fighting – he was the organizer of the armed workers' brigades destined to head the (aborted) German revolution of 1923 – nor running spy networks diverted him. No doubt he also enjoyed the thrills of that kind of life, but he did not strike me as a man who chose it for that reason. He did what needed doing. 'When we were young,' he told me, 'Rakosi [the former Hungarian communist leader and dictator, at the time of this conversation retired in exile in the USSR] used to say to me "Sandor, why not become a full-time professional revolutionary?" Well, look at him and look at me. It was a good thing that I had a proper trade and never gave it up.' Communist Parties were not for romantics.

On the contrary, they were for organization and routine. That is why bodies of a few thousand members – like the Vietnamese CP at the end of the Second World War – could, given the occasion, become the makers of states. The secret of the Leninist Party lay neither in dreaming about standing on barricades or even Marxist theory. It can be summed up in two phrases: 'decisions must be verified' and 'Party discipline'. The appeal of the Party was that it got things done when others did not. Life in the Party was almost viscerally anti-rhetorical, which may have helped to produce that culture of endless and almost aggressively boring and, when reprinted in Party publications, sensationally unreadable 'reports' which foreign Parties took over from Soviet practice. Even in operatic Italy the young postwar red intellectuals made fun of the traditional style of speech at the great public meetings on which the faithful still insisted. Not that we were unmoved by powerful oratory, and we recognized its importance on public occasions and in 'mass work'. Even so, speeches are not a major part of my communist memories, except for one in Paris in the first months of the Spanish Civil War by La Pasionaria, large, black in widow's weeds, in the tense emotion-charged silence of a packed Vel d'hiv indoor arena. Though hardly any of the audience knew Spanish, we knew exactly what she was telling us. I can still remember the words '*y las madres, y sus hijos*' (and the mothers, and their sons) floating slowly from the microphones above us, like dark albatrosses.

The Leninist 'vanguard party' was a combination of discipline, business efficiency, utter emotional identification and and a sense of *total* dedication. Let me illustrate. In 1941, pinned down by a fallen beam, our comrade Freddie thought she would die in the fire set off by the only enemy bomb that hit Cambridge during the Second World War. My friend Tedy Prager, who vainly tried to free her until the fire services came – he lived in what had been my old cottage in Round Church Street, almost within arm's reach of the explosion – tells the story:

My feet, she screamed, it's burning my feet, and I kept chopping at the beam, but nothing moved. Poor Freddie . . . It's no good, she was now crying, I'm done for. And then, as I wept with desperation and smoke, too exhausted to lift the axe any longer, she cried out: Long live the Party, long live Stalin ... Long live Stalin, she cried out, and Good-bye boys, good-bye Tedy.[3]

Freddie did not die, though she has spent the rest of her life with legs amputated below the knees. At the time it would not have struck any of us as surprising that the last words of a dying Party member should be for the Party, for Stalin and for the comrades. (In those days among foreign communists the thought of Stalin was as sincere, unforced, unsullied by knowledge and universal as the genuine grief most of us felt in 1953 at the death of a man whom no Soviet citizen would have wanted, or dared, to call by a pet name like 'Uncle Joe' in Britain or 'Big whiskers' [baffone] in Italy.) The Party was what our life was about. We gave it all we had. In return, we got from it the certainty of our victory and the experience of fraternity.

The Party (we always thought of it in capital letters) had the first, or more precisely the only real claim on our lives. Its demands had absolute priority. We accepted its discipline and hierarchy. We accepted the absolute obligation to follow 'the line' it proposed to us, even when we disagreed with it, although we made heroic efforts to convince ourselves of its intellectual and political 'correctness' in order to 'defend it', as we were expected to. For, unlike fascism, which demanded automatic abdication and service to the Leader's will ('Mussolini is always right') and the unconditional duty of obeying military orders, the Party – even at the peak of Stalin's absolutism – rested its authority, at least in theory, on the power to convince of reason and 'scientific socialism'. After all, it was supposed to be based on a 'Marxist analysis of the situation', which every communist was meant to learn how to make. 'The line', however predetermined and unchangeable, had to be justified in terms of such an analysis, and, except where circumstances made this physically impossible, 'discussed' and approved at all levels of the Party. In Communist Parties outside power, where members were not too scared to pursue the ancient left-wing tradition of argument, the leadership had to go through the process of repeating its case for the official line until there was no room for doubt about what we were expected to vote for. (The technical term for this process was 'patiently explaining'.) After the vote, 'democratic centralism' required that argument should give way to unanimous action.

We did what it ordered us to do. In countries such as Britain it did not order us to do anything very dramatic. Indeed, but for their conviction that what they were doing was saving the world, communists might have been bored by the routine activities of their Party, conducted in the usual ritual of the British labour movement (comrade chairman, branch minutes, treasurer's report, resolutions, contacts, literature sales and the rest) in private homes or unwelcoming meeting rooms. But whatever it had ordered, we would have obeyed. After all, most Soviet and Comintern cadres in the period of Stalin's terror, who knew what might await them, followed the order to return to Moscow. If the Party ordered you to abandon your lover or spouse, you did so. After 1933 the German Party in exile ordered Margaret Mynatt (later the inspiration behind the English-language *Collected Works of Marx and Engels*) to go to England from Paris, since they needed someone in London and, as known German communists were not admitted, a comrade with valid British documentation was needed. Without a moment's hesitation she abandoned the love of her life (or so she later told me) and went. She never saw him (or was it a her?) again. Party dues in Auschwitz, I was told after the war by a former inmate, were paid in the inconceivably precious currency of cigarettes, and it says something about the Party's capacity for collective resistance that they could procure them.

To have a serious relationship with someone who was not in the Party or prepared to join (or rejoin it) was unthinkable. Admittedly, since Party members were also apt to be emancipated in their attitude to sex, it is to be supposed that not all militants eschewed completely apolitical sex, but even for the Comintern agent in Brecht's wonderful poem *An die Nachgeborenen* (To Those Born Later), his casual couplings ('*der Liebe pflegte ich achtlos*') were yet another proof that the Party's work came before everything that was personal. I confess that the moment when I recognized that I could envisage a real relationship with someone who was not a potential recruit to the Party was the moment I recognized that I was no longer a communist in the full sense of my youth.

It is easy in retrospect to describe how we felt and what we did as Party members half a century ago, but much harder to explain it. I cannot recreate the person I was. The landscape of those times lies buried under the debris of world history. Even the image – if there was one – of the wonderful hopes we had for human life has been overlaid by the range of goods, services, prospects and personal options which are today available to the majority of men and women in the incredibly wealthy and technologically advanced countries of the West. Marx and Engels wisely refrained from describing what communist society would be like, but most of what little they said about what individual life would be like under it, now seems to be the result, without communism, of that social production of potentially almost unlimited plenty, and that miraculous technological progress, which they expected in some undetermined future, but which is taken for granted today.

Rather than reconstruct in my eighties what made us communists, let me quote from shortly after the 1956 crisis, when I was closer to the convictions of youth. I wrote that even the most sophisticated revolutionaries share 'that utopianism or "impossibilism" which makes even very modern ones feel a sense of almost physical pain at the realization that the coming of socialism will not eliminate all grief and sadness, unhappy love-affairs or mourning, and will not solve or make soluble *all* problems'. I observed that 'revolutionary movements . . . appear to prove that almost no change is beyond their reach'.

Liberty, equality and above all fraternity may become real for the moment in those stages of the great social revolutions which revolutionaries who live through them describe in the terms normally reserved for romantic love. Revolutionaries not only set themselves a standard of morality higher than that of any except saints, but at such moments actually carry it into practice . . .Theirs is at such times a miniature version of the ideal society, in which all men are brothers and sacrifice everything for the common good without abandoning their individuality. If this is possible within the movement, why not everywhere?

By this time I had recognized, with Milovan Djilas, who has written wonderfully well of the psychology of revolutionaries, that 'these are the morals of a sect', but that is precisely what gave them such force as engines of political change.[4]

It was easy enough in Europe during and between the world wars to conclude that only revolution could give the world a future. The old world was in any case doomed. However, three further elements distinguished communist utopianism from other aspirations to a new society. First, Marxism, which demonstrated with the methods of science the certainty of our victory, a prediction tested and verified by the victory of proletarian revolution over one sixth of the earth's surface and the advances of revolution in the 1940s. Marx had shown why it could never have happened before in human history, and why it could and was destined to happen now, as indeed it did. Today the foundations of this certainty that we knew where history was going have collapsed, notably the belief that the industrial working class would be the agency of change. In the 'Age of Catastrophe' they looked firm.

Second, there was internationalism. Ours was a movement for *all* humanity and not for any particular section of it. It represented the ideal of transcending selfishness, individual and collective. Time and again young Jews who began as Zionists became communists because, obvious as the sufferings of the Jews were, they were only part of universal oppression. Julius Braunthal wrote, describing his conversion to socialism in Vienna at the start of the century: 'I felt sorry for my Zionist friends whom I had deserted; but I hoped I would be able to persuade them one day to understand that the smaller aim has to give way to the bigger.'[5] With retrospective bitterness disguised as cynicism my New York colleague the philosopher Agnes Heller describes her conversion to communism in a Hungarian Zionist work camp in 1947 at the age of eighteen:

> We lived in community, we felt we belonged together. We needed neither money nor the rich ... I didn't like the rich, today I am ashamed of it. I abominated the black market dealers, the dollar speculators, the men of rapacity and greed. No problem! I'd stay loyal for ever to the poor. So, crazy chick that I was, I joined the Communist Party to be with the poor.[6]

In practice, national or other collective or historical identities were far more important than we then supposed. Indeed, communism probably made its greatest impact outside Europe, where it had no effective rival in the fight against national or imperial oppression. Ho Chi Minh, the liberator of Vietnam, chose as his *nom-de-guerre* in the Comintern 'Nguyen the Patriot'. Chin Peng, who led the communist insurgency and jungle guerrillas in Malaya, though less successfully, began as a youthful patriot who first turned to communism when he abandoned hope in the ability of the Kuomintang Party to liberate China. He told me so himself, an elderly Chinese gentleman of intellectual interests looking most unlike a former jungle guerrilla leader, in the improbable environment of the Athenaeum's Coffee Room. Nevertheless, even for those who began with limited aims, even for those who abandoned the wider hope when it disappointed the narrower one, like the many communist Jews who left the Party under the impact of Stalin's anti-Semitic campaigns, communism represented the ideal of transcending egoism and of service to all humanity without exception.

But there was a third element in the revolutionary convictions of Party communists. What awaited them on the road to the millennium was tragedy. In the Second World War communists were vastly overrepresented in most resistance movements, not simply because they were efficient and brave, but because they had always been ready for the worst: for spying, clandestinity, interrogation and armed action. Lenin's vanguard Party was born in persecution, the Russian Revolution in war, the Soviet Union in civil war and famine. Until the revolution communists could expect no rewards from their societies. What professional revolutionaries could expect was jail, exile and, quite often, death. Unlike the anarchists, the IRA or movements of Islamic suicide bombers, the Comintern did not make much of a cult of individual martyrs, though the French CP after liberation appreciated the attraction of the (true) fact that during the Resistance it had been '*le parti des fusillés*' (the party of those executed by firing squad). Communists were undoubtedly the quintessential enemy for almost every government, including even the relatively few which allowed their Parties legal existence, and we were constantly reminded of the treatment they could expect in jails and concentration camps. And yet we saw ourselves less as sufferers or potential casualties than as combatants in an omnipresent war. As Brecht wrote in his great 1930s elegy on the Comintern professionals, *An die Nachgeborenen*:

> I ate my meals between battles
> I lay down to sleep among the murderers.

Hardness is the soldier's quality, and it ran even through our very political jargon ('uncompromising', 'unbending', 'steel-hard', 'monolithic'). Hardness, indeed ruthlessness, doing what had to be done, before, during and after the revolution was the essence of the bolshevik. It was the necessary response to the times. As Brecht wrote:

> You, who will emerge from the flood
> In which we have perished
> Remember also
> When you speak of our weaknesses
> The black times
> You have escaped

But the point of Brecht's poem, which speaks to communists of my generation as no other does, is that hardness was forced upon the revolutionaries.

> We, who wanted to prepare the ground for kindness
> Could not be kind ourselves.

Of course we did not, and could not, envisage the sheer scale of what was being imposed on the Soviet peoples under Stalin at the time when we identified ourselves with him and the Comintern, and were reluctant to believe the few who told us what they knew or suspected.[7] Nobody could anticipate the scale of human suffering in the Second World War until it happened. However, it is anachronistic to suppose that only genuine or wilful ignorance stood between us and denouncing the inhumanities perpetrated on our side. In any case, we were not liberals. Liberalism was what had failed. In the total war we were engaged in, one did not ask oneself whether there should be a limit to the sacrifices imposed on others any more than on ourselves. Since we were not in power, or likely to be, what we expected was to be prisoners rather than jailers.

There were Communist Parties and functionaries, such as André Marty, who appears in Hemingway's *For Whom the Bell Tolls*, who took pride in their necessary 'steel-hard' bolshevism, not least the Soviet Communist Party, where it combined with the absolutist tradition of unlimited power and the brutality of everyday Russian existence to produce the hecatombs of the Stalin era. The British CP was not among them, but Party pathology appeared in more masochistic and peaceful forms. To take a case in point: the late Andrew Rothstein (1898–1994). Andrew was a rather boring, round-faced petit-bourgeois figure, who defended whatever needed defending in the Soviet Union, the son of a more dramatic Russian old bolshevik, Theodore Rothstein, who had once been a Soviet diplomat and had written a pioneering book of Marxist labour history. We shared a cold bedroom once at a conference of the Association of University Teachers, and I still recall him carefully unpacking his toilet set and slippers. Possibly I was mandated to protest against the failure of the University of London's School of Slavonic Studies, where he taught Soviet Institutions, to renew his time-limited contract as a lecturer. A founder member of the British CP, and obviously with good Russian connections, he had been a leading figure in the Party in the 1920s, but in 1929–30 his opposition to the Comintern's ultra-left course, not to mention his vitriolic temper and lack of proletarian bona fides, led to his fall. He was exiled (minus his wife and children) to Moscow, his Party member-ship transferred to the CPSU. Luckily for his survival he was soon allowed back into Britain and the British CP on condition that for the rest of his career he occupied only local functions in the Party. Yet he remained a totally loyal, totally committed communist. Indeed, I had the impression that for him, as for others like him, the test of his devotion to the cause was the readiness to defend the indefensible. It was not the Christian '*credo quia absurdum*' (I believe it is because it is absurd), but rather the constant challenge: 'Test me some more: as a bolshevik I have no breaking-point.' When the British CP finally went out of existence in 1991, he became, at the age of ninety-three, the first member of the tiny hard-line Communist Party of Britain which succeeded it.

I doubt whether any communist of my generation would have been inspired to join the Party, or stayed in the Party, by the career of Rothstein. And yet we had our heroes and models – Georgi Dimitrov, in the Reichstag fire trial of 1933 who stood up alone in the Nazi court, defying Hermann Göring and defending the good name of communism and, incidentally, of the small but proud Bulgarian nation to which he belonged. If I did not leave the Party in 1956, it was not least because the movement bred such men and women. I am thinking primarily of one such figure, barely known in his lifetime, unremembered except by comrades and friends today. I still recall him, small, sharp-eyed, quizzical, as we walked on a Sunday morning through the sun-dappled and carefully marked footpaths of the Wienerwald hills, among occasional couples of hiking acquaintances, white-haired men and women, who had organized illegal Party and socialist meetings in the remoter parts of those woods before they survived the concentration camps. The open air had always been the characteristic environment of Austrian revolutionaries. There is probably no man for whom I have a greater admiration.

In mid-August 1944 he had written his last words in cell 155 of block 2 and cell 90 of block 1 of Fresnes prison in Paris:

> Franz Feuerlich, communist
> Franz Feuerlich, Austrian
> will be executed 15 August 1944
> On the eve of liberation?[8]

But Ephraim Feuerlicht (1913–79), whom we all knew by his Party name Franz Marek, was lucky. The liberation of Paris saved him. He had been a leading figure in the French Communist Party's MOI (Main d'Oeuvre Immigrée) organization, under the Czech Artur London (later victim of the Stalinist trials), whose Spaniards, Jews, Italians, Poles and others played such a disproportionately large and heroic part in the armed Resistance in France. (Those whose image of Jews under fascism is that of eternal victims, should remember the fighting record of socialist and communist Jews, from the 7,000 who fought in the International Brigades to the MOI and their equivalents in other occupied countries.) Among other things Franz was in charge of work with the German troops themselves. He did not talk about those times, except once to our son Andy, then about ten, who wanted to know what sort of things you did in the Resistance. He said that mostly you kept out of the way of the people who wanted to arrest you, but that he had had a few narrow escapes. Born in Przemysl, which is today in the Ukraine, brought up in the deepest poverty in interwar Vienna – Franz claimed that he never had a *new* jacket and trousers until he became a professional revolutionary – he became politicized as a Zionist at the age of fifteen, but converted to communism from the most Marxist of the Zionist groups, the Hashomer Hazair, though he did not join the Communist Party until after the Austrian civil war of 1934. Not surprisingly, it was the immediate consequence of a few months spent wandering round pre-Hitler Germany in 1931–2. He became a professional almost from the start, having demonstrated what were clearly exceptional abilities for clandestine work to the comrade sent to instruct the Austrians in the unaccustomed situation of illegality. Though he insists that the secret of such work was punctuality and pedantry about details, in short, the strict bolshevik 'rules of conspiracy', as a man in his early twenties he enjoyed the romantic side of the work. He liked to recall that he occupied what had once been the office of Dimitrov in the ninth district – Vienna had always been the International's centre for the Balkans. Soon he was setting up a Vienna office for the Romanian CP (all 300 of them) and organizing its participation in the forthcoming Seventh World Congress, before being promoted to head the 'Apparat' of the illegal Austrian Party – communications, safe houses, frontier crossings, and the provision and distribution of literature – and later its entire agit-prop activities. No doubt it was this that brought him to Paris after the Anschluss.

He returned to Austria after the war as a member of the Austrian CP's Political Bureau, wrote a brief and luminous book on France, and edited the Party's theoretical journal. In 1968 he briefly succeeded in decoupling the Austrian CP from the USSR after condemning its invasion of Czechoslovakia, but Moscow soon reasserted itself. Marek was expelled, but continued as editor of an independent left-wing monthly the *Wiener Tagebuch* and (together with myself and some others) planner and editor – his only regular income now came from it – of Giulio Einaudi's ambitious *Storia del Marxismo*. He fell to a long-awaited heart attack in the summer of 1979. He died a communist. The Italian Communist Party was represented at his funeral. What he left at his death, give or take a few books, could be packed into two suitcases.

A man of strong, lucid intelligence and remarkable learning, he could have been a thinker, a writer, an eminent academic. But he had chosen not to interpret the world but to change it. Had he lived in a larger country and in other times, he might have been a major political figure in a humanized communism. He continued on this road to the end, resisting the temptations of a post-political refuge in literature or graduate seminar. In his way, he was a hero of our times, which were and are bad times.

II

I have so far written about communists outside power. What about the Party members I have known who faced the very different situation in communist regimes, where it brought not persecution but privilege? They were not outsiders but insiders, not opposers but rulers, often of countries most of whose inhabitants did not like them. The police was not their enemy but their agency. And for them glorious future after the revolution was not a dream but now.

They did not have the advantage, which maintained our morale, of enemies who could be fought with conviction and a clear conscience: capitalism, imperialism, nuclear annihilation. Unlike us, they could not avoid responsibility for what was being done in the name of communism in their countries, including the injustices. This is what made the Khrushchev Report of 1956 especially traumatic for them. 'If "the laws of history" could no longer take the blame for these terrors, but Stalin as a person, then what about our own co-responsibility?' wrote an exiled Czech reform-communist of my acquaintance.[9] He had been in the public prosecution service in the 1950s.

In my lifetime there were three generations of such communists who had crossed this threshold of power: the pre-Stalinist 'old bolsheviks', few of whom survived the 1930s and none of whom I knew; those who made or experienced the great change – the interwar and resistance generations of communists; and those who grew up under the regimes which collapsed in 1989. There is nothing to be said about the last of these. By the time they joined what was a public elite, they knew the rules of the game by which their countries lived. Nor is there anything I can say about the Soviet Union. I have real personal acquaintance with only one member of the Soviet generation, though he was not a Russian but a second-generation foreign communist brought up in the USSR before returning to his own country, the late Tibor Szamuely of Hungary.

He was a very bright, squat, ugly and witty historian, nephew of one of the most eminent figures in the 1919 Hungarian Soviet Republic, who had been brought up in the USSR, where his father was executed and his mother deported. He himself, after almost starving in the siege of Leningrad, claimed also to have had the usual spell in a camp during the dictator's final lunacies. He returned to Hungary after Stalin's death, cynical, but officially communist, and Party secretary in the university history faculty, where his line was ultra-hard, but somehow no students or colleagues were expelled or penalized. However, when I first met him in London in about 1959 he made a beeline for the most anti-communist contacts. Like so many central European Jews, he was a passionate anglophile. Perhaps he was already preparing to jump ship as a freedom-lover, which he did a few years later, becoming an anti-communist publicist for Conservative publications and a close friend of the writer and drinker Kingsley Amis, equally reactionary and funnier but notably less intelligent. In spite of what he must have regarded as my illusions we liked one another and got on extremely well. It was through him that I first went to Hungary in 1960, though, as a high official – I think he was then vice-rector of the university – he was not pleased at my insistence on visiting the great Marxist philosopher George Lukács, who had recently been allowed by the Russians to return to Budapest. Lukács had been seized and exiled after the 1956 revolution and now sat in his apartment above the Danube once again like an ancient high priest in civilian clothes, smoking Havana cigars. It was in Tibor's flat that I had the memorable Christmas dinner with the master spy. It was to our flat in Bloomsbury that he chose to come directly from the airport with wife and children when he had finally arranged (via a posting to Ghana) to get the whole family out of socialism for good.

It was not the horrors of socialism that had finally driven him out, but excess of cynicism. For, though he was received in Britain as a victim of Soviet repression, in fact he had taken no part in the 1956 revolution. Indeed, after its defeat he reestablished the Party unit at the university. Szamuely's career therefore advanced rapidly in the next years. Unfortunately in the course of those years, under the benevolent eye of the Kadar government, the sympathizers with the 1956 movement, that is to say the bulk of communist intellectuals and academics, quietly re-established their positions. The career of the Soviet collaborator who had risen so steeply after 1956 went into a decline. But, of course, he had no doubt been as contemptuous of the illusions of the 1956 revolutionaries as of the Soviet regime. Taking another step away from the Party world of my youth, in subsequent years I successfully resisted the temptation to say anything in public about the 1956 record of the great freedom-lover. It was more than the reluctance to score what would have been, after all, no more than a passing political debating point at the cost of embarrassing a personal friend. Marlene and I recognized that there was a principle here: there are times when a line must be drawn between personal relations and political views. And yet, excellent company, charming and witty as he was, we and the Szamuelys drifted apart. Perhaps private and public lives are not as separable as all that.

Czechs, East Germans and Hungarian academics were the Party members in the Soviet bloc I saw most of. Of the major political figures of the regimes I met only one or two briefly, notably Andras Hegedüs, the last Hungarian premier under Rakosi, who recycled himself as an academic sociologist after 1956, travelled, protected dissidents but said little, though allowing it to be understood that the quality of the Party leadership had declined after his day. None of my friends was a Party figure, although Ivan Berend turned down the offer to become a minister of education in his country, Hungary. He was and is a superb historian, President of his country's Academy of Sciences under communism, whose merits were recognized, after the end of communism, by election as President of the International Committee of Historical Sciences. Almost all the Czechs I knew, some of whom dated back to the pre-war English emigration, became supporters of the Prague Spring of 1968, and some, such as my friend Antonin Liehm, played a notable part in it as editor of the leading cultural-political journal of the time, *Literarny listy*. We first met not through politics but as jazz-lovers at a Prague festival, but jazz, like the rehabilitation of Kafka, was an oppositional activity in the run-up to 1968, though I am not aware of any political background to the publication of my *The Jazz Scene*, the only one of my books translated into Czech under communism. After 1968 the Party reformers were either forced into emigration or into window-cleaning, coal-heaving or similar activities, if not old enough to be pensioners. Some, like Edward Goldstücker, a major figure in the Prague Spring as President of the Writers' Union, had already been jailed for years in the Stalinist persecution of the early 1950s. (We saw him in 1996 in Prague shortly before his death: the authorities of the new Czechoslovakia had denied him the status of one persecuted by communism.) They lost their country for good for, when communism ended, nobody wanted them any more.

The Hungarians I got to know best, too young for pre-war politics or resistance – Ivan Berend and his long-time collaborator George Ranki both returned from the Nazi camps in 1945 to high school – were reform communists, except for the brilliant Peter Hanak, young star of Hungarian Marxist history in 1955, insurgent in the revolution of 1956, and strongly anti-communist afterwards. But the post-'56 mood in Hungary was both modestly reformist and tolerant, even of some dissidence. Of all Party regimes Hungary probably came closest to normal intellectual life under communism, perhaps largely thanks to its wealth of intellectual talent, which it reinforced by good relations with its western émigrés. Some of its most remarkable non-political minds rejected emigration even in the worst times, such as the mathematical genius Erdös, who insisted on maintaining his Hungarian passport while also insisting on travelling round the world's mathematics departments, never staying in any place for more than a few months, carrying all his worldly possessions with him in his suitcase. He managed this extraordinary and perhaps unique achievement by a private citizen at the height of the Cold War, thanks to the unanimous support of the international mafia of mathematicians. When, unable to talk number theory with him, I asked him, on an agreeable evening in Cambridge, why he wanted the permanent right to go back to Budapest, he said: 'Is good mathematical atmosphere.' Hungary, of course, was the only part of central Europe that had not lost most of its Jews.

In some countries of 'real socialism', as for instance Poland, it was possible to avoid the Party in one's dealings with colleagues and friends. Not so in the German Democratic Republic where nothing was outside its supervision, certainly not the contacts of its citizens with foreign communists. Moreover, there was no scope for dissidence there or even doubt about the line that came down from the commanding heights. In some ways, and not least for linguistic reasons, I therefore found it easiest to discover there what Party membership meant under socialism.

East German communists, at least those within my knowledge, were and most remained believers, whether old KPD cadres from before 1933; youthful enthusiasts who joined in the ruined landscape of 1945 to build a new future, such as Fritz Klein, son of the editor-in-chief of one of the Weimar Republic's most respected Conservative newspapers; second-generation communists such as my friend Siegfried Bünger, son of a worker from rural Mecklenburg; or Gerhard Schilfert, converted as a Soviet prisoner-of war, a man incapable of being other than sincerely convinced by and loyal to authority, old or new. (All these were historians.) In a way, they selected themselves. Those who could not stand the heat got out of the kitchen, which was really quite easy until the building of the Berlin Wall in 1961.

I had little direct contact with the Old Guard, except with the Kuczynskis and, through my friend the painter Georg Eisler, with his admired father Hanns, partner of Brecht and official state composer of the GDR, whom I met in the unproletarian ambiance of the Waldorf Hotel. Hanns had abandoned his wife and son, whose exile had taken them from Vienna via Moscow and Manchester back to Vienna. A more recent wife, Lou, he lost to another communist veteran from Moscow, the brilliant and romantic charmer Ernst Fischer, son of a Habsburg general and postwar star of Austrian culture and the Austrian CP until it expelled him after the Prague Spring. I owe an intellectual debt to Fischer, acknowledged in my *Age of Revolution*. All remained in friendly contact, as Fischer did with his first wife, a handsome aristocratic girl from Bohemia who became a Soviet agent, whose revolutionary credentials went back to the German communist insurrection of 1921. The Leipzig-Viennese Eislers were almost the quintessential Comintern family. Aunt Elfriede (known to history as Ruth Fischer) had been the young communist believer in free love who moved Lenin to his criticism of casual sex ('the glass of water theory'). Some years later, she emerged as part of the ultra-left leadership of the KPD before disappearing into expulsion and exile having picked the wrong side in Soviet and Comintern politics. She reappeared after the war in the USA, among other things as a denouncer of her brother Gerhart Eisler. He, also a defeated (but more moderate) leader of the KPD, had become a Comintern agent of importance in China, the USA and elsewhere. He was expelled from the USA, jumping ship en route in Britain, and returned to East Germany where, during the mania of late Stalinism, he was – or so it is claimed – cast as a potential and no doubt in due course self-confessed traitor in a show trial. Fortunately the East German regime, though occupied by the Soviet forces, never joined this murderous Stalinist fashion, though it is rarely given credit for such restraint. Gerhart Eisler spent the rest of his life in politically minor jobs in the GDR, such as head of the broadcasting services, gently fending off his nephew's questions about his past. Had he written his memoirs, which he refused to do, they would have been as meaningless as those of most diplomats: his generation did not talk. Hollywood, where he spent his exile, suited Hanns, the musician, fat, witty, cynical, and far better at succeeding there than his partner Brecht, but he went back none the less and wrote the new state's national anthem. One can hardly accuse them of having many illusions about the reality of Comintern communism, the USSR and least of all the GDR. They stayed, controlled and harassed by a rigid political hierarchy to whom they were from time to time denounced by rivals and ambitious juniors, constantly watched, even as they were publicly honoured, by the largest permanent policing system ever operated in a modern state, the Stasi. But they stayed.

In one way the peculiar situation of the GDR made it easier. The East German regime suffered from the patent fact that it had no legitimacy, initially almost no support, and would have never in its lifetime won a freely contested election. The successor to the SED (Socialist Unity Party) has probably more genuine popular support today than when the old regime totted up the habitual 98 per cent of votes. To this extent East German communists were still, speaking globally, in embattled opposition, especially under the threat and temptation of their overpowering neighbour, the vastly larger Federal Republic. This justified measures which would otherwise have horrified communists, even allowing for their Party's rejection of liberal democracy. One remembers Brecht's bitter wisecrack about government dissolving the people and electing another. On that very occasion, 17 June 1953, my friend Fritz Klein, a devoted communist of twenty-nine, supported the Soviet intervention after the great workers' revolt, because he thought the regime socially more just and politically more reliably anti-fascist than the Federal Republic. Similarly, in 1961 he supported the building of the Berlin Wall. 'My view then,' he writes, 'was that it had to be accepted as the lesser evil, faced with the inevitable alternative: to abandon the still legitimate experiment of building a new society.'[10] The most they could hope for was that the socialist society they were constructing would work and eventually win over the people. Without doubt the best and most intelligent East German Party members were both critics of the system and remained hopeful reformers to the end. But they were powerless. It was, of course, easier for Party members to abdicate their judgement and play it by the book (that is, at the top, ask for advice from Moscow) or simply do whatever the Party told them had to be done. And the Party was run by old hardliners from before 1933 or their successors of the next generation.

The passions of the Cold War have presented the East European regimes as gigantic systems of terror and gulags. In fact, after the years of blood and iron under Stalin (who was in two minds whether he wanted a GDR at all), the GDR's system of justice and repression, leaving aside the victims of the Berlin Wall, has been well described authoritatively by a Harvard historian as 'continuously shabby but relatively unsanguinary'.[11] It was a monstrous all-embracing bureaucracy which did not terrorize but rather constantly chivvied, rewarded and punished its subjects. The new society they were building was not a bad society: work and careers for all, universal education open at all levels, health, social security and pensions, holidays in a firmly structured community of good people doing a honest day's work, the best of high culture accessible to the people, open-air leisure and sports, no class distinctions. At its best it settled down into – Charles Maier's words again – something between 'socialism and *Gemütlichkeit*', or a 'Biedermeier collectivism'.[12] The drawback, apart from the fact, unconcealable from its citizens, that it was far worse off than West Germany, was that it was imposed on its citizens by a system of superior authority, as by strict nineteenth-century parents on recalcitrant or at least unwilling minors. They had no control over their lives. They were not free. Since West German television was generally accessible the constant presence of compulsion and censorship was evident and resented. Nevertheless, as long as it looked permanent, it was tolerable enough.

All this affected Party members as much as, perhaps more than, the rest. Their conversations were not only recorded by rivals or the omnipresent Stasi informers, but, if deemed unacceptable, brought demands for public self-criticism or demotion by dour but unconvincing functionaries from the self-contained ghetto of the national rulers, rigidly laying down the line. Dissidents were worried rather than harried into conformity. In the worst cases, they were nagged or extruded to the West, like Wolf Biermann, whom I remember visiting with Georg Eisler, in his room in a back court of East Berlin where he sang the protest songs that had already made him famous.

Most Party members in the GDR, and almost certainly most Party intellectuals, believed in some kind of socialism to the end. It is hard to find among them, as among Soviet emigrants, reform communists who had become 100 per cent pro-American cold warriors. But they were increasingly downhearted. When did communists begin to suspect – or to believe – that the 'really existing' socialist economy, clearly inferior to the capitalist one, was not working at all?

Markus Wolf, the head of GDR espionage, a man of visibly impressive ability, whom I got to know when a Dutch TV station organized a conversation between him and myself on the Cold War, told me that he had come to the conclusion in the late 1970s that the GDR system would not work. Even so, in the last moments of the GDR he came out publicly as a communist reformer – an unusual stance for an intelligence chief. In 1980 the Hungarian Janos Kornai's book *The Economics of Shortage* already provided the classical analysis of the self-contradictory operations of Soviet-style economies. In the 1980s, a decade when these economies were visibly running down (unlike the post-Mao Chinese economy), communists in the Soviet bloc countries with elbow-room – Poland and Hungary – were already, it was clear, preparing for a shift. The hard-line regimes in Prague and Berlin had nothing to rely on except the potential intervention of the Soviet army, which was no longer on the cards since Gorbachev had taken over in the USSR. In Eastern Europe as in the West, Communist Parties were decomposing. Soon the Soviet Union itself would decompose. An historical epoch was ending. What was left of the old international communist movement lay beached like a whale on a shore from which the waters had withdrawn.

Late in the 1980s, almost at the end, an East German dramatist wrote a play called *The Knights of the Round Table*. What is their future? wonders Lancelot. 'The people outside don't want to know any more about the grail and the round table . . . They no longer believe in our justice and our dream . . . For the people the knights of the round table are a pile of fools, idiots and criminals.' Does he himself still believe in the grail? 'I don't know,' says Lancelot. 'I can't answer the question. I can't say yes or no . . .' No, they may never find the grail. But is not King Arthur right when he says that what is essential is not the grail but the quest for it? 'If we give up on the grail, we give up on ourselves.' Only on ourselves? Can humanity live without the ideals of freedom and justice, or without those who devote their lives to them? Or perhaps even without the memory of those who did so in the twentieth century?

10

War

I

I arrived back in England just in time for the war to start. We had expected it. We, or at least I, had even feared it, though no longer in 1939. This time we knew we were already in it. Within a minute of the prime minister's old, dry voice declaring war, we had heard the wavy sound of the sirens, which to this day brings back the memory of nocturnal bombs to any human being who lived through the Second World War in cities. We were even surrounded by the visible landscape of aerial warfare, the corrugated iron of shelters, the barrage balloons tethered like herds of silver cows in the sky. It was too late to be afraid. But what the outbreak of war meant for most young men of my generation was a sudden suspension of the future. For a few weeks or months we floated between the plans and prospects of our pre-war lives and an unknown destiny in uniform. For the moment life had to be provisional, or even improvised. None more so than my own.

Until my return to England I had not really come to terms with the implications of the family's emigration. I now discovered myself not only without a known future for an unpredictable period, but also without a clearly discernible present, unanchored and alone. The family home was gone, and so was the family. Outside Cambridge I had nowhere in particular to go, though I would not be short of comrades and friends to put me up, and I was always welcomed in the only available household of London relatives, the ever-reliable Uncle Harry's. I had no girlfriend. In fact, for the next three years, when I came to London I lived a nomadic sort of existence sleeping in spare beds or on the floors of various flats in Belsize Park, Bloomsbury or Kilburn. From the moment I got called up, my only permanent base was in a few crates of books, papers and other belongings which the head porter of King's allowed me to store in a shed. I packed them after my call-up. I thought of them reemerging after the war, with luck, like a Rip van Winkle whose life had stopped in 1939 and who now had to get used to a new world. What world?

The war had begun to empty Cambridge. As the former staff of *Granta* had already dispersed, I asked the printers to close the journal down for the duration, thus formally burying an essential component of pre-war Cambridge. Research on my proposed topic of French North Africa was now pointless, though I went through the motions, background reading, hitchhiking to the British Museum when necessary and when the snowdrifts of an unusually freezing winter made it possible.

What is more, since the line-change of the autumn of 1939, it was not the war we had expected, in the cause for which the Party had prepared us. Moscow reversed the line which the Comintern and all European Parties had pursued since 1935 and had continued to pursue after the outbreak of war, until the message from Moscow came through. Harry Pollitt's refusal to accept the change demonstrated that the leadership of the British Party was openly split on the issue. Moreover, the line that the war had ceased to be antifascist in any sense, and that Britain and France were as bad as Nazi Germany, made neither emotional nor intellectual sense. We accepted the new line, of course. Was it not the essence of 'democratic centralism' to stop arguing once a decision had been reached, whether or not you were personally in agreement? And the highest decision had obviously been taken. Unlike the crisis of 1956 (see chapter 12) most Party members – even the student intellectuals – seemed unshaken by the Moscow decision, though several drifted out in the next two years. I am unable to remember or to reconstruct what I thought at the time, but a diary I kept for the first few months of my army service in 1940 makes it clear that I had no reservations about the new line. Fortunately the phoney war, the behaviour of the French government, which immediately banned the Communist Party, and the behaviour of both French and British governments after the outbreak of the Soviets' winter war against Finland made it a lot easier for us to swallow the line that the western powers as imperialists were, if anything, more interested in defeating communism than in fighting Hitler. I remember arguing this point, walking on the lawn in the Provost's garden in King's with a sympathetic sceptic, the mathematical economist David Champernowne. After all, while all seemed quiet, if not somnolent, on the western front, the only plans of the British government for action envisaged sending western troops across Scandinavia to help the Finns. Indeed, one of the comrades, the enthusiastic public school boy and boxing half-blue J. O. N. ('Mouse') Vickers – he actually looked more like a large weasel than a mouse, thin, quick and mobile – was due to be sent there with his unit when the Russo-Finnish war ended. For communist intellectuals Finland was a lifeline. I wrote a pamphlet on the subject at the time with Raymond Williams, the future writer, critic and guru of the left, then a new, militant and obviously high-flying recruit to the student Party. Alas, it has been lost in the course of the alarums and excursions of the century. I have been unable to rediscover a copy. And then, in February 1940, I was at last called up.

The best way of summing up my personal experience of the Second World War is to say that it took six and a half years out of my life, six of them in the British army. I had neither a 'good war' nor a 'bad war', but an empty war. I did nothing of significance in it, and was not asked to. Those were the least satisfactory years in my life.

Although I was clearly not the military type, and still less a potential commander of men, the main reason why I wasted my country's time and my own during most of my twenties was almost certainly political. I had, after all, some qualifications relevant to a war against Nazi Germany; not least a native knowledge of German. Moreover, as a rather bright history student at King's, whose intelligence veterans of the First World War were given the responsibility of recruiting for the future staff of Bletchley, and which sent seventeen of its dons there, it is inconceivable that my name would not have crossed the mind of one of these. It is true that I lacked at least one conventionally accepted qualification for intelligence work, namely doing the *Times* crossword puzzle. As a central European I had never grown up with it, nor did it interest me. It is also true that I did not rate highly on the other traditional qualification, the one that had got my uncle Sidney into codebreaking in the First World War, namely chess. I was an enthusiastic but very far from distinguished player. Still, had I not been quite so public and prominent a bolshevik as an undergraduate, I rather think that I would not simply have been left in Cambridge to await the decisions of the East Anglian call-up authorities.

On the other hand, the official view that someone of such obvious and recent continental provenance and background could not, in spite of his and his father's passports, be a 100 per cent *real* Englishman, may well have played some part. (Such a sentiment was far from uncommon in the Cambridge of the 1930s and was shared perhaps by my supervisors.) After all, plenty of Party members did serve in intelligence during the war, including some who made no secret of their membership. Certainly my nomination a few weeks after call-up for what turned out to be a divisional cipher course (two officers, seven NCOs, three other ranks) was aborted for this reason. 'Nothing personal, but your mother was not British,' said the captain as he told me to take the next train from Norwich back to Cambridge. 'Of course you're against the system now, but naturally there's always a bit of sympathy for the country your mother belonged to. It's natural. You see that, don't you?' 'Yes, sir.' 'I mean I have no national prejudices. It's all the same to me what the nations do, so long as they behave themselves, which the Germans aren't doing now.' I agreed. He promised to recommend me for an interpreter's job. Nothing further was ever heard about it. Curiously enough, my memory completely wiped out this episode, although I recorded it at the time.

Did I already have an intelligence file when I was at Cambridge? There is no way of knowing. I had certainly acquired one by the middle of 1942, when a friendly sergeant in Field Security told me that I was supposed to be watched. It is possible that I acquired one in 1940 shortly after I was called up, for as a good communist I made arrangements to stay in contact with the Party, which meant that when in London, I met Robbie (R. W. Robson), a sallow, lined, hard-smoking working-class full-time cadre since the early 1920s, in one of those small, dusty, second-hand-looking offices up a dark staircase in WC1 or WC2, in which such people were to be found. These were very likely bugged by Security.

Whenever I acquired my file, I was clearly seen as a suspicious character, to be kept out of sensitive areas such as abroad, even after the USSR became Britain's ally and the Party devoted itself to winning the war. While the war lasted (and indeed from 2 September 1939 until my first postwar visit to Paris in 1946) I never left the soil of Great Britain – the longest unbroken period I have ever spent without crossing some sea or land frontier. Nobody after May 1940 appeared to take an interest in my languages. At one moment I got as far as an interview on the subject in what I took to be a secret service office at the top of Whitehall, but nothing came of it. Reluctantly I got used to the idea that I would have no part in Hitler's downfall.

What could the officers do who found themselves lumbered with an intellectually overqualified and practically underqualified oddball with minimal gifts for the military life? Since I could drive a car I was called up as a driver, but I did not take to the company's requisitioned 15-cwt- and 3-ton trucks, or to motorbikes, and soon became merely a pair of unskilled arms. What could be done with such a figure? I was presumably regarded as unpromotable. In the end the 560th Field Company of the Royal Engineers found a way of getting rid of me. I was recommended for transfer to the Army Education Corps, which – since this was a people's war – was being rapidly expanded. I was sent on the required course to a building behind the jail in Wakefield, taking with me – why should I still remember this so vividly? – Thomas Mann's *Lotte in Weimar*. There I discovered the enormous superiority of northern fish-and-chips to what I had hitherto been used to, and passed, in the company of another historian and future vice-chancellor of London University.

My transfer came through some time later, in the early autumn of 1941, a few days after we had moved to Hay-on-Wye, on the Welsh borders, near which, exactly fifty years later, I found myself buying the Breconshire cottage in which I write these lines. It may well have saved my life, for in the meantime the unit had been ordered abroad, and we already had our embarkation leave behind us. As usual, I spent it among the bombs in London. Naturally nobody told us where we were bound for, though the Middle East seemed the most likely. But the 15th East Anglian Division, including the 560th Field Company RE, did not set sail for the Middle East, but via Cape Town and Mombasa for Singapore, where they were captured by the Japanese in February 1942. Those who survived spent the next three years building the Burma railway. About a third of them did not. I never saw my mates again. Would I have survived? Who knows. In any case, I did not find out how lucky I was until much later.

II

My army career thus falls into two sharply distinct parts. The first of these, my time with the Royal Engineers, was by far the more interesting. As might be expected, a field company of sappers was a purely working-class unit, except for its few officers. I was the only intellectual in it, indeed almost certainly the only other rank in it who habitually read the news pages of the daily newspaper before or instead of the racing pages. This unusual habit gave me my nickname during the weeks when France collapsed: 'Diplomatic Sam'. For the first time in my life I found myself a member of the proletariat whose emancipation was to bring freedom to the world, though an uncharacteristic one. To be more precise, I found myself living in the country in which the majority of the British people spent their lives, and which had only a marginal contact with the world of the classes above them. Being called up in Cambridge dramatized the contrast, since for two or three months I lived in both worlds. After duty (i.e. mainly learning the elements of drill on the green turf of Parker's Piece) I moved from one to the other as I walked to the centre of university Cambridge from the working-class street where the military authorities had quartered me and a barber's assistant and former hotel porter from Lowestoft called Bert Thirtle, on an elderly widow, Mrs Benstead, We shared what had been the Benstead matrimonial bed which was fortunately a wide one. It was not an ideal introduction to the world of the proletariat, since Thirtle lacked the social reflexes which I found so striking in my otherwise politically disappointing mates, and which explains so much about British trade unionism. Most of my mates saw themselves essentially as civilians who put on uniforms as their dads had done in 1914–18. They saw no special virtue in the martial life or look: civvy street was where they hoped to go back to as soon as possible. But Thirtle had always secretly dreamed of wearing a uniform, although it did not get him far with the girls (any girl was a 'tart' in our jargon) he picked up in Petty Cury. His fiancée, a seventeen-year-old who worked in a kitchen, wrote him daily letters and sent parcels containing the local papers, *The Wizard*, *Comic Cuts* and American strip cartoons.

In retrospect I am amazed how powerful an instinctive sense or tradition of collective action was in a bunch of young working men, ranging from the unskilled to some apprenticed tradesmen, mostly builders, assembled in the same NAAFI canteen or games room by the accidents of conscription. This struck me less at the time than their wavering uncertainty – and indeed my own – about what we should all do at moments that called for some action, and the general sense of helplessness in the face of authority. And yet, as I read the notes of my diary, what impresses me is the familiarity with the procedures of collective action, the constant, almost intuitive, potential for militancy. They were at home in the 'public sphere' of the British working class. Had not someone, during one protest, suggested that we should organize a proper meeting at The Locomotive like a real union, with a table and a bell and a glass of water?

The proletarian experience was novel in other respects. I think it is safe to say that in 1940 few Kingsmen had had occasion to operate a road drill, and I found the experience of doing so tiring but exhilarating. The Sappers were essentially a formation of workers skilled and less skilled, more from general manufacture and the building trades (for a lot of metal workers were in reserved occupations and those needed by the army went into other, more specialized corps) from many parts of Britain – the Black Country, London, Nottingham, a sprinkling from the Northeast and Scotland – but mainly from the eastern counties, since ours was essentially an East Anglian division. A few anomalous Cantab recruits found themselves in its ranks – myself, slightly older friends and acquaintances such as Ian Watt, later a distinguished professor of literature, whose work on the origins of the English novel the student Marxists were already discussing, and slightly younger ones such as the witty graphic satirist, *Granta*'s cartoonist Ronald Searle. Both returned, marked for life, from Japanese gulags. Ronald, whom I occasionally saw during our common time in the division, was already being discovered by the admirable Kaye Webb, then commissioning editor at *Lilliput*, a pocket-sized and very hip magazine founded by an emigrant Mitteleuropean, and much appreciated by our generation, who later married him. (She also took a few articles from me during and after the war, until the magazine disappeared.) Meanwhile, he became one of the most successful cartoonists of his time, thanks largely to the invention of St Trinian's, a girls' school peopled by the most appalling pupils, inspired, one understood, by the small terror-bringing Japanese of his wartime prison camps.

By and large in my days as a Sapper I lived among workers – overwhelmingly English workers – and in doing so acquired a permanent, if often exasperated, admiration for their uprightness, their distrust of bullshit, their sense of class, comradeship and mutual help. They were good people. I know that communists are supposed to believe in the virtues of the proletariat, but I was relieved to find myself doing so in practice as well as in theory.

Then Hitler invaded Norway and Denmark and the war really began. As soon as the Germans – we could hardly believe it – began to overrun the Low Countries, the 560th Field Company had something real to do. For anything up to fourteen hours a day, virtually isolated from the civilian life of Norfolk which went on around us, we improvised defences for East Anglia against a potential invasion. We shifted sandbags, revetted the walls of giant anti-tank trenches round the town that were being dug ahead of us by a civilian excavator, inexperienced, clumsy and above all utterly unconvinced that the ditch would stop any tanks, especially since there were no anti-tank guns or anything else, but our main work was mine-laying and attaching explosive charges to bridges, ready to blow them in case of need. As spring turned into summer, we had absolutely miraculous weather for this work. I can still feel the wonderful elation of climbing (a bit nervously) up the sides of the girders of the great bridge across Breydon Water, just outside Great Yarmouth, to work on the high span between blue sky and salt water, the (deceptive) sense of power that comes from the routine handling of explosives, fuses and detonators. I can remember the holiday idleness of lazing in small detachments of three or four posted to some remote lock or bridge with a tent and 200 lb of explosives, waiting for the invaders. What would we have done, had they come? We were raw, without military experience or even arms: in addition to our clumsy Lee-Enfield rifles the company had exactly six Lewis guns with which to keep enemy aircraft at bay. We would not have made an impressive first line of defence against the Wehrmacht.

The lads' reaction to the German invasion of Denmark and Norway was a confident indignation. Gloom, depression and even defeatism had been the mood by the time they invaded the Low Countries, in the middle of the political crisis that finally threw out Neville Chamberlain. 'What kind of English soldiers are you?' said the company Irishman, Mick Flanigan, surrounded by barrack-room talk about how much better the German army obviously was than ours, and what things might be like under a German government. Chamberlain's fall cheered them up again, for he had obviously been a major cause of the general depression. Patently the new Churchill government was welcomed by our company. (I noted at the time how strange it was that the heroes of the British workers were Churchill, Duff Cooper and Eden, 'aristocrats, not even demagogues'.)

Discouragement grew again in the next few weeks of back-breaking physical work and virtually complete isolation in our camps. Whatever the effect on civilians of Churchill's famous radio addresses, the one on 'We shall fight on the beaches', including presumably those of Norfolk, was given at a time when we could not have heard it. Indeed, at the time I described the mood of the lads as 'terrible'. We were working all hours of day and night, virtually confined to barracks and workplace ('our biggest entertainment,' I wrote, 'is going to have the weekly shower'), without explanation, recognition or appreciation and, above all, ordered about, anonymous and inferior. Middle-class recruits dreamed of getting to the front where 'they'd forget about blanco and polishing cap-badges and we'd all be in it together'. Most of my mates simply concluded: 'This is no life for a human being. If the war finishes, OK. I want to get out of this and back into civvy street.' Did they mean it? Plainly they did not, as their reaction to the fall of France on 17 June was witness.

I heard the news on a trip to a nearby pub from our post by the small bridge we were guarding on the table-flat road to Great Yarmouth. None of us had any doubt about what it meant. Britain was now alone. Let me transcribe what I wrote a few hours later in my diary:

'Who was responsible?' Half an hour after the radio announcement the English are already asking the question. In the pub where I heard the news, in the car that gave me a lift back to the bridge, in the tent with the two mates. Only one answer: it was old Chamberlain. The unanimous view: whoever is guilty must pay for it somehow. It's something, even if it should turn out to be just a passing impulse . . .

A car stops at our bridge. I'd guess the driver, specs and false teeth, is a commercial traveller. 'Have you heard the news on the radio?' I say, 'Yes, we have.' 'Bad, bad,' says the man shaking his head. 'Bloody bad, terrible.' Then he drives on. We call after him, 'Thanks, anyroad' and go back to lying on the bank in the long grass and talking things over, slowly and in dismay.

The other two cannot believe it.

Not only could my mates not grasp what had happened. They could neither take in nor even imagine that this might mean the end of the war or making peace with Hitler. (Actually, reading my own immediate reactions to the fall of France, and in spite of the official Party line since September 1939, neither could I. A victory for Hitler was not what we had had in mind.) They could envisage defeat at the end of a fighting war – nothing was easier in June 1940. It was also clear to anyone near the East Anglian coast that, if Hitler invaded, as everyone expected him to, there was nothing much to stop him. What they could not envisage was not going on with the war, even though it was plain to anyone with a sense of political realities (even one reduced to an occasional sight of the *Daily Telegraph* on the East Anglian marsh), that Britain's situation was desperate. This feeling that Britain was not defeated yet, that it was *natural* to go on with the war, was what Winston Churchill put into words for them, though with a tone of heroic defiance which, pretty certainly, none of my mates felt. He spoke for a British people of ordinary folk, such as those of the 560th Field Company, who (unlike many of the better-informed) simply could not imagine that Britain might give up.

As we now know, in the words of Hitler's Chief of General Staff, General Halder, 'the Führer is greatly puzzled by England's persistent unwillingness to make peace', since he believed himself to be offering 'reasonable' terms.[1] At this point he saw no advantage in invading and occupying Britain which (to quote Halder again) 'would not be of any benefit to Germany. German blood would be shed to accomplish something that would benefit only Japan, the United States and others.' In effect, Hitler offered to let Britain keep her empire as what Churchill, writing to Roosevelt, correctly described as 'a vassal state of the Hitler empire'.[2] In the 1990s a school of young Conservative historians argued that Britain should have accepted these terms. If Lord Halifax and the powerful peace party in the 1940 Conservative Party had prevailed it is not imposs-ible – indeed, it is not unlikely – that the bulk of Britons would have gone along with them, as the bulk of Frenchmen went along with Marshal Pétain. Yet nobody who now remembers that extraordinary moment in our history could believe that the defeatists had a real chance of prevailing. They were seen not as the peace-bringers but as the 'guilty men' who had brought the country to this pass. Confident in this massive popular backing, Churchill and the Labour ministers were able to hold their own.

We knew none of this – neither of the peace party in Churchill's government (though the left suspected there was one), nor of Hitler's offers and hesitations. Luckily in August 1940 Hitler began the mass aerial attack on Britain, which became the nightly bombing of London in early September. From being a people that went on with the war because we could not think of anything else to do, we became a people conscious of our own heroism. All of us, even the ones not directly affected, could identify with the men and women who continued with everyday life under the bombs. We would not have put it in Churchill's bombastic terms ourselves ('This was their finest hour'), but there was considerable satisfaction in standing up to Hitler alone.

But how were we to go on? There was not the slightest chance of returning to the continent within the foreseeable future, let alone winning the war. Between the Battle of Britain and the time the East Anglian division was sent to its doom, we moved across vast stretches of Britain, from Norfolk to Perthshire, from the Scottish Borders to the Welsh Marches, but during this entire period nothing that the 560th Field Company did appeared to its members to have any bearing on fighting the war against Germany, except the time in

1941 when we found ourselves stationed on Merseyside during the great German raids on Liverpool and consequently mobilized to clear up among the ruins on the mornings after. (A picture of myself in a tin hat being fed tea at a Liverpool street canteen by friendly ladies may well be my first appearance in a newspaper.) On the other hand, there was no way in which Hitler could get Britain out of the war either. Nor could he simply leave things as they were. In fact, as we now know, the failure to defeat Britain in the west decided him to turn east against the Soviet Union and, in doing so, to make the war winnable again for Britain.

At all events, from the summer of 1940 one thing was clear even to Party members as passionate and devoted as myself: in the army nobody would listen to the official Party line against the war. It made increasingly little sense and, from the moment when the Germans swept into the Balkans in the spring of 1941, it was clear to me (and indeed even to most in the Party leadership) that it made no sense at all. We now know that Stalin became the chief victim of its unrealism, stubbornly and systematically *refusing* to accept the accumulation of detailed and utterly reliable evidence of Hitler's plan to attack the USSR, even after the Germans had crossed its borders. The probability of Hitler's attack on Russia had been so great that even the British Party appears to have expected it by early June 1941, worried only about Winston Churchill's reaction to it.[3]

Both communists and non-communists, therefore, felt the same sense of relief and hope when Hitler invaded the USSR on 22 June 1941. In what was essentially a working-class unit like our company, there was more than relief. Generations brought up during the Cold War are not aware how widely British workers and even Labour leaders before the war had thought of Soviet Russia as in some sense 'a workers' state', as well as the one great power committed to opposing fascism, as it were *ex officio*. And, of course, everybody knew that its support against Hitler was indispensable. There was no shortage of deeply hostile observers and critics, but until the Cold War the dominant image of the USSR in the British labour movement was not that of totalitarianism, mass terror and the gulag. So in June 1941 Party members, sighing with relief, returned to what they had been saying before the war, and rejoined the masses of ordinary Britons. On my suggestion, I got a football signed by every member of the 560th starting with the company sergeant-major, and sent it to the Soviet Embassy in London for transmission to an equivalent engineers' unit in the Red Army. I think the *Daily Mirror*, already very much the forces' paper, published a photo. After 22 June 1941 communist propaganda more or less made itself.

III

However little I contributed to Hitler's downfall or to the world revolution, there was a lot more to be said for serving in the Royal Engineers than in the Army Education Corps. It is far from clear what the traditional army thought of an outfit that claimed to teach soldiers things they did not need to know as soldiers, and to discuss non-military (or any) matters. It was tolerated, because its head, Colonel Archie White, was a professional soldier who had won a VC in his time and because most serving soldiers in the war were undeniably past and future civilians, whose morale required more than the inculcation of regimental loyalty and pride. The army did not like the AEC's link with the new Army Bureau of Current Affairs (ABCA), which issued regular monthly discussion pamphlets on political subjects, as like as not written by Labour sympathizers. Conservative politicians were later to hold ABCA responsible for the radicalization of the armed forces who, in 1945, massively voted Labour.

This is to overestimate the interest of the bulk of servicemen and women in specifically political literature. ABCA appealed to and aimed at the reading minorities, but did not excite the masses. If any reading-matter shaped the squaddies' politics, at all events in or within reach of the UK, it was the *Daily Mirror*, a brilliantly produced and certainly Labour-sympathizing tabloid more widely read and discussed by the troops than any other. Nor can I claim to have made any greater contribution to the political radicalization of the British army's Southern Command than to the defeat of Hitler. After June 1941 the Party line was winning the war, and this aligned communists with everyone else, though it made them more reluctant to criticize the government than less aligned and disciplined leftwingers, except on issues suggested by the USSR, such as demanding an invasion of western Europe much sooner than Roosevelt and the even more reluctant Churchill wanted. Public opinion did not need the Party to arouse passionate admiration and enthusiasm for the Red Army and Stalin. During the war my then father-in-law, a retired and non-political sergeant-major in the Coldstream Guards (though a Labour voter in 1945) liked to remind visitors proudly that he looked like Vishinsky, the notorious prosecutor in the Stalinist show trials of the 1930s.

Since the army did not quite know what to do with them, AEC sergeant-instructors like me (the lowest rank in the Corps) found themselves in a curious military limbo, rather like military chaplains, except without the officers' pips and the ritual occasions for which the padre's presence was mandatory. They were distributed in ones and twos throughout the training camps or base camps, or attached, without any very clear function, to operational formations. We did not really belong to the outfits that were technically responsible for our rations, quarters and pay; nobody troubled us much. We had arms, but they were so irrelevant that, when I was finally demobilized, there was no available mechanism for handing in my rifle. On the other hand, wherever stationed, I had no difficulty finding a place for my typewriter and a few books. I cannot recall that anyone in the Guards Armoured Division, to which I was attached for a while, ever commented on the appearance of a sergeant whose dress and bearing made no serious attempt to live up to the notoriously exigent requirements of the Household Brigade. Nobody but an Education sergeant would have got away with it. At least until we went overseas, the army allowed us to live a life of semi-detachment. I cannot remember how often I went to London from the various places in southern England to which the AEC took me, but in the end – and particularly after I married in the spring of 1943 – I spent practically every weekend there.

So, for practical purposes I increasingly found myself living like a civilian weekend commuter. Indeed, there were times when even my daily life was hard to distinguish from that of civilians, except for the fact that I wore a uniform. Thus in my last eighteen months I lived in Gloucester, billeted on a Mrs Edwards, an agreeable middle-class lady, friend and supporter of past and future Labour MPs in the area, whose sitting room contained a Matisse of medium quality which her financial adviser – evidently a good one – had persuaded her to buy for investment in 1939 for £900. In the election campaign of 1945 I even canvassed there for the Labour Party, amazed like so many others at the unexpectedly massive support I encountered on the doorsteps. I even found myself, representing the army, addressing the workforce at one of the great aircraft plants along the road from Gloucester to Cheltenham, which were the strongholds of the local CP. I concluded that I was not a natural mass orator.

Nevertheless, London was where I really lived as an adult human being. That is where I had spent all my leaves anyway, in the days of the Blitz of 1940–41, discovering on night-time walks that only a degree of desensitized fatalism ('it will only hit you if it's got your name on it') makes it possible to conduct the usual activities of life under bombardment. That was also where, since I could now get there so often, a less irregular and unpredictable private life became possible. In May 1943 I married Muriel Seaman, whom I had vaguely known as a very attractive LSE communist girl, and who was now working in the Board of Trade. This enables me to say that I was once married to one of the few literal Cockneys ('born within the sound of Bow bells'), for she was born in the Tower of London, her mother the daughter of a Beefeater (the Wardens of the Tower), her father a sergeant of the Coldstream Guards detachment detailed to guard its treasures. It also helped to clarify my postwar future. As someone married to a full-time senior civil servant, I would have to change my postwar field of research, or face leaving a wife in London while I spent a couple of years in French North Africa. After consulting my old teacher Mounia Postan, now also a temporary civil servant in London, I hit on the history of the Fabian Society, practically all of whose sources were in the metropolis. The subject turned out to be disappointing. But then, so also did my own marriage, like a number of other wartime marriages, although I did not think so at the time. Fortunately, we had no children.

I had met Muriel again through my main London friends, Marjorie, an old flame from the LSE, and her partner, the charming economist Tedy Prager, another old LSE red, who had returned from the temporary exile (Isle of Man, Canada) to which the British government had almost automatically sent so many of the passionately anti-Nazi young Austrian and German refugees. After his Cambridge doctorate he worked in what would today be called a think-tank, PEP (Political and Economic Planning), before returning to Austria in 1945 as a loyal Party member; by then with another wife. From the point of view of his career, professional or perhaps even political, he would have done better to stay. They were among the rare couples of my student generation or age group who lived and worked permanently in wartime London – my cousin Denis Preston's ménage was another – for most of the physically fit men were in uniform, and only a few servicemen, mostly in staff and intelligence work, were based in the metropolis. On the other hand, the place was full of women one had known in student days, for the war provided far more significant jobs for women than before. By age, health and gender, one's London friends and contemporaries were thus a curiously skewed community. The men blew in and out, visitors from outside, as I was myself. The regular residents were the women, and those unfit and past military age. But there was one more constantly present scene: the foreigners, which, so far as I was concerned, meant those who operated in the German language. So it was natural that Tedy Prager should bring me into the broad ambit of the Free Austrian Movement, in which, of course, as a communist he was deeply involved.

I expect that, at a loose end and a regular visitor to London, I would sooner or later have found my way into the refugee milieu. Indeed, I had come across them from the start in the course of my military duties on Salisbury Plain, for nobody was more likely to be found in restrooms and libraries than the miscellaneous collection of musicians, former archivists, stage-managers and aspirant economists from central Europe whom Britain was employing as unskilled labourers in the Pioneer Corps. (In due course many of them were more rationally employed in the armed forces.) Although I had absolutely no emotional tie to Germany, and little enough to Austria, German had been my language, and since leaving Berlin in 1933 I had made enormous efforts not to forget it in a country where I no longer had to use it. It still remained my private language. I had written my voluminous teenage diaries in it, and even in wartime the diaries I occasionally kept. While English was my regular literary idiom, the very fact that my country refused to make any use of my bilinguality in the war against Hitler made me want to prove I could still write the language. In fact, in 1944 I became a freelance contributor to a poorly printed German exile weekly, financed by the Ministry of Information, *Die Zeitung*, for which I wrote various literary pieces. Whatever the political or propagandist object of this journal was, it failed to achieve it, and so its disappointed backers shut it down immediately the war ended. The paper was bitterly opposed both by the German social-democratic and socialist exiles and by the communist émigrés. From this I infer that I cannot have consulted the Party about it, or, in other words, that I did not think of it as 'political' at all. I had written out of the blue to the paper's literary editor 'Peter Bratt', who turned out to be one Wolfgang von Einsiedel, a wonderfully cultured, soft-faced, homosexual relative of Bismarck and numerous Prussian generals, literary editor on the *Vossische Zeitung* before 1933. He treated me with exemplary kindness, understanding and friendship, no doubt correcting my German. We used to meet and talk in wartime Soho pubs. I lost contact with him after he moved to Munich, but perhaps this book is a suitable place to give thanks to one of the few persons in wartime outside my family and the Communist Party to whom I owe a personal debt.

The Free Austrian Movement, into which Tedy Prager brought me, was a much more serious matter, politically and culturally. Though behind the scenes it was organized by the communists, and therefore run with great efficiency, it succeeded in mobilizing the great bulk of the not very heavily politicized Austrian emigrant community (including my future father-in-law in Manchester), on the basis of a simple and powerful slogan: 'Austrians are not Germans'. This was a dramatic break with the tradition of the first Austrian Republic (1918–38) in which all parties, with the exception of the handful of surviving Habsburg loyalists – and since about 1936 the communists – assumed the opposite and emphasized that their country was *German* Austria, and (until Hitler) looked forward to an eventual unification with Germany. Ideologically Hitler's Anschluss in March 1938 therefore disarmed its opponents: the old socialist leader Karl Renner (who was to become the first President of the second Austrian Republic in 1945) had even welcomed it. The communists had for some time developed an interesting argument in favour of the historic and even cultural separateness of Austria from Germany, for which I was also eventually mobilized, being both a communist and an available qualified historian. (From April 1945 to the time I was demobilized in 1946 I wrote a series of historical articles along these lines in the Free Austrian journals, probably my first published historical work.) Not being Germans was a line that naturally appealed to the overwhelmingly Jewish Austrian emigrant community, which, with all its gratitude and admiration for Britain, in any case seems to have found it harder to assimilate to local society than the emigrant Germans. It also fitted in with the postwar policy of the Allies, which meant that the Free Austrian Movement – by far the best-organized section of the continental refugees – enjoyed some official respect and was largely free from the more public squabbles so typical of émigré politics. It was also unusually successful in giving the Austrian child and teenage refugees of the 1938–9 *Kindertransporte* a sense of community and future in its 'Young Austria'. At all events, they returned to Austria with the warmest memories of their British exile. Several of my later friends, notably the poet and translator Erich Fried and the painter Georg Eisler, came from this milieu.

Life in semi-detachment from the army was thus acceptable enough, even if hardly demanding. I had a wife, friends and a cultural scene in London, and (thanks to my cousin Denis, who was associated with a tiny periodical for intellectual and mostly left-wing aficionados, *Jazz Music*) I got to know and learn from the small community of serious jazz and blues fans in and out of London. Indeed, one of my more successful army educational enterprises was a jazz record class I organized for a so-called Young Soldiers training unit in deepest Dorset, for which I travelled regularly to Bournemouth to borrow records, and improve my own knowledge from one of them, Charles Fox. Moreover, though I was not formally organized in any Party branch, as far as I recall, there was plenty of politics to discuss, since in 1943 Moscow seemed to put the entire future of the communist movement into question. It dissolved the Communist International. In the same year the Tehran meeting between Stalin, Roosevelt and Churchill moved Stalin to announce the prospect of a continued postwar collaboration between capitalism and socialism. The Communist Party of the USA was consequently dissolved. The American communist leader Earl Browder announced that 'Capitalism and Socialism have begun to find a way to peaceful coexistence and collaboration in the same world'[4] – a proposition no communist would have maintained in public without prior clearance with Stalin – and the British CP based its plans for the future on the assumption that this is what 'the Tehran line' meant. Indeed, someone at King Street – I suppose it must have been Emile Burns, the culture commissar at the time – actually asked me to prepare a memorandum for their discussions on the economic possibilities of postwar capitalist–communist development. Loyal and disciplined as we were, not all revolutionaries found these 'new perspectives' easy to swallow, even when we could see why it might be sensible to dissolve the Comintern, and had no doubt that socialism was not going to come to the USA in anyone's lifetime.

And yet, not surprisingly, every day of this existence was a reminder that I was doing nothing to win the war, and that nobody would let me near any job, however modest, where my qualifications and gifts, such as they were, might have been of some use for this purpose. The division to which I was attached prepared to go overseas, but without me. From the cliffs of the Isle of Wight I could see what was clearly the gathering of the invasion fleet for France, while I had nothing better to do than to play the uniformed tourist in Queen Victoria's camp residence Osborne, and to buy a second-hand copy of Hazlitt's *Spirit of the Age* in a bookshop. I volunteered to go abroad, but nobody wanted to know. I was sent to Gloucester. As far as the greatest and most decisive crisis in the history of the modern world was concerned, I might as well not have been there.

And yet, although I did not realize it, I was to see something indirectly of the war after all. I was posted to the Military Wing of the City General Hospital, Gloucester, where I acted as a sort of general welfare officer or liaison with civilian bodies offering help. It specialized in serious casualties, increasingly the battle casualties from Normandy, and especially in the treatment of severe burns. It was a place of penicillin, blood and skin transfusions, limbs wrapped in cellophane and men walking around with things like sausages suspended from their faces, dressed in the curiously strident 'hospital blue' with the red ties of military patients. It dealt with everybody, even with wounded Germans (one officer explained to me that he had not been a Nazi, but he had given a personal oath of loyalty to the Führer) and Italians (one of them, in bed and reading Strindberg in an Italian translation, talked and talked and would not let me go, though I could barely understand Italian: about Italian officers, Britain and Italy, the future of Italy, the war, anything). We were naturally prouder of our 'Allies', whom I recorded in a fortnightly bulletin: the Pole from Torun, who had fought in both armies, deserting from the Germans in Normandy and back there again with the Poles after a night in Edinburgh; and the ward's showpiece, the little Moroccan, with his thin, high-cheeked Berber face, in bulging hospital blues with a much-unfolded citation for exemplary bravery of 'le jeune spahi Amor Ben Mohammed' at Himeimat, who communicated with us via a French Algerian, Private Colleno of the Free French.

It was a place of disaster. And yet, the most extraordinary thing about this place of blood was that in it a death surprised us. It was a place of hope, rather than tragedy. Let me quote what I wrote at the time:

The unexpectedness of seeing people with only half a face and others rescued from burning tanks, has now passed. Occasionally someone comes in whose mutilation is a shade more gruesome, and we hold our breath when we turn to him, for fear our face might give away our shocked repulsion. We can now reflect at leisure that this is how Marsyas looked when Apollo had finished with him; or how unstable the balance of human beauty is, when the absence of a lower jaw will completely unhinge it.

The reason for this callousness is that mutilation is no longer an irrevocable tragedy. Those who come here know, in general, that they will leave in the end as, approximately, human beings. It may – it will, in fact – take them months or even years. The process of completing them, a delicate living sculpture, will take dozens of operations and they will pass through stages when they will look absurd and ridiculous, which may even be worse than looking horrific. But they have hope. What faces them is no longer an eternity shut away in some home, but human life. They lie in saline baths because they have no skin, and joke with one another because they know they will get some. They walk round the ward with faces striped like zebras and pedicles dangling like sausages from their cheeks.

It is only in a hospital such as this that one begins to realize the meaning of Hope.

And not only hope for the body. As the end of the war, and certain victory, drew nearer, hope for the future was in the air. Here are two news items from the bulletin I published for the Military Wing.

> I used to be in agricultural work, but my feet are gone, and I can't do it any longer. Mr Pitts asked me what I wanted to do and I said, having been a motor-mechanic in the Army, how about it? So I'm going to a training school in Bristol . . . to polish up my i.c. engines, 45/ a week if I live at home, and I'm not forced to stick to the job . . . I think this plan for setting disabled soldiers on the road is pretty good.

And again: 'The ABCA Discussion on Friday will be opened by Sgt. Owen RA of Hut 9 who will give his idea of "How I'd set about rebuilding".' And Sgt Owen, a foreman bricklayer and once TUC delegate for his union, wondered whether 'any other men in Building have any ideas to bring forward'. The end of the war was near, there would be a General Election (some wards actually asked for the voting forms before they had been distributed) and things would be different. Who did not share this belief in 1944 and 1945, even if the first of our worries after the end of the war was naturally when we would get demobilized?

It was mine too. Pointless as my military service was, while the war lasted it was both normal and necessary. I had no complaints. Once the war was over, as far as I could see, every day in the army was a day wasted. As the summer of 1945 turned to autumn and then to winter, I was approaching the end of my sixth year in uniform, but the army showed no sign of wishing to get rid of me. On the contrary. Early in 1946, to my utter astonishment, it proposed to send me, attached to, of all things, an airborne unit, to, of all places, Palestine. The army seemed to think being sent to fight Jews or Arabs was a compensation for not being sent to fight Germans.

This, finally, was the straw that broke the camel's back. Communist Jews were, of course, anti-Zionists on principle. And yet, whatever my sympathies, antipathies and loyalties, the situation of a Jewish soldier dropped into the middle of a tripartite dispute between Jews, Arabs and the British was filled with too many complications for me. So, for the first time I pulled strings. I telephoned Donald Beves, the Tutor at King's, saying I wanted to get out of the army to take up my 1939 research studentship. He wrote the necessary letters, saying how indispensable it was for me to return to Cambridge, and they did the trick. On 8 February 1946 I handed in my uniform, though keeping a gas mask case, which turned out to be a useful shoulder bag, received my civvie clothes and fifty-six days' demobilization leave. At the age of twenty-eight and a half years, I returned to London and to human life.

11

Cold War

I

In 1948 the borders between East and West in Germany became front lines in the Cold War. During the 'Berlin Crisis' which began when the Russians cut land communications to that city in early April, and the long months of the subsequent Berlin airlift, East and West were locked into a dangerous and nerve-racking confrontation of forces. Communists in the West, however insignificant, were 'on the other side'. As far as I was concerned, the Cold War therefore began in May 1948, when the Foreign Office informed me that it was unfortunately unable to confirm my invitation to take part for a second time in the British Control Commission's course to 're-educate' the Germans. The reasons, it was abundantly obvious, were political. A silent but comprehensive effort to eliminate known Party members from any positions connected with British public life began about that time. While it was neither as hysterical nor as thorough-going as in the USA, where by the mid-1950s communists, or even self-described Marxists, had virtually disappeared from college and university teaching, it was a bad time to be a communist in the intellectual professions. Public policy encouraged discrimination and treated us as potential or actual traitors, and we were deeply suspect to our employers and colleagues. Liberal anti-communism was not new, but in the Cold War, with ample assistance from propaganda financed by the US and British authorities, the loathing of Stalinism and the belief (not shared by the British government[1]) that the USSR was bent on immediate world conquest gave it a new hysterical edge.

Until then the political temperature, in Britain at least, had been much less overheated. Within the country, Labour now ruled and nobody, certainly not the defeated Conservatives, seriously challenged the far-reaching reforms of the new government. By general agreement, a return to the 1930s was unthinkable or at least unmentionable; the 1945 government enjoyed unquestioned electoral and moral legitimacy, and were, in any case, no more 'revolutionary' than the state-directed war effort of the past six years, which had brought the British people a victory that they felt to be profoundly *theirs*. Internationally, the grand alliance of Britain, the USSR and the USA had won the war, and, diplomats and intelligence services apart, frictions between the wartime allies had not yet erased the consciousness of that common struggle.[2] In 1945–7 Communist Parties were represented by ministers in the governments of most belligerent and occupied countries in western Europe as well as non-communist ones in eastern Europe.

Men and women returned from the war, or turned from wartime occupations, to peacetime civilian life – to resume their old careers or plans, or to consider what to do next. Friends, who might not have seen each other for years, met again. Most of them would still be alive, for Britain had had a comparatively easy war, compared to the Russians, the Poles, the Yugoslavs and, of course, the Germans. The 1914 war, still known, and for good reason, as the 'Great War', killed one quarter of the Oxford and Cambridge students serving in the forces, but I can think of only five or six out of the 200 or so Cambridge contemporaries I knew or knew of, who did not return from the Second. It was a time of comparing notes and for pre-war communists to ask the question: 'Are you still in the Party?' A considerable number of pre-war students no longer were.

I returned from the army first, for about a year, to a curious double existence in London and for several days a week as a research student in Cambridge, but from February 1947 to September 1950 as a full-time Londoner. We lived in Gloucester Crescent, a middle-class sliver on the edge of Camden Town, the westernmost outpost of the vast zone of London's bombed and as yet totally ungentrified East End, which attracted intellectuals both because it was then still extraordinarily cheap and wonderfully accessible: ten minutes by public transport from the university and the British Museum. (Nobody one knew in those days had a car.) It had not yet become the headquarters of a band of very bright 1950s Oxbridge ex-students (actually, more 'bridge' than 'Ox') gently satirized in strip-cartoons in broadsheet newspapers when middle-class intellectuals became lifestyle setters in the 1960s. Many of them were friends acquired in Cambridge during the Cold War years. In 1946 Gloucester Crescent was not classy, but, as I wrote in a tender piece on Camden Town commissioned for *Lilliput* by Kaye Webb (then married to the cartoonist Ronald Searle, just returned from the Japanese gulag), one could just pretend the roar of the lions in Regent's Park Zoo was audible from there. In 1947 we moved to a far more stylish flat behind an early eighteenth-century façade on the north side of Clapham Common opposite the church where the Clapham Sect had worshipped, a barn with a tower. Outside, I recall seeing my new colleague at Birkbeck College, Nikolaus Pevsner, perambulating the area for his great *Buildings of England* like an examiner giving marks to the past. Inside I struggled, in the end successfully, with my fellowship-cum-doctoral dissertation and, in the end unsuccessfully, with what I did not quite recognize as the problems of my first marriage. As it happens, fifteen years later I was to move into a Victorian house a few minutes away – the first one I ever lived in as owner and not tenant – with Marlene.

Intellectual communists or fellow-travellers were not yet marginalized. Indeed, when the BBC began transmitting its groundbreaking Third Programme, a pre-war (non-communist) Cambridge historian, Peter Laslett, who acted as a talent-scout for it, introduced me to the elderly, worldly-wise, culture-watching Anna ('Nyuta') Kallin, its Russian talks producer, who helped my first, initially stumbling, steps in the world of microphones. (Of course it did not matter much: one spoke at most to only a few tens of thousands.) I did several pieces for her in 1947, including what may well have been the first-ever radio talk in English on Karl Kraus.

Party members as yet had no difficulty in getting academic jobs and several historians (including myself) did so, or could have done. I became a lecturer at Birkbeck College in 1947 though the head of my department was well aware of my politics. (Students reassured him, when he asked whether I was trying to indoctrinate them.) I went to the World Youth Festival in Prague with my then wife, who took time off from her job as a Principal in the Board of Trade, that is to say a member of the tiny policy-making elite of the civil service. She was, of course, also a communist, having rejoined when we married – in those days I would have found it inconceivable to marry a non-Party member – and the senior civil service branch met in our Clapham flat.[3] As far as I can remember, she did not at the time suggest that it might be better for her career in the civil service not to go to Prague. Ten years or so later, when I offered to sublet half my flat in Bloomsbury to a friend who had gone from Cambridge into the Treasury, he told me sadly that, given my known politics, he simply could not take the risk.

In my case, the end of the war even brought a brief relaxation of anti-communism. The British government, having totally refused to employ my knowledge of German for any purposes whatever during my six years in the army, now found it useful. In 1947 I was asked, presumably via some pre-war Cambridge acquaintance now in the Foreign Office, to help in 're-educating' the Germans in what had once been an imperial hunting-lodge on the Lüneburger Heide in North Germany, a few kilometres from the zonal border with the East, to and from which the railway transported the travelling and smuggling traffic of several thousands a day, plainly winked at by both the British and Russian authorities.[4] The 'democratizing' team, which contained at least one other man banned in the following year, could not possibly be described as politically or even economically 'sound'. The students were a well-assorted lot, from both West and – still – East: my first experience of the Germans who had stayed in Germany. I note in retrospect that the largely Jewish 're-educators' from Britain – actually the idea that we came to these intelligent people from across the Channel with some patent formula for a democratic future was a bit embarrassing – did not feel the sort of visceral anti-German reaction which the knowledge of Auschwitz and the camps, already common, is today expected to have provoked. We – or at least I – did not.

Certainly one could not help wondering all the time (as I wrote) 'what may these harmless-looking people not have done between 1933 and 1945?' Every Ashkenazi Jew lost relatives in the camps: in my case Uncle Victor Friedmann, transported east with Aunt Elsa, a small Sephardic lady, from somewhere in France; Uncle Richard Friedmann with Aunt Julie, who would not leave their fancy goods store in agreeable Marienbad; and Aunt Hedwig Lichtenstern. (As so often among Austrian and German, but not among East European Jews, the old died, while the young got out in time.) Their names were entered in the only memorial I know worthy of the Jewish genocide, the whitewashed walls of the Altneuschul, the ancient synagogue in Prague. These walls, surrounding an empty interior, were completely filled with the names of all Czechoslovak Jews who perished under Hitler, line below line of tidy writing, names, dates, places, in alphabetical order from roof to floor. Nothing at all except the uncountable names of the dead. I read Uncle Richard's and Aunt Julie's names there through tears, not long before the Prague Spring of 1968. Some time in the 1970s the Czech regime took the astonishing decision to desecrate the memorial by painting out all the inscriptions. The official excuse is said to have been that no particular group among the many victims of fascism ought to be singled out for special commemoration. They were restored with some delay after the end of communism.

I had not then met people who had survived the camps, Buchenwald and Auschwitz. Some of them were to become colleagues and friends, apparently unmarked by their experiences, and even, much later, prepared to talk about the time when every day of a survivor's life was bought at the price of someone else's death. Like Primo Levi they were not unmarked. At least one of them, dear, witty, enthusiastic Georges Haupt, who had entered Auschwitz as a Romanian schoolboy, suddenly collapsed and died at the age of fifty. Still, both conviction and realism saved us from turning the Nazis' own racist anti-Semitism inside out into an equivalent anti-Teutonism. Even later we (certainly I) blamed not Germans as such but National Socialism, especially as the first serious description and analysis of the *univers concentrationnaire* I read, Eugen Kogon's remarkable *Der SS-Staat* (Frankfurt, 1946) was written by a German, about a camp – Buchenwald – that dehumanized, tortured and killed many, but did not primarily target Jews. Moreover, one look at West German cities, gigantic fields of barely cleared rubble, at the apparently total collapse of the economy in the period before the currency reform, at the yellow-faced people living on barter and camped on station platforms with sacks of potatos, suggested that whatever ordinary Germans had done under Hitler, in 1947 they were paying for what had been done by them or in their name.

As I wrote at the time, it was not hard 'to understand what [these men and women] have gone through in the past 8 years . . . raids, expulsions, hunger etc. Men, women and children.' Anyone who had returned from a Russian prisoner-of-war camp, or even had experienced 'the awful shocks of the behaviour of the Russians in the first weeks after liberation' could talk of hard times. Not because the Russians necessarily took it out on the Germans, although the rank-and-file of the Red Army unquestionably had reasons for doing so and did so. ('They showed no fear whatsoever and their vision of the future was the rape and pillage of Berlin.'[5]) As one of our students, returned from captivity, who has since become one of the most eminent German historians,[6] explained to me: 'They did not treat us worse than themselves. It was simply that they were physically so much tougher than we were. They could stand the cold better. That scared us, when we were at the front, and we suffered from it as prisoners. They would dump us on a central-Asian plain in winter and say: build a camp. Start digging.'

It was not surprising that hatred and fear of Russia penetrated the atmosphere in Germany, among both the natives and the vast numbers of refugees – particularly numerous in our part of Lower Saxony – who made Russia responsible for their mass flight or mass expulsion. In 1947 it was a curious, sometimes schizophrenic, combination of feelings: repulsion, superiority, but also respect for the victor, and the contrast between the image of uncontrolled social disintegration in the West and the vague feeling that the discipline 'over there' (in the Soviet zone) got people to do a day's work, controlled the black market, etc. The Marshall Plan and the 1948 currency reform were about to change all this, but in the summer of 1947 a sense of total impotence and blankness about the future still dominated public opinion in the British zone. There could be no German reconstruction without a third world war, one heard in Hamburg. I felt this helplessness myself. 'Frankly, the more I'm here the more depressed I get,' I wrote. 'Hope? I can't see any.' This was a spectacularly wrong assessment of West German prospects, but Germany did not look encouraging in 1947.

But what did it make a western communist feel like about the Soviet Union, whose shadow so patently darkened the German scene? No illusions could survive the immediate postwar contact with the Soviet occupation, direct or indirect, just as the hopes of postwar international amity, which were not confined to communists, had a hard time surviving the postwar frictions between the western and eastern military and officials on the ground. The young Austrian refugees from the London wartime emigration who followed their Party's instruction to return to rebuild their country amid the smell of hungry people in wintry trams and in high-ceilinged, commandeered offices had expected physical hardships, but few had anticipated the actual pervasive anti-Russian mood. For those who lived under, or even had direct contact with, the realities of Soviet-occupied central Europe, being communist was no longer as simple as before the war. We did not lose our faith and our confidence in the eventual superiority of socialism to capitalism, nor our belief in the world-changing potential of Communist Party discipline, but our, or at least my, hopes were now edged with that sense of inevitable tragedy of Walter Benjamin's 'angel of history'.[7] Paradoxically, what made it easier or, for many, possible to maintain the old faith was, more than anything else, the crusading global anti-communism of the West in the Cold War.

II

But let me return to the time of the Berlin airlift. As the wartime alliance broke up, so did the fading hope of postwar co-operation between the two superpowers. In 1947 the communist ministers in western governments began to be edged out of their offices, and so were the non-communist ministers in the countries under communist rule. For purely European purposes a new Communist International (the so-called Communist Information Bureau or Cominform) was set up, to publish a journal which, even by the exacting standards of the Soviet era, must have been the all-time champion of unreadability.[8] The eastern regimes, deliberately *not* set up as communist, but as pluriparty 'new' or 'peoples' democracies' with mixed economies, were now assimilated to the 'dictatorship of the proletariat', i.e. the standard Communist Party dictatorships. And for the West, as confrontation became more overt, communists became fifth columnists.

In Britain things began to change, but in a relatively low-key, gentlemanly manner. There was no overt purge of Party members from the civil service, though, where known, they were removed from jobs with access to sensitive information. Those in the politically sensitive 'administrative' class were discreetly informed that there was no future for them in the service, but there would be no publicity, if they were to choose to leave of their own free will. One who chose to stay served the rest of his career in those remote corners which large bureaucracies reserve for those who can neither be sacked nor given any job of the slightest responsibility.

There was no actual purge in the universities. Birkbeck College, where I had just begun teaching, was exceptional – at least until the arrival of an ambitious new Master in 1951 – in showing no discernible signs of anti-communism among staff or students. Its students earned their living during the day, and such political tradition as it had was on the left. The mood in the small, crowded and friendly staff common room suggested that it was overwhelmingly composed of Labour voters. Such Tories as there were – I suppose my colleague and later boss Douglas Dakin was one – were hardly typical. He had been secretary of the local branch of the union, the Association of University Teachers, in the intervals of running the entire student side of the college as part-time Registrar (with one secretary), playing cricket and teaching, and handed the union job on to me as soon as I arrived. Moreover, by far the most prestigious member of the college staff was a communist, and employer of Party members in his department, a man closely identified with the USSR, J. D. Bernal, crystallographer and so universal a genius (but for a total blank in music) that he could never concentrate on any topic long enough to win a Nobel Prize, although he was the inspirer of several. Even those who had their doubts about his loyalty to Moscow could hardly forbear to admire this short, bushy-haired man who looked like the essential scientist in a strip-cartoon, walked like a sailor on shore or, as he said, 'the pobble who had no toes', and entertained the staff room with well-honed anecdotes about his extraordinarily distinguished time as scientific adviser to Combined Operations during the war. Picasso himself, held up on his way to take part in a Soviet-sponsored meeting in Sheffield, had drawn a spirited mural on the wall of Bernal's flat in Torrington Square, which many years later was to become a sort of logo of Birkbeck. The great artist shared not only Bernal's communism, but also his legendary polygamy; with the difference only that Bernal genuinely treated the women drawn to him as equal partners, both sexually and intellectually. This reputation for gender equality was what attracted the brilliant Rosalind Franklin to Birkbeck from King's College, London, dissatisfied with her treatment by the other (male) workers – the ones who got the Nobel Prize – on the famous Double Helix. Though she was notoriously, and understandably, touchy about macho assumptions in colleagues, she was, at least when we talked, full of praise for Bernal as man and scientist, even when she made fun of the Party-line loyalists in his department.

I was lucky to teach at a college which provided a built-in, unforced protection against the pressures of the Cold War outside. Nevertheless, the academic situation was not good. To the best of my knowledge, all communists who had been appointed to academic posts before the summer of 1948 remained in their jobs, and no attempt was made to dismiss them, unless by the non-renewal of short-term contracts, which were extremely rare in those days. On the other hand, to the best of my knowledge, no known communists were appointed to university posts for ten years or so from 1948, nor, if already in teaching posts, were they promoted. In the course of that decade, for instance, I was turned down for several posts in economic history in Cambridge – I supervised and examined this subject in the Economics Tripos – and I did not get promotion to a Readership in London until 1959. Even people who had had only a few months' connection with the Party, such as the economic historian Sidney Pollard, were seriously held back. This was frustrating, but a long way from the American witch-hunting. (No British academic posts, to my knowledge, were made conditional on the formal abjuration of past sin, as happened when the University of Berkeley offered a chair to Pollard several years later – a condition which he refused to accept.) Curiously, there was more of a political purge in parts of Adult Education, a field which attracted a substantial number of reds and other radicals on ideological grounds, notably in the Extramural Delegacy of Oxford University, which had been run for some years by Thomas Hodgkin, a particularly charming member of the British intellectual aristocracy (Quaker branch) who had been expelled from Palestine for joining the Communist Party during his time as aide-de-camp to the British High Commissioner;

the Party was the only place where Jews and Arabs mixed as friends and equals. Unfortunately the formidable Ernest Bevin, Foreign Secretary and still boss of the Transport and General Workers' Union, had accused the delegacy of harbouring red activists who fomented strikes at what was then the major Morris car plant at Cowley – those were the days when Oxford could be described as 'the Latin Quarter of Cowley'.[9] However, even here there was no general purge of communists.

We accepted that 'this tacit and often half-conscious discrimination, similar to, though less systematic than, the exclusion of social democrats from German university posts before 1914'[10] was relatively mild and concentrated on denouncing American academic McCarthyism – those were the days when the US government refused an entry visa even to the great physicist P. A. M. Dirac – and the dangers that would follow if the American model were to spread to Britain. Nevertheless, in 1950 the historian E. H. Carr was reported as thinking, correctly, that 'It had become very difficult . . . to speak dispassionately about Russia except in "a very woolly Christian kind of way" without endangering, if not your bread and butter, then your legitimate hopes of advancement.' In any case, there is no question that the principle of freedom of expression did not apply to communist and Marxist views, at least in the official media.[11]

What made communist intellectuals feel members of a harried minority was not so much official or quasi-official victimization, as exclusion. Naturally we were convinced, and sometimes had evidence, that our letters were read, our phone bugged, and that, in case of real war, we would find ourselves interned, hopefully with plenty of time to read and work, on some suitable smaller island of the British archipelago. We resented it, even as we could not deny that, given the Cold War, it was logical behaviour for the government. We were the enemies of NATO, after all. What made the rhetoric of Cold War liberals so intolerable was their conviction that all communists were simply agents of the Soviet enemy and their denial that any communist could therefore possibly be a member in good standing of the intellectual community.

Perhaps friendship might have survived politics – after all, I remained on good terms with Mounia Postan, even though I knew that every one of his job references was a poisoned arrow – but it requires more than the small change of social life. And even the taste of genuine friendship could have the bitter tang of Cold War distrust. When I received my first invitation to the USA, anticipating problems, I asked a colleague and friend (a moderate Labour supporter at the time) whether he would be prepared to write a letter testifying to my academic standing. 'Of course I will,' he said. I still remember the momentary sense of abandonment as he added: 'Of course it has nothing to do with it, but could you just tell me – I mean, not that it matters in the least, but are you still in the Communist Party?'

That is why my most resented memory of the Cold War is not of jobs lost, or letters obviously opened, but of my first book. I had proposed it in 1953 to the publishers Hutchinsons, now long buried in some transatlantic publishing conglomerate, for their University Library, a series of compact texts addressed to students: a short comparative volume on *The Rise of the Wage Worker*. The proposal was accepted, but when I submitted the finished manuscript, it was turned down on the advice of an anonymous but presumably authoritative reader or readers. It was, they said, too biased, and therefore unacceptable under the contract. No suggestions for modifications were made. I protested. The firm agreed that I had put in a good deal of work, and therefore offered me a good-will payment of 25 guineas.[12] What stuck in my gullet was not only the contemptible amount of the sum – even in the mid-fifties it amounted to the proceeds of two or three book reviews – but the knowledge that the book had almost certainly been turned down on the advice of some senior colleague, as like as not – given the subject – a supporter of the Labour Party. And there was nothing I could do about it. I was sufficiently furious to consult my lawyer, the astute Jack Gaster, about suing Hutchinsons. He told me not to think of it. 'You may find people to testify to your academic standing, but they will find more to testify that you are biased.' He was right. I never published the book, though I used parts of it in other publications. What makes the incident so typical of that miserable phase of the Cold War is that some years later my then publisher George Weidenfeld, having asked my advice, published a book of the same length on precisely the same subject, and, in my view, ideologically more obviously controversial, as part of one of those global co-production series which he was then promoting.

Under these circumstances, and even though by 1958 the ideological temperature of the Cold War had become a shade less icy, the decision of George (now Lord) Weidenfeld to commission me to write, for an advance on publication of £500, a volume in a gigantic and still not completed history of civilization he was then planning, was admirable and not without courage. It turned out to be *The Age of Revolution 1789–1848*, the first volume of a four-volume history of the nineteenth and twentieth centuries. I was quite well known for my identification with the Communist Party. He was a commercial publisher and a person not uninterested in good relations with the social and political establishment. I owe him a lasting debt of gratitude. Who recommended me to him? I can only speculate, since Lord Weidenfeld himself claims not to remember. I suspect it was J. L. Talmon, of the Hebrew University, Jerusalem, who had been his first choice for the volume in question, but who wanted to drop out. Talmon and I had found ourselves arguing about the nature of democracy and the Jacobins in the French Revolution, and respected each other, though we disagreed on most other things, notably Zionism.

III

The darkest period of public anti-communism, the years of the Korean War and, incidentally, of the opening instalment of the great 'Cambridge Spy' serial – the defection of Burgess and Maclean in 1951 – coincided with a dark moment in my own life. In the summer of 1950 my first marriage, rocky for some time, broke up in circumstances which left me wounded and for some years acutely unhappy. After I left our flat in Clapham Common, I never saw Muriel again except at the moment of our divorce. Fortunately I had won a Fellowship at King's the year before, and the college – such things were then possible – at a moment's notice found me a set of rooms in the wonderful Gibbs Building next to the chapel. King's was my permanent base for the next five years, though I continued to teach at Birkbeck, either returning to Cambridge by a late train, or staying a night or two in the room I rented in the house of Jack and Barbara Tizard in Clapham. Those were black times, both politically and personally. What was more painful: my divorce or the execution of the Rosenbergs, which so many communists at the time felt as a personal defeat and a personal tragedy? It is difficult to separate the two strands that merged in a common mood of determination to survive them: by work, by travel, even by political defiance, as when I invited the physicist Alan Nunn May, just released from jail for nuclear espionage, to a King's Feast. I may add that, as so often, King's behaved impeccably on this occasion; and so did Cambridge when a former mayor and owner of the local newspaper demanded the dismissal of the Assistant Schools Medical Officer, the Austrian refugee Hilde Broda, on the grounds that she had married Alan Nunn May since taking her job. The motion was thrown out without a division. Britain was not the USA.

Looking back, I have mixed feelings about my postwar years at Cambridge. On the one hand I did not take to village life – even in a village of dons – where the range of social relations was both constricted and, to some extent, obligatory. My instincts are and were metropolitan, and in Cambridge there was neither anonymity nor privacy, except in one's own room behind the closed outer door or 'sported oak'. (In those days all doors to students' or dons' living quarters were left unlocked, unless the inhabitant was either not in Cambridge or wished to indicate that [s]he did not want to be disturbed.) What is more, every day I spent there reminded me of the fact that the university did not want me. The posts for which I applied, then and later, went to others. I applied for them really only out of pride. Neither I nor, after I remarried, Marlene, would have wanted to live permanently in Cambridge, or in any other small university-dominated town. The only lengthy visiting posts we really enjoyed have been in capitals: Paris and, above all, Manhattan. In short, when, after six years of my Fellowship, I moved back to London, I felt I had returned to my proper territory.

On the other hand, being a single man living in college, Cambridge gave me another bite at the cherry of student life. Of course it was not the life of the 1930s: for one thing, those among my contemporaries who had become dons had changed their views, and the general depoliticization of the undergraduates was acutely depressing. The sort of political student I remembered, and felt at ease with, was now to be found only among South Asians and Chinese – who were admittedly not rare in the economics faculty, for which I supervised and examined: students such as the young A. K. Sen, who had come to Trinity as a graduate from Presidency College, Calcutta, to sit at the feet of Maurice Dobb and Piero Sraffa, his brilliance already evident. Of course, one saw student life differently as a Fellow, and was treated differently by the undergraduates, even in free-and-easy King's. (The pre-war atmosphere of cultured homosexuality was still strong in the college, although from 1952 on the turn to heterosexuality became obvious, with patently woman-oriented new arrivals on King's fashion scene, such as the future journalist and writer Neal Ascherson, and the transformation of young men such as the future media designer Mark Boxer, who having established themselves in the old mode, transferred to the new.) I did, however, have one asset that brought me closer to the life and mood of the 1950s male student mood than I could otherwise have been, but not – at this time – to the young women (although supervising those studying history and economics in Newnham helped). I was an Apostle, and therefore on close terms with some of them. This may therefore be a suitable moment to say something about this odd Cambridge institution: still extant and flourishing, still keeping its actual active membership secret, although most of its pre-1939 history is by now a matter of public record, and few of its retired members make any secret of their apostolicity. It was and is a small community, essentially of brilliant undergraduates or early postgraduates, co-opting others to maintain itself in being, whose purpose is to read and discuss papers written by its members at weekly meetings. Undergraduates were the core of the Apostles. Indeed, by definition they *are* 'the Society', since those who left 'the real world' of its meetings for 'the phenomenal world' outside, by graduating or leaving Cambridge ('taking wings' and therefore being known as 'Angels') necessarily had to defer to the active brethren.

I had been elected to the Cambridge Conversazione Society in my last undergraduate term in 1939, together with another Kingsman, the later Walter Wallich of the BBC, son of the director of the Deutsche Bank and descendant of its founder who, after the

Kristallnacht of 1938, having sent wife and children abroad in good time, took a train from Berlin to Cologne and jumped off the bridge into the Rhine. It was an invitation that hardly any Cambridge undergraduate was likely to refuse, since even revolutionaries like to be in a suitable tradition. Who would not wish to be associated with the names of earlier Apostles, which were more or less the great names of nineteenth-century Cambridge: the poet Tennyson, the marvellous physicist Clerk Maxwell, the greatest of Cambridge historians, Frederick Maitland, Bertrand Russell and the glories of Edwardian Cambridge – Keynes, Wittgenstein and Moore, Whitehead and, in literature, E. M. Forster and Rupert Brooke. Only the greatest of nineteenth-century Cambridge names was missing, Charles Darwin of Christ's. Actually, the bulk of the Victorian and Edwardian Apostles, who have been exhaustively and perceptively analysed by an American professor,[13] were by no means in that class, and, since greatness of intellectual (or other) achievement often requires running the risk of boring friends whose interests do not coincide completely with your own – and no Apostle would have wanted to bore the other brethren – many of them suffered in later life from their inability to live up to the exemplars of their great tradition.

It may be worth observing that communism had nothing to do with my election, although the famous photo of six Apostles that appears in every book on the Cambridge spies contains four communists. It is no surprise that the Party was heavily represented in the society of the Spanish Civil War years. However, neither John Cornford and James Klugmann nor any of the heads of the Party in my time were Apostles, nor (with one exception) was any Marxist don of the 1930s. The criterion for being elected to the society was, and presumably still is, not subject or belief, or even intellectual distinction, but 'being apostolic', whatever that meant – and it was, and no doubt continues to be, endlessly discussed among the brethren. For that matter, neither were the Cambridge spies recruited primarily through the Apostles (except via Anthony Blunt): of the Cambridge Five three had nothing whatever to do with the society (Philby, Maclean and Cairncross).

The war had suspended the 'real world' in Cambridge, although a number of senior Angels continued in at least intermittent residence as dons. If I am not mistaken, only two pre-war active brethren returned to Cambridge as research students, myself and the late Matthew Hodgart, a black-haired, moon-faced, hard-drinking literary Scot, perhaps the most brilliant of my undergraduate friends, by then no longer a communist. We were, or rather, since he was not present, I was charged by the assembled Angels at the society's first postwar annual dinner in 1946 (at Kettners in Soho) to revive it. We did this by recruiting among pre-war friends who had returned to Cambridge, and the students sent to me for supervision by King's. When I became a Fellow, I recruited a college friend, the Canadian economist Harry Johnson. Since I also supervised economics students in economic history, the postwar Apostles thus found themselves continuing the tradition of Maynard Keynes. However, increasingly, the arts, i.e. history and English, tended to fill the society of the 1950s – together with the unclassified multiple brilliance of Jonathan Miller, who read natural sciences. Before the 1939 war many of them would have gone into the civil service, but now the non-economists among them flocked into two expanding occupations: 'the media' and university teaching, sometimes in succession. Women began to be elected only in the 1960s.

After the war the most famous surviving Apostle, the novelist E. M. Forster, moved into King's College, and, loyal as ever to the society, offered his rooms for its Sunday evening meetings, sitting quietly in the corner – he probably never said much even in his youth – listening to the young brethren speaking literally (in the society's argot) 'on the hearth-rug', since fireplaces fed from coal-scuttles were still the main Cambridge line of defence against the raw eastern climate. Never a habitual scribbler, by this time Morgan had virtually stopped writing, although he took enormous trouble to avoid the slightest hint of cliché or platitude in such few texts as he still composed. He had no family, except that of his old policeman lover. I do not think he was ever as much at ease in the postwar world as he would have liked to be, but he was consoled by the unchanging nature of the youth surrounding him. In the early 1960s I once tried to introduce him to the later twentieth century by taking him to see the American soliloquist – one could hardly call him a 'comedian' any longer – Lenny Bruce, who was briefly performing at the Establishment, a shortlived Soho club, on his way to rapid self-destruction. Morgan was, as always, courteous and endlessly considerate, but this was not his wavelength.

It has been said by a perceptive observer of the society's first century that 'the Apostles devoted themselves to two things above all else, and did so with a pure intensity which to an unkind eye might look absurd, but to a kind eye absolutely admirable. These were friendship on the one hand, and intellectual honesty, on the other.'[14] Both were still very central to the Apostles of my time, though the dons who participated in these sessions, being older, probably injected a dose of diplomacy into the 'intellectual honesty' they brought to their personal relations. Still, both crossed the barriers of age and temperament, and I, as well as my family, owe to the undergraduate Apostles of the early fifties (and to the young men and women I met with and through them) a number of lasting friendships.

III

I cannot say that the first half of the 1950s was a happy time for me in my personal life. I filled it with work, with writing, thinking and teaching, with a lot of travel during university vacations, and, dutifully, with Party work. Fortunately, moving out of London had put me out of the range of London local branch work – organization, canvassing, selling the *Daily Worker* (renamed *Morning Star* after 1956) – for which I had no natural taste or suitable temperament. From then on, in effect, I operated entirely in academic or intellectual groups.

Intellectually, though, those were good years. The mind of most people is at its sharpest and most adventurous in their twenties, but I returned from the army passionately determined to catch up on the ideas of the lost war years, and just young enough to do so. There is nothing for the self-education of academics like the need to prepare lectures, and, since the four or five of us in Birkbeck's history department had to cover all history since antiquity, I had to have a very wide range as a lecturer, even without the additional demands made on me as a supervisor in Cambridge. Academic careers might be blocked, but the historical world was not. What happened in the wider world of historians in those years is the subject of another chapter. For the present purposes it is enough to note that I began to publish in the professional journals from 1949, to play a part in international congresses and in the Economic History Society (to the council of which I was elected in 1952). Above all, from 1946 to 1956 we – a group of comrades and friends – conducted a continuous Marxist seminar for ourselves in the Historians' Group of the Communist Party, by means of endless duplicated discussion papers and regular meetings, mainly in the upper room of the Garibaldi Restaurant in Saffron Hill and occasionally in the then shabby premises of Marx House on Clerkenwell Green. Those who know only the buzzing, gentrified Clerkenwell of 2000 cannot imagine the empty, cold, grey dankness of those streets at weekends fifty years ago, when the Dickensian fog, which disappeared after 1953, was still likely to fall like a vast yellow-grey blindfold on London. Perhaps this was where we really became historians. Others have spoken of 'the astonishing impact of [this] generation of Marxist historians' without whom 'the worldwide influence of British historical scholarship, especially since the 1960s, is inconceivable'.[15] Among other things it gave birth to a successful and eventually influential historical journal in 1952, but *Past & Present* was born not in Clerkenwell, but in the more agreeable ambience of University College, Gower Street.

The Historians' Group broke up in the year of communist crisis, 1956. Until then we, and certainly I, had remained loyal, disciplined and politically aligned Communist Party members, helped no doubt by the wild rhetoric of crusading anti-communism of the 'Free World'. But it was far from easy.

The Soviet Union, God knows, made it harder and harder. Intellectuals were, of course, under particular pressure, since from 1947 on the beliefs to which they were committed were reduced to a catechism of orthodoxies, some only faintly related to Marxism, and several – especially in the natural sciences – absurd. After the official triumph of 'Lysenkoism' in the USSR this was a major problem in the Cambridge graduate branch, several, perhaps most, of whose older members were natural scientists. Were they, like the great geneticist J. B. S. Haldane, quietly to withdraw from the Party, unable to accept untruth? Were they, like J. D. Bernal, to ruin their public standing by trying, if not quite managing, to defend the Soviets? Were they simply to shut their eyes, say nothing, and go on with their work as before? The peculiarities of Stalinist science were not quite so damaging elsewhere. Communist psychologists, for instance, found Moscow's insistence on Pavlov ('conditioned reflexes') less constricting, partly because of the experimental, positivist, behaviourist and strongly anti-psychoanalytical slant of British psychology departments. But these were the special problems of intellectuals, and for various reasons they did not seriously affect British communist historians who kept away from Russian and Communist Party history. Obviously, none of us believed the version of Soviet Party history contained in the, pedagogically brilliant, text of Stalin's *History of the CPSU (b): Short Course*. But there were more general problems, even if we leave aside the horrors of the Soviet camps, the extent of which communists did not then recognize.

What were British, and even more Cambridge, communists, who had been deeply involved in wartime relations with the Yugoslav Partisans, to think of the 1948 split between Stalin and Tito? We were close to Yugoslav communism. Young Brits by the hundred flocked into the country to build the so-called 'Youth Railway', including notably Edward Thompson, not yet a historian, whose brother Frank had his wartime base among the Macedonian Partisans, until he went on to fight and die with the Bulgarian ones. How could one possibly believe the official Soviet line that Tito had to be excommunicated because he had long prepared to betray the interests of proletarian internationalism in the interests of foreign intelligence services? We could understand that James Klugmann was forced to disavow Tito, but we did not believe him and, since he had until recently told us the opposite – and so had the newly formed Cominform, whose headquarters were initially in Belgrade – we knew he did not believe it either. In short, we stayed loyal to Moscow because the cause of world socialism could dispense with the support of a small, if heroic and admired, country, but not with that of Stalin's superpower.

Unlike what happened in the 1930s, I cannot recall any serious efforts to compel Party members to justify the succession of show trials which disfigured the last years of Stalin, but this may merely mean that intellectuals like myself had given up the effort to be convinced. Few of us knew anything about Bulgaria, so the first of the trials, against Traicho Kostov (executed in 1949), left me unhappy but not unduly sceptical. The trial of Laszlo Rajk in Hungary in the autumn of 1949 was another matter. Among the 'agents of the British Secret Service' alleged to have undermined communism, the indictment named (and suitable confessions doubtless confirmed) someone I knew personally: the journalist Basil Davidson. I simply did not believe this. A big, tough man with a sharp mind, already grizzling wiry hair, an eye for women and a very attractive wife, Basil had had what they called a 'good' but unorthodox war. He had fought with the Yugoslav Partisans in the flat, fertile Vojvodina adjoining Hungary – terrible guerrilla territory – then with the Italian Partisans in the Ligurian mountains, and written a good book, *Partisan Picture*, about both. (It gave him the necessary training for his later footslogging with African liberation fighters in the hinterlands of Portuguese Guinea and Angola.) We became, and still remain, friends. The Hungarian accusation was not incredible in itself. In fact, though I did not then know it, Davidson had in his time, like other British journalists on the continent, been recruited by the Secret Intelligence Service and sent to Hungary. It would not have surprised me if he had known Rajk then. What made me sceptical, apart from my personal judgement of the man, was the fact that his career as a journalist had taken a sharp turn for the worse with the Cold War. After leaving the (London) *Times* he was, in effect, edged out of the *New Statesman and Nation*, then at its height as the organ of the respectable left, as a fellow-traveller. Nobody wanted him. He was about to construct for himself a new freelance career as a highly respected pioneer historian of Africa, and an expert on the anti-imperialist liberation movements south of the Sahara. The accusation simply made no sense.

The last and biggest set of East European show trials, in Czechoslovakia, sounded even less convincing; quite apart from the markedly anti-Semitic tinge which they shared with the notorious 1952 'doctors' plot' against Stalin in the USSR itself. My student generation knew many of the young Czech emigrants to Britain. We knew at least one of the executed 'traitors' well: Otto Sling, married to the ever-reliable Marion Wilbraham from the pre-war Youth Peace

Movement, had returned to his country to become Party chief of Brno, Czechoslovakia's second city. By this time even the – expected – official Party defence of the Czech trial seemed to show a certain lack of conviction.

Patently people like myself did not remain in the Communist Party because we had many illusions about the USSR, although undoubtedly we had some. For instance, we clearly underestimated the horrors of what had gone on in the USSR under Stalin, until it was denounced by Khrushchev in 1956. Since a good deal of information was available about the Soviet camps, which could not easily be ignored, it is no excuse to point out that even western critics did not document the full extent of the system until 1956.[16] Moreover, after 1956 many of us did leave the Party. Why, then, did we remain?

Perhaps the best way to recapture the mood of the peak years of the Cold War – essentially the period from Hiroshima to Panmunjom – is by an episode from the life of Bertrand Russell, which the great philosopher did not like to have recalled in his later days as an anti-nuclear activist. Shortly after the dropping of the Hiroshima and Nagasaki bombs, Russell concluded that the American monopoly of nuclear arms would be only temporary. While it was, the USA should exploit it, if need be by a pre-emptive nuclear attack against Moscow. This would prevent the USSR launching on the course of imminent world conquest to which he believed it to be committed, and would it was hoped destroy a regime which he regarded as utterly appalling. In short, as far as the people of the USSR were concerned, he believed in the then familiar western Cold War slogan 'Better dead than red'. In practice *other* peoples were the only ones to whom this literally senseless slogan was applied. If it had any sense it meant, not that Cubans or Vietnamese or, if it should so happen, Italians should commit suicide rather than live under a communist government, but that they should be killed by the arms of the Free World to prevent this awful contingency. (No sane person seriously expected mass suicide in either Britain or the USA.)

Fortunately, though the possibility of American pre-emptive nuclear strikes worried Whitehall,[17] nobody listened to Russell, who in any case changed his mind when both superpowers had the capacity to destroy one another, thus turning world war into global suicide. Yet before then people, including even some serious politicians, undoubtedly talked in terms of something like an apocalyptic global class war. The issues were enormous. Whichever side one stood on, there was no limit to the price to be paid. The war, especially since Hiroshima and Nagasaki, had got the world used to human sacrifices by the hundreds of thousands, even millions. Those who opposed nuclear arms were accused of depriving the West of a necessary, an indispensable arm. We too – I say this with retrospective regret – recognized no limit to the price we were prepared to ask others to pay. It is no mitigation to say that we were prepared to pay it ourselves.

On the one hand, communists saw the USA and its allies threatening the total destruction of a still besieged and vulnerable USSR, in order to bring to a halt the global advance of the forces of revolution since the defeat of Hitler and Hirohito. They still saw the USSR as its indispensable guarantee. On the other hand, for the USA and its allies the USSR was both the threat to the world and a system totally to be rejected. Everything would be so much simpler if it were not a superpower. Everything would be even simpler if it were not there. To us it was obvious that the USSR was not in a position to conquer the world for communism. Some of us were even disappointed because it appeared not to want to. It was – at least western communist intellectuals thought, even if they did not say so – a system with severe defects, but with titanic achievements and still with the unlimited potential of socialism. (Though it now seems incredible, in the 1950s, and not only to its sympathizers, the Soviet Union did not yet look like a foundering economic hulk but like an economy which might well outproduce the West.) To most of the world, it did not seem to be the worst of all possible regimes, but an ally in the fight for emancipation from western imperialism, old and new, and a model for non-European economic and social development. The future of both communists and the regimes and movements of the decolonized and decolonizing world depended on its existence. As far as communists were concerned, supporting and defending the Soviet Union was still the essential international priority.

So we swallowed our doubts and mental reservations and defended it. Or rather, because it was easier, we attacked the capitalist camp for preferring a West Germany run by old Nazis, and soon actually to be rearmed against the USSR, to an East Germany run by old prisoners of Nazi concentration camps; for preferring the old imperialism to the movements of anti-imperial liberation, and a USA which made Franco's Spain its military base against those who had supported the Republic.

Even so, it was not easy. Being a communist in the West was no problem. The trouble was the experience of communism in the East. But I was soon to see this myself. There were the first signs of some slight thawing on the fringes of the frozen ice-cap of Stalin's USSR. In 1952, even before the terrible old man died, the historian E. A. Kosminsky was allowed a brief visit to Britain with his wife for the first time since, long ago in the 1920s, he had worked in London on those problems of English manorial history in the Middle Ages that had made him famous in the world of historical scholarship. I took him to the British Museum, for he wanted to use the great round Reading Room again. Could he have a short-term ticket? A lady librarian asked whether he had ever used the library before. He had. 'Ah,' she said, looking his name up in the files. 'No, of course there will be no problem. Do you still live in Torrington Square?' It was a moment of great emotion for him. A few months later, after Stalin's death but before post-Stalinism, he arranged for the Soviet Academy of Sciences to invite a group of British Marxist historians to the USSR. It was my first, but not quite my only, experience of the country of the October Revolution. I did not much want to go there again. That visit helped to prepare me for the crucial turning-point in the lives of all communist intellectuals, and in the world communist movement, which is the main subject of the next chapter: the crisis of 1956.

12

Stalin and After

I

I am among the relatively few inhabitants of the world outside what used to be the USSR who has actually seen Stalin; admittedly no longer alive but in a glass case in the great mausoleum in Moscow's Red Square: a small man who seemed even smaller than he actually was (about 5ft 3in) by contrast with the awe-inspiring aura of autocratic power that surrounded him even in death. Unlike Lenin, who is still on view, having so far (2002) resisted eleven post-Soviet years of attempts to remove him, Stalin was displayed only in the brief period between his death in 1953 and 1961. When I saw him in December 1954, he still towered over his country and the world communist movement. As yet he had no effective successor, although Nikita Khrushchev, who inaugurated 'destalinization' not many months later, was already occupying the post of General Secretary and getting ready to elbow his rivals aside. However, we knew nothing of what was happening behind the scenes in Moscow.

'We' were four members of the Historians' Group of the British Communist Party invited by the Soviet Academy of Sciences during the academic Christmas vacation of 1954–5, as part of the still painfully slow process of extricating Soviet intellectual life from its isolation: Christopher Hill, already well known as a historian of the English Revolution, the Byzantinist Robert Browning, myself and the freelance scholar Leslie (A. L.) Morton, whose Marxist *People's History of England* enjoyed the official imprimatur of the Soviet authorities. Probably only Robert Browning, a Scotsman of amazingly wide-ranging erudition and linguistic competence, who gave a paper on the recent decipherment of the Cretan Linear B inscriptions, realized quite how cut off Soviet scholars had been from literature in the English language. (Contacts with France had never been quite so decayed.) Since none of the visitors specialized in Russian history, where the real strength of our hosts naturally lay, on balance they probably benefited more from our conversations than we did.

What did we expect to find in the USSR? We were not totally dependent on the official guide/translators provided for us by the academy, for two of us knew Russian – Christopher Hill, who had spent a year in the USSR in the mid-1930s and had friends there, and the apparently almost accentless Robert Browning. Nevertheless, the USSR two years after Stalin's death, and indeed for several years thereafter, was not a place given to informal communication with foreigners even in Russian. Not that an official 'delegation' invited by the academy, a body with considerable status and clout in Soviet society at that time, left much room for informal contacts or free time. For even the programme of entertainments and cultural visits was geared to the importance of the host organization and, by extrapolation, of its foreign guests. Outside buildings, our feet were barely allowed to touch the ground.

In short, as intellectual VIPs – an unfamiliar role – we almost certainly were treated to more culture than other visiting foreigners, as well as an embarrassing share of products and privileges in a visibly impoverished country. We would, for instance, be whisked straight off the famous Red Arrow Moscow–Leningrad overnight train, to a matinée children's performance of *Swan Lake* at the Kirov, installed in the directors' box, to which, after the performance, the prima ballerina – I think it was Alla Shelest – was brought straight from the stage and still sweating, *to be presented to us*, four foreigners of no particular importance who found themselves momentarily in the location of power. Almost half a century later, I still feel a sense of curious shame at the memory of her curtsy to us, as the children of Leningrad prepared to go home and the – overwhelmingly Jewish – musicians filed out of the orchestra pit. It was not a good advertisement for communism. But of Russia and Russian life we saw little except the middle-aged women, presumably war widows, hauling stones and clearing rubble from the wintry streets.

What is more, even the intellectuals' basic resource, 'looking it up', was not available. There were no telephone directories, no maps, no public timetables, no basic means of everyday reference. One was struck by the sheer impracticality of a society in which an almost paranoiac fear of espionage turned the information needed for everyday life into a state secret. In short, there was not much to be learned about Russia by visiting it in 1954 that could not have been learned outside.

Still, there was something. There was the evident arbitrariness and unpredictability of its arrangements. There was the astonishing achievement of the Moscow metro, built in the iron era of the 1930s under one of the legendary 'hard men' of Stalinism, Lazar Kaganovich, a dream of a future city of palaces for a hungry and pauperized present, but a modern underground which worked – and, I am told, still does – like clockwork. There was the basic difference between the Russians who took decisions and the ones who did not – as we joked among ourselves, they could be recognized by their hair. The ones who took action had hair that stood up on their heads, or had fallen out with the effort, the ones who didn't could be recognized by the lankness above their foreheads. There was the extraordinary spectacle of an intellectual society barely a generation from the ancient peasantry. I recall the New Year's Eve party at the Scientists' Club in Moscow. Between the usual toasts to peace and friendship, someone suggested a contest in remembering proverbs – not just *any* old saws, but proverbs or phrases about sharp things, such as 'a stitch in time saves nine' (needles) or 'burying the hatchet'. The joint resources of Britain were soon exhausted, but the Russian contestants, all of them established research scientists, went on confronting each other with village wisdom about knives, axes, sickles and sharp or cutting implements and their operations until the contest had to be stopped. That, after all, was what they brought with them from the illiterate villages in which so many of them had been born.

It was an interesting but also a dispiriting trip for foreign communist intellectuals, for we met hardly anyone there like ourselves. Unlike the 'peoples' democracies' and 'really existing socialisms' of the rest of Europe, where communists fighting oppression came from persecution to power at the end of the war, in the USSR we found ourselves in a country long governed by the Communist Party of the Soviet Union, in which having a career implied being a member of that Party, or at least conforming to its requirements and official statements. Probably some we met were convinced as well as loyal communists, but theirs was an inward-looking Soviet conviction rather than an ecumenical one, although it is likely that we would have had more in common with some of those we asked to meet but who were 'unfortunately prevented from coming to Moscow by problems of health', 'temporarily absent in Gorki' or not yet returned from the camps. It was much easier to sense what the 'Great Patriotic War' meant, privately and emotionally, to the people we saw – particularly in Leningrad, survivor of the terrible wartime siege – than what communism meant to them. At all events I am certain that, standing by the Finland Station in the marvellous winter light of that miraculous city I shall never get used to calling St Petersburg, what we thought about the October Revolution was not the same as what our guides from the Leningrad branch of the Academy of Sciences thought.

I returned from Moscow politically unchanged if depressed, and without any desire to go there again. I did return but only fleetingly, in 1970 for a world historical congress, and in the last years of the USSR for brief tourist excursions from Helsinki, where I spent several summers at a UN Research Institute.*

The trip to the USSR in 1954–5 was my first contact with the countries of what was later called 'really existing socialism', for my visit to the 1947 World Youth Festival in Prague occurred before the Party had taken full power in the new 'peoples' democracies'. Indeed, in Czechoslovakia it had just emerged, with 40 per cent, as by far the largest party in a genuine multiparty general election. Apart from getting to know several of their historians personally, I made direct contact with the other socialist countries only after the Twentieth Congress of the Soviet CP which inaugurated the global crisis of the communist movement, though in the case of my first visit to the German Democratic Republic in April–May 1956, before the publication of Khrushchev's public attack on Stalin. But by that time everything had changed.

---

* It may be worth mentioning in passing that none of my books was ever translated into Russian or any other Soviet language during the communist period, but then, the only 'real socialist' languages any of them were translated into before the fall of the Berlin Wall were Hungarian – fairly consistently – and Slovenian. However, my book on jazz was translated into Czech.

II

There are two 'ten days that shook the world' in the history of the revolutionary movement of the last century: the days of the October Revolution, described in John Reed's book of that title, and the Twentieth Congress of the Communist Party of the Soviet Union (14–25 February 1956). Both divide it suddenly and irrevocably into a 'before' and 'after'. I cannot think of any comparable event in the history of any major ideological or political movement. To put it in the simplest terms, the October Revolution created a world communist movement, the Twentieth Congress destroyed it.

The world communist movement had been constructed, on Leninist lines, as a single disciplined army dedicated to the transformation of the world under a centralized and quasi-military command situated in the only state in which 'the proletariat' (i.e. the Communist Party) had taken power. It became a movement of global significance only because it was linked to the USSR, which in turn became the country that tore the guts out of Nazi Germany and emerged from the war as a superpower. Bolshevism had transformed one weak regime in a vast but backward country into a superpower. The victory of the cause in other countries, the liberation of the colonial and semi-colonial world, depended on its support and on its sometimes reluctant but real protection. Whatever its weaknesses, its very existence proved that socialism was more than a dream. And the passionate anti-communism of the Cold War crusaders, which saw communists exclusively as agents of Moscow, welded them more firmly to the USSR.

As time went on, and especially during the years of the battles against fascism, the effectively organized revolutionary left had become virtually identified with the Communist Parties. They had absorbed or eliminated other brands of social revolutionaries. While the Communist Universal Church gave rise to one set after another of schismatics and heretics, none of the rebel groups it shed, expelled or killed had ever suceeded in establishing itself more than locally as a rival, until Tito did so in 1948 – but then, unlike any of the others, he was already head of a revolutionary state. As 1956 began, the joint strength of the three rival Trotskyite groups in Britain has been estimated as fewer than 100 persons.[1] In practice since 1933 the CPs had virtually cornered Marxist theory, largely through the Soviets' zeal for the distribution of the works of the 'classics'. It had become increasingly clear that, for Marxists, 'the Party' – wherever they lived, and with all their possible reservations – was the only game in town. The great French classicist J. P. Vernant, a communist before the war, broke with the Party by joining the Gaullist Resistance from the start against the then Party line, and had a most distinguished war as 'Colonel Berthier', and *compagnon de la Libération*, but he rejoined the Party after the war, because he remained a revolutionary. Where else could he go? The late Isaac Deutscher, the biographer of Trotsky, but in his heart a frustrated political leader, said to me, when I first met him at the peak of the communist crisis of 1956–7: 'Whatever you do, don't leave the Communist Party. I let myself be expelled in 1932 and have regretted it ever since.' Unlike me, he never reconciled himself to the fact that he was politically significant only by having become a writer. After all, was not the business of communists *changing* the world and not merely interpreting it?

III

Why did Khrushchev's uncompromising denunciation of Stalin destroy the foundations of the global solidarity of communists with Moscow? After all, it continued a process of managed destalinization that had been advancing steadily for more than two years, even though other Communist Parties resented the familiar Soviet habit of suddenly, and without previous information, confronting them with the need to justify some unexpected reversal of policy. (In 1955 Khrushchev's reconciliation with Tito particularly exasperated comrades who, seven years earlier, had been forced, almost certainly against their will, to hail his excommunication from the True Church.) Indeed, until the leaking of the Khrushchev speech to a wider public, including that of the Communist Parties, the Twentieth Congress looked simply like another, admittedly rather larger, step away from the Stalin era.

I think we must distinguish here between its impact on the leadership of Communist Parties, especially those who already governed states, and on the communist rank-and-file. Naturally, both had accepted the mandatory obligations of a 'democratic centralism', which had quietly dropped what measure of democracy it might originally have contained.[2] And all of them, except perhaps the Chinese CP which nevertheless acknowledged the primacy of Stalin, accepted Moscow as the commander of the disciplined army of world communism in the global Cold War. Both shared the extraordinary, genuine and unforced admiration for Stalin as the leader and embodiment of the Cause, and the well-attested sense of grief and personal loss which communists unquestionably felt at his death in 1953. While this was natural enough for the rank-and-file, for whom he was a remote image of poor people's triumph and liberation – 'the fellow with the big moustache' who might still come one day to get rid of the rich once and for all – it was undoubtedly shared by hard-bitten leaders like Palmiro Togliatti, who knew the terrible dictator at close quarters, and even by his real or prospective victims. Molotov remained loyal to him for thirty-three years after his death, though in his last paranoiac years Stalin had forced him to divorce his wife, had her arrested, interrogated and exiled, and was plainly preparing Molotov himself for a show trial. Anna Pauker, of the Comintern and Romania, wept when she heard of Stalin's death, even though she had not liked him, had indeed been afraid of him, and was at the time being prepared to be thrown to the wolves as an alleged bourgeois nationalist, agent of Truman and Zionism. ('Don't cry,' said her interrogator. 'If Stalin were still alive you'd be dead.'[3]) No wonder that the impassioned attack on his record, and on the 'cult of personality', by Khrushchev sent shockwaves through the international communist movement.

On the other hand, much as their leaders admired Stalin and accepted the 'guiding role' of the Soviet Party, Communist Parties, in or outside power, were neither 'monolithic', in the Stalinist phrase, nor simple executive agents of CPSU policy. And since at least 1947 they had been told to do things by Moscow, often politically prejudicial, which they, or at least substantial sections of their leadership, would never have done themselves. While Stalin lived and the Moscow leadership and power remained 'monolithic', that was the end of it. Destalinization reopened closed options, especially since the men in the Kremlin patently lacked the old authority, and still faced strong opposition from the old Stalinists. Because Moscow was (briefly) no longer under monolithic rule. In short, the cracks in the structure of the region under Soviet control could now open. Within a few months of the Twentieth Congress they did so, visibly, in Poland and Hungary. And this in turn aggravated the crises within the non-governmental Communist Parties.

What disturbed the mass of their members was that the brutally ruthless denunciation of Stalin's misdeeds came, not from 'the bourgeois press', whose stories, if read at all, could be rejected a priori as slanders and lies, but from Moscow itself. It was impossible not to take notice of it, but also impossible to know what loyal believers should make of it. Even those who 'had strong suspicions . . . [about the facts revealed] amounting to moral certainty for years before Khrushchev spoke'[4] were shocked at the sheer extent, hitherto not fully realized, of Stalin's mass murders of communists. (The Khrushchev Report said nothing about the others.) And no thinking communist could escape asking himself or herself some serious questions.

Nevertheless, I think it is safe to say that at the start of 1956 no leadership of any non-state Communist Party seriously thought that destalinization implied a fundamental revision of the role, objectives and history of such Parties. Nor did they expect major troubles from their membership, since the people who remained Party members were those who had resisted the propaganda of the cold warriors for ten years. Yet, probably because of their very confidence, this time they failed to carry a substantial number of their members with them.

In retrospect the reason is obvious. We were not told the truth about something that had to affect the very nature of a communist's belief. Moreover, we could see that the leadership would have preferred us not to know the truth – they concealed it until Khrushchev's off-the-record speech had been leaked to the non-communist press – and they manifestly wanted to bring any discussion about it to a close as soon as possible. When the crisis broke out in Poland and Hungary they went on concealing what our own journalists reported. One could understand why as Party organizers they might find this convenient, but it was neither Marxism nor genuine politics. When the familiar call to unswerving loyalty failed, their immediate instinct was to blame the unfortunate vacillations of those well-known elements of instability and weakness, petty-bourgeois intellectuals. It took the Party authorities from March to November to recognize what the Committee of the Communist Party's Historians' Group had seen almost immediately, namely that this was 'the most serious and critical situation the Party was in since its foundation'.[5] Indeed, after the Hungarian Revolution and Soviet armed intervention later that year, not even the most blindly loyal Party members could reasonably deny it. When the leadership had re-established itself in 1957, after fending off an outburst of open opposition without precedent, the British Communist Party had lost a quarter of its members, a third of the staff of its newspaper, the *Daily Worker*, and probably the bulk of what remained of the generation of communist intellectuals of the 1930s and 1940s. But, though it lost several of its leading trade unionists, it rapidly regained its national industrial influence, which reached its peak in the 1970s and early 1980s.

It is difficult to reconstruct not only the mood but the memory of that traumatic year, rising, through a succession of lesser crises, to the appalling climax of the Soviet army's reconquest of Hungary, and then stumbling and wrestling to an exhausted defeat through months of doomed and feverish argument. Arnold Wesker's play *Chicken Soup with Barley*, about a Jewish working-class family struggling with its communist faith, gives a good idea of what has been called 'the pain of losing it and the pain of clinging to it'.[6] Even after practically half a century my throat contracts as I recall the almost intolerable tensions under which we lived month after month, the unending moments of decision about what to say and do on which our future lives seemed to depend, the friends now clinging together or facing one another bitterly as adversaries, the sense of lurching, unwillingly but irreversibly, down the scree towards the fatal rock-face. And this while all of us, except a handful of full-time Party workers, had to go on, as though nothing much had happened, with lives and jobs outside, which temporarily seemed unwanted distractions from the enormous thing that dominated our days and nights. God knows 1956 was a dramatic year in British politics, but in the memory of those who were then communists, everything else has faded. Of course we mobilized against Anthony Eden's lying government in the Suez crisis together with a for once totally united

Labour and Liberal left. But Suez did not keep us from sleeping. Probably the simplest way of putting it is that, for more than a year, British communists lived on the edge of the political equivalent of a collective nervous breakdown.

What made things worse was that the family-sized British Communist Party was in many ways, to quote an apocryphal critique by the Comintern, 'a party of good friends'. Unlike other Parties, it had no history of clamorous expulsions and excommunications. It lacked the particular version of the 'bolshevik' house-style of leadership which created ruthless, complacent bullies such as André Marty in the French CP. We were likely to have met and talked to our leaders, liked most of them and at least some of us could understand the pressures upon them. None of the critics wanted to leave the Party, the Party did not want to lose us. Wherever our political future was to take us – and even those who left or were expelled from the Party overwhelmingly remained on the left – all of us lived through the crisis of 1956 as convinced communists.

I would have been in the thick of the crisis in any case, but I was close to the centre of it, since in 1956 I was the chairman of the Communist Party's Historians' Group – one of the few times I have been chairman of any organization – and the group emerged almost immediately as the nucleus of vocal opposition to the Party line, when it was brought to us by a King Street spokesman on 8 April 1956, shortly after the Khrushchev speech, or rather after the subsequent British Party Congress which had (vainly) tried to bypass the whole issue. We rebelled and the group made the two most dramatic challenges to the Party. In the first, one of the group's leading members, Christopher Hill, acted as spokesman for the Minority Report of the Commission on Inner-Party Democracy, i.e. virtual leader of the opposition at the Party Congress of May 1957. In mid-July John Saville of Hull University and E. P. Thompson, then a lecturer in the extramural department of Leeds, launched an unprecedented and by Party convention entirely illegitimate bulletin of opposition within the Party, *The Reasoner*. (After they left the Party it was revived as *The New Reasoner* in 1957, with contributions from various sympathetic hands, including myself.) The Soviet intervention in the Hungarian Revolution moved several of us to a second and even more flagrant breach of Party discipline, technically punishable by expulsion, a collective letter of protest, signed by most of the better-known historians (including the usually silent loyalist Maurice Dobb), rejected by the *Daily Worker* and demonstratively published in the non-Party press.[7] Only Party members of that generation will appreciate how unpardonable such a breach of discipline was. A few years later this letter allowed me, on an emotional evening in an Austrian pub, to checkmate a very drunken and ill-tempered Arthur Koestler who wanted to know whether people like me had ever opposed the Russians over the Hungarian Revolution.

The historians had been the most consistently flourishing of the Party's 'cultural groups', and a notably loyal one politically. Why did we – more than the writers, more than the scientists, groggy from the impact of the absurdities of Lysenko and official Soviet ideology – find ourselves in the front line of opposition from the start? Essentially, because we had to confront the situation not only as private individuals and communist militants, but in our professional capacity. The issue of what had been done under Stalin, and why it had been concealed, was literally a question about history. So were the open but undiscussed questions about episodes in our own Party's history which were directly linked to Moscow decisions in the Stalin era, notably the abandonment of the anti-fascist line in 1939–41. So, indeed, was our own political attitude. As someone said on the day of our first rebellion: 'Why should we simply approve Khrushchev? We do not know, we can only endorse policy – but historians go by evidence.'[8]

This accounts for our only collective intervention as a group in the affairs of the Party in 1956. We demanded a serious history of the CP. King Street, which, as I can now see in retrospect, was desperate to conciliate a troublesome bunch of intellectuals whom they nevertheless recognized as an asset, agreed to set up a commission to discuss the matter. Harry Pollitt, Chairman and unquestioned leader of the Party during our lifetime, Palme Dutt, the ideological guru, and James Klugmann, represented the leadership, I as group chairman and Brian Pearce spoke for the historians. (Brian, once a Tudor specialist, now a superb translator from French and Russian, had long been critical of the myths and silences of CP history. He was to leave the Communist Party for one of the Trotskyite groups.)

I recall frustrating meetings. Not that the historians were faced with a single co-ordinated line. Harry had admired Stalin and, like most old-time Party leaders, neither approved nor respected Khrushchev. He was a working-class leader of major stature with more charisma than any Labour Party leader except Bevan and, as an old boiler-maker, far more sense than Bevan of what the trade unions were about. His instincts and long experience made him sceptical of researchers on Party history. As a politician he knew that coroners' inquests on ancient quarrels, especially among comrades still living, tended to cause trouble. As an old Comintern hand, he realized that a lot of things could not be told and some had better stay untold. None of us could have known then that in 1937 Pollitt had intervened in Moscow in defence of a former Comintern representative in Britain and his wife, who had just been arrested – possibly going up even to Stalin. This extraordinarily brave and honest step had landed him in serious trouble in those days of paranoiac terror. The Comintern considered replacing him as leader of the Party, and the scenario of a possible show trial was sketched out. He had been saved from the worst, with the aid of a British passport, by Dimitrov, and perhaps by the stubborn refusal under torture of the Comintern's former organizational chief Osip Piatnitsky to make the required 'confession' implicating the designated victims.[9] Would it have done the movement any good if someone had published this episode in the Party's history, even if it undoubtedly reflects credit on it and especially on Pollitt himself ? He made it clear that in his view the only kind of history that helped the Party was the regimental kind – a record of battles fought, heroic deeds, sacrifices for the cause, red banners waved – to fill the comrades with pride and hope.

The Indo-Scandinavian intellectual Palme Dutt, one of those implausibly tall upper-class figures one occasionally meets among Bengalis, belonged through his mother to an eminent Swedish kindred – Olof Palme, the socialist premier assassinated in 1986, was another member.* Unlike Harry, Dutt was a natural intellectual as

* So was Professor Sven Ulric Palme of Stockholm University, who proposed me for my first honorary degree, crowned by a real laurel wreath, which our cleaning lady in Clapham later threw in the dustbin. (Swedish academia takes itself sufficiently seriously not to see anything out-of-the-way in a collection of middle-aged scholars in dark suits

well as an instinctive hardliner. Many years earlier the night he spent in my little house in Cambridge after a meeting had left me with a lasting admiration for his acute mind and a lasting conviction that he was not interested in truth, but used his intellect exclusively to justify and explicate the line of the moment, whatever it was. I now think I was unfair to the intellectual instincts still buried somewhere deeply inside him, or perhaps to his hope of posthumous recognition as something better than a gifted sophist in the service of authority. He granted that a genuine history of the Communist Party was essentially the history of its policies, that is to say of the changes in the line. And this must of course involve critical consideration, and, where necessary, negative judgement. But had the moment for this yet come? He doubted it.

And our old hero James Klugmann? He sat on the far right-hand corner of the table and said nothing. He knew we were right. If we did not produce a history of our Party, including the problematic bits, they would not go away. The history would simply be written by anti-communist scholars – and indeed, within less than two years such a history was written.[10] But he lacked what the great Bismarck once called '*Zivilcourage*', civilian as distinct from military courage. He knew what was right, but shied away from saying it in public. (In this he was like a rather different political figure, Isaiah Berlin, about the policies of the State of Israel.) He said nothing, and agreed to take on himself the task of writing an acceptable official history of the CPGB, which he knew to be impossible. Twelve years later he published a first volume which went up to 1924. My fairly savage demonstration that he had been wasting his time did not spoil our relations.[11] Before his death he published a second volume which went up to 1927, just before he would have to face the most controversial episodes. He would never have written more. In the meanwhile he edited *Marxism Today*, founded as a sop to critics who stayed in the Party in 1957, not exactly encouraging open discussion but not exactly discouraging it either.

and laurel wreaths conversing, with glasses of champagne, as in a modern-dress production of *Julius Caesar*.)

IV

When I consider what effect the Twentieth Congress had on the larger historical scene, I feel a little embarrassed to insist on the storms in our British teapot. Following strikes by Polish workers and demonstrations by Polish Catholics – a powerful combination even then – a new communist leadership took over in Poland under Vladislav Gomulka, purged in 1949 and only recently let out of prison. (Fortunately the Poles had evaded organizing the prearranged trials and executions that disfigured Bulgaria, Hungary and Czechoslovakia, and could therefore 'rehabilitate' living people rather than corpses.) The Chinese, then still part of the international movement, prevailed on the Russians to avoid military action. The Hungarian Revolution which immediately followed was less lucky, almost certainly because its new leadership went beyond what the Soviets could be expected to tolerate, by leaving the eastern military alliance of the Warsaw Pact and declaring their neutrality in the Cold War. None of this, least of all Khrushchev himself, impressed the Chinese, whose relations with the USSR then began to deteriorate sharply. Within a year or two the two communist giants had split. There were now two rival communist movements, though in fact almost all existing Communist Parties remained loyal to the Soviet centre. The so-called 'Maoism' of the 1960s created no real parties but small and squabbling activist sects. Even the most serious ostensibly pro-Chinese group, the Communist Party of India (Marxist), which seceded from the CPI, was not really Maoist. It carried with it such mass support as there was for communism in India, notably in the state of Kerala, where trucks decorated with the picture of Stalin are still to be seen on country roads, and West Bengal whose 68 million citizens the CPI(M) has now (2002) governed with solid popular support for decades.

In Britain the main effect of the great 1956 earthquake was that it made some 30,000 members of the Communist Party feel terrible, and scattered the forces of the small extreme left. Most of those who left the Party probably quietly dropped out of political activism. (So also did some who remained, like myself, convinced that, since the Party had not reformed itself, it had no long-term political future in the country.) Some joined the three main Trotskyist groups, although these grew not so much by transfers from the CP as by the general cracking of the world communist monolith and the loss of the CP's virtual monopoly in Marxism. The militant young now had the choice of lefts. Most of the critics from the Historians' Group, which did not effectively survive the crisis, groped for, or rather tried to build, some 'New Left' undefiled by the bad memories of Stalinism.

Saville and Thompson's *New Reasoner* (1957–9) became the home for most of the ex-CP intellectuals. Eventually it merged with the *Universities and Left Review* founded by the youngest former member of the Historians' Group, Raphael Samuel, together with another ex-communist, Gabriel Pearson, and two rather impressive unattached younger Oxford radicals, the Jamaican cultural theorist Stuart Hall and the Canadian philosopher Charles Taylor. The average age of the editors was twenty-four. From the early 1960s this uneasily merged *New Left Review* was taken over by a new team of young Oxford post-CP Marxists, the core of which came from the old Anglo-Irish milieu in the Irish Republic. Its chieftain was the remarkably able Perry Anderson (aged twenty-two), who also largely financed it. Unlike the little Britons of the older 'New Lefts', its interests were distinctly international, more theoretical, and much less tied to the labour movement or socialist politics. Although it moved into the orbit of the Fourth International it succeeded in establishing itself as the major periodical of a new generation of Anglo-Saxon Marxists.

In practical terms these 'New Lefts', although intellectually productive, were negligible. They did not reform the Labour Party (about which they remained ambivalent) or the Communist Party (as happened in Sweden). They produced neither new parties of the left (as in Denmark), nor lasting new organizations of significance, nor even individual national leaders. Thompson himself eventually became nationally famous as a spokesman for nuclear disarmament, but although CND (Campaign for Nuclear Disarmament), by far the most important movement of the post-1945 British left, was founded about the same time (1958) it had nothing to do with the crisis in the CP.

In some ways the brief episode of the Partisan Coffee House symbolizes the combination of ideology, impracticality and sentimental hope of those early post-1956 'New Lefts'. Like so much else it was the brainchild of Raphael Samuel who, with Edward Thompson, another and greater natural Romantic, emerged as the most original influence among the ex-CP intellectuals. Anyone who knew Raphael during an impassioned life cut short by cancer has exactly the same memories of him: a thin, enthusiastic face with mild, quick-witted eyes under a waterfall of eventually thinning dark hair, rushing from place to place alone, carrying with him wherever he went a vast collection of notes and files from which he struggled to retrieve the right piece of paper. All the work he ever published was part of an infinite all-embracing work-in-progress. He found it impossible to choose between the many marvels of the (overwhelmingly British) past, which is why he never got far with the doctoral thesis I was supposed to supervise – I think it was on Irish labour in Victorian London – or any other project. Not unnaturally for so ingrained an activist, he found his place in Ruskin College, where he taught trade unionists within earshot of the mostly uncaring dons of Oxford University. His history had neither structure nor limits. It was an unending and astonishingly learned perambulation round the wonderful landscapes, of memory and the lives of common people, with an occasional intellectual pounce suggested by some particularly fascinating sight glimpsed on the way.

This eager vagabond figure, the absolute negation of administrative and executive efficiency, carried inside him an explosive charge of energy, an endless capacity to generate ideas and initiatives, and above all a quite astonishing capacity to talk others into realizing them. The *Universities and Left Review* was one of them, the 'History Workshop' movement, origin of the *History Workshop Journal* (the most influential meeting-point of the post-Marxist historians of the left), was another. The Partisan Coffee House was a third. With two generations of Jewish revolutionary Marxists from Eastern Europe behind him, he dreamed of replacing the Stalinist authoritarianism of the Party with a free-wheeling creative mobilization of political minds, and what better centre for doing so than a café? Not one of those neo-baroque quick-consumption coffee bars which were then filling the side streets of the West End with the newly popular Gaggia Espresso machines, but a real Soho café, in which people could discuss theoretical issues, play chess, consume *strudel* and hold political meetings in a back room, as on the continent in the days before innocence was lost. The profits of the café would pay for the *Review* itself, whose offices would be above it. The Partisan would express both the new spirit of politics and the new spirit of the arts. It would be designed by the cutting-edge young architects of the moment, who were obviously going to be in sympathy with the project. I cannot remember whether jazz sessions were part of the dream. More likely folk sessions. To ensure its bona fides (and perhaps win the support of the older generation) some suitable left-wing personalities would preside over it. I let myself be talked into one of these directorships, against my better judgement. An eminent tweed-suited ex-CP architect with a house in Keats Grove was another. I cannot remember any of the others. Raph took not the slightest notice of any of us.

In retrospect it seems incredible that this hare-brained project got beyond the initial pitch. And yet it did. Even Raphael's genius as a salesman could not have raised the very substantial amount of money needed without the prior collapse of the Communist Party's so-called 'Business Branch', which had previously provided much of the CP's income. Until 1956 they had been a solid bastion of loyal orthodoxy who asked visiting Party speakers (actually, me, on the occasion I talked there) to address them on such subjects as 'The Paris Commune of 1871'. Now prosperous, some of them even very rich, the revelation of what had been done to Soviet Jews in the last Stalin years was too much for these overwhelmingly Jewish East Enders recruited to the Party during the anti-fascist era. Whoever backed the Partisan must have known that it was not a serious business proposition, but something about the youth and the sheer utopian confidence of Raph must have appealed to middle-aged men whose moral universe lay in ruins around them. Somehow Raph got the money, a house was bought or leased in Carlisle Street, Soho, within sight of Marx's old residence in Dean Street, and the Partisan Coffee House was installed.

It was a scheme designed for disaster. The then current fashion among architects preferred austere interiors looking like station waiting rooms. These attracted the more demoralized bums and the fringe hangers-on of Soho, who were neither welcomed in nor attracted by establishments with a more elaborate decor, especially at night, as well as the Metropolitan Police in search of drug-busts. The large expensive tables and square chunky seats were designed to encourage drafting thesis chapters and long debates on tactics, while minimizing the space for, and the rate of consumption of, income-generating customers. In any case, the management of the Partisan was not strong on checking cash receipts and keeping accounts. In short, though Raphael attempted to explain all this away to the increasingly gloomy directors, the place went out of business within two years. Only nostalgia and the need to maintain contact between the pre- and post-1956 generations of the left can explain why I found myself involved in this lunatic enterprise. And yet, it was not more predictably doomed than the various other political enterprises of those who left the Party in 1956–7. Like the Partisan Coffee House the political projects of the 'New Left' of 1956 are now a half-remembered footnote.

Intellectually 1956 left rather more behind – not least the remarkable impact of E. P. Thompson, who was to be recorded by the *Arts and Humanities Citations Index* (1976–83) as one of the 100 most-cited twentieth-century authors in any field covered by the *Index*. Before 1956 he was little known outside the CP, in which he had spent the years since returning from the war as a brilliant, handsome, passionate and oratorically gifted activist in Yorkshire, and his adult classes, whose members saw him as 'a tall, rangy sort of fellow' overloaded with nervous energy, explicating poems by William Blake.[12] For his original passion had been for literature rather than history as such, although he was marginally involved in the Historians' Group. It was 1956 that made him primarily into a historian. His later fame is essentially based on *The Making of the English Working Class* (1963), an erupting historical volcano of 848 pages which was immediately accepted as a major work even by the world of professional historians, and which captured young radical readers on both sides of the Atlantic overnight, and continental European sociologists and social historians not long after. And this in spite of its almost aggressively brief chronological span and narrowly English – not even British – subject matter. Escaping from the cage of the old Party orthodoxy, it allowed him as well to join a collective debate with other hitherto isolated thinkers of the left, old and new, also often rooted in the adult education movement, notably the other major figure of the first 'New Left,' the literary scholar Raymond Williams.

Edward was indeed a person of quite extraordinary gifts, not least the sort of palpable 'star quality', which led every eye to turn towards his increasingly craggy good looks whenever he was present on any scene. His 'work combined passion and intellect, the gifts of the poet, the narrator and the analyst. He was the only historian I knew who had not just talent, brilliance, erudition and the gift of writing, but . . . "genius in the traditional sense of the word" ',[13] and all the more obviously so since he fitted the Romantic image of the genius in looks, life and work – especially with the suitable landscape of the Welsh hills behind him.

In short, he was a man showered by the fairies at birth with all possible gifts except two. Nature had omitted to provide him with an in-built sub-editor and an in-built compass. And, with all his warmth, charm, humour and rage, it left him in some ways insecure and vulnerable. Like so many of his other works, *The Making* had begun as the first chapter of a short textbook on British labour history from 1790 to 1945, and had just got out of hand. Within a few years he suspended the remarkable studies of eighteenth-century society begun after *The Making* had turned him temporarily into an orthodox academic, which did not fit his style, to plunge into years of a theoretical struggle against the influence of a French Marxist, the late Louis Althusser, who inspired some of the brightest of the contemporary young leftists at that time. At the end of the seventies all his energy was diverted into the anti-nuclear movement, of which he became the national star. He never returned to history until he was too ill to complete his projects. He died in 1993 in his Worcestershire garden.

One could not fault a scholar for giving up writing for anti-nuclear campaigning in the early 1980s, but the Althusserian episode had no such justification. I told him at the time that it would be criminal to turn from his potentially epoch-making historical work to controverting a thinker who would be dead as an influence in another ten years' time. And indeed, Althusser was already getting close to his sell-by date in the French *Marxisant* milieu even then. Though he helped at the time to open theoretical debate on the left, he survives today not as a philosopher but chiefly by virtue of his tragic personal trajectory. He was a manic-depressive who was to kill his wife. But even this was not then predictable, although Althusser in his manic phases was already a somewhat disturbing experience. Shortly before the tragedy he came to London, officially for a seminar at University College, unofficially to mobilize support for some hare-brained stratospheric initiative in which he wanted to involve *Marxism Today* and myself. His host handed him over to us after a night's hospitality and Marlene looked after him for a morning, during which, inspired by our modest instrument, he insisted on ordering a grand piano from a local store for delivery to Paris. When picked up by his next caretaker he expressed an immediate interest in a Rolls-Royce (or maybe a Jaguar) from a car showroom in Mayfair which he insisted on visiting. It seemed clear that this brilliant mind was already accelerating the ride of his mental motor-bike round some wall of death to a fatal climax.

The truth is that Edward suffered bitterly from the failure of the 1956 'New Left'. None of the ex-communist generation expected much of the Labour Party. The new generation of the intellectual young, with whom he wanted desperately not to lose touch, were moving in new and, for him, undesirable directions. Had they his (and Raymond Williams's) feeling for the moral strength of the British working class? The new theoretically minded continental Marxism was not his, and he detected an 'irrationalist' 'revolting bourgeoisie' behind the new international student movement. He was on the outer margin of politics. It hurt him. I think this was one reason why he threw himself into the anti-nuclear movement with such passion.

Though I remained in the CP, unlike most of my friends in the Historians' Group, my situation as a man cut loose from his political moorings was not substantially different from theirs. In any case my relations with them remained the same. The Party asked me to change them, but I refused. They sensibly chose not to expel me, but that was their choice, not mine. Party membership no longer meant to me what it had since 1933. In practice I recycled myself from militant to sympathizer or fellow-traveller or, to put it another way, from effective membership of the British Communist Party to something like spiritual membership of the Italian CP, which fitted my ideas of communism rather better. (The Italian CP returned my sympathies.)

In any case, the individual political activities of none of us mattered much any more. We had influence as teachers, as scholars, as political writers or at best 'public intellectuals', and for this – at least in Britain – our membership of Party or organization was irrelevant, except to people who had strong a priori feelings about the CP. If we maintained or acquired influence among the left-wing young, it was because our left-wing past and our present Marxism or commitment to radical scholarship gave us what is today called 'street cred', because we wrote about important matters and because they liked what we wrote. From the point of view of this reading public, old or young, the political and ideological differences between Thompson, Raymond Williams and Hobsbawm were less important than that all three belonged to the small minority of 'names' – intellectually reputable thinkers and writers – flagged as belonging to the left.

Still, the question remains why, unlike many of my friends, and however much of a dissident, I stayed in the Party. In the course of time I have had to answer this question a number of times. I have been asked it by almost every journalist who has ever interviewed me, for the quickest way of identifying a personality in our media-saturated society is by one or two unique peculiarities: mine are being a professor who likes jazz and who remained in the Communist Party longer than most. I have given substantially the same answer at varying length.[14] It represents my justification in subsequent decades of remaining in the Party, and not necessarily what I felt at the time. It is impossible to reconstruct those feelings now, although, then as later, I was strongly repelled by the idea of being in the company of those ex-communists who turned into fanatical anti-communists, because they could free themselves from the service of 'The God that Failed' only by turning him into Satan. There were plenty of them about in the Cold War era.

In retrospect, and seeing the person I was in 1956 as a historian rather than an autobiographer, I think two things explain why I stayed in the Party, though, obviously, considering leaving it. I did not come into communism as a young Briton in England, but as a central European in the collapsing Weimar Republic. And I came into it when being a communist meant not simply fighting fascism but the world revolution. I still belong to the tail-end of the first generation of communists, the ones for whom the October Revolution was the central point of reference in the political universe.

The difference in background and life history was real enough. It had been obvious to me and to others even within the Party. No intellectual brought up in Britain could become a communist with the same sense as a central European of

> the day the heavens were falling
> the hour the earth's foundations fled

because, with all its problems, this was simply not the situation in the Britain of the 1930s. Yet in some ways, having become a communist before 1935 was even more significant. Politically, having actually joined a Communist Party in 1936, I belong to the era of anti-fascist unity and the Popular Front. It continues to determine my strategic thinking in politics to this day. But emotionally, as one converted as a teenager in the Berlin of 1932, I belonged to the generation tied by an almost unbreakable umbilical cord to hope of the world revolution, and of its original home, the October Revolution, however sceptical or critical of the USSR. For someone who joined the movement where I came from and when I did, it was quite simply more difficult to break with the Party than for those who came later and from elsewhere. In the last analysis I suspect that this was why I allowed myself to stay. Nobody forced me out and the reasons for going were not quite strong enough.

But – and here I speak as autobiographer rather than historian – let me not forget a private emotion: pride. Losing the handicap of Party membership would improve my career prospects, not least in the USA. It would have been easy to slip out quietly. But I could prove myself to myself by succeeding as a known communist – whatever 'success' meant – in spite of that handicap, and in the middle of the Cold War. I do not defend this form of egoism, but neither can I deny its force. So I stayed.

13

Watershed

Some moments in history – the outbreaks of the two world wars, for instance – are recognizably catastrophic, like earthquakes or volcanic eruptions. There are similar moments in private life, or at all events, as earlier chapters show, there have been such moments in mine. However, if we want to stay with geological similes, there are other moments that can best be compared with watersheds. Nothing very obvious or dramatic seems to be happening, but after you have crossed an otherwise nondescript bit of territory you notice that you have left an epoch in history, or in your own life, behind. The years on either side of 1960 – my early and middle forties – formed such a watershed in my life. Perhaps also in the social and cultural history of the western world. Certainly of Britain.[1] This seems to be a good moment to break my long walk through the short twentieth century for a pause to view the landscape.

The second half of the 1950s forms a curious interim in my life. After the end of my King's Fellowship I moved back to a permanent base in Bloomsbury, a large, partly dark flat full of books and records, overlooking Torrington Place, which, until my marriage in 1962, I successively shared with a series of communist or ex-CP friends: Louis Marks and Henry Collins of the Historians' Group, the old Marxist literary critic Alick West and the Spanish refugee Vicente Girbau. Since it was central and had enough spare capacity, it also attracted out-of-town and metropolitan overnight visitors and other temporary attachments. It was, to be honest, much more fun than living in a Cambridge college, even though I lived through the worst periods of the crisis of communism and the tearing of political roots there. It had the additional advantage of being so close to Birkbeck that I could, if necessary, go home between lectures. London was a good place to live in. This was the setting in which I lived through the watershed.

219

That my personal and professional life changed in these years is obvious enough. I met a Viennese-born girl in an ocelot coat in a setting of world politics. We fell in love. She had recently returned from the United Nations' vain attempt to intervene in the Congo, I was about to go to Castro's Havana, and Marlene and I married during the Cuban missile crisis of 1962. It was three years after publishing my first books, and a few weeks before *The Age of Revolution, 1789–1848*. Professionally, I was beginning to acquire some international reputation, and therefore to travel outside what had been my habitual range in the 1950s, France, the Iberian Peninsula and Italy. In the 1960s I began my academic trips to the USA and Cuba, I discovered and started to explore Latin America, found myself in Israel and India, and returned to the Mitteleuropa I had not seen since childhood. What is more, I had begun to notice that I no longer lived in the constant expectation of seismic catastrophe as Mitteleuropeans had done in the days of my youth. I began to notice – I do not recall exactly when – that I was operating in a time-frame of decades rather than years or even, as before 1945, months. I did not consciously abandon the basic precautions of the potential refugee which people of my kind learned to observe, whether as Jews or as Reds, against the sudden hazards of economic and political life between the wars: a valid passport, enough immediately available money to buy a ticket to the chosen country of refuge at a moment's notice, a way of life that permitted quick departures and a rough idea of what to take, if one had to go. In fact, when, shortly after marrying Marlene, and in the middle of the Cuban missile crisis of October 1962, I had to go abroad, I reacted accordingly. I made some financial arrangements, fixed a provisional appointment with Marlene in Buenos Aires, where I was due to be in a week or two, in case things began to look really drastic, and left her enough money for the fare. Nevertheless, though it was quite evident that the Cuban missile crisis was a matter of global life and death, I cannot actually have expected nuclear world war to break out. Had I done so, I suppose I should, logically, have taken Marlene with me immediately, at least to get both of us out of the immediate firing-line. If the worst came to the worst, South America was the least likely battlefield. I already found myself operating on the assumption that the danger to the world came not from the global ambitions or aggressiveness of the USA (the USSR was too weak to have them) but the risks inherent in politicians and generals on both sides playing a game with nuclear bowls which they knew it would be suicide to use – but which might easily slip out of control. In fact we now know that this was precisely the lesson which Kennedy and Khrushchev, neither of whom wanted a war, drew from the Cuban missile crisis in 1962. In short, as far as I was concerned, from 1960 on the Cold War was not over, but it had become dramatically less dangerous.

As for long-term planning, anyone who enters upon marriage can no longer avoid it even if he or she wanted to. I had already been forced to consider the problem a couple of years earlier, when a child was impending from an earlier relationship – my children's half-brother Joshua – and only the refusal of the woman concerned to leave her husband had removed him from my life into others' lives. By the middle of the 1960s I was the father of Andy and Julia, the first-time owner of a small car in which I transported them to a holiday cottage in North Wales and first-time house-owner of a large house in an as yet very incompletely gentrified part of Clapham, divided in two by an austere architect friend, which Marlene and I had bought jointly with the taciturn Alan Sillitoe and his wife, the poet Ruth Fainlight. 'Has he won the pools or something?' the local newsagent asked Marlene, since in those days of full employment he could not understand what an obviously healthy and respectable-looking youngish fellow was doing not going out to work in the morning and coming back of an evening like other men. Though Alan was as much of a workaholic as most writers, this guess was not totally off target: he had, after all, written *Saturday Night and Sunday Morning* and *The Loneliness of the Long Distance Runner*, which, thanks to their merits and the enormous growth of secondary education, became two of those contemporary classics which, set for O-level and A-level examinations, generate a lasting flow of royalties. He could afford to live off his books, and could avoid the treadmill of freelance journalism. I, though writing at home, did conform to type, for I went to work at Birkbeck on the Northern Line and came back from there late at night. On the other hand, I remained peculiar, inasmuch as I showed no enthusiasm for garden-ing, and, unlike the Caribbean electricians and transport workers in the short street that led to the Wandsworth Road outside our front door, I did not spend Sunday mornings cleaning our car.

Clearly I was well on the way to the everyday life of academic and middle-class respectability. At this point, except for travel, nothing much happens any longer to the subject of autobiography except inside his or her head or in other people's heads. This is also true for that matter of the subjects of biography, as generations of the writers of intellectuals' lives have learned to their cost. However towering the achievement of Charles Darwin, once he returned from the voyage of the *Beagle* and married, there is not much more to be said about the material events in his life for his last forty years than that 'he passed his time at Down, Kent, as a country gentleman'[2] and to speculate about the reasons for his poor health. The life of the respectable academic is not full of professional drama, or rather its dramas, like those of office politics, are of interest only to those directly involved in them. Again, though there is plenty of drama in family life, especially when parents and teenage children confront each other, third parties, such as the readers of biographies, are usually less gripped by the drama of life inside other families than their own. The scenario is familiar. So the years around 1960 form a watershed not only in my life, but in the shape of this autobiography.

But private lives are embedded in the wider circumstances of history. The most powerful of these was the unexpected good fortune of the age. It crept up on my generation and took us unawares, especially the socialists among us who were unprepared to welcome an era of spectacular capitalist success. By the early 1960s it became hard not to notice it. I cannot say that we recognized it as what I have called 'The Golden Age' in my *Age of Extremes*. That became possible only after 1973, when it was over. Like everyone else, historians are best at being wise after the event. Nevertheless, by the early 1960s it had become evident to my generation in Britain, that is to say the ordinary run of those who had come out of the war in their twenties, that we were living far better than we had ever expected to in the 1930s. If we belonged to the social strata whose male members expected to have 'careers' rather than just 'go to work' (at that time this was not yet a game played much by women), we discovered that we were doing rather better, sometimes considerably better, than our parents, especially if we had passed more examinations than they had. True, this did not apply to two sections of our generation: those whose careers had reached their peak during the war, and who therefore looked back with nostalgia from the comparative lowlands of postwar civilian life, and the members of the established upper strata, whose parents, as a group, already enjoyed as much wealth, privilege, power or professional distinction as their children could expect to inherit or achieve. Indeed, they might see themselves as also-rans, if they went into the fields in which their fathers had been unusually successful – politics, science, the old professions, or whatever. Who has not been sorry for the political son overshadowed by his father – Winston and Randolph Churchill are the classic example – or the decent but run-of-the-mill natural scientist sons of FRS or Nobel Prize fathers? Like any academic with a Cambridge background, I have known a few.

But for most of us postwar life was an escalator which, without any special effort, took us higher than we had ever expected to be. Even people like myself, whose career progress was unusually retarded by the Cold War, moved along it. Of course this was partly due to my historical luck in entering the academic profession at a time when it was still fairly small, its status was high, and it was consequently quite well paid by the standards the Benthamite, Liberal and Fabian reformers had established for the public service in Victorian and Edwardian days. For though, unlike in other European countries, university teachers were not civil servants, they were under the wing of the state, which provided the funds for the collective five-year forward planning of the universities, but kept at arm's length. So long as the profession remained small, and free market ideology was held at bay, it was understood that the salary, like the status, of the averagely successful lecturer should take him or her to the level equivalent to an averagely successful civil servant in the administrative grade: not wealth beyond the dreams of avarice, but a decent middle-class existence. The costs were still modest, at least for those of progressive views who wanted to send their children to state schools, and could as yet see no reason for not doing so. The welfare state benefited the middle classes relatively more than the workers. Those were the days when, largely for reasons of principle – and not yet discouraged by the experience of the National Health Service in practice – people like me refused to take out medical insurance. The price of houses remained within reach until the boom of the early 1970s, and the rise in their value gave us a natural bonus. Just before they began their move towards the stratosphere, it was possible to buy a freehold house in Hampstead for just under £20,000 gross, or, allowing for the profit on the sale of the previous house, £7,000 net. For those who married and had children young, there were no doubt a few years of relative tightness, holidays on caravan sites and scrabbling for extra income from schools examinations and the like, but a previously childless academic like myself, halfway up the university scale, who remarried in his forties, had no real problem in maintaining a family. Indeed, I cannot recall a time when my bank account was overdrawn. Such problems as arose were eventually eased by rising earnings from royalties and other literary activities, but around 1960 these were still very marginal additions to my income.

The generations who had become adults before the war could compare their postwar lives to those of their parents, or their own pre-war expectations. It was not so easy for them to see, especially when already facing the unchanging imperatives of bringing up a family, that their situation in the new 'affluent society' of the West was different in kind as well as in degree from the past. After all, the permanent household chores were not fundamentally changed but only made easier by new technology. Once married, earning a living, looking after children, house and garden, the washing and washing-up still filled most of a couple's time and thinking. Only the young and mobile could recognize, and utilize, all the possibilities of a society that for the first time gave them enough money to buy what they wanted, enough time to do what they wanted, or that made them independent of the family in other ways. Youth was the name of the secret ingredient that revolutionized consumer society, and western culture. This is dramatically evident in the rise of rock and roll, a music which depends almost exclusively on customers in their teens or early twenties, or those once converted to this music at that age. US record sales grew from $277 million in 1955, the birth-year of rock and roll, to more than $2,000 million in 1973, of which 75–80 per cent represented rock music and similar sounds.

I certainly do not belong to the rock generation. Nevertheless, I was lucky enough to be present at, and to recognize, the birth of that generation in Britain. For, as it happens, in this country a form of jazz created a bridge between the older forms of youthful pop music and the rock revolution. From 1955, when my King's Fellowship ran out and I returned to live permanently in London, it happened that I found myself professionally involved in the affairs of jazz. Since I now faced paying rent in London, having lived gratis in a Cambridge college, I thought of a way of earning some extra income. It was about this time that the London cultural establishment, stung by the challenge of the so-called 'angry young men' of the 1950s, thought it advisable to pay attention to jazz, for which they advertised their passion. The *Observer* had hired one of them, Kingsley Amis, as a jazz critic. He was already on the way from left-wing youth to conservative old age, but still quite far from the role of reactionary club-bar buffer into which he was later to settle. Having felt inferior to erudite jazz experts since the early 1930s, I knew very well that I was quite unqualified to be one, but it seemed to me that I understood at least as much about the subject as Kingsley Amis and had been familiar with it much longer. I therefore suggested to Norman Mackenzie, an ex-comrade from LSE days, then working on the *New Statesman and Nation*, that they also needed a jazz critic. The journal was in its glory days under its great editor Kingsley Martin, who neither knew nor cared about jazz, but could see that one had to keep up with this new cultural fashion, at least by a monthly column. He explained to me that in writing for the paper I should bear in mind its ideal typical reader, a male civil servant in his forties, and handed me over to the then commander of the cultural half of the mag, the admirable Janet Adam Smith, who knew almost everything about literature and mountain climbing, and a very great deal about the rest of the arts, but not about jazz. Because I wanted to keep the personalities of the university teacher and the jazz critic apart, for the next ten years or so I wrote under the pseudonym Francis Newton, after Frankie Newton, one of the few jazz-players known to have been a communist, an excellent but not superstar trumpeter who played with Billie Holiday on the great Commodore Records session that produced 'Strange Fruit'.

Jazz is not just 'a certain type of music' but 'a remarkable aspect of the society in which we live',[3] not to mention a part of the entertainment industry. Besides, relatively few readers of the *New*

Statesman were likely to go to jazz gigs or buy Thelonious Monk, although I discovered, to my intense pleasure, that the second half of the fifties was a new golden age for the music, whose American stars were now coming to Britain, after being kept out of our island for twenty years by a union dispute. I therefore wrote not only as a reviewer of concerts, records and books but as a historian and reporter. What is more, pretty soon I found myself in contact (probably through my cousin Denis) with the small but culturally hip publishing house of McGibbon and Kee, then financed by a moody millionaire supporter of the Labour Party, Howard Samuel, which had already published books by what was probably the only Old Etonian jazz band leader, Humphrey Lyttelton, and by the difficult, lonely and haunted social explorer of 1950s London, Colin Mac-Innes, connoisseur of, and guide to, the new black London and the beginnings of the music-saturated teenage culture. They wanted me to write a book about jazz. It appeared as *The Jazz Scene* in 1959, the same year as my first history book, and was well received though it did not make much money.[4] It encouraged me to explore the scene more systematically. This was not hard, for at least some of the jazz aficionados of the early 1930s had gone into the music business as agents or promoters, not least cousin Denis, who was establishing himself as probably the leading British record producer in the field of indigenous jazz and ethnic music. Indeed, his fortunes rose with those of the artists he recorded, such as Lonnie Donegan, whose 'Rock Island Line' (a jailhouse song originally recorded by the great Leadbelly) exploded into the big time in the spring of 1956. Fortunately also I was at the time unmarried and, teaching in an evening college which did not lecture until six p.m., I could adapt to the rhythm of life of the late-sleeping night people who make up the entertainment scene. Also I lived in Bloomsbury, within ten minutes' walk of any action anywhere in the West End. So I found myself dropping without difficulty into my habitual role of 'participant observer' or *kibitzer*.

The jazz people were by no means teenagers. And yet both my contemporary sketch of the public for 'trad jazz' and 'skiffle' and Roger Mayne's photographs for the first edition of *The Jazz Scene* show clearly that what the music they made inspired was essentially a somewhat older children's crusade. They were part of the youth

1. Three sisters Grün: (*left to right*) Mimi, Nelly, Gretl (Vienna, 1912)

2. Three brothers Hobsbaum: (*left to right*) Percy, Ernest,
Sidney (Vienna, early 1920s)

3. Nelly and Percy Hobsbaum in Egypt, *c.*1917

4. Second mother: Aunt Gretl (England, *c.* 1934)

5. Mother, Nancy, cousin Peter, EH outside alpine TB sanatorium (Austria, 1930)

6. Camping in England with Ronnie Hobsbaum (1935)

7. School-leaving photograph (sans EH) of my class at the
Prinz-Heinrichs-Gymnasium (Berlin, 1936)

8. Paris 1936: the Popular Front government celebrates Bastille Day. EH (*top right*) and uncle Sidney (*centre*) on French Socialist Party newsreel truck

9. Paris 1937: world student conference with Spanish Civil War posters. EH (*seated*) interpreting

10. Red Cambridge: James Klugmann *(top row, centre of window)* with Cambridge helpers and international delegates to Congress of World Student Assembly (Paris, August 1939). To his right are Pieter Keuneman (Sri Lanka) and P. N. Haksar (India)

11. Red Cambridge: the photo of John Cornford (Cambridge 1915–Spain 1936) which stood on so many of our mantelpieces

12. Moscow 1954: British Communist historians' delegation under portraits of Stalin and Lenin. (*left side, left to right*) Christopher Hill, A. L. Morton, interpreter, EH

13. USSR 1954: historians at Zagorsk. (*second left to right*) Hill, Morton, interpreter, EH)

PICTURE DOCUMENTARY

THE DAY OF MASS ARREST

The police warning is defied. Hundreds of Bertrand Russell's supporters flock to Trafalgar-square and get arrested, to demonstrate against Britain taking part in preparations for nuclear defence. Herald photographers record the drama of the day.

1 Deadline is 5 p.m. In and around Trafalgar-square 4,000 police are on duty. Supporters of the passive resistance campaign, organised by the Committee of 100, sit in the roadway. Their purpose: to be arrested for obstruction, go to court and by their very numbers focus attention on their policy of unilateral disarmament for Britain. Over 5,000 people are in the Square. The police link arms as a wall between the squatters and those behind—many just onlookers, many sympathisers. Bertrand Russell hears the news in prison.

2 Canon John Collins, chairman of the Campaign for Nuclear Disarmament, does not support the sit-down. He comes as an observer but is arrested.

3 A squatter goes limp as police take him away. He neither resists nor helps them as they obey their orders. He'd be disappointed if they hadn't taken him. On the pavement some onlookers applaud.

4 Actress Vanessa Redgrave (current success: "The Taming of the Shrew") gets what she squatted three-and-a-half hours for. She's a leader of the protest.

How to be over 60 — and still fit as a fiddle!

Many of today's health problems can be traced directly to deficiencies in our modern diet. Vital health salts are missing from much of today's devitalised food, and often the natural goodness of our meals is destroyed by modern cooking.

Bemax is enriched wheat-germ—richest natural source of the vital health salts and important vitamins. A simple way to keep your health, strength and energy.

Next day, for the trouble "One to we work by and sell fit as a fiddle", to Vitamin B included, village-laid. Upper Mill, London, 9d.

Keep your health, strength and energy with

BEMAX every day

14. Trafalgar Square 1961: sit-down demonstration against nuclear arms (*Daily Herald*, 18 September 1961)

15. Trafalgar Square 1961: historian among policemen

culture that was by then becoming sufficiently visible for those of us who roamed on its outskirts for whatever reason to recognize its existence, although only someone like Colin MacInnes with a special private affinity for adolescent rebellion and independence, could tune in on its wavelength. Nevertheless, apart from a distinct relaxation of female sexual conventions in the vicinity of musicians and singers, it had not yet become married to a counter-culture. That did not happen, at least in Britain, until the 1960s.

Much of what symbolized the youth counter-culture of the 1960s was nevertheless to be taken over from the old jazz scene – notably drugs and the patterns of life of what I once described as 'the floating, nomadic community of professional black [and white] musicians living on the self-contained and self-sufficient little islands of the popular entertainers and other night people', the places where the day people got rid of their inhibitions after dark. This was not necessarily a counter-culture in the later sense, for jazz musicians had an almost limitless toleration for any variant of human behaviour, but did not usually make a manifesto of it. The nearest thing to a counter-culture around the jazz scene was to be found on its fringes and among its hangers-on or outside admirers, as among the musicians' girlfriends on the game who could earn a few hundred pounds in a few hours on the street – good money in the 1950s – and take off for a quick holiday in Morocco, among the conscious rejecters of traditional middle-class conventions, such as Ken Tynan, or among the middle-aged bourgeois insiders asserting outsider status by drinking sessions in the watering-hole of the painter Francis Bacon, Muriel Belcher's Colony Club in Frith Street, Soho. Not that Muriel's mostly homosexual crowd was particularly jazz-oriented, although I was introduced into this shabby first-floor room by an admiring reviewer of *The Jazz Scene*, and was quite likely to meet Colin MacInnes there, who praised jazz but did not understand it, and George Melly, who sang it and did. Melly was part of a fringe of the British jazz scene made up of refugees from middle-class respectability or people who combined their music with activities in the world of words and images. To the fans he was known as a self-parodying blues singer close to a music-hall act, as Wally Fawkes was known as a clarinet player. In the straight world both were much better known as the joint creators of a highly popular strip-cartoon which gently satirized the recognizable members of what was not yet known as the media world.

The third change, this one more readily recognized, was the change in the political or ideological mood after 1956. I can now see that the new factor that brought it about was the end of empires, but in Britain this did not become clear until the 1960s.

The Cold War remained, but, outside western governments, the public's commitment to an emotional anti-communism began to decline. However much it was denounced, from 1960 the Berlin Wall stabilized the frontier between superpower empires in Europe, neither of which was seriously expected to cross it. We still lived under the black cloud of nuclear apocalypse. It came close in the Cuban missile crisis of 1962 and in 1963 Stanley Kubrick produced its definitive version, the film *Doctor Strangelove* – but by then it could already be played for laughs, however black. But CND, the new Campaign for (unilateral British) Nuclear Disarmament (1959), by far the largest public mobilization of the British left, was not intended to, and plainly could not, affect the USA's and the USSR's nuclear arms race, although many Britons were sincerely moved by the idea of setting a good moral example to the world. It was about keeping out of the Cold War or, perhaps more exactly, about getting Britain used to no longer being a great power and a global empire. (The argument that Britain's own nuclear capability was necessary to deter a Soviet attack made no sense, especially as we now know that the bomb had originally been constructed by British governments to maintain their status and independence against the USA rather than to frighten Moscow.)

However, looking back, it is clear that what increasingly shaped the post-1956 politics of the left was a by-product of decolonization and, certainly in Britain, of the mass immigration from the Caribbean parts of the old empire. The crisis of the Fourth Republic in France had little to do with the Cold War, and everything to do with the liberation struggle of the Algerians. I still recall a 1958 mass meeting in Friends' House to protest against the military coup which ended it, addressed by the red-haired and impassioned journalist Paul Johnson, then a maverick left-wing Catholic, who denounced General de Gaulle as the next fascist dictator. It was largely the shocking and widely publicized French use of torture in Algeria that turned

Amnesty International (1961), into a western international campaigning body not primarily directed against eastern abuses of human rights.

With the American civil rights movements and the influx of coloured immigrants to Britain, racism became a far more central theme on the left than it had been. Through jazz I found myself associated with an early anti-racist campaign in Britain after the so-called Notting Hill (actually Notting Dale) race riots of 1958, the so-called 'Stars Campaign for Interracial Friendship' (SCIF), which was not so much a real political operation (though Colin MacInnes went about the area, a favourite stamping ground of his, posting its news-sheet through letter boxes) as an example of the modern media operation which, like others of its kind, fizzled out after a few months of rather successful publicity. It did indeed mobilize the 'stars', mainly of jazz – most of the big British names were there, Johnny Dankworth and Cleo Laine, Humphrey Lyttelton and Chris Barber, as well as some pop stars – but its strength lay in the operators who could get stories into the press and programmes on to television, and produced newsworthy ideas such as the televised interracial children's Christmas party of 1958. While it lasted, it enjoyed the invaluable help of the remarkably able and admirable Claudia Jones, a US Communist Party functionary born in the West Indies and expelled as a 'non-citizen' from the USA in the witch-hunt days, who did her best, with indifferent success, to bring some Party efficiency and some political structure into the Caribbean immigration in West London and to get adequate backing for her efforts from the British CP. An impressive woman, she has been unjustly forgotten, except perhaps as one of the inspirations behind what has become the annual, and no longer political, Notting Hill Carnival.

Third World passions did not become a major inspiration for the left until the 1960s, and, incidentally, weaken the hold of the Cold War crusading ideologists on western liberals and social democrats. Yet by the end of the 1950s the Cuban Revolution was already in power, about to add a new image to the iconography of world revolution, and to turn the USA into a highly visible Goliath facing the defiance of a bearded young David. In 1961 the reaction to the attempted Bay of Pigs invasion was immediate – as immediate as the reaction to the Soviet invasion of Hungary had been in

1956 – and it extended far beyond the usual parties, signers of petitions, and indeed the usual range of protesters. Ken Tynan telephoned me desperately the morning the news came through: something must be done! As soon as possible. How could we set about it? Though a genuine man of the left, whose political sincerity both Marlene and I always defended against those who accused him of posing, he was far from the usual member of the 'stage army of the good'. Had he been, he would have known what to do himself. When we had set up the usual committee, rounded up the usual suspects for letters of protest, and organized a march to Hyde Park – I cannot for the life of me remember whom we had as speakers – I recall noting with agreeable surprise how unlike the usual left-wing demo this one was, at least in appearance. The call to defend Fidel Castro, through Tynan, or perhaps more likely Tynan's Man Friday Clive Goodwin, actor, agent and activist, had mobilized a remarkable mass of younger theatrical males and females, and young women from the fashion agencies. It was the best-looking political occasion I can remember, a wonderful sight, and all the happier since we knew by then that the American invasion had been defeated.

So, almost without noticing, I found myself – and the world – slipping into a new mood as the 1950s turned into the 1960s. Even politically, although after 1956 I had neither decided to leave the CP nor been expelled, I no longer found myself as isolated as Party members had once been. Party labels were no longer decisive for those who supported the new political campaigns – anti-nuclear, anti-imperial, anti-racist or whatever. When some communist historians founded a new historical journal, *Past & Present*, in 1952, about as bad a time in the Cold War as can be imagined, we deliberately planned it not as a Marxist journal, but as a common platform for a 'popular front' of historians, to be judged not by the badge in the author's ideological buttonhole, but by the contents of their articles. We desperately wanted to broaden the base of our editorial board, which at the start was naturally dominated by Party members, since only the rare, usually indigenous, radical historian with a safe academic base, such as A. H. M. Jones, the ancient historian from Cambridge, had the courage to sit at the same table as the bolsheviks. The eminent art historian Rudolf Wittkower was actually warned not to accept our invitation and it was another ten years before Moses Finley, the victim of US McCarthyism welcomed in Cambridge, was prepared to write for us. We were equally keen to extend the range of our contributors. For several years we failed in the first task, although, thanks to our excellent reputation among younger academics, we soon did better on the second. In 1958 we succeeded. A group of non-Marxist historians of subsequent eminence, led by Lawrence Stone, shortly about to go to Princeton, and the present Sir John Elliott, later Regius Professor at Oxford, who had sympathized with our objectives but until then had found it impossible formally to join the former red establishment, offered to join us collectively on condition that we dropped the ideologically suspect phrase 'a journal of scientific history' from our masthead. It was a cheap price to pay. They did not ask us about our political opinions – actually orthodox communists were no longer easy to find on the board – we did not enquire into theirs, and no ideological problems have ever arisen on its board since then. Even the Institute of Historical Research, which had steadfastly refused to include the journal in its library, relented.

So both my personal life became in some sense 'normal' and (in spite of the rhetoric to the contrary) the world I lived in was – or at least looked like – a less insecure and provisional place, and was certainly a more prosperous one. The first observation was undeniable, even though my academic career was still taking its time to develop. I was not to get my chair, or the usual marks of official recognition – academies, the first honorary degrees – until the 1970s, when I was well into my fifties. In retrospect I can see this was a stroke of luck, for nothing is worse for a career than to reach the peak too soon and face the long march along the flat plateau of the establishment or, even worse, the lengthening distance between present achievement and the work that once made one's reputation. Just because I had started late, and been held up for so many years, I continued to have better things to look forward to at an age when others could expect only to postpone decline.

As for the world, we knew quite well that its stability was only apparent, even though its extraordinary economic and technological leap forward was plain. Nevertheless, for those of us lucky enough to live in central and western Europe, it was not an illusion. We may not have fully recognized our good fortune yet, but we lived in the lands of the blessed: a region without war, without the prospect or fear of social upheaval, in which most people enjoyed a life of wealth, a range of choices in life and leisure, and a degree of social security beyond the reach of all but the very rich in our parents' generation, and beyond even the dreams of the poor. Ours was a better place to live in than any other part of the world.

I was soon to discover that this could not be said of other parts of the globe. Nor, as the 1960s were soon to show, did it satisfy the inhabitants of the lands of the blessed.

14

Under Cnicht

In 1961, shortly after sitting down with Bertrand Russell and perhaps 12,000 others, on a famous anti-nuclear occasion in Trafalgar Square, fortunately unarrested by the police, I was told by my friend and brother-Apostle Robin Gandy that I looked a bit stressed, and that he thought a few days with him in North Wales would do me good. He had a small, almost aggressively primitive cottage there, next to a dying chapel, where, between hill walks and rock scrambles, he pondered the problems of mathematical logic. In those days, before the wonderful network of small rural railway lines in Britain had been destroyed, it was still possible to travel gently between trees through the heartlands of central Wales and, once the coast was reached, by a not entirely misnamed Cambrian Coast Express to Penrhyndeudraeth in what was still for Anglophones the county of Merioneth, the last area in the British Isles that still voted to ban the sale or public consumption of alcohol on the Lord's day. There Robin met me on his motorbike, in his habitual black leather gear, to save me a few miles' trudge across the coastal ridge and the table-flat plain (The Traeth) that had been a sea inlet until it was drained in the early nineteenth century by the seawall built by a Mr Maddocks, after whom the new port of Portmadoc was to be named. The enterprise had been much admired by progressive visitors, among them the poet Shelley. Before that, ships had been able to sail to the foot of the mountains, using the dramatic and unmistakable triangle of Cnicht (The Knight) as a landmark. The name suggests that it reminded them of a medieval helmet. Where the road left the Traeth and started to climb gently to the high Croesor valley just below Cnicht was the frontier of Clough's kingdom. There I and, when I remarried, Marlene and the children, would spend most of our holidays for the next quarter of a century.

The ruler, indeed the maker, of this kingdom, Clough Williams-Ellis, was a tall, straight, affable, roman-nosed figure, invariably in a tweed jacket, breeches and yellow stockings – he was the only man to wear this gear on his visits to the Athenaeum – by then in his later seventies. The best way to introduce him to a generation for whom the Britain he came from is as alien as Tolstoy's Russia, is to say that when he married during the First World War, his fellow-officers asked him what he wanted for a wedding present. He wanted to build a folly – a fragment of a mock medieval fortress with a view of the sea. It was built. One got to it through an iron gate, painted in 'Clough's green', the unmistakable colour of iron and woodwork in Clough's kingdom, opposite the main entrance to his house, Plas Brondanw, a small ancient pile with a wonderful formal garden opening on a vista of the peak of Snowdon framed by Clough's characteristic urns and arches. From the gate one strolled a couple of hundred yards along a gently rising avenue whose trees he had also planted. (Trees were one of his many passions. He was so outraged at the proposal to sell off for property development the wonderful Grand Avenue of trees which led to the great house of Stowe, which he was engaged in turning into a public school, that he bought it himself and saw to it that it was preserved. It was perhaps his major contribution to the project.) Our children loved to play in the tower, climbing the stairs that went nowhere except to a view over the sea and a damp stretch of moorland beyond which, a few miles away, one saw the Big and Little Moelwyn, the other two mountains of the kingdom, after which Clough had named his son, who had not returned from the war. It had once served as a set for a movie about China. Clough was enormously pleased about this. It was not romantic absurdity as such that he loved, but play, not to mention celebrities. Besides, it is almost certain that the film company had come to Merioneth not because a small piece of it could be made to look more Chinese than any other part of Great Britain, but because star and crew could stay at the best-known of Clough's creations, the greatest of his follies, Portmeirion. This was and remains a life-size quasi-baroque toy-town pretending to be on the Italian Riviera, colours and all, which suddenly emerges from rhododendron-covered rocks across the grey waters of the wide shallow estuary that leads into Cardigan Bay. He paid for its constant extension by turning part of it into the sort of hotel and holiday village which slightly bohemian showbusiness people found irresistible (with fireworks rather than golf courses), and eventually, perhaps more reluctantly, with the money spent by day trippers. (Friends of the family were let in free.) Nothing about Portmeirion was or is quite real – although it was filled with authentic statues and bits of architectural decor saved by Clough from destruction – but everything represented daydreams, not, however, without the potential for nightmares. It was later chosen as the setting for a cult British television series, *The Prisoner*, in which a Kafkaesque victim found he could not escape from an environment full equally of charm and menace. Neither could the makers of the series, which therefore came to a sudden stop after seventeen episodes. It is still repeated from time to time for a large community of aficionados.

In some ways Clough, proud of his standing as a professional architect, also became the victim of the environment he had created and could not escape. As the younger son of a landowning family, he had to earn a living, and architecture, his passion from childhood, fitted both his background and his inclinations. He had only one term's formal training. What he lacked in professional qualifications, he made up for in country roots, informed enthusiasm and the sort of contacts a handsome and charming young man of good family could easily make in the weekend-party environment of Edwardian Britain, which was, after all, his own. Friends, or friends of friends, gave him the chance to build stables, then estate cottages, then wings of country houses, and public schools, even a complete and massive Edwardian pile, Llangoed Hall, on the Breconshire banks of the Wye, which survives as a hotel. (Actually the great majority of his buildings were of modest size.) And yet Portmeirion typecast him as 'not a serious architect' by the standards of the highly developed professional puritanism of the era of Le Corbusier and Mies van der Rohe. He got the official recognition of a knighthood as Sir (Bertram) Clough Williams-Ellis only at the age of eighty-seven.

This was a complete misunderstanding of the man. For him buildings without trees, walls, views, roads leading to farmyards, cottages or water, had no real meaning. What he wanted to create or shape was not buildings but small worlds in which people lived and worked in a unity of masonry, landscape wild and tame, vistas, symbols and memorials, no doubt also to be admired as an ensemble by visiting travellers. Because it was not a place in which people went about their usual business, but a fun place, a *jeu d'esprit*, or, more seriously, a momentary dream of utopia, Portmeirion was not typical of what he was about. His ideal was not Lutyens but Squire Headlong, the lord and enthusiastic shaper of, and guide to, a wild Welsh estate in Thomas Love Peacock's *Headlong Hall*. (The novels, or rather conversation pieces, of Peacock, friend of Shelley and amused admirer of Wales, were required reading in Clough's kingdom.) And the essence of such an estate must be the characteristic combination of wild natural beauty, poverty and the inhabitants' indifference to visual aesthetics, so surprising in a people as receptive to music and words as the Welsh. Though he thought it essential to embellish them with suitably symbolic masonry and metalwork, and to draw attention to their romantic potential, his environments were not supposed to be 'beautiful' but to be themselves. And, above all, to remain themselves. His campaigns for the conservation of rural landscape against 'the octopus' of unplanned 'development' went back to the 1920s. Largely to preserve them as they were, he had between the wars bought up the bare hillsides, moors and mountains that constituted his kingdom. Fortunately – for he was comfortably off rather than rich – they had virtually no market value at that time. 'A ten-guinea fee earned in London paid for many acres of hill-land.'[1]

And indeed, though it contained marvellous things, Clough's kingdom was not conventionally 'beautiful'. How could it be? Much of it consisted of a spectral, twice-destroyed stony country, always poor, and laid waste by the decline of small uneconomic hill farms and the final collapse of the great slate quarries which, supplying the builders and real-estate developers of Victorian Britain with their roofing, had for a while lifted a barren mountain region out of bare subsistence. It was, literally, a landscape of post-industrial ruins. One could climb from the giant dead quarries of Blaenau Ffestiniog up to the lunar landscape of the abandoned quarry and workers' barracks below the choughs at Cwmorthin, then down again along the abandoned railway track that led through the bare Cwm Croesor. Serving also the abandoned quarry of Croesor, one of whose former cottages was ours for some years, it led to the abandoned long incline down which the full trucks ran by gravity to the Traeth and eventually across it to be loaded at Portmadoc. It was also a landscape of post-agricultural ruins, such as the one the great poet of the region, R. S. Thomas, speaks of in his 'The Welsh Hill Country':

> The moss and the mould on the cold chimneys
> The nettles growing through the cracked doors
> The houses stand empty at Nant-yr-Eira
> There are holes in the roofs that are thatched with sunlight
> The fields are reverting to the bare moor

Even in the 1960s tourism was only slowly beginning to fill the gap – for, though Snowdon dominated the view, the major beauty spots (and mountain climbing centres) of Snowdonia were a few miles away. The ruined Ffestiniog Railway, the narrow-gauge line on which 200 men from Llanfrothen and Penrhyndeudraeth had once travelled daily to the great quarries at Blaenau Ffestiniog, was just beginning to be restored by passionate amateurs for the benefit of grateful tourist parents wondering what to do with their children. For most of our years in North Wales it still stopped dead on an overgrown mountainside before returning to Portmadoc.

Much of Clough's work as ruler of his kingdom was literally making ruins habitable and filling empty walls on still depopulating hillsides. Our first cottage was one of a windswept row of four, built somewhere in the scooped-out bare mountain valley outside the quarry village of Croesor for the local quarry. Its only permanent inhabitant by then was our cherished Nellie Jones, who brought up three children by various fathers, and a dog, in an approximate kitchen, and acted as caretaker for some almost equally rackety English visitors. (The village, or rather hamlet, of Croesor itself was just about to lose its shop-cum-sub-post office, and only a constant battle against the authorities – assisted by Clough's policy of letting empty cottages to unmarried or abandoned mothers – kept its tiny schoolhouse from closing.) Our second was a sixteenth-century ruin, once part of the complex of buildings that formed the seat of the Anwyl family, fallen on bad times after the eighteenth century, which Clough had transformed into a habitable house for Londoners who did not mind living in extreme discomfort, but in romantic surroundings. Typically, he had left part of a projecting wall of three-feet stone blocks out of which, in the centuries of ruin, a tree had grown so vast and tall that we insisted on a clause in our lease to protect us in case it was toppled by some storm, destroying most of the house. I doubt whether a single inhabited building on his estate was not either first built, restored or made fit for human occupation by him. But the inhabitants belonged to at least two entirely different and barely overlapping species: the second-homers or incomers and the native Welsh.

The incomers were a network of middle-class British intellectuals and a scattering of attached bohemians. In some ways most of them were linked directly or indirectly with the Williams-Ellises. Most of their connections came through Cambridge, which had also been Clough's own university, and that of his dead son Kitto, whose friends from King's became part of the Brondanw scene as regular visitors and (in one case) son-in-law. That is how Robin Gandy had first come to the valley. Each of the initial settlers in turn tended to attract their friends, contemporaries, teachers and students, who also came, saw and were conquered: the Hobsbawms, one by one, plus two children, followed by Marlene's brother, Walter Schwarz, plus wife and five offspring, the historians E. P. and Dorothy Thompson, from the lower slopes of the Moelwyns, and various sons and daughters of the Bennett family whose parents, both English dons, were pillars of Cambridge academic society. In one way or another a substantial set of Cambridge names was already linked with Clough's kingdom: the philosopher Bertrand Russell on the Portmeirion peninsula; the Nobel Prize physicist Patrick Blackett, settled in retirement in what had been a holiday cottage just above Brondanw, not far from his daughter's house in Croesor; Joseph Needham, the great historian of Chinese science, spent regular holidays at Portmeirion with one of his two ladies – his wife presumably remaining at home in Cambridge. John Maddox, for many years the editor of *Nature*, had a spell as a tenant in one of Clough's cottages on the Traeth; and my teacher, the economic historian Mounia Postan, and his wife Lady Cynthia (Keppel) had a house, once a school, on the outskirts of Ffestiniog. To talk of a 'Welsh Bloomsbury set' – the phrase comes from Rupert Crawshay Williams, a locally resident charming and sad philosopher who brought Bertrand Russell into the area – is pushing it a bit. However, an intensive social life flourished among the Anglophones of the Portmeirion peninsula, the Croesor valley and Ffestiniog. One of the most characteristic sounds of holidays in North Wales was that of guests shaking the rain off their waterproofs and dumping wet wellingtons in lobbies as they got ready to entertain and be entertained under some low-slung rural ceiling. And as so many of them lived by the word, there is at least poetic truth in the joke that in the Croesor valley on windless nights one was never out of earshot of some typewriter.

Though science and Cambridge went together, I suspect that it was Clough's wife, the writer Amabel Williams-Ellis, who got much the greatest satisfaction out of the accumulation of great brains in the local hinterland. A Strachey from a landed and intellectual family with long Indian links, her family connection (both Oxford and Cambridge) was, if anything, with politics. Her journalist father, St Loe Strachey, had carried considerable political weight, and her brother, John Strachey, broke away, first to follow the (then) hope of radical Labour, the dashing womanizer Sir Oswald ('Tom') Mosley, until he became the leader of British fascism, then to become the most widely known Communist Party intellectual of the 1930s. He turned away from communism in 1940 and became a prominent, though not notably successful, minister in the Labour governments after 1945. Amabel herself had joined the Communist Party unofficially, and remained a little homesick for the days when the Party was a semi-conspiratorial embattled band of brothers and sisters. She welcomed me as a reminder of those times, someone with whom she could gossip about the comrades, but perhaps chiefly as a reliable conversationalist on intellectual themes. For this purpose she would drive up to our cottage, full of memories, with the excessive care and dangerous slowness of the very aged motorist. Since few except the locals used the Croesor Road, traffic made the necessary allowances for her. Amabel, far more than Clough, had a passion for the intellect. As a girl she had dreamed of becoming a scientist, but that is not what 'gels' in her type of family did. Indeed, she was not sent to school at all. She became a writer, in the end best known as a children's writer, while as was usual in her generation her considerable contribution to Clough's own writing and thinking was subsumed under his. Amabel was not the tragic kind – indeed, she enjoyed the sweetnesses of life and the new emancipation of women, including (it would seem) a fairly free-wheeling approach to marital fidelity, but, had she not been brought to keep the stiff upper lip of her class, she might have shown some bitterness. She would have made a very professional scientist and she saw to it that at least one of her daughters became a marine biologist. I grew very fond of the old lady, even though sometimes taking avoiding action against her expeditions in search of intellectual enlightenment. We talked a great deal, especially in her last years, after Clough's death, when she waited for visitors, wanting to die. She did not complain, but made no secret of wanting an end to lying alone bedridden and in pain behind thick stone walls in a damp old house. She had lived enough. However, even political solidarity could never move her to tell me how to find the entrance of the underground workings, somewhere under Clough's kingdom, where the treasures of the National Gallery had been stored during the Second World War. A communist past was one thing, state secrets quite another.

Apart from the minority who came to do some serious climbing, what brought the rest of us outsiders to the Welsh mountains? Certainly not the search for comfort. In our Welsh cottages we voluntarily lived under the sort of conditions we condemned capitalism for imposing on its exploited toilers. None of us, even given the spartan middle-class styles of the 1950s, would have dreamed of accepting such standards in our everyday lives in London or Cambridge, not even my brother-in-law Walter Schwarz, with his boundless enthusiasm for primitive discomfort as indicating environmentally sound living close to nature. Even so, the only people we could rely on regularly to share the discomforts and the marvels of life in Parc Farm were close and weather-proof friends such as Dorothy Wedderburn. To guarantee even approximate dryness on our first night, we had to pack all blankets and bedclothes into vast airtight plastic bags every time we left Parc. It took two or three days after arrival to dry the house out enough to make it roughly habitable, and even then it was almost impossible to keep warm except in odd corners, in spite of paraffin-heaters – basic equipment, though not much good for outdoor toilets – and the fuel for our fireplaces which metropolitan intellectuals, dressed in the local style like tramps, could be seen chopping in the drizzle outside their back doors. Perhaps the sheer physical discomfort of life in

Wales was part of its attraction: it made us feel closer to nature, or at least to that constant struggle against the forces of climate and geology which gives such satisfaction. My most vivid memories of North Wales are of these confrontations: taking our two small children along stony, snow-covered tracks to shelter and giving them chocolate in a mountainside cave, returning from a long hike with Robin in persistent, drenching rain, scrambling along sheep-tracks on steep hillsides – if a sheep could do it, why not a middle-aged historian? – above all, walking, balancing and clambering round the steep rocky sanctuary of the Arddy, west of the ridge of Cnicht, rewarded by the familiar but always unexpected sight of the cold lakes hidden in its folds.

But these were visitors' pleasures. Our part of North Wales also attracted a curious population of permanent or semi-permanent settlers, or rather refugees, from outside: freelance writers, displaced bohemians from Soho, searchers for spiritual salvation on low or irregular incomes, and the odd anarchist intellectual. The presence of Bertrand Russell, the aged guru of anti-nuclear militancy, in Clough's kingdom brought a number of them into the area; not counting members of his own dysfunctional family. Ralph Schoenman, the young American militant who acquired such remarkable influence over the ancient philosopher at this time, never became part of the local scene. He was too busy whizzing round claiming to save the world, ostensibly in the name of Russell. However, after retiring from this battle Pat Pottle, secretary of the activist Committee of a Hundred (and co-liberator of the Soviet spy George Blake from Brixton jail), settled down in Croesor, attracted by his fellow anti-nuclear activist and revolutionary, the painter Tom Kinsey (later the only known anarchist master of foxhounds, but, Snowdonia being what it is, on foot rather than horseback). After the Cuban missile crisis of 1962 he had organized a demonstration in Portmeirion of thanks to Russell for saving the peace of the world – for it was in a telegram to Russell (in answer to one which Kinsey claimed he had drafted) that Khrushchev had actually made the official public announcement that the crisis was over.

This community of incomers lived side by side with the indigenous Welsh, but divided from them, not only by language but, perhaps even more, by class, lifestyle and the growing separatism of the locals. Sex apart, there were really very few close friendships across the 'interracial' divide, and little of that easy neighbourliness and village spirit that made coming to our present, equally remote and even more agricultural community in (Anglophone) Mid-Wales such a relief, especially to that spontaneous socializer, Marlene, after the growing tensions of Croesor.

Unlike the passionately Welsh but 100 per cent Anglophone native gentry, e.g. the Williams-Ellises, by the 1970s permanent settlers from outside began to learn the language themselves, not to communicate, but in deference to the increasingly obvious nationalistic feeling in the region. By the 1960s all except the very oldest and isolated locals were bilingual, bilinguality being essential to any Welsh person, even in the most Cymric village, who expected to watch television and have dealings with people from outside the neighbourhood, including the 80 per cent of his or her country's non-Welsh-speaking inhabitants. That, indeed, was the fundamental problem for Welsh-speaking areas like ours, and the basis of their increasingly strident nationalism. Even the full linguistic assimilation of a few score foreigners was as nothing compared to the irresistible Anglophone flood of modern civilization.

For most of the mountain people the Welsh language was chiefly a Noah's Ark in which they could survive the flood as a community. They did not so much want to convert and converse: people looked down on visiting South Walians with their 'school Welsh'. Unlike Noah, they did not expect the flood to end. They turned inwards because they felt themselves to be in that most desperate of situations, that of a beleaguered, hopeless and permanent minority. But for some there was a solution: compulsory Cymricization, imposed by nationalist political rule. In the meantime the incoming invaders could be discouraged by burning down their second homes. Those who claimed to know said that some of the activists came from Clough's kingdom, though it was not a centre of cottage-burning. People distinguished between the neighbouring summer visitors they knew and 'the English' in general. And although nothing can be kept secret in the countryside, unlike in the big city, no case of terrorist cottage-burning was ever solved by the police.

In some respects the indigenous inhabitants of Clough's kingdom, and of the mountains of North Wales in general, were therefore as uprooted as the seasonal or even most of the permanent English immigrants, who moved into the farms and cottages abandoned by the natives. Like a house built on subsiding land, the foundations of their society were breaking; unlike such a house, they could not be shored up. Isolation had kept the society together in the past, along with poetry, puritanism and the general poverty of an essentially rural society. All this was now going. The chapels stood empty. (I cannot recall meeting any ministers of religion in our years in the Croesor valley, except the highly anomalous, because Anglican, R. S. Thomas, who came to bury our neighbour and his fellow-poet, in English, Thomas Blackburn, in a steeply sloped graveyard with an unforgettable view of Snowdon.) Total abstinence from alcohol, which had to be the defining criterion of puritan Protestantism in a population so energetically interested in (officially non-existent) non-marital sex, was in retreat. The locus for the new culture of militant Welsh nationalism was not the chapel but the pub. (Clough had built one, the Brondanw Arms, with a beautifully wrought metal wreath as the inn sign, but this motif meant nothing to the inhabitants of Garreg and Llanfrothen, who called it, and the pub, simply The Ring.) Only a tolerant silence about illegitimate babies remained, even the ones that could not be quietly disguised as unexpected younger siblings of their mothers. The hillsides were abandoned for lowland council housing with central heating. Even money now divided communities more, for within the Welsh language community, wealth had not been decisive in the past, since the really rich and powerful were or became anglicized, that is to say they were outside it.

If anything, the hierarchy of status had been spiritual or intellectual – that of minister of religion (that is to say orator), poet and scholar – who might be anyone, a postman with a gift for improvising the complex metres of Welsh verse or, like the great antiquarian and scholar Bob Owen, the pride of Croesor, whose library now forms part of the National Library of Wales in Aberystwith, a clerk at the quarry. (His son and his family – Tudwr, Gaynor and their children Bob, Eleri and the baby Deian – were and remained our friends in the village.) A less cultural, but still locally recognized male status also came with distinction as a poacher, a widely practised and universally approved sport. Even in our times, when a Welsh friend from an old quarry village wanted to give us salmon for dinner and asked the weekly itinerant fish-seller for the price, the response naturally was: 'Are you buying or selling?' R. S. Thomas's great poems should not mislead us into thinking of most North Wales hill farmers as unintellectual hulks. A lot of Welsh reading and thinking went on under those low roofs, ancestrally designed to combine a maximum view of approaching strangers with maximum shelter from rain and storm. In many ways our neighbour Edgar from Croesor Ychaf, explaining the regular collective pre-shearing round-up by the local farmers and their dogs of all the sheep running free on the mountain, was as knowledgeable about the ecology of the terrain as the college-trained and sullenly nationalist nature warden who had moved into the former village post office, and at least as articulate.

Whether Clough's kingdom was typical of mountain Wales, I cannot tell, but it was an unstable and unhappy place full of underlying tension. It found expression in a growing, resentful and sometimes rancorous, anti-English feeling, a withdrawal from personal relations which came more naturally to adults than to children.[2] There were also other signs of social malaise. When what were locally called 'the orange people' (the 'sanyasins' or followers of the Indian guru Shri Bhagwan) came into the valley in the early 1980s, they won converts among the native Welsh as well as, less surprisingly, in the English bohemian diaspora. And clearly not only because their way to salvation encouraged a lot of free sex. Croesor was a marvellous place for family holidays, but it was not a happy valley.

By the time I retired from Birkbeck in 1982 we had spent time in Clough's kingdom every year for almost two decades. Bryn Hyfryd, and even more Parc Farm, flanked by the old Manor House (Big Parc), with its visitors and the tiny Gatws bursting with Schwarz cousins, was part of our, and even more of our children's, lives, and friendships. Just because it was not blanketed by the permanent routines of everyday and professional life, the memories associated with North Wales – even the domestic and family rows – stand out with special vividness: the terrible news of the Russian invasion of Prague in 1968, news of the death of my aunt Mimi brought by telegram – there were still such things – to a phone-less cottage, the car-door torn from its hinges by the storm as we got out to make our way to Edward Thompson's New Year's Eve party down the torch-lit path, our drive with Dorothy Wedderburn to picnic past Aberdaron on the far point of the Lleyn peninsula on a sunny Christmas Day, the ancient well in Parc that went on supplying us with water even in the great drought of 1976. Except for the landscape, it was not perfect: living in Boy Scout discomfort became less attractive (it had never appealed to Marlene), and the growth of nationalism soured relations with the Welsh. But, though I was now about to spend four months a year in New York, we would probably have stayed in the Croesor valley to the end of our lives.

But after Clough died in 1978 and Amabel in 1984 things changed. Clough's grandson, who took over the estate – his parents were busy running the factory and the marketing of Portmeirion pottery – was a passionate Welsh nationalist, who showed no interest in his grandparents' collection of Cambridge antiques, occupying houses which ought to be re-echoing to the Welsh language of their restored Cymric families. In short, the leases of the outsiders were not renewed. The official reason was that leases would henceforth be given only for permanent residence. We were allowed to stay on year by year until a suitable Welsh tenant could be found, or the estate could raise the money to make the premises of Parc Farm habitable for anyone except a romantic second-homer. We stayed on those terms for a year or two while we looked for another home in Wales, but no longer in North Wales. In any case our friends were also losing their cottages and, by the time I got into my seventies, clambering up Cnicht was no longer so attractive. We found it in the milder landscape and political climate of Powys, from whose hills I can see Cader Idris on a clear day.

My daughter still goes to the valley from time to time. Neither Marlene nor I have been there since we moved away in 1991. I have not the heart to see the place again. But I cannot forget it.

15

The Sixties

I

Sometime in early May 1968 I found myself in Paris, where one of the offshoots of UNESCO had organized a giant conference on 'Marx and Contemporary Scientific Thought' to commemorate the 150th anniversary of his birth. Like most such gatherings, its obvious function was to give a number of academics a free trip to an agreeable tourist centre; and, like most conferences on Marx, especially those to which a platoon of ideological bureaucrats from the USSR contributed extremely boring papers of no interest, it encouraged participants to get out of the conference hall and into the streets. But on 8, 9 and 10 May the streets of Paris – at least those of the 5th and 6th *arrondissements* – were full of demonstrating students. By sheer chance, the commemoration of Marx's anniversary coincided with the the climax of the great Paris student rebellion. Within a day or two it was to become more than a student rebellion, namely a nationwide workers' strike and a major political crisis of the regime of General de Gaulle.[1] Within a few months 'the events of May' were recognized as the epicentre of a bicontinental outburst of student rebellion, crossing political and ideological frontiers from Berkeley and Mexico City in the west to Warsaw, Prague and Belgrade in the east.

As I write this, I look at the pictures of those Paris days in the anthology of 1968 photographs, published as a volume thirty years later.[2] Several of the most impressive were taken on the final day of the Marx Conference – I can still recall the sting of tear-gas after the burning of the Latin Quarter – but my most lasting memory is captured in Henri Cartier-Bresson's undated picture of a massive student march of protest – a vast, overwhelmingly male, tie-less, clenched-fist concourse of juveniles, still, almost without exception, with the respectable short bourgeois haircuts of the pre-hippy age, almost concealing the presence of an occasional adult face. Yet these occasional adult faces are what I remember most vividly, because they represent both the unity and the incompatibility of the old generation of the left – my own – with the new. I remember my old friend and comrade Albert ('Marius') Soboul, holder of the chair in the history of the French Revolution at the Sorbonne, upright, solemn-faced, dressed in the dark suit and tie of an academic grandee, marching abreast of men young enough to be his children who shouted slogans of which he profoundly disapproved as a loyal member of the French Communist Party. But how could a man in the tradition of Revolution and Republic not '*descendre dans la rue*' on such an occasion? I remember Jean Pronteau – still a senior Party member at that time – who had commanded the 1944 Paris insurrection against the Germans in the Latin Quarter, telling me how moved he was by the sight of barricades going up, spontaneously, at the exact corner of the rue Gay-Lussac where they had been built in 1944, and no doubt where they had been during the revolutions of 1830, 1848 and the Paris Commune of 1871. If *noblesse oblige*, then so, surely, does a revolutionary tradition.

And indeed, nothing shocked me more at the time than the meeting to which I and several other visiting Marxists from the UNESCO jamboree were invited by, was it the Institut Maurice Thorez or some other academic adjunct to the French Communist Party?, at which points of Marxist interpretation were to be discussed, while the students marched. Nobody appeared to take cognizance of what was happening outside. I caused a few moments of awkwardness by pointing this out. Did we have nothing to say, I asked, about what was happening on the very streets through which we had passed on our way to the meeting? Could we not at least declare our general support? Alas, thirty-four years later I cannot for the life of me remember whether those of us who felt as I did managed to shame the gathering into making such a declaration. It seems unlikely.

The Magnum 1968 collection includes another picture that encapsulates at least part of my feelings at the time. (It is also, I need hardly add, by Henri Cartier-Bresson, that genius at catching the historic moment.) An elderly member of the middle class stands, with arms folded behind his back, looking reflectively at a poster-covered Parisian wall and a rough wooden door – presumably to some yard or building site. The top layer of posters has been half-stripped from the wall, leaving breeze-blocks and older movie posters half-visible. On the door there is an accumulation of political posters – a Communist Party poster on top of some text about student power, a half-torn sheet calling for struggle for a democratic society opening the way to socialism, and on top of it all a large graffito written with the basic armament of the 1968 revolutionary, the spray-paint can. It reads '*Jouissez sans entraves*', which the editors have translated bashfully as 'Let it all hang out'. (It really means: 'Let nothing stop orgasms'.) We cannot tell what Cartier-Bresson's elderly citizen made of the walls of Paris, which were the chief victims and public witnesses of the student revolt. My own reaction was sceptical. As every historian knows, revolutions can be recognized by the vast floods of words they generate: spoken words, but in literate societies words written in enormous quantities by men and women who do not usually express themselves in writing. By this criterion May 1968 was something like a student revolution – but its words record an odd kind of revolution, as anyone could see who watched the walls of Paris at the time.

The truth is that the characteristic posters and graffiti of 1968 were not really political in the traditional sense of the word, except for the recurring denunciations of the Communist Party, presumably by the militants of the various left-wing groups and factions, almost invariably descended from some Leninist schism. And yet, how rare were the references to the great names of that ideology – Marx, Lenin, Mao, even Che Guevara – on the walls of Paris![3] They would later appear on badges and T-shirts, as icons symbolizing the overthrow of systems. The student rebels reminded theorists of a long-forgotten Bakuninist anarchism, but if anything they were closest to the 'situationists', who had anticipated a 'revolution of everyday life' through the transformation of personal relations. That (and their very Gallic brilliance in devising memorable slogans) is why they became the mouthpieces of an otherwise inchoate movement, although it is almost certain that hardly anyone until then had heard of them, outside a small circle of left-wing painters. (I certainly had not.) On the other hand, the 1968 slogans were not simply the expressions of a drop-out counter-culture, in spite of an obvious interest in shocking the bourgeoisie ('*LSD tout de suite!*'). They wanted society *overthrown* and not simply side-stepped.

For middle-aged leftwingers like me, May 1968 and indeed the 1960s as a whole were both enormously welcome and enormously puzzling. We seemed to be using the same vocabulary, but we did not appear to speak the same language. What is more, even when we participated in the same events, those of us old enough to be the parents of the youthful militants patently did not experience them as they did. Twenty postwar years had taught those of us who lived in the states of capitalist democracy that social revolution in these countries was not on the political agenda. In any case, when one is past fifty, one does not expect the revolution behind every mass demonstration, however impressive and exciting. (Hence, incidentally, our – and everyone's – surprise at the disproportionate political effectiveness of the 1968 student movements which, after all, overthrew the presidents of the USA and, after a decent face-saving interval, of France.) Moreover, for us brought up on the history of 1776, 1789 and 1917, and old enough to have lived through the transformations since 1933, revolution, however intense an emotional experience, had a political objective. Revolutionaries wanted to overthrow old political regimes, domestic or foreign, with the aim of substituting new political regimes which would then institute or lay the foundations of a new and better society. Yet, whatever drove most of these youngsters on to the street, it was not this. Unsympathetic observers, such as Raymond Aron (seeing himself in the role of de Tocqueville commenting on the Paris of 1848), concluded that they had no objective at all: 1968 was simply to be understood as collective street-theatre, 'psychodrama' or 'verbal delirium', because it was merely 'a colossal release of suppressed feeling'.[4] Sympathetic ones, such as the sociologist Alain Touraine, author of one of the first and still one of the most illuminating books written about those extraordinary weeks, thought their implicit aim was a reversion to the pre-1848 utopian ideologies.[5] But one could not really read utopia into the general antinomianism of slogans such as 'It is forbidden to forbid', which probably came as close to expressing what the young rebels felt – whether about government, teachers, parents or the universe. In fact, they did not seem to be much interested in a *social* ideal, communist or otherwise, as distinct from the individualist ideal of getting rid of anything that claimed the right and power to stop you doing whatever your ego and id felt like doing. And yet, insofar as they found public badges to pin on private lapels, they were the badges of the revolutionary left, if only because they were by tradition associated with opposition.

The natural reaction of old lefties to the new movement was: 'These people have not yet learned how to achieve their political objectives.' That is presumably why, referring to the French title of my book *Primitive Rebels*, then recently published in Paris,[6] Alain Touraine, who had every sympathy with the 1968 rebels, wrote on the fly-leaf of my copy of his book 'Here are the Primitives of a new Rebellion'. For the purpose of my book had indeed been to do historic justice to social struggles – banditry, millennial sects, pre-industrial city rioters – that had been overlooked or even dismissed just because they tried to come to grips with the problems of the poor in a new capitalist society with historically obsolete or inadequate equipment. But supposing the 'new primitives' were not pursuing our ends at all, but quite different ones? Because it was so clearly and passionately on the side of the eternal losers I wrote about, my own book, available in English since 1959, had given me more street credibility among the Anglophone 'new lefts' than Party members usually enjoyed. Nevertheless, I was astonished and a little baffled to be told by a colleague from the University of California, Berkeley, the epicentre of the US student eruption, that the more intellectual young rebels there read the book with great enthusiasm *because they identified themselves and their movement* with my rebels.

Having both taught in the USA at the peak of the anti-Vietnam movement in 1967 and watched the Paris events in 1968, I wrote an equally uncomprehending article on 'Revolution and Sex' in 1969. If there was any correlation between the two, I pointed out, it was negative: rulers kept slaves and the poor quiet by encouraging sexual freedom among them and, I might have added, remembering Aldous Huxley's *Brave New World*, drugs. As a historian I knew that all revolutions have their free-for-all libertarian aspect, but 'taken by themselves cultural revolt and cultural dissidence are symptoms, not revolutionary forces'. 'The more prominent such things are' – as obviously in the USA – 'the more confident can we be that the big things are not happening'.[7] But what if the 'big things' were to be not the overthrow of capitalism, or even of some oppressive or corrupt political regimes, but precisely the destruction of traditional patterns of relations between people and personal behaviour *within existing society*? What if we were just wrong in seeing the rebels of the 1960s as another phase or variant of the left? In that case it was not a botched attempt at one kind of revolution, but the effective ratification of another: the one that abolished traditional politics, and in the end the politics of the traditional left, by the slogan 'the personal is political'. Looking back after thirty-odd years it is easy to see that I misunderstood the historic significance of the 1960s.

One reason for this was that I had been immersed since 1955 in the small and mostly nocturnal universe of jazz musicians. The world I lived in after hours in the second half of the fifties had already seemed to anticipate much of the spirit of the 1960s. This was an error. It was quite different. If there is anything that symbolizes the 1960s it is rock music, which began its world conquest in the second half of the 1950s and immediately opened a profound gap between the pre- and post-1955 generations.

It was impossible not to be aware of this gap, as when my wife and I, in Berkeley and San Francisco for a few days at the height of the 'flower-power' year of 1967, visited a former au pair of Andy and Julia in Haight-Ashbury, where she was then discovering herself. It was obviously marvellous for the girl, usually as level-headed a Netherlander as you could hope for, and fun to watch, but how could it be our scene? We were taken to the Fillmore, the giant ballroom throbbing with strobe lights and excessive amplification. I cannot even remember what Bay Area groups we heard – the only act that made any sense to me that night was one of the Motown girl groups – was it the Marvelettes or the Supremes? – which swung in the familiar way of black r&b. Perhaps this is not surprising. To enjoy that year in San Francisco one really had to be permanently high on something, preferably acid, and we were not. Indeed, by virtue of our age, we were a textbook illustration of the phrase 'If you can remember anything of the 1960s, you were not part of them.'

Nor could the jazz world, with the rarest exceptions, understand rock. It reacted to rock music with the same sort of contempt as it had traditionally reacted to the Mickey Mouse music of the old pit and commercial bands. Perhaps even with greater contempt, since the men who played the most boring of barmitzvah gigs were at least professionals. Conversely, within a few years rock almost killed jazz. The generational gap between those for whom the Rolling Stones were gods and those for whom they were just a creditable imitation of black blues-singing was virtually unbridgeable, even when both sides might from time to time find themselves in agreement on some talent. (As it happens I rather admired the Beatles and recognized the fragments of genius in Bob Dylan, a potential major poet too idle or self-absorbed to keep the muse's attention for more than two or three lines at a time.) Whatever the appearances, my generation would remain strangers in the 1960s.

And this despite the fact that for a few years in the 1960s the language, culture and lifestyle of the new rock generations became politicized. They spoke dialects recognizable as deriving from the old language of the revolutionary left, though not, of course, of orthodox Moscow communism, discredited both by the record of the Stalin era and the political moderation of the Communist Parties. Anyone who reads the best book on the 1960s written in Britain, *Promise of a Dream*, by my friend and former student Sheila Rowbotham, will realize that for some years it really was almost impossible for someone of her generation (born 1943) to distinguish between what was personal and what was political. It was 'the left-wing Alexis Korner' – I remember him, dark and quiet in Bayswater – who inspired 'the clear-cut throbbing sexuality of the blues bands'[8] such as the Rolling Stones, whose Mick Jagger wrote 'Street Fighting Man' after a dramatic Vietnam Solidarity demonstration in 1968 and published it in the flamboyant Pakistani Trotskyite Tariq Ali's new radical paper, *The Black Dwarf* ('PARIS, LONDON, ROME, BERLIN. WE WILL FIGHT. WE SHALL WIN'). Pink Floyd, 'The Dialectics of Liberation', Che Guevara, Middle Earth and acid belonged together. Not that the line was totally erased. A subsequent holder of a Cambridge economics chair proposed that principled socialist men should protest publicly against the spread of Soho strip clubs, e.g. by stripping outside them. ('The *New Left Review* men had told him he was being "puritanical and old-fashioned in his attitude to socialism".') Wearers of 'the sombre "struggle gear", increasingly worn . . . on the left' shook their heads over an equally devoted militant who came to an occupation of the London School of Economics 'in an olive-green bell-bottomed trouser suit, bought in my September spending spree'.[9] Most of this passed the older left by, even though the young British radicals – perhaps thanks to my generation of red historians – were probably more deeply impregnated with history, especially labour history, than any other. We knew most of the chief activists as fellow-protesters, pupils or friends. I did not bother to read the *Black Dwarf*, although I was asked to write an article for it and naturally did so. People like me were mobilized by the young for such things as Vietnam teach-ins – I was put up against the spectacularly ill-chosen Henry Cabot Lodge, former American Big Brother in Saigon in the Oxford Union teach-in of 1965 organized by Tariq Ali. Fortunately in my own college I did not face the bruising experience of a student occupation, a considerable strain on intergenerational relations, although I was invited to address a crowd of occupying forces in the Cambridge Old Schools by one of their leaders, the son of old friends. I think my suggestion that even the history of eras lost in the mists of antiquity such as the nineteenth century could be 'relevant' – the buzzword of the moment – disappointed them.

We did not understand how deeply even the unquestionably *political* ultra-left, the armed revolutionaries and neo-terrorists who emerged from the 1960s, were influenced by, indeed were part of, the 'counter-culture'. The Weathermen in the USA took their name from a song by Bob Dylan. The Red Army Faction, better known as the Baader-Meinhof Gang, lived in the German version of a counter-culture of outsiders by choice and behaviour.

My age group did not understand that the student generations of the West in the 1960s believed, as we had once done, though in a manner far less easy to specify as 'politics', that they lived in an era when all would be changed, because around them everything was already being changed, by revolution. We, or at least congenitally pessimistic middle-aged reds such as myself, already bearing the scars of half a lifetime of disappointment, could not share the almost cosmic optimism of the young, as they felt themselves to be 'caught in that maelstrom of international rebellion'.[10] (One of its byproducts was the fashion for global revolutionary tourism, which was to see Italian, French and British left-wing intellectuals simultaneously converging on Bolivia in 1967 at the death of Guevara and for the trial of Regis Debray.)

Of course all of us were caught up in these great global struggles. The Third World had indeed brought the hope of revolution back to the First in the 1960s. The two great international inspirations were Cuba and Vietnam, triumphs not only of revolution, but of Davids against Goliaths, of the weak against the all-powerful. 'The guerrilla' – an emblematic word of the era – became the quintessential key to changing the world. Fidel Castro's revolutionaries, recognizable by their youth, long hair, beards and rhetoric as heirs of 1848 – think of the famous image of Che Guevara – could almost have been designed to be world symbols of a new age of political romantics. It is difficult to recall, and to understand even now, the almost immediate global repercussions of what in January 1959 was after all a not unusual event in the history of one Latin American island of modest size. Small, scrawny Vietnamese on jungle trails and in paddy-fields checkmated the giant destructive force of the USA. From the moment in 1965 that President Johnson sent in his troops, even middle-aged non-utopians such as myself had not the slightest doubt about who would win. More than anything else in the 1960s, it was the grandeur, heroism and tragedy of the Vietnamese struggle which moved and mobilized the English-speaking left and linked both its generations and almost all its usually feuding sects. I met contemporaries and pupils in Grosvenor Square, demonstrating in front of the American Embassy. I went on marches with Marlene and our small children, chanting 'Ho-Ho-Ho-Chi Minh', like the rest. I was a declared sceptic about the Guevarist guerrilla strategy, which in any case proved uniformly disastrous (see chapter 21), but Vietnam remains engraved on both our hearts. Even at the very end of the century, the emotion was still there, and palpable in Hanoi, as Marlene and I watched a party of tiny, hard-bitten elderly men in formal suits, wearing their campaign medals, make their way under the trees to visit Ho Chi Minh's home. They had fought for us, instead of us.

Apart from sharing in the campaigning for it, I had no particular connection with Vietnam during the war, nor did I visit it until a quarter of a century after victory, and then purely on holiday. On the other hand, like so many leftwingers who were inspired by the Cuban revolution, I visited Cuba several times in the 1960s, and thus, incidentally, saw a good cross-section of the world's itinerant left. My first trip there was in 1960, the irresistible honeymoon period of the young revolution. I found myself coinciding and joining forces with two economist friends who represented that rare phenomenon, the old US Marxist left identified neither with the CP nor with its opponents: the tall Paul Sweezy, all slow-speaking New England Yankee, and Paul Baran. Since their embattled little journal, the *Monthly Review*, had kept the red flag flying in Cold War USA, they were welcomed by Castro and the ex-guerrillas of the Sierra Maestra. My own contacts came rather through a formidable CP leader with an exceptional gift for political adaptation, Carlos Rafael Rodriguez, whose insistence on making common cause with Fidel while he was in the Sierra Maestra paid off after the victory. Havana was still sufficiently close to the free-swinging paradise for shady tourists of the musical *Guys and Dolls* to radiate rumba and cultural tolerance, and the island looked sufficiently fertile to give the revolutionary regime what looked like an easy future. We agreed that it ought to have no difficulty in feeding its 10 million inhabitants, with enough left over for Cuba Libres (rum and Coca-Cola), cigars and those wonderful tiny street-corner coffees which disappeared as the economy foundered. Eighteen months after victory the honeymoon between people and revolutionary government was still tangible. Dodging radical young Americans with movie-cameras we toured the country in an optimistic haze.

My second visit, in 1962, via Prague, Shannon and Gander, was with a British left-wing delegation of the usual composition: a left-wing Labour MP; unilateral nuclear disarmers; a hardnosed, usually Party-line union leader, not without an interest in foreign nooky; the odd radical conspirator; CP functionaries and the like. A young, fast-talking African had somehow attached himself to us, claiming to represent an undefined 'Youth Movement' in a vaguely defined region of West Africa, whose first action on arriving in Prague was to make tracks for the Foreign Ministry where he hoped to find somebody to fund Third World revolution through him. The Cubans refused to have anything to do with him. At the time I saw him as that curious by-product of that age, a black confidence man exploiting the ignorance or anti-imperialist reflexes of white progressives: one of the Good Soldier Schwejks or *picaros* of the Cold War. The liberal left became familiar with, and sometimes let itself be exploited by, such figures – in Britain the highly uncongenial 'Michael X', halfway between a bad beginning as a West London hustler and a grim end on the scaffold in Trinidad and on the pages of V. S. Naipaul's harsh novel, was at one time familiar at London parties. Certainly these examples of the flotsam and jetsam of a disintegrating empire were less impressive than the black militants from the USA who were soon to look to Cuba for aid, but behind the unpersuasive scams of people such as the young African there was a tragedy of uprooted lives among white aliens which I did not sufficiently appreciate. As for the delegation itself, all I can remember about it is that I found myself translating for Che who (in Fidel's place) received us for lunch in the former Hilton hotel. (He was indeed as fine a figure of a man as he looks on the famous photo, though he said nothing of interest.) However, thanks to the invaluable Argeliers León, expert in the affairs of Afro-Cuban secret societies and cults and director of the Institute of Ethnology and Folklore which the new regime had just established, I was able to listen to some wonderful music in the black *barrios* of Havana.

My third visit was to a somewhat extravagant gathering, the Havana Cultural Congress, 'the last episode in Fidel Castro's affair with the European intelligentsia', in January 1968, to which Fidel, at that point on cool terms with Moscow, had pointedly omitted to invite cultural figures from the Soviet bloc or (except in Italy, where culture and the PCI still went together), orthodox CP intellectuals. Instead, he brought in an impressive range of independent, dissident and heterodox leftists from various cultural scenes, including most of the older generation of the Parisian avant-garde political outgroups. Their most memorable contribution to the congress was to produce a politico-artistic 'incident', when old surrealists physically attacked the Mexican artist Siqueiros, who had once been associated with the plans to assassinate Trotsky, at the opening of an art show, though it was not clear how far this was on grounds of artistic or political disagreement. Yet the curious thing about this invasion of the past from the Latin Quarter is how little it had in common with, or anticipated, the student rebellion that was about to sweep through Paris. Nevertheless, it was an exciting occasion, though a somewhat depressing one, considering the evident mess Cuba had made of its economy. At all events it gave me the opportunity to get to know the remarkable Hans Magnus Enzensberger in his Fidelista phase, with his Russian wife, the enchanting Masha, a lost soul whose life was to end tragically in London, child of the dark night of the Stalinist Soviet Union. For her father had been Alexander Fadeyev, General Secretary of the Writers' Union in the years of the Great Terror, that is to say a state bureaucrat drinking his way through the task of administering his friends' lives and deaths before committing suicide in 1955.

I do not know what Fidel made of this strange influx of Europeans. He was presumably more at ease with Giangiacomo Feltrinelli, a moustached outdoor-looking figure recently expelled from both Bolivia and for good measure Peru, who was telling the Cubans 'in a Spanish comprehensible only to an Italian' that 'his function as a European publisher was at an end, and he now saw himself wholly as an anti-imperialist combatant'.[11] Fortunately the publishing house he had founded in 1955, equally distinguished in politics and litera-ture, first to publish both Boris Pasternak's *Dr Zhivago* and Lampe-dusa's *The Leopard*, still flourishes. I cannot remember whether I met him on that occasion, though I had known this intense young multi-millionaire slightly since the early 1950s when he was an impassioned Communist Party activist and financier of CP culture. I remember a summery conversation with him in his office in Milan in the nerve-racking period of the international communist crisis of 1956–7, about where the movement could or should go, between phone calls arranging a weekend with a girl in some castle on the Adriatic coast. It must have been just when he was leaving the Party. His dissidence was to take him into the underworld of armed revolutionary struggle. As a teenager he had fought with the commu-nist partisans for revolution, against fascism and against all his family and the super-rich Milan bourgeoisie stood for. The spirit of Che Guevara revived these memories. Soon after 1968 he went underground – or as far underground as a rich and socially prominent international headline-maker can go – and was killed in 1972, in obscure circumstances while attempting to blow up a high-tension pylon in Segrate, in the Milan hinterland.

Whether Fidel himself knew the charming young French-Canadian intellectuals who failed to convince me that their plan to create a new Sierra Maestra in the forests of Quebec would advance the cause of world revolution, I do not know. I suspect that someone in Cuba did. I tried to phone the most intelligent and agreeable of them repeatedly a couple of years later when I found myself in Montreal. There was no answer. Such was my lack of rapport with the spirit of the times that it only struck me much later that he must have been one of the terrorists of the nationalist Front de la Libération du Québec who kidnapped the British Trade Commissioner and strangled a Quebec minister, perhaps one of those allowed a safe exit to Cuba in return for the British diplomat. But those were the days when even the ultras of ethnolinguistic nationalism, such as the early Basque E T A, presented themselves in the garb of international revolution.

II

For a moment in the late 1960s the young, or at least the children of the old middle classes and the new masses rising to middle-class status through the explosion in higher education, felt they were living the revolution, whether by a simple collective private exit from the world of power, parents and past or by the constant, accumulating, almost orgasmic excitement of political or apparently political action, or gestures that took the place of action. The mood of the political young during 'that hectic spring and summer' of 1968 was recognizably revolutionary, but incomprehensible to old lefties of my generation, and not only because the situation was plainly not revolutionary in any realistic sense. Let me quote Sheila Rowbotham, who has described it with wonderful perception:

Personal feelings removed themselves from the foreground. My sexual encounters were snatched in between meetings and somehow the customary emotions didn't settle upon them. It was as if intimacy had acquired an almost random quality. The energy of the external collective became so intense, it seemed the boundaries of closeness, of ecstatic inwardness, had spilled over on to the streets ... I thus caught a glimpse of the peculiar annihilation of the personal in the midst of dramatic events like revolution ... In retrospect revolutions seem puritanical, but that is not how they are experienced at the time ... Caught in that maelstrom of international rebellion, it felt as if we were being carried to the edge of the known world.[12]

Nevertheless, as soon as the dense clouds of maximalist rhetoric and cosmic expectation turned into the rain of every day, the distinction between ecstasy and politics, real power and flower power, between voice and action, became visible once more. Jericho had not fallen to the sound of Joshua's collective trumpets. The political young had to consider what action was needed to capture it. Since both the older and the younger generation of revolutionaries spoke the same language, mainly in one or another Marxist dialect, a semblance of communication became possible again, especially since the activist groups broke with the vague belief in spontaneous inspiration and often returned to the tradition of disciplined vanguard organizations. In fact, however, there was still a vast gap between the old and the young left. Revolution was not on the agenda in our countries. For revolutionaries of my generation the central problem remained what Marxist parties should do, indeed what their function could be, in non-revolutionary countries. And elsewhere? Where successful insurrection or guerrilla conquest was realistically on the agenda, we – at least I – were still in favour of it.

The old instinct to be on the side of any insurrectionaries and guerrillas who talked the language of the left, however stupid and pointless, died hard. It was not until the 1980s that, confronted with the phenomenon of the Peruvian 'Shining Path' guerrillas – admittedly based on an ideology eccentric even on the lunatic fringes of Marxism–Leninism – I frankly admitted to myself that this was a left-wing revolutionary movement I simply did not want to win. (Fortunately good Vietnamese communists had put a stop to Pol Pot's killing fields.) Perhaps sympathy for the rebels was no more than the intellectuals' version of the age-old *omertà* of the poor, the reflex of not telling on those harried by the state and its men in uniforms. Perhaps this came naturally to the author of *Primitive Rebels* and *Bandits*, who still finds it hard to withhold admiration from embattled, even if plainly mistaken, losers. In the USA my own sympathies were with the Black Panthers. I admired their courage and self-respect. I was touched by the simple-minded

Leninism of their publications, but it was plain to me that they had not the slightest chance of achieving their objectives.

With most of the organizations of insurrectionists, or rather small armed action-groups which emerged in Europe from the debris of the great rebellion of 1968, I found myself entirely out of sympathy. There was room for reasoned disagreement with their opposite numbers in the very different political situation of Latin America (see chapter 21), but in Europe their activities were either pointless or counter-productive. The only operations of this kind which might claim some political feasibility were those of separatist nationalists, Quebecois, Basque or Irish, to whose political project I was strongly opposed. Marxists are not separatist nationalists.[13] In any case, one of the two most lasting separatist movements of the kind born in this period, the Provisional IRA, did not claim to be on the left at all, but, on the contrary, broke away in 1969 from the old-established ('Official') IRA which *had* turned left.

So I found myself both out of sympathy and out of contact, if only by virtue of age, with these new practical revolutionaries. Not that there were all that many. In Britain there were none, except the shortlived, ineffective anarchist Angry Brigade. In West Germany the armed action people amounted to a few dozen at most, probably relying for support on 1,500 or so sympathizers, plus perhaps another handful who moved from action in their own country to international action in anti-imperialist solidarity with some body of Third World rebels, usually the Palestinians. It was a world I did not know, unless one or other of the often very radical young West German historians of those years had some connections with them. I had no contact with the Red Brigades and their like in Italy, much the most formidable of the armed action-groups in Europe other than the Basque ETA. I doubt whether the active members of these groups numbered more than a hundred or two. For reasons I have never understood, no significant armed revolutionary groups of the left seem to have emerged from the ruins of 1968 in France, although a small but quite effective terrorist group operated for a number of years in Belgium. On the other hand, had I been in touch with such groups, I would not have asked them what they did, and they would not have told me, even if they thought I was politically with them.

And where did it all lead to? In politics, nowhere much. Since a revolution was not on the cards, the European revolutionaries of 1968 had to join the political mainstream of the left, unless, being very bright young intellectuals, as so many of them were, they escaped from real politics into the academy, where revolutionary ideas could survive without much political practice. Politically the 1968 generation has done well enough, especially if one includes those recruited into civil services and think-tanks and the burgeoning numbers of advisers in politicians' private offices. As I write the French Prime Minister, Lionel Jospin, is an ex-Trotskyist, the German Foreign Secretary, Joshka Fischer, is an ex-street-fighting man, and even the 'New Labour' government of Tony Blair contains, among its lesser members, more than one firebrand of those days. Only in Italy, where the extreme left retained a strong independent presence, has the mainstream left not been rejuvenated by the young 68 radicals. Is this any more or any less than the inevitable seepage of former revolutionaries from radicalism to moderation in every intellectual generation since 1848?

What has really transformed the western world is the *cultural* revolution of the 1960s. The year 1968 may prove to be less of a turning-point in twentieth-century history than 1965, which has no political significance whatever, but was the year in which the French clothing industry for the first time produced more women's trousers than skirts, and when numbers training for the Roman Catholic priesthood began visibly to collapse. I always taught the students in my labour history courses that the great dockers' strike of 1889, which is prominent in every textbook, may be less significant than the silent adoption by masses of Britain's industrial workers, some time between 1880 and 1905, of a form of headgear recognizable as a badge of belonging to their class, the familiar peaked cap. It may be argued that the really significant index of the history of the second half of the twentieth century is not ideology or student occupations, but the forward march of blue jeans.

But, alas, I am not part of that history. For Levis triumphed, like rock music, as the badge of youth. By then I was no longer young. I had no great sympathy for the contemporary equivalent of Peter Pan, the adult who wants to stay an adolescent for ever, nor could I see myself as credibly performing the role of oldest teenager on the scene. I therefore decided, almost as a matter of principle, never to wear this gear, and I have never done so. This handicaps me as a historian of the 1960s: I stood outside them. What I have written about the 1960s is what an autobiographer can write who never wore jeans.

16

A Watcher in Politics

I

Looking back, I am surprised how little direct political activity there was in my life after 1956, considering my reputation as a committed Marxist. I did not become a figure in the nuclear disarmament movement, addressing vast crowds in Hyde Park like Edward Thompson. I did not march at the head of public demonstrations like Pierre Bourdieu in Paris. I did not save from jail a Turkish editor who had published one of my articles by offering to stand trial myself by his side, as Noam Chomsky did in 2002. True, I cannot compare with the eminence or the star quality of these friends, but even at the level of lesser celebrity, there was plenty to be done. I did not even take any active part after 1968 in the bitter political struggle within the small Communist Party between the Soviet hardliners and the Eurocommunists, which finally killed the Party in 1991, though (obviously) indicating where I stood. Essentially, apart from a lecture here and there, my political activity consisted of writing books and articles, notably for that most original of editors, Paul Barker, in his days at *New Society*, as a historian or a historically minded journalist, a Marxist one, which obviously gave my writings a political dimension, as did my special field of labour history. Even my most political writings of the 1960s and 1970s were only obliquely tied to current matters.

So I was not really prepared for the moment when, for the first and only time in my life, I found myself with a brief cameo part on the national scene of British politics. For about ten years from the late seventies I was deeply involved in the public debates about the future of the Labour Party and, after the beginning of what turned out to be eighteen unbroken years of Conservative government, the nature of the new 'Thatcherism'. Most of my contributions were republished in two volumes of political writing.

It grew from a seed unintentionally planted in September 1978 in the pages of the Communist Party's 'theoretical and discussion journal', *Marxism Today*, which was to play an unexpectedly important part in political debate in the 1980s under the recently appointed editor, a brilliant, bald, jogging, motor-race watcher, politico-intellectual entrepreneur and former university lecturer, my friend Martin Jacques. It published a lecture I had given in the annual series of Marx Memorial Lectures under the title 'The Forward March of Labour Halted?' It was not intended as a political intervention, but as a Marxist historian's survey of what had happened to the British working class over the past century. I argued that the apparently irresistible though not continuous rise of the British labour movement in the first half of the century seemed to have come to a halt. It could not now necessarily be expected to realize the historic destiny once predicted for it, if only because the modern economy had changed, relatively diminished and divided the industrial proletariat. If my lecture had a political edge, it was turned against the Labour Party leadership under Harold Wilson, Prime Minister from 1964 to 1970 and again in 1974–6, who presided over a brief moment of labour revival in 1966, and did not recognize it. Nevertheless, 'The Forward March Halted?' amounted to a public warning that in the late 1970s the movement was heading for serious trouble.

One part of my presentation was immediately singled out for irritated criticism by Ken Gill, a member of the TUC General Council and perhaps the leading CP trade union leader, namely my comments on the sharp increase of sectionalism in the industrial movement. I had pointed out that the trade unions' militancy, so plain in the 1970s, was essentially for their members' narrow economic benefits, and that even under left leadership this did not necessarily indicate a resumption of the forward march of labour. On the contrary, 'it seems to me that we now see a growing division of workers into sections and groups, each pursuing its own economic interest irrespective of the rest'. Given the new mixed economy, the group relied not on the potential loss strikes caused to employers, but on the inconvenience they might cause to the public, that is on putting pressure on the government to settle. In the nature of things this not only increased potential friction between groups of workers, but risked weakening the hold of the labour movement as a whole.

Nobody could live through the strike-happy 1970s in Britain without being aware of union militancy and the tensions between unions and governments. It reached its peak in the autumn and winter of 1978–9. However, I was sufficiently remote from the political scene on the industrial labour left to be surprised to find that my lecture led to an intense and politically charged controversy in *Marxism Today* over the next year. Without particularly intending to, I had touched several very raw nerves. The fact that within a few months of my article the weak and struggling Labour government had been comprehensively defeated in a General Election by the Conservatives under their new militantly class-warrior leader, Margaret Thatcher, made the pain even more intolerable. By the time the last criticism of my paper appeared in *Marxism Today* the Thatcher era had already begun. By the time the post-electoral debate on my paper was added to the pre-electoral, and both were published in 1981 in a book jointly sponsored by *Marxism Today* and Verso Editions,[1] the Labour Party itself had been split by the secession of the so-called social democrats, and the remaining rump of the party was struggling to survive.

In retrospect, the illusions of the mixed coalition of lefts which almost destroyed the Labour Party between 1978 and 1981 are harder to understand than the trade union leaders' illusions of power which had undermined it since the late 1960s. Since the General Strike of 1926 the British ruling class had been careful not to seek a head-on confrontation with the unions, i.e. with the 70 per cent or so of Britons who saw themselves as workers. The golden age of the post-1945 economy had even taken the edge off the built-in anti-unionism of industrialists. For twenty years giving in to union demands had not put pressure on profits. The seventies had begun to worry both politicians and economists, but they were a triumphant period for trade union leaders, who had blocked a Labour government's plans to limit their power, and who had twice defeated a Conservative government by national miners' strikes. Even those union leaders who realized that there had to be some limit on uncontrolled free market bargaining, saw themselves as negotiating a 'wages policy' with governments from a position of impressive strength.

As it happened, the glory years of seventies unionism were also those of the trade union left. For though the CP was small, declining, politically divided between Moscow hardliners and a 'Eurocommunist' leadership, and harassed on the left by younger Trotskyist militants, it probably played a larger part on the national trade union scene in the 1970s than ever before, under the leadership of its formidably able industrial organizer, Bert Ramelson, whose remarkable wife Marian, a Yorkshire textile worker, had been an amateur historian herself and an active supporter of the Historians' Group. The CP was not merely part of the 1970s militancy. With the blessing (not unqualified) of the two figures closest to national Godfathers in the TUC, Hugh Scanlon, of the Engineering Union, and Jack Jones, the former International Brigader, of the Transport and General Workers, the TUC left, largely marshalled by Ramelson and Ken Gill, co-ordinated the unions' fight against the two Wilson governments' attempts to clip their wings. Moreover, the long-hoped-for shift in the balance of the (still) great National Mineworkers' Union had happened in the 1960s. Yorkshire had swung left, bringing to national prominence a – then – CP protégé, the young Arthur Scargill. Together with the always solid and Party-led bastions of Wales and Scotland, the left now outvoted the equally reliable moderate bastions of northeast England. The fifteen years after 1970 were the era of the great national miners' strikes – victorious in 1972 and 1974, disastrous in 1984–5, thanks to the combination of Mrs Thatcher's determination to destroy the union and the delusions of the union's by then national leader, Arthur Scargill. By chance my lecture in the autumn of 1978 coincided with the tensest moment in relations between the unions and the Labour Party.

The illusion of trade union power under left-wing leaders and activists fuelled the even greater illusion of a conquest of the Labour Party, and hence of future Labour governments, by the socialist left. A mixed coalition of lefts within the Labour Party and 'entryist' revolutionaries who had joined it, had increasingly come together behind the project of winning control of the party under the banner of the increasingly radical ex-minister Tony Benn. Unlike the industrial militancy, which had substantial backing from the members of the unions, then at the peak of their numbers, the political militants reflected the decline in the political interest, votes and party membership among workers. In fact their strategy relied on the ability of small groups of militants among a largely inactive membership to capture Labour Party branches and, reinforced by the politically decisive 'block vote' of left-led unions at party conferences, to impose a more radical leadership and policy on the party. This was an entirely practicable strategy. Indeed, it almost succeeded. The illusion lay in the belief that the Labour Party thus captured by a mixed minority of sectarian leftwingers would somehow remain united, gain in electoral force, and would have a policy capable of standing up to the attack of Mrs Thatcher's class warriors, whose force they systematically failed to grasp.

Consequently this illusion led to disaster. Many traditional voters – one third of the actual self-described working-class electors – were in any case abandoning Labour and voting for the Conservatives. The party split, and for some years the alliance between the new Social Democratic Party and the Liberals actually came close to gaining more votes than the Labour Party. Two and a half years after the victory of Mrs Thatcher's Conservatives Labour had lost another one in five of its voters and no longer had majority support in *any* group of the working class, even the unskilled and unemployed. And this at a time when the Conservative government itself had lost votes since the election of 1979. As I wrote at the time, 'The triumph of Thatcher is a by-product of the defeat of Labour.' What made things worse was what I then described as 'the sheer refusal of some of the left to look unwelcome facts in the face'.[2]

In short, the future, perhaps the very existence, of the Labour Party was at stake in the years following the victory of Mrs Thatcher's Conservatives in 1979. The new Social Democrats had written it off, and aimed to replace it by an alliance, eventually a merger between themselves and the Liberals. I remember the occasion – a dinner in the house of Amartya Sen and his wife Eva Colorni – to which one of their Kentish Town neighbours came late, with apologies. Bill Rogers had just been meeting with the rest of the so-called 'Gang of Four' (Roy Jenkins, David Owen and Shirley Williams, all eventually in the House of Lords) to draft the declaration establishing what became, a few weeks later, the Social Democratic Party. It was joined by a substantial number of the Labour middle and professional classes, some of whom were to return to the party when it stopped pursuing its visibly suicidal course. On the other hand, the militant left, and many socialist intellectuals such as my old friend Ralph Miliband (whose sons were to become important figures in the offices of Prime Minister Tony Blair and Chancellor Gordon Brown), also wrote off the Labour Party until the moment when it had been captured and was ready to become 'a real socialist party', whatever that meant. I outraged some of my friends by pointing out that they were not seriously trying to defeat Mrs Thatcher. Whatever they thought, 'they acted as though another Labour government like the ones we have had before from time to time since 1945 were not just unsatisfactory, but worse than no Labour government ... (i.e.) worse than the only alternative government on offer, namely Mrs Thatcher's'.[3] The question was, could the Labour Party be saved?

In the end it was saved, but only just, at the Labour Conference in 1981, when Tony Benn stood for the deputy leadership of the party and was defeated in a photo-finish by Denis Healey. The future of the party was not certain until after the disastrous election of 1983, when Michael Foot, who had been elected leader in 1980 (as the candidate of the left, also against Healey), was succeeded by Neil Kinnock. On the eve of his election I spoke at a fringe meeting on that occasion, organized either by the Fabian Society or by *Marxism Today*. Kinnock himself made a point of being there, and signing a copy of my book 'with warm thanks', so, if I recall, were David Blunkett and Robin Cook, then also on the non-Bennite Labour left, at the time I write pillars of the Labour government since 1997. Whatever his limitations, Neil Kinnock, whose candidature I had strongly supported, was the leader who saved the Labour Party from the sectarians. After 1985, when he secured the expulsion of the Trotskyite 'Militant Tendency' from the party, its future was safe.

This was the only occasion on which I actually met Neil Kinnock, apart from the time when I interviewed him for *Marxism Today* a little later, returning rather depressed about his potential as a future prime minister. Hence the absurdity of the habit of some political journalists for the next year or two of linking my name with his ('Kinnock's guru'). Nevertheless, there was a sound political reason why the name of a Marxist intellectual who was not even in the Labour Party should, at a few moments of the battle for the survival of that party, have been useful for those who wanted to save it. I had been among the very few who predicted serious trouble for Labour, which gave me some standing in the controversy. I was among the few known socialist intellectuals who were openly sceptical of the project of taking over the party and argued against its proponents with passion and (I hope) some effectiveness.* But in those difficult times it was particularly useful for the opponents of the sectarians to be able to cite support from someone known to most activists in the party – at least to those who read books and periodicals – and with a long and incontrovertible track record on the far left as a Marxist. For in 1980 and 1981 constitutional changes had given the sectarian leftists what looked like a built-in majority within the party and thus virtually handed its fortunes over to them. The future of the party depended essentially on detaching enough activists of the Labour left from the sectarians to offset this, at least at crucial moments.

The case for doing so had to be made from the left, all the more so since until 1983 the chief alternative candidate for the Labour leadership was Denis Healey, formerly Minister of Defence and Chancellor of the Exchequer, who represented everything the left disliked, who did not try to conceal his contempt for most of them, and who had established a justified reputation as a political bully-boy. The Labour Party under Tony Blair has moved so far to the right of its traditional position that there is probably less ideological difference between Healey and myself when we meet today, old men looking back on a better past, than there has been since we first met in the student CP, but by the standards of the 1970s he was the man of the Labour right. In private life he was and is a person of charm, high intelligence and culture, underneath the battlements of his trademark eyebrows, and the author of one of the few British politicians' memoirs that can be read with enjoyment as a book.

---

* 'Trade unionism, with all its limitations, is never able to overlook the masses, because it organizes millions of them all the time, and has to mobilize them quite a lot of the time. But capturing the Labour Party for the left can be done in the short run without reference to the masses. It could, in theory, be achieved pretty well entirely by . . . a few tens of thousands of committed socialists and left Labour people by means of meetings, the drafting of resolutions and votes. The illusion of the early 1980s is that *organization* can replace politics,' in Martin Jacques and Francis Mulhern (eds), *The Forward March of Labour Halted?* (London, 1981), p. 173.

However, the public Healey was easier to respect than to love. He would certainly have made a far better political leader than any of the other candidates, although the sectarians would have done their best to destroy him. The situation at the time was such that probably only a leader with left-wing credentials could have got the party out of its crisis.

Michael Foot, who beat him, was not constructed to be a party leader or potential prime minister, and should not have been elected to the leadership. He was and is a marvellous man. For years he and I used to meet at the Hampstead bus stop from which we travelled together, I to the university, he to the House of Commons or the office of the journal *Tribune*, an increasingly stooped, casually dressed old man with a limp and a fine profile, shaking his white head of hair with passion. Walking – he belonged to the generation of the great hiking British intellectuals – and public transport were his forms of locomotion. Since he became a government minister only briefly in the 1970s, the official car was not part of his ego.

He was and is a Labour politician who attracts genuine love, as well as admiration for patent moral integrity and for his considerable talents and literary culture. He had eloquence of the kind that belonged to the era of mass meetings and great House of Commons occasions, before the days of the small TV screen: the oratory of the flashing eye, the gesture, the elocution reaching to the last row. He was a highly professional journalist of great rhetorical power, superb at denouncing injustice and reaction. He was a voracious reader and easy writer of some style, never tired of singing the praises of those he admired most, Jonathan Swift and William Hazlitt. Perhaps his capacity for enthusiasm, or his unwillingness to hurt, made him too uncritical. His life of Aneurin Bevan, the great leader of the Labour left, whose parliamentary seat in the South Wales valleys he inherited and in due course passed on to Neil Kinnock, was too hagiographical, his numerous book reviews, including those of my own books, not critical enough. I cannot think of anyone who actually disliked him.

He seemed, even to his contemporaries and colleagues, to belong to an older, almost a pre-1914 generation, the first from the old dissenting provincial middle class to abandon their traditional loyalty to the Liberal Party for the cause of the workers. He was not built for authority but for opposition, a 'tribune of the people' who defended it against the presumption of its rulers. For almost all his career in the Labour Party he was the spokesman of the left against the leadership, although they could always rely on his utter loyalty to the movement – notably in 1964, when the left had Harold Wilson's first Labour government with a tiny majority of three at its mercy. He was not an organization man. He lacked the unfortunately useful gifts of intrigue and horse-trading that give the term 'politician' a bad name, and the sense of egoism and personal ambition that drives so many of the most formidable of them. The three years of his leadership were a disaster.

Tony Benn, a good and honest man who almost brought the party to ruin, lacked neither ego nor ambition. After all, he had spent a great deal of time and energy fighting for the right to disclaim his title as a hereditary peer to win the right to shorten his name and to enter the real politics of the House of Commons. In some ways he was extremely well fitted to be what he plainly wanted to be more than anything else, namely leader of the party and, in due course, prime minister. Handsome, looking remarkably young, physically robust – politics is an exhausting game like rugby or chess – and eloquent, he was and remains one of the few faces and voices almost immediately recognizable by the general public. Even his air of eagerness, like a Boy Scout looking for an occasion to do a good turn, his trademark pipe, his proletarian preference for mugs of tea, were assets. Though he had no great political profile in the past, he was moving left in the 1970s. Had he wanted to, he would almost certainly have been able to hold the Labour Party together and see it through difficult times. He looked like winning the leadership sooner or later, and, like many others, I thought he was probably the best man for the job – until he threw it away. I interviewed him at some length for *Marxism Today* in October 1980, and was impressed, if not completely reassured, by his insistence that in his view the Labour Party should remain 'a very broad church'.

Yet a few months later it became entirely clear that Benn was totally unsuited for the job. He had put his money entirely on the sectarians. In January 1981 a special conference of the party in effect handed over its fortunes to the left. The details do not matter. It was now evident that only his own political stupidity could stop Benn from becoming the leader of the Labour Party fairly soon. At this point anyone with minimal political sense, knowing how deeply the party was split, would have played the card of generosity, reconciliation and unity. Instead of this Benn issued a triumphant call for the victorious left to take over and to demonstrate its power by electing him against Healey for the deputy leadership. Whether a more conciliatory approach would have prevented the secession of the future Social Democrats, no one can tell. However, Benn's total identification with the left sectarians made it evident to anyone who did not want the Labour Party to be reduced to a marginalized socialist chapel that its future required him to be defeated. And this was achieved, if only just. Tony Benn himself retreated to an honourable position as a backbench defender of the constitution, democracy and civil liberties and a propagandist for socialism, but his career as a serious politician was at an end.

II

Such as they were, my interventions in the political debate were almost entirely through *Marxism Today*. One would not have expected this modest monthly to become, in the course of the 1980s, and in spite of its association with the CP, essential reading in the media and political world – and not merely among the left. Even some eminent Conservative politicians – Edward Heath, Michael Heseltine, Christopher Patten – wrote for it or allowed themselves to be interviewed for it. A young Labour politician of no left-wing sympathies whatever, elected to Parliament in 1983, claimed he was a regular reader and allowed himself to be interviewed for it: Tony Blair. Most of the already established names who were to become major personalities of the future Labour government had their say in it: Gordon Brown, Robin Cook, David Blunkett, Michael Meacher. The journal was bitterly attacked by the hardliners within the Communist Party, which was about to be destroyed by its own internal battles and the collapse of the communist regimes, but its political leadership, firm supporters of the Prague Spring and the Italian kind of communism, gave it solid political and, of course, financial support as long as it could. (It went out of existence at the end of 1991 with the Party and the USSR.) In an era of crisis for the Labour Party the ideas for its future came from a communist journal. Its success was overwhelmingly due to the combination of political nous and journalistic flair of Martin Jacques, and not least to the decision to open its pages to writers far from the Party line, and the orthodoxies of the old socialists. Nevertheless, we also benefited by the almost total disarray of the traditional politico-intellectual universe in Britain in the Thatcher era. This chiefly affected the sectors left of centre, but even the Conservatives were exploring an unknown new territory. What must or could be done in the new era? How, even where, was it to be discussed? *Marxism Today* provided a space where these questions could be considered outside the established frameworks, above all because it insisted that with the arrival of Mrs Thatcher, 'The Great Moving Right Show' as the cultural theorist Stuart Hall called it in an article in 1979 which coined the term 'Thatcherism', all bets were off. The game was new. And *Marxism Today* said so, before the rest.

In retrospect nothing is more obvious. The Thatcher era was the nearest thing in the twentieth century to a political, social and cultural revolution – and not one for the better. Armed with the most uncontrolled and centralized power available to government in any electoral democracy, it set out to destroy everything in Britain that stood in the way of an unholy combination of unrestricted profit-maximizing private enterprise and national self-assertion, in other words greed and jingoism. It was moved not only by the justified belief that the British economy needed a kick in the pants but by class feeling, by what I called 'the anarchism of the lower middle class'. It was directed equally against the traditional ruling classes and their mode of rule, in practice including the monarchy, the country's established institutions, and the labour movement. In the course of this largely successful endeavour it obliterated most of the traditional British values and made the country unrecogniz-able. Most of my generation probably feel like an American friend who decided to settle in England in the new century after retiring from an academic career in Massachusetts, and who was asked whether he missed the USA. He answered: 'Nowhere near as much as I miss the Britain I knew when I first came here.' This, at bottom, was the reason for the overwhelming dissidence of, even the widespread visceral hatred of Thatcher, felt in intellectual and cultural Britain, and the increasing dissidence of the bulk of the college-educated middle class, symbolized by the spectacular refusal of Oxford University to grant her an honorary degree. Not that this prevented the ideological advance of the Thatcherite belief that the only way to run the public and private affairs of a nation was by businessmen with business expectations using business methods. What made the triumph of Thatcherism so bitter was that, after 1979, it was not based on any massive conversion of opinion in the country, but primarily, though not exclusively, on the deep division of its opponents. There was no wave of Thatcherite voting in the 1980s like that which lifted Ronald Reagan in the USA. It consistently remained a minority of the electorate. My own calls for some electoral arrangement between Labour and the Liberal–Social Democratic Alliance or, at the very least, systematic 'tactical voting'* by anti-Conservative electors, were (naturally) dismissed by both, although in the end the voters had more sense than the parties and voted tactically in large numbers and to good effect. What made the situation so frustrating was that neither Labour nor the Liberal–Social Democratic Alliance had an alternative to offer. Thatcherism remained the only strategy in town. In the end all we had to rely on was that it would eventually become so unpopular that it would lose against any opposition, which is indeed what happened – but only after eighteen years. We warned that much of the Thatcherite revolution might prove irreversible. In this also we were right.

On paper it was easy to analyse the situation realistically, dismissing the 'cries of betrayal against those who insist on looking at the world the way it is'.[4] In practice it was hard, since many of those against whom I wrote were comrades (or at least former comrades) and friends. Apart from myself and Stuart Hall, *Marxism Today* could not rely on the steady support of any established intellectuals of the old and the original (post-1956) new left. Most of the socialist and Marxist intellectuals outside the *Marxism Today* milieu were hostile, including such prestigious figures as Raymond Williams, Ralph Miliband and the eminences of the *New Left Review*. I was denounced at trade union meetings. This is not surprising. For

* I may have been the first to bring the term into the electoral debate.

many of them the line of *Marxism Today* meant the betrayal of the traditional hopes and policies of socialists, not to mention of the proletarian revolution which the Trotskyites still looked forward to. It could even look like disloyalty to the organized working class, battered with the full force of state power by a government waging class war, especially during the great national coalminers' strike of 1984–5, which mobilized the full force of the left's (and not only the left's) emotional sympathy. Mine too, although it was patent that the delusions of an extremist leadership of the union, relying on the rhetoric of militancy and the traditional unionist refusal to break ranks in the middle of battle, were leading the union and the coalfield communities to certain disaster. Even we were not immune to the sheer force of the movement's rhetorical self-delusion. *Marxism Today*, surveying the wreckage after the strike with a degree of realism, could not bring itself to admit the scale of the defeat.[5]

This, indeed, was the general predicament of socialists in Britain from the middle 1970s on. Things fell apart for moderate reformist social democrats as well as for communists and other revolutionaries. For Marxists and non-Marxists, revolutionaries and reformists, we had in the last analysis believed that capitalism could not produce the conditions of a good life for humanity. It was neither just nor in the long run viable. An alternative socialist economic system, or at least its forerunner, a society dedicated to social justice and universal welfare, could take its place, if not now then at some future time; and the movement of history was plainly bringing this nearer through the agency of state or public action in the interest of the mass of the wage-earning classes, implicitly or explicitly anti-capitalist. Probably never did this look more plausible than in the years immediately following the Second World War, when even European conservative parties were careful to declare themselves anti-capitalist and US statesmen praised public planning. None of these assumptions looked convincing in the 1970s. After the 1980s the defeat of the traditional left, both political and intellectual, was undeniable. Its literature was dominated by variations on the theme 'What's Left?' I contributed to it myself. Paradoxically, the problem was far more urgent in the non-communist countries. In almost all the communist regimes the collapse of a widely discredited 'really existing socialism', the only socialism officially extant, had eliminated any other kind from the political scene. Moreover, it was reasonable enough for people there to place their hopes, even sometimes their utopian hopes, in an unknown western capitalism, so obviously more prosperous and efficient than their own broken-down systems. It was in the west and south that the case against capitalism remained convincing, especially that against the increasingly dominant ultra-*laissez-faire* capitalism favoured by transnational corporations, backed by economic theologians and governments.

Marxism Today could see that the simple refusal to acknowledge that things had changed dramatically ('Let cowards flinch and traitors sneer, we'll keep the red flag flying here'), however emotionally attractive, was not on the cards. Indeed, that is why the traditional Labour left, always present and significant in the party's history, though rarely decisive, disappeared from sight after 1983. It no longer exists. On the other hand, we could not accept – until Tony Blair became leader in 1994 we could barely even envisage – the alternative of 'New Labour', which accepted the logic as well as the practical results of Thatcherism, and deliberately abandoned everything that might remind the decisive middle-class voters of workers, trade unions, publicly owned industries, social justice, equality, let alone socialism. We wanted a reformed Labour, not Thatcher in trousers. The narrow failure of Labour to win the 1992 election eliminated this prospect. I am not alone in recalling that election night as the saddest and most desperate in my political experience.

The logic of electoral politics as perceived by politicians whose programme consisted of permanent re-election, and after 1997 the logic of government, drove us out of 'real' politics. Some of the Young Turks of *Marxism Today* went where the power was. When, eighteen months after Labour had returned to power, Martin Jacques revived the journal for a single issue to survey the new era of Blair, one of them looked down on us – myself and Stuart Hall specifically – from the heights of 10 Downing Street, as people viewing society from the seminar room, 'as if from the outside, without any sense of membership or responsibility', unlike 'intellectuals who are able to combine critique, vision and practical policy'. In short, academic or not, 'critique was no longer enough'.[6] The time had come for the political realists and the technicians of government. And both must operate in a market economy and fit in with its requirements.

True enough. But our point – certainly mine – was and is that if critique is no longer enough, it is more essential than ever. We criticized New Labour not because it had accepted the realities of living in a capitalist society, but for accepting too much of the ideological assumptions of the prevailing free market economic theology. Not least the assumption which destroys the foundations of all political movements for improving the condition of the people, and with them therefore the justification of Labour governments, namely that the efficient conduct of a society's affairs can only be by the search for personal advantage, i.e. by behaving like businessmen. Indeed, the critique of neo-liberalism was all the more necessary, since it not only appealed to businessmen and to governments who wanted to remove their traditional suspicion of Labour, and needed a justification for appealing to middle-class 'swing voters', but because neo-liberalism claimed the authority of a 'science' increasingly identified with the interests of global capitalism, namely economics, as consecrated for almost a quarter of a century by its highest authority, the Nobel Prize for Economics. Not until the very end of the century, when it was finally awarded to Amartya Sen, and then to a vocal critic of 'the Washington consensus', Joseph Stiglitz, was it given again to economists known to be outside the prevailing orthodoxy; and not until (so it is understood) the electors for the Nobel prizes in the natural sciences had expressed dissatisfaction at the consistent ideological bias of what was intended to be a scientific distinction. Perhaps the bursting of the great speculative bubbles of the *fin-de-siècle*, 1997–2001 have finally broken the spell of market fundamentalism. The end of the hegemony of global neo-liberalism has been predicted and indeed announced long enough – I have done so myself more than once. It has already done more than enough harm.

III

In the meantime Soviet socialism was dying.

Unlike the end of the Cold War and the implosion of the Soviet Empire, the end of the USSR took place in comparative slow motion, between the time Gorbachev came to power in 1985 and its formal death in late 1991. It had its moments of headline drama – Yeltsin on the tank in Moscow resisting the attempted coup of August 1991 – but its basic action took place in the darkness of the Soviet corridors of power, such as the unpublicized but fundamental decision in 1989 to abandon the last of the Five-Year Plans (1986–92) in mid-course. As it happens, I was working on the Soviet economy at the UN university's World Institute of Development and Economic Research (WIDER) and watched the process in the agreeable and acutely Russia-watching city of Helsinki, a few hours by land, a few minutes by air from the Soviets, where I spent some summers during those final years. If it did nothing else, it gave me an insight into the disastrous blindness of the western economists who passed through there, moving comfortably between airport, transnational hotel chain and limo, preparing to put the Russian economy to rights by the untrammelled operations of the free market, as certain of the possession of eternal truth as any Islamic theologian.

By the 1980s the idea that the socialism of the USSR or its followers was what those of us inspired by the October Revolution had in mind was dead. A case could still be made for it as the necessary counterweight to the other superpower, and with greater moral conviction as the supporter of the liberation of oppressed peoples, notably in South Africa. The Moscow regime supported the ANC struggle, financed and armed it for decades when there was no foreseeable prospect of its success or of Soviet benefit. A devotion to colonial liberation was probably the last relic of the spirit of world revolution. Indeed, what had kept me immune to the appeal of Maoism was that, in spite of its internationalist rhetoric in the days of the Sino-Soviet split, Chinese Communism and Maoist ideology seemed to me essentially national if not nationalist, an impression not weakened by a few weeks' visit to that impressive country in 1985. Unlike the USSR, which would never have backed a movement as remote from social revolution as the thuggish UNITA in Angola, Maoist China, which advertised its vocation as the centre of global armed struggle, actually supported guerrilla movements very selectively, and almost entirely on anti-Soviet and anti-Vietnamese grounds.

We, or at least I, no longer had many hopes. My friend Georg Eisler recalls how, returning from Cuba in the 1960s, I wondered how long it would take before Havana became assimilated to Sofia. The Soviet invasion of Czechoslovakia, which I remember as vividly as others do the death of Kennedy, made it unthinkable even to visit Prague again, but would one want to retire from the West even to a relatively liberal country like Hungary? The answer was no, even though, for an old central European, it was intellectually and culturally far more lively and less provincial than its radiantly prosperous neighbour, Austria.

What did old communists and the general left expect from the USSR in the 1980s except that it should be a counterweight to the USA and by its very existence frighten the rich and the rulers of the world into taking some notice of the needs of the poor? Nothing, any longer. And yet we felt a strange sense of relief, even a glimmer of hope, when Mikhail Gorbachev came to power in 1985. In spite of everything he seemed to represent our kind of socialism – indeed, to judge by early statements, the sort of communism represented by the Italians or the 'socialism with a human face' of the Prague Spring – which we had thought almost extinct there. Curiously, our admiration was not to be significantly diminished by the tragedy of his dramatic failure inside the Soviet Union, which was almost total. More than any other single man, he became responsible for destroying it. But he had also been, one might say, almost single-handedly responsible for ending half a century's nightmare of nuclear world war and, in Eastern Europe, for the decision to let go of the USSR's satellite states. It was he who, in effect, tore down the Berlin Wall. Like so many in the West I shall go on thinking of him with unalloyed gratitude and moral approval. If there is one image from the 1980s that has stayed with me, it is the multiple face of Mikhail Gorbachev on the display screens in a TV shop which suddenly stopped me in my tracks somewhere on West 57th Street in New York. I listened to him addressing the United Nations with a sense of wonder and relief.

That he would fail at home was, alas, soon obvious; perhaps even that he and his fellow-reformers were too foolhardy or, if one prefers, neither big nor knowledgeable enough about the nature of the world they were ruling, to know quite what they were doing. Perhaps nobody was, and the best thing for the Soviet Union and its peoples would have been to continue its slow descent hoping for piecemeal improvement under a less ambitious and more realistic reformer. So, as I wrote from Helsinki in a commentary on the 1991 failed coup that ended the Gorbachev era, 'he chose glasnost in order to force perestroika; it should have been the other way round. And neither marxism nor western economists had either experience or theory that helped.'[7] Like a crippled giant tanker moving toward the reefs a rudderless Soviet Union therefore drifted towards disintegration.[8] Finally it foundered. And the losers, in the short and medium term, were not only the peoples of the former USSR, but the poor of the world.

'Capitalism and the rich have, for the time being, stopped being scared,' I wrote in 1990.

Why should the rich, especially in countries like ours where they now glory in injustice and inequality, bother about anyone except themselves? What political penalties do they need to fear if they allow welfare to erode and the protection of those who need it to atrophy? This is the chief effect of the disappearance of even a very bad socialist region from the globe.[9]

Ten years after the end of the USSR, it is possible that fear has returned. The rich and the governments whom they have convinced of their indispensability may once again discover that the poor require concessions rather than contempt. But, thanks to the weakening of the fabric of social democracy and the disintegration of communism, the danger today comes from the enemies of reason: religious and ethno-tribal fundamentalists, xenophobes, among them the heirs of fascism or parties inspired by fascism, who sit in the governments of India, Israel and Italy. It is one of the many ironies of history that, after half a century of anti-communist Cold War, the only enemies of the Washington government who have actually killed its citizens on the territory of the USA are its own ultra-right zealots and fundamentalist Sunni Muslim militants once deliberately financed by the 'free world' against the Soviets. The world may yet regret that, faced with Rosa Luxemburg's alternative of socialism or barbarism, it decided against socialism.

17

Among the Historians

What has happened to the writing of history in my lifetime? Readers not interested in this somewhat specialized subject may skip this chapter, although it is unfortunately not as academic as it seems at first sight. There is no getting away from the past, i.e. from those who record, interpret, argue about and construct it. Our everyday lives, the states we live in, the governments we live under, are surrounded by, drenched in, the products of my profession. What goes into school textbooks and politicians' speeches about the past, the material for writers of fiction, makers of TV programmes and videos, comes ultimately from historians. What is more, most historians, including all good ones, know that in investigating the past, even the remote past, they are also thinking and expressing opinions in terms of and about the present and its concerns. Understanding history is as important for citizens as for experts, and Britain is lucky in having a powerful tradition of serious but accessible writing by experts for a wider public: Adam Smith, Edward Gibbon, Charles Darwin, Maynard Keynes. Historians should not write only for other historians.

In my generation what Marc Bloch called 'the trade of the historian' was not taught in any systematic way in Britain. We picked it up as best we could. Very much depended on whom we encountered as undergraduate students. In my days at Cambridge there was only one teacher whose lectures, though given at nine o'clock in the morning, I attended regularly, in common with most of the bright young radical history students of that time.[1] The astonishing M. M. ('Mounia') Postan, recently arrived in Cambridge from the London School of Economics, was a red-haired man who looked like a lively ape or Neanderthal survivor, which did not stand in the way of his impressive appeal to women, and he lectured in a heavy Russian accent on economic history. Economic history was the only branch of the subject then on the Cambridge programme which was relevant to the interests of Marxists, but the Postan lectures, with their air of intellectual revivalism, attracted even some such as the young Arthur M. Schlesinger who made no bones about his 'lack of skill (and interest) in economic history', not to mention his lack of interest in Marxism. Every one of those lectures – intellectual-rhetorical dramas in which a historical thesis was first expounded, then utterly dismantled and finally replaced by Postan's own version – was a holiday from interwar British insularity, of which the Cambridge history faculty provided a particularly self-satisfied example. What other don would have told us in 1936 to read the recent French *Annales d'histoire économique et sociale*, not yet famous even in its own country, to invite the great Marc Bloch to lecture in Cambridge, presenting him to us, justifiably, as the greatest living medievalist? (Alas, I can remember nothing of his lecture except the image of a small pudgy man.) Though passionately anti-communist, Postan was the only man in Cambridge who knew Marx, Weber, Sombart and the rest of the great central and East Europeans, and took their work sufficiently seriously to expound and criticize it. He knew nevertheless that he attracted the young Marxists, and, though denouncing their belief in Russian bolshevism, welcomed them as allies in the fight against historical conservatism.[2] During the Cold War, when I depended on his references as my doctoral supervisor, he also helped to keep me out of jobs by pointing out to anyone concerned that I was a communist. I cannot exactly say that he was my teacher, or indeed anyone's teacher – he formed no school and had no disciples – but he was my bridge to the wider world of history. And he was certainly the most surprising figure to be found in a senior history chair in Britain, or probably anywhere, between the wars – impressive, charming and absurd.

For Mounia Postan, somewhat improbably for a historian, was a lifelong fantasist and romancer. Without corroboration you could not believe a word of what he said. If he did not know the answer to a question – about the middle ages or the love-affairs of his students – he invented one. Since he was also very obviously an outsider in interwar Britain, whose highest ambition was to be an insider, the scope for fantasy was vast. Moreover, he lied with an utterly disarming shamelessness or *chutzpah*. Many years later when he was due to retire from his Cambridge chair but did not want to, he told the university that he was one year younger than his documented age, claiming that his birth record in what had then been Russia and was now Romania, no longer existed. As usual, he did not convince. As usual, people shook their heads, smiled, and said: 'That's Mounia!'

In some ways the greatest of his fantasies was the construction of a new identity in Britain, where he arrived from Soviet Russia via Romania in 1921. His early history was very much what one might have expected of a middle-class Jewish youth from the south-western borders of Tsarist Russia. He had studied at Odessa University until the Revolution, which he welcomed, joining a radical Marxist-Zionist group, divided only between those who wanted to go to Palestine to build a socialist society immediately, and those who wanted to organize the world revolution first. Mounia belonged to the second tendency. When Soviet power, distrustful of Zionism, was firmly institutionalized in the Ukraine after the civil war, he found himself imprisoned, he claimed for a few months, and then released. (During the Second World War this made him unacceptable to the Soviet authorities as a representative of the British Ministry of Economic Warfare.) He then came to England where, beginning as a part-time student, he made his career in the London School of Economics as a medieval agrarian historian. He did not so much conceal his background as allow the world to choose between an assortment of stories of varied continental adventure, mostly implying non-Jewishness, although no Jew who met him, and even in interwar England few non-Jews, could have been deceived for a moment. And yet, he succeeded by sheer brilliance, absurd charm, immigrant determination and not least the help of his teacher and first wife, the medieval economic historian Eileen Power (1889–1940), in climbing the peaks of his new environment, ending his life as Sir Michael Postan, married to Lady Cynthia Keppel, sister of the Earl of Albemarle. In this he was more successful than the other implausible and intellectually brilliant historiographic import from Eastern Europe, the very consciously Jewish L. B. (Sir Lewis) Namier, who got his knighthood but failed to get a chair in his cherished Oxford.

One obvious difference between the two was that one was an international figure engaged in a global field, while the other's main historical interests were insular. At one of our first meetings Fernand Braudel asked me: 'I understand in England there is much talk about a historian called Namier and his school. Can you tell me something about him?' Neither he nor any other economic historian would have asked this question about Postan, if only because from 1934 on he had edited the internationally known journal in the field, *Economic History Review*. Moreover, while nobody outside England except a few specialists cared much that Namier had (it was then thought) revolutionized the approach to the esoteric subject of English eighteenth-century parliamentary history, all economic historians in the effective academic universe recognized Postan's topics in medieval agrarian history as important, cared about them and were prepared to engage in debate on them across the borders of state and ideology – from Harvard to Tokyo. Unlike research on national politics of the past, economic history in those days had an accepted universe of discourse, even an accepted framework by which to judge the interest of the questions asked, whatever the disagreement about the answers.

In some ways the contrast between Postan and Namier symbolized the major conflict that divided the profession of history, and the major tendency of its development from the 1890s to the 1970s. This was the battle between the conventional assumption that 'history is past politics', either within nation-states or in their relations to each other, and a history of the structures and changes of societies and cultures, between history as narrative and history as analysis and synthesis, between those who thought it impossible to generalize about human affairs in the past and those who thought it essential. The battle had begun in Germany in the 1890s, but in my student days the most prominent champions of rebellion, apart from the Marxists, were in France: Marc Bloch and Lucien Febvre through their review *Annales*. Paradoxically Bloch and Postan's field of medieval history, which one might have expected to appeal to conservatives, actually encouraged original thinking about the past. Even the most conventional historian found it impossible to cut medieval life into neat and separable slices – political, economic, religious or whatever. It almost demanded comparisons and a rethinking of contemporary assumptions and, incidentally, cut across the borders of modern states, nations and cultures. Like ancient history, and perhaps for similar reasons, medieval history is a subject which has attracted some of the best as well as the most stuffy historical minds in my lifetime, though fewer brilliant Marxist scholars than antiquity. On the other hand, it was a field which contained a large number of figures such as my boss at Birkbeck College, the late R. R. Darlington, whose dream in life was to produce an exhaustive edition of a minor twelfth-century chronicler, and who appeared genuinely appalled when I, a young lecturer, suggested that a seminar by a South African social anthropologist then attached to the college might be of interest to students of his special paper on Anglo-Saxon England. What archives had he worked in?

Into this battle between the old and the new history young Marxists like myself at the start of their professional careers as historians, now found themselves precipitated as they joined what was still a small field, measured both in the number of its practitioners and in their output. The enormous expansion of universities old and new, and the stratospheric rise in 'the literature', did not get under way until the 1960s. Even in countries like Britain and France, or in fairly broad academic fields such as economic history worldwide, virtually everyone knew of, and could get to know, everyone else. Fortunately the first international congress of historical sciences after the Second World War was held in Paris in 1950. Before the war the historical establishment had ruled supreme – for by driving the best of their social sciences into emigration fascism if anything reinforced it. The innovators had at best managed to establish a foothold in a broadly defined zone of 'economic and social history', as in France and Britain. However, the war had so disrupted the old structures that for a brief moment the rebels had actually taken charge. The congress, organized by an *Annales* man, Charles Morazé, shortly but politely to be eliminated from power in the review by the rising star Fernand Braudel, was planned on heterodox lines, essentially by the French, with some input by the Italians and some from the Low Countries and Scandinavia, plus by some very uncharacteristic Anglo-Saxons: Postan himself, the Australian historical statistician Colin Clark, and a Marxist ancient historian. The Germans were, of course, virtually absent, even though it was not known at the time quite how much their eminent historians had been involved in the Nazi system. The historians of the USA attended the congress in droves – when have Americans not been keen on visiting Paris? – but they had plainly not been much consulted about the planning. Apart from one report on ancient history, and a last-minute Texan disquisition on world history as frontier history, they were kept outside the main planned sections. The Soviet Union and all its dependencies were absent, with the one exception of Poland. They all turned up in full force in 1955 after Stalin's death, at the next international congress in Rome. Times were tense in those months immediately after the outbreak of the Korean War when the (French) President of the International Committee said gloomily that 'the congress would provide future historians of historiography with an important record of the mentality of historians after the crisis of the second world war . . . while they waited for the third'.[3]

One innovation in which I found myself involved directly was a section on Social History, probably the first in any historical congress. In fact, there was as yet very little of it, at all events for the nineteenth and twentieth centuries, nor was it at all clear in the minds of the planners what the term implied. It was obviously more than the somewhat narrow study of labour and socialist organizations which had previously had first claim on the name (that is the Amsterdam International Institute for Social History, holder of the Marx–Engels manuscripts). Equally obviously it should be concerned with labour, with social classes and social movements, and with the relations between economic and social phenomena, not to mention 'the reciprocal influences between economic facts and political, juridical, religious, etc. phenomena'.[4] To my surprise, since I had barely published my first article in a learned journal, I found myself nominated as the official chairman of the 'Contemporary' session, presiding over a splendid report by a crippled Marxist scholar on fifteenth to sixteenth-century Poland. I assume Postan must have proposed me, since nobody else could have. My session was attended by an odd collection of anomalies and the unestablished, soon due to move closer to the centre of the historical world. There was J. Vicens Vives, a lone visitor from Franco's Barcelona in search of intellectual contact, who was to become the inspirer of his country's historians. There was Paul Leuillot, secretary of the *Annales*, who saw himself as spokesman for Marc Bloch and Fernand

Braudel, as well as myself, about to become co-founder of *Past & Present*. There were the often brilliant French researchers with uncompleted but vast theses, such as Pierre Vilar and Jean Meuvret, and therefore not yet integrated into the university system, who would shortly be fitted into Braudel's new rival to the Sorbonne, the 6th Section of the Ecole Pratique des Hautes Etudes (now Ecole des Hautes Etudes en Sciences Sociales). There were the Marxists and their critics. In short, the face of historiography in the 1950s and 1960s was becoming visible.

The crucial point to note is that, in spite of patent ideological differences and Cold War polarization, the various schools of historiographic modernizers were going the same way and fighting the same adversaries – and they knew it. Essentially, they were against 'positivism', the belief that if you got the 'facts' right, the conclusions would take care of themselves, and against the traditional bias of conventional historians in favour of kings, ministers, battles and treaties, i.e. top-level decision-makers both political and military. In other words, they wanted a much broadened or democratized as well as methodologically sophisticated field of history. They were in favour of a history fertilized by the social sciences (including notably social anthropology), which is why the *Annales* broadened out from economic and social history to the subtitle *Economies, Sociétés, Civilisations*. When, fifteen years after the end of Hitler, a postwar generation of modernizers began to make its mark on German history, in the German Federal Republic it chose the banner of 'Historical Social Science'.

As I have already hinted, the historical modernizers, though united against historical conservatives, were neither ideologically nor politically homogeneous. The inspiration of the French was in no way Marxist, except for the historiography of the French Revolution, which, being safely anchored in the harbour of the Sorbonne, had nothing to do with the *Annales* school. (Braudel once told me regretfully that the trouble with French history in his lifetime was that its two major figures, he and Ernest Labrousse of the Sorbonne, were brothers who could not get on.) In Britain, on the other hand, the Marxists were unusually prominent, and the journal *Past & Present*, which emerged from the discussions of the Communist Party Historians' Group, became the modernizers' chief medium.

The rebel Germans, a postwar generation, were largely formed by their studies in Britain and the USA, and tended to Max Weber rather than Marx, as against the home-grown Marxism of the British Communist Party Historians' Group. Yet we all recognized each other as allies. *Past & Present* acknowledged the inspiration of *Annales* in the first paragraph of its first issue. For *Annales* Jacques Le Goff ('a reader from the beginning, an admirer, a friend, almost (if I may say so) a secret lover'[5]) compared *Past & Present* with his journal, while the chief of the new Germans appears to regard 'the astonishing effect of the Marxist historians' generation' as the main factor behind 'the global impact of English historiography since the 1960s'.[6]

At this stage history in the USA (as distinct from the US social sciences) still played a relatively minor international role. In fact, there was little real contact between it and the old world, except in fields of traditional interest to US Europeanists, such as the French Revolution, and in the fields brought with them from Europe by the German exiles after 1933. But Europeanists were a minority, distrusted as cosmopolitan Ivy Leaguers by the great bulk of generally monoglot historians whose subject was the history of the USA, a subject which, as treated by most of them, had very little in common with what historians elsewhere were doing. Only slavery was a subject that aroused international interest, but the younger historians of this subject who were to make a mark abroad were very untypical of the profession in the fifties and sixties. They included several young postwar members of the American Communist Party – Herb Gutman, the brilliant Gene Genovese and the former national secretary of the Young Communist League and subsequent Nobel Prize laureate, the endlessly ingenious Bob Fogel.

Curiously enough, this was true even of so patently global a subject as economic history, which may explain why, when an international association was founded in this field, it was basically run as an Anglo-French condominium of Braudel and Postan. Stateside historical innovations – economic history in terms of businessmen ('entrepreneurial' history) in the 1950s, 'psychohistory' (that is Freudian interpretations of historical figures) and the much more dramatic 'cliometrics' (history as retrospective and often imaginary econometrics) in the 1960s – found it hard to cross the

Atlantic. Not until 1975 was the quinquennial World Congress of Historical Sciences held in the USA, presumably on diplomatic grounds, to balance the Moscow session of 1970.

On the whole, in the thirty years following the Second World War the historical traditionalists were fighting a rearguard engagement in a losing battle against the advancing modernists in most western countries where history flourished freely. Perhaps they would have defended themselves more effectively if the garrison of the central stronghold of traditional historical scholarship, Germany, had not been put out of action by its association with National Socialism. (The situation of historians in communist countries was not comparable to the West, but, as it happened, the Marxism to which they were officially and sometimes genuinely committed fitted in with the western modernizers more than with traditionalist, mainly nationalist, history in their own countries.) In 1970 a rather optimistic, not to say triumphalist, meeting was organized by the American journal *Daedalus* to survey the state of history. Except for the (defensive) spokesmen for political and military history, the gathering was dominated by the modernizers – British, French and, among the under-forties, American.[7] By that time a common flag had been found for the far from homogeneous popular front of the innovators: 'social history'. It fitted in with the political radicalization of the dramatically expanding student population of the 1960s. The term was vague, sometimes misleading, but as I wrote at the time, noting the 'remarkably flourishing state of the field': 'It is a good moment to be a social historian. Even those of us who never set out to call ourselves by this name will not want to disclaim it.'[8]

There was some cause for satisfaction. Not least because, somewhat unexpectedly, the Cold War had not substantially interfered with developments in history. Indeed, it is surprising how little it penetrated the world of historiography, except, obviously, on such matters as the history of Russia and the USSR. *Capitalism and the Historians*, a volume published in the 1940s under the auspices of Friedrich von Hayek, argued that historians who pointed out the negative effects of the Industrial Revolution on the poor were systematically biased against the benefits of the free enterprise system. This led to a lively polemic which entertained students, the so-called 'Standard-of-Living Debate' when the left (i.e. myself, speaking for the communist historians) responded, but it cannot be said that this debate, which has continued at intervals ever since, was subsequently conducted on ideological lines. Explosive subjects such as Russia, especially in the twentieth century, and the history of communism were, of course, ideological battlefields, although the debate was one-sided, since the orthodoxies enforced in the Soviet Empire crippled both their historians and their interpretations. If one was a serious Soviet historian, the best thing was to stick to the history of the ancient East and the Middle Ages, although it was touching to see how the modernists rushed to say (within the constraints of the permissible) what they knew to be true every time the window seemed to be slightly opened – as in 1956 and in the early 1960s. I myself became essentially a nineteenth-century historian, because I soon discovered – actually in the course of an aborted project of the CP Historians' Group to write a history of the British labour movement – that, given the strong official Party and Soviet views about the twentieth century, one could not write about anything later than 1917 without the likelihood of being denounced as a political heretic. I was ready to write about the century in a political or public capacity, but not as a professional historian. My history finished at Sarajevo in June 1914.

Luckily I abstained from twentieth-century history until it was almost over, but it went against the grain of the historiographical movement, which was away from the remote past and towards the present. Until well past 1945 'real' history finished, at the latest, in 1914 after which the immediate past reverted to chronicle, journalism or contemporary commentary. Indeed, since the archives remained closed in Britain for several decades, it simply could not be written to the standards of traditional historians. In most countries, even the nineteenth century had not yet been fully absorbed by academic history departments, except by the economic historians. The great historiographical debates had not been about it, although political radicalism, not least in the form of a new passion for labour history, now drew attention to an era which had been seriously neglected by historians in a number of countries. Even in Britain, until the 1960s politicians, serious journalists, relatives and essayists wrote the biographies of the great figures of Victorian Britain, not professors. Nevertheless, the gap between past and present narrowed, perhaps because so many professional historians had actually been involved in the Second World War.

At the same time, academic history in the western sense was still largely confined to the First and Second worlds and Japan. Broadly speaking, outside these regions it did not exist, did not flourish, or continued along traditional lines, except for minorities of Marxists and (as in parts of Latin America) patches of modernist Parisian influence. Moreover, most academic history was overwhelmingly Eurocentric, or – in the term preferred in the USA – concerned with 'Western Civilization'. The globe entered Cambridge history only as 'The Expansion of Europe'. With rare exceptions such as Charles Boxer it was not historians but geographers, anthropologists and language specialists, as well naturally as imperial administrators, who occupied themselves with 'non-western' affairs. Before the war extra-European history as such interested few historians except (by reason of their anti-imperialism) the Marxists and non-European historians such as the Japanese, who were then also under strong Marxist influence. In Cambridge a succession of historians convened the so-called 'colonial group' of the student Communist Party (over-whelmingly South Asians). The Canadian E. H. Norman, later a diplomat and pioneer historian of modern Japan who committed suicide in 1957 under pressure from the US witch-hunters, was followed by my old friend V. G. (Victor) Kiernan, a man of dis-arming charm and universal, elegant erudition about all continents who also wrote on the poet Horace and translated Urdu poetry, by the Canadian Harry Ferns, whose field was Argentina and who became extremely conservative in later years, and by the brilliant, original and self-destructive Jack Gallagher, who never got up before midday and later occupied the chairs of imperial history in both Oxford and Cambridge. My own interest in extra-European history also derives from my association with that group.

Extra-western history came into its own with the decolonization of the old empires and the simultaneous rise of the USA as a world power. World history as the history of the globe emerged in the 1960s, with the obvious progress of globalization. Historians from the Third World, notably a group of brilliant Indians, spun off from the local schools of Marxist debate, gained worldwide recognition only in the 1990s. The interests of world empire as well as the extraordinary resources available to US universities made the USA the centre of the new post-Eurocentric world history and, incidentally, transformed its history textbooks and journals. How could historical perspectives remain the same? Fidel Castro brought about the systematic development of Latin American studies in Britain in the early 1960s. Indeed we understood at the time that it was influenced by suggestions from President Kennedy's Washington that it would be convenient to supplement locally distrusted North American experts on this region with the more acceptable Europeans. (If so, the project misfired. Latin American history overwhelmingly attracted young radicals.) However, the histories of Europe, the USA and the rest of the world remained separate from each other – their publics coexisting but barely touching. History remains, alas, primarily a series of niche markets for both writers and readers. In my generation only a handful of historians has tried to integrate them in a comprehensive world history. This was partly because of the almost total failure, largely for institutional and linguistic reasons, of history to emancipate itself from the framework of the nation-state. Looking back, this provincialism was probably the major weakness of the subject in my lifetime.

Nevertheless, around 1970 it seemed reasonable to suppose that the war for the modernization of historiography that had begun in the 1890s had been won. The main railway network along which the trains of historiography would roll had been built. Not that the modernizers, at least outside the French enemies of the 'history of events', necessarily proposed a hegemony of economic and social history, or even a relegation of political history, let alone the history of ideas and culture. The modernizers were far from reductionists. Though they believed that history must explain and generalize, they knew it was not like the natural sciences. However, they believed that history had a comprehensive project, whether it was Braudel's 'total' or 'global history, integrating the contributions of all the sciences of man', or, if I may quote my own definition, of 'what history in the broadest sense is about: how and why Homo sapiens got from the palaeolithic to the nuclear era'.[9] Yet within a few years the scene had changed utterly. As Braudel himself complained about the *Annales* he no longer directed in the 1970s, the sense of priorities, the distinction between significance and triviality, which was essential to the old project, had gone. Just so old hands from *Past & Present* complained about Raphael Samuel's new *History Workshop Journal* (the last remote offspring of the old CP Historians' Group), that it discovered all sorts of corners of the past interesting to enthusiasts, but showed no sign of wanting to ask questions about them. History as the exploration of an objectively recoverable past had not yet been challenged. That only came with the fashion for 'postmodernism', a term which was virtually unknown in Britain before the 1980s, and which, fortunately, had made only marginal inroads into the field of serious historical writing by the start of the new century. Nevertheless, sometime in the early seventies the historiographical tide turned. Those who thought they had won most of the battles from the 1930s on, now found it running against them. 'Structure' was on the way down, 'culture' was on the way up. Perhaps the best way of summarizing the change is to say that the young historians after 1945 found their inspiration in Braudel's *Mediterranean* (1949), the young historians after 1968 in the anthropologist Clifford Geertz's brilliant tour de force of 'thick description', 'Deep Play: Notes on the Balinese Cock-Fight' (1973).[10]

There was a shift away from historical models or 'the large *why* questions', a shift from 'the analytical to the descriptive mode',[11] from economic and social structure to culture, from recovering fact to recovering feeling, from telescope to microscope – as in the enormously influential little monograph on the world-view of one sixteenth-century eccentric Friulian miller by the young Italian historian Carlo Ginzburg.[12] Perhaps there was also an element of that curious intellectual distrust for the rationalism of the natural sciences which was to become much more fashionable as the century drew to its end. Not that one can see much of a return from structural to narrative history among academics, or to old-style political history. At any rate, as far as I know historians of younger generations in the past thirty years have so far produced no masterpiece of non-analytic narrative history to be compared to that acknowledged triumph of traditional scholarship in this genre, Steven Runciman's *The Crusades* (1951–4). However, the sheer extent to which patently important matters had been concealed or passed in silence in the half-century since 1945 left a vast scope for straight, archive-based filling of gaps, or the 'history of events'. One has only to think of the hidden continent of Soviet archives which came into public view in the 1990s, the history of the Cold War or the long official silences or public myths about France under German occupation, or about the foundation and early years of Israel.

Although the historiographical moderns who had battled so successfully against the ancients until the late 1960s were an alliance which contained the Marxists, the challenge to their supremacy did not come from the ideological right. If my generations of Marxist historians formed in the years from 1933 to 1956 had no real successors, it was not because the cold warriors gained ground in schools and history faculties – probably the opposite was the case – but because the generations of the post-1960s left mostly wanted something else. But once again, this was not a specific reaction against Marxism. In France the virtual hegemony of Braudelian history and the *Annales* came to an end after 1968, and the international influence of the journal dropped steeply.

At least some of the change in history echoed the extraordinary cultural revolution of the late 1960s, which had its epicentre in the universities, and more particularly in the arts and humanities. It was not so much an intellectual challenge as a change of mood. In Britain the 'History Workshop' movement was the most characteristic expression of the new post-1968 'historical left'. Its object was not so much historical discovery, explanation or even exposition, as inspiration, empathy and democratization. It also reflected the remarkable and unexpected growth of a mass public interest in the past which has given history a surprising prominence in print and on screen. History Workshop meetings, which brought together amateurs and professionals, intellectuals and workers, and vast numbers of the young in jeans, flanked by sleeping-bags and improvised crèches, resembled gospel sessions, especially when addressed with the required *hwyl* by star performers such as the wonderful historian of Wales, Gwyn Alf Williams, a low-slung dark man whose superb management of his stammer served to underline his platform eloquence. It is typical that the first Women's Liberation Conference in Britain (to which Marlene was taken by the females of our 'New Left' friends) grew out of a proposed History Workshop at the end of the 1960s. Sheila Rowbotham's historical manifesto of feminism which followed was characteristically called *Hidden from History*.

These were people for whom history was not so much a way of interpreting the world, but a means of collective self-discovery, or at best, of winning collective recognition.

The danger of this position was, and is, that it undermines the universality of the universe of discourse that is the essence of all history as a scholarly and intellectual discipline, a *Wissenschaft* in both the German and the narrower English sense.[13] It also undermines what both the ancients and the moderns had in common, namely the belief that historians' investigations, by means of generally accepted rules of logic and evidence, distinguish between fact and fiction, between what can be established and what cannot, what is the case and what we would like to be so. But this has become increasingly dangerous. Political pressures on history, by old and new states and regimes, identity groups, and forces long concealed under the frozen ice-cap of the Cold War, are greater than ever before in my lifetime, and modern media society has given the past unprecedented prominence and marketing potential. More history than ever is today being revised or invented by people who do not want the real past, but only a past that suits their purpose. Today is the great age of historical mythology. The defence of history by its professionals is today more urgent in politics than ever. We are needed.

We also have much to do. While the actual affairs of humanity are now conducted mainly by the criteria of problem-solving technologists, to which it is almost irrelevant, history has become more central to our understanding of the world than ever before. Quietly, amid the arguments about the objective existence of the past, historical change has become a central component of the natural sciences, from cosmogony to revived Darwinism. Indeed, through molecular and evolutionary biology, palaeontology and archaeology human history itself is being transformed. It has been reinserted into the framework of global, indeed of cosmic, evolution. DNA has revolutionized it. Thus we now know how extraordinarily young *homo sapiens* is as a species. We left Africa 100,000 years ago. The whole of what is usually described as 'history' since the invention of agriculture and cities consists of hardly more than 400 human generations or 10,000 years, a blink of the eye in geological time. Given the dramatic acceleration of the pace of humanity's control over nature in this brief period, especially in the last ten or twenty generations, the whole of history so far can be seen to be something like an explosion of our species, a sort of bio-social supernova, into an unknown future. Let us hope it is not a catastrophic one. In the meanwhile, and for the first time, we have an adequate framework for a genuinely global history, and one restored to its proper central place, neither within the humanities nor the natural and mathematical sciences, nor separated from them, but essential to both. I wish I were young enough to take part in writing it.

Still, it was good to be a historian even in my generation. Above all, it was enjoyable. In a conversation on his intellectual development my friend, the late Pierre Bourdieu, once said:

> I see intellectual life as something closer to the artist's life than to the routine of the academy . . . Of all the forms of intellectual work, the trade of sociologist is without doubt the one the practice of which has given me happiness, in every sense of the word.[14]

Substitute 'historian' for sociologist, and I say amen to that.

18

In the Global Village

How can the autobiographer who has been a lifelong academic and author write about his professional life? What happens in writing occurs essentially in solitude on screens or pieces of paper. When writers are engaged in any other action, they are not writing, though they may be accumulating material for it. This is true even of the literary activity of men (or women) of action, such as Julius Caesar. There is plenty to be said about conquering Gaul, and, as secondary schoolboys used to know, Caesar said it very well, but there is little to be said about the process of writing *On the Gallic War* except, presumably, that the great Julius dictated it to some slave secretary in the intervals of doing more important things.

Again, academics spend most of their working time on the routines of teaching, research, meetings and examining. These are unadventurous and lacking in unpredictability by the standards of more high-profile living. They spend much of their leisure time in the society of other academics, a species which, however interesting as individuals, is not thrilling company en masse. Half a century ago it could be plausibly argued that an assembly of historians, such as could be seen at the annual meetings of their societies, was even less distinguishable from an assembly of insurance company executives than collections of other university teachers, but since the generation of 1968 has entered the academy, this may no longer be so.

As for students, en masse they are certainly more interesting for anyone who likes being a teacher, but mainly by virtue of their youth and all the things that go with it, such as enthusiasm, passion, hope, ignorance and immaturity, rather than because much is to be expected by facing crowds of them. Admittedly, this is not strictly true of the two institutions in which I spent most of my teaching career, Birkbeck College in the University of London and the Graduate Faculty of the New School for Social Research (now New School University) in New York. Both, being somewhat anomalous parts of academia, have singular student bodies. Birkbeck, the successor of the London Mechanics' Institution of 1825, remains an evening college, teaching those who earn their living during the day. One of the reasons why I spent my entire British career there, was the pleasure of teaching extraordinarily motivated men and women, usually older and hence more mature than the normal post-school student. They faced their teachers weekly with the acid test of the profession: how to keep a bunch of people interested in what is being said to them between eight and nine p.m., knowing that they have come to college after a full day's work, swallowed a quick meal in the cafeteria, sat through one or two earlier lectures, and face maybe an hour's journey home after I get through. Birkbeck was a good school, not least of learning how to communicate.

The peculiarity of the New School's Graduate Faculty was its combination of heterodoxy and internationalism. The New School for Social Research itself had been founded after the Great War by educational and ideological and politically radical reformers rebelling against what they regarded as the tyranny of examinations. It found first-class people, of whom there was no shortage in New York City, to teach anything for which there was a demand, from classical philosophy to yoga. The Graduate Faculty had been set up in 1933 to provide for the academic refugees from Hitler's Germany, followed by those from the rest of occupied Europe. It is on record as the first academic institution to give lectures on jazz and almost certainly the first to give a seminar on structuralism (by Claude Lévi-Strauss and Roman Jakobson), both during the Second World War. Its reputation for heterodoxy and radicalism attracted unusual students from the USA, and even more interesting and able ones from western and Latin American countries. In the 1980s it developed a relationship with the countries about to shake off their communist regimes. The Poles, Russians, Bulgarians and Chinese joined the Brazilians, Spaniards and Turks in our classes. I once counted twenty nationalities in my own. Since they knew more about their own countries and special fields than I did, I learned at least as much from them as they did from me. There was almost certainly no more varied and stimulating a body of students anywhere.

Communication is the essence both of teaching and of writing.

Fortunate the author who likes both, for it rescues him or her from the desert island on which we usually sit, writing messages for unknown recipients in unknown destinations to be launched across the oceans in bottles shaped like books. But the teacher–author speaks directly to the potential readers. Lecturing was probably still the major form of teaching in my academic generation, and in many ways lecturers relate to any room full of students as actors relate to the faces before them in the theatre except that their house lights don't go out. We are both performers, they are what we perform for. There is nothing like lecturing to tell us when we are losing the attention of the audience. Nevertheless, the lecturer's task is harder, for he or she expects the audience to carry away a load of specific information and ideas which they should remember and digest, and not only the emotional satisfaction of the occasion. Even a good lecturer communicates only what radiates from any other performer with stage presence, namely the projection of a personality, a temperament, an image, a mind at work – and, with a bit of luck, he or she may strike a corresponding spark in the imagination of some people out there. It is through class discussion that we establish whether we have actually communicated what we wanted to. That is one reason why, during my whole career as a university teacher, I preferred general to specialist courses. Indeed, my books on general historical subjects either grew out of student lectures or, after more specialized origins, were tested in student lectures.

The satisfaction of a teacher's job comes essentially from relations with individuals, but these form only a small part of the very large body of men and women with notebooks in lecture theatres, the vast pile of examination scripts or term papers that fill a university teacher's working life in the course of his or her career. And even they are part of a pretty unchanging routine. Experienced from inside, a research seminar may be unforgettable, but seen from the outside it merely looks like – and I am thinking of my own at the Institute of Historical Research in London in the 1970s and 1980 – a couple of dozen people in the late afternoon, surrounded by books, sitting along a table discussing a paper read by one of them or an outside visitor, and then going a couple of hundred yards to a pub for a drink or two. Considered as a potential movie, it is not even art-house material.

In memory the academic autobiographer's years stretch back like the wagons on those endless freight-trains, observed from some hill as they carry containers across the American landscape. Seen in retrospect, the succession of trucks is less interesting than the changing territory through which they pass. In my case they have passed through cities and campuses in three continents – four, if the Americas count as two – though before retirement mostly on relatively brief visits, except for a semester as a visiting professor at the Massachusetts Institute of Technology (1967) and a half-year's teaching and research in Latin America (1971), both with my family. However, a peripatetic life with small children is not ideal for academics, and eventually their schooling made it impossible. I never tested the anti-communism of the US authorities by accepting a permanent appointment in their country. If I was tempted by visiting spells at one or another of the great North American universities, Marlene's veto stood in the way: small-town academic life was not for her. Only one such place broke her resistance, the Getty Center – then still at Santa Monica – the nearest thing to paradise for scholars, where we spent some time in 1989. However, Los Angeles can hardly be regarded as the sticks. I too had been immunized against the campus life by my own brief experience in the summer quarter at Stanford, then as now a superb university, one of the half-dozen finest in the world, but embedded in Palo Alto, sensationally boring as a community for living in. For many years afterwards I could not even bring myself to revisit this nowhere space of empty streets in which cars visited each others' owners in beautiful homes.

The ideal arrangement for both of us was a stable metropolitan base varied by the increasingly available academic trips abroad, which the revolution in air transport made easy from the 1960s. They have taken us from Finland to Naples, from Canada to Peru, from Japan to Brazil. Our times have added the roving professor to the other profession which likes to recall the pleasures, embarrassments and absurdities of a life of changing places, but which still remains essentially the same, namely the foreign correspondent. I have had the luck to teach and live for most of my professional life in or near the centre of the two major cultural cities of the late twentieth-century world: within a stone's throw of the British Museum in one, in a Greenwich Village office above Bradley's, the quintessential jazz location of Manhattan, in the other. (Alas, Bradley's folded in 1996 and New York has not been the same for me since.)

Nevertheless, careers and freight-trains do not roll across the land at an absolutely steady rate. The war had delayed the start of my own career, and the Cold War had slowed it down considerably. It continued in the doldrums, but by the middle 1960s, when other offers in Britain and abroad began to come in, this was so eccentric as to be widely regarded as scandalous.[1] Still, I had begun to publish books only in my forties, and by the time I could actually call myself 'Professor' in Britain, I was in my middle fifties, a time of life when most professionals have got as far as they, and the world, expects them to get in their career. At that stage for most of us the promise is in the past, and so is such achievement as it has produced. Professionally speaking, people in this position are left to face half a lifetime of endless tomorrows no better than today, apart from the gowns and ribbons – professional and maybe public honours – which (at least in the humanities) usually signify that the honorand's future will add nothing to his or her past, except the slow decline of age. World war and Cold War saved me from all this. By an unexpected twist of fortune, they prolonged the period of youth and promise into middle age. At the same time remarriage and children gave a new start to my private life.

In fact, only the war had genuinely delayed my career – but probably no more than that of most men in my age group. (In Britain it had actually advanced the prospects of women graduates.) The Cold War of the 1950s blocked jobs and publishers' contracts, but 'on the street', as the *fin-de-siècle* phrase has it, that is to say among the working historians, my reputation was serious from the start, certainly in the unofficial world of the younger historians. I was clearly a rising star in the rather narrower community of the Marxist ones.

Pride and intellectual vanity made me worry whether my reputation was carried only by the sympathies of the left, or rested only on the relative scarcity of Marxists to fill the niche which, since the Second World War, even conventional history reserved for this version of a recognized 'opposition'. It is not that I minded then or mind now being identified as 'Hobsbawm the Marxist historian', the label which I still carry round my neck to this day, like the decanters circulating after dinner in combination rooms to prevent dons from confusing their port with their sherry. Young historians need to have their attention drawn to the materialist interpretation of history as much, perhaps even more, today, when even left-wing academic fashions dismiss it as in the days when it was being damned as totalitarian propaganda. After all, I have been trying to persuade people for over half a century that there is more to Marxist history than they have hitherto thought, and if the association of one historian's name with it helps to do so, so much the better. What troubled my vanity was rather the fear of a mere ghetto reputation, such as that from which figures prominent inside another character-istic twentieth-century cultural ghetto, the Roman Catholic com-munity in Britain, have so often found it difficult, even impossible, to escape. G. K. Chesterton, the dimensions of whose talent have been concealed from non-Catholics by the very closeness of his association with the Church, is a good example. (No British writer would dream of thinking about him like Italo Calvino who once said it was one of his ambitions to become 'the Chesterton of the Communists'.) Getting good reviews from friendly critics was not the problem. The test of success was to get them from the neutral and hostile ones.

From about 1960 on it became increasingly evident that I was getting beyond a ghetto reputation. My first book, *Primitive Rebels* (1959), was well received in the USA, both among the historians and the social scientists. Within a few years it had been translated into German, French and Italian. My second book, *The Age of Revolution 1789–1848* (1962), aimed at a broader public, was a success. At least it impressed an established literary agent, the bulky, white-haired and moustached *bon vivant* David Higham, enough to ask me whether I wanted to join his stable and to offer me periodic lunches at his window table in the Etoile restaurant in Charlotte Street. As I write this both the Etoile (with much the same menu) and the table are still there, under the supervision of another protector of agents and authors, Elena, whose reputation as the queen mother of literary restaurants had been acquired earlier in Soho, and I am still under the wing of old Higham's successor in the firm still named after him, my friend Bruce Hunter. History may move at the speed of a missile, but some continuities remain. Since *The Age of Revolution* was part of an international co-production series organized by George Weidenfeld, it would have been translated very quickly anyway, whatever its merits. Nevertheless the seven translations and foreign editions that appeared in the 1960s were helpful, and the book was well received everywhere. I later discovered that a notoriously poor Spanish translation in 1964 was welcomed by the rapidly growing anti-Franco movement in the Spanish universities, since, unlike most Marxist publications, it was legally available.

I published a good deal in the 1960s: a collection of earlier pieces on the history of labour (*Labouring Men*, 1964), a text on British economic history since the eighteenth century (*Industry and Empire*, 1968), a small study of the myth and reality of the world's Robin Hoods, written in Wales as the Russians put an end to the Prague Spring (*Bandits*, 1969), and in the same year, jointly with my friend George Rudé, a rather larger research monograph on the English farm-labourers' rising of 1830 (*Captain Swing*, 1969). By 1971 when I finally got the official professorial title in the University of London, I was already entering the zone of academies (at least in the USA) and honorary degrees (at least in Sweden).

So by the 1970s I was an academically, if not politically, respectable and recognized figure. That decade reinforced this situation. My membership of the Communist Party of Great Britain was by then seen as little more than the personal peculiarity of a well-known historian, one of that new species the jet-plane academic. Only America refused to forget about Hobsbawm the subversive, for, until the abrogation of the Smith Act in the late 1980s, I remained ineligible for a visa to enter the USA and required a 'waiver' of this ineligibility every time I went there, which was more or less every year. I was a founder and active member of the editorial board of one of the most prestigious English-language historical journals, a member of the councils and committees of learned historical societies. Seminars and graduate courses in London, doctoral students, national and international, kept the new professor busy. The invitations to lectures and appointments elsewhere continued and multiplied. In my last year at Birkbeck I was simultaneously attached to establishments in London, Paris (at the Collège de France and the Ecole des Hautes Etudes en Sciences Sociales) and the USA (as

'Professor-at-large' of Cornell University). It was all the more enjoyable, even if slightly absurd, since this take-off in my professional fortunes was something I had neither looked for nor expected. One way or another, we had a splendid, if occasionally surrealist, time in the 1970s, not least (with a young family) in Mexico, Colombia, Ecuador and Peru and (without family) in Japan. It is not every academic wife who finds herself travelling thirty miles with small children and recorders on a chicken-filled bus in the Peruvian central Sierra to a joint music lesson with the children of a British anthropologist, while her husband, very very slowly – for the buildings are above 4,000 metres – inspects the records of a recently nationalized *hacienda* shortly to go to the country's newly established Agrarian Archive.

Perhaps this explains why, though producing learned articles, I wrote fewer academic books in this decade – effectively only *The Age of Capital* (1974), which made me aware that, without having meant to, I was engaged in writing a wildly ambitious general history of the nineteenth century. Actually much of the most intensive work I did during that decade, planning and writing for an equally ambitious *History of Marxism*, which was published by Einaudi in Turin in 1978–82, never reached the public entirely in languages other than Italian, since the public interest in these matters dropped precipitately at the end of the 1970s. However, in the 1980s my production speeded up again, largely thanks to the wonderful conditions available in New York and Los Angeles. I published a new collection of papers on labour history (*Worlds of Labour*, in the USA *Workers*) in 1984, the third volume on the nineteenth century in 1987 (*The Age of Empire 1875–1914*), and two books based on invited lectures, *Nations and Nationalism Since the 1780s* (what other subject was there to lecture on in Belfast in 1985?) and *Echoes of the Marseillaise: Two Centuries Look Back on the French Revolution*, both in 1990. I also co-edited and contributed to a volume based on a *Past & Present* conference I had organized a few years earlier, and which proved to be unusually influential: *The Invention of Tradition* (1983). My image as I went into my eighth decade was that of an eccentric elderly grandee of the historical profession, who happened to insist that he was a Marxist, but who continued in full production.

Indeed, the history of the twentieth century I wrote in the happy conditions of the New School (where I had been teaching for a semester a year since 1984), *The Age of Extremes 1914–1991* (1994), was my most successful book, both in sales and critical reception. It was well received across the entire ideological spectrum of the globe – with the single exception of France – winning prizes in Canada as well as Taiwan, being translated both into Hebrew and Arabic, into Taiwan and Mainland Mandarin, into Croatian and Serbian editions of what my generation still thinks of as the Serbo-Croat language, and into both Albanian and Macedonian. By the second year of the new century it had been or was about to be published in thirty-seven languages.

And yet, in a field as steeped in politics, its own and the world's, as the writing of history, it would be quite unrealistic to separate the two. Much as someone in my position resented being placed into a Marxist ghetto, my reputation as a historian (and certainly in the 1960s and 1970s my sales) undoubtedly benefited from my reputation as a Marxist. Paradoxically, it was in the world of 'really existing socialism' that my books were not published, outside Hungary and Slovenia. The local theologians did not know what to do about a historian who could not be published as an unbeliever ('not of course, a marxist, but worth consulting in certain respects'), nor as a Marxist, since the only 'marxist interpretation' they recognized was a restatement of the officially recognized orthodoxy.

In the West, and even more in what was then called the Third World, the 1960s were a good time for my kind of history, or more exactly, for the alliance of historical modernizers whose fortunes I have discussed in the last chapter. Consider the three-volume *Economic History of Britain* which Penguin Books commissioned at that time, on the advice of Jack (later Sir John) Plumb, perhaps no longer the young radical of 1930s Cambridge, but not without memories of that era: the authors were M. M. Postan, Christopher Hill and myself. Marxists, no longer in the ghetto unless they wanted to be, were, for the time being, part of the historical mainstream. At the same time a new politico-intellectual left was emerging in the universities and schools of Europe and the USA, which actively sought out people with radical credentials. That is why E. P. Thompson's marvellous *Making of the English Working Class* triumphed in the middle sixties, lifting its author, deservedly but to everyone's surprise, to international fame practically overnight. For a while older teachers complained that the students read virtually no other book. I had neither Edward's genius and charisma nor his sales, but I also wrote on the subjects, and with the sentiments, which attracted radicalized young student readers.

Nowhere were scholarship and politics more closely linked than in the so-called Third World, where, of course, Marxism, being anti-imperialist, was not just the label for a small academic minority, but the prevailing ideology among the younger intellectuals. Brazil may serve as an example. Even during the military regime (1964–85) which had forced out of public life virtually everyone known to have associations with the left who was not in jail or driven into emigration, people like me were consulted on the staffing of a new university. And, indeed, invited to lecture, as I was in 1975 at a vaguely defined conference on 'History and Society' at the new university about which I had been consulted, whose student body – perhaps not surprisingly – was passionately hostile to the regime. This was no accident. The press, which devoted quite disproportionate space to a provincial academic occasion, though otherwise approximate (the *Estado de São Paulo* described me as 'Irish by birth'), went out of its way to stress my 'marxist formation'. In fact, as I was told by friendly journalists, by the middle seventies the regime was beginning to relax a little, and the entire Campinas conference was part of an operation to test how much liberalization it was willing to tolerate. What more effective test than to announce the invitation of a known Marxist, and one whose non-academic ideas were likely to be loudly applauded by the students – as indeed they were[2] – and to give plenty of publicity to the occasion? This was a characteristic example of the admirable Brazilian combination of civic courage and intelligence, never accepting the dictatorship, never ceasing to press just beyond the limits of its tolerance. True the Brazilian generals were not quite so murderous as some others in Latin America but the regime was bloodstained enough, and the risks of jail and torture were real. As it happens, the opposition had calculated right: the regime was ready to cede.

It is perhaps no surprise that I may have subsequently benefited as a writer from my minimal and unconscious part in the struggle against the Brazilian military dictatorship. And indeed from the extraordinary fact, not commonly noticed by western liberals, that between 1960 and the mid-1980s, what the USA called 'the free world' passed through the most widespread phase of non-democratic government since the fall of fascism, typically in the form of military regimes. Intellectuals, and certainly students, were heavily in opposition to these, though sometimes silenced by sheer terror, whether in Greece, Spain, Turkey, among the usual suspects in Latin America, or in countries such as South Korea. Making available and reading oppositional literature was the obvious first step towards political democratization, as soon as these regimes gave even the slightest ground. Since the universities were the places where the non-business elite of these countries was educated – outside the USA the triumph of business schools and MBAs was still in the future – in those decades a very high proportion of those destined to go into politics, public service, academic life, journalism and the other media were made familiar with the names that stood for left-wing social and historical thought. Since the number of contemporaries with this reputation was small, our names became quite well known in reading circles, even though the actual circulation of our writings, legal or pirated, was modest. Naturally after democratization it could become much larger, though nowhere else quite as large as in Brazil, where more copies of the first edition of my history of the twentieth century were to be sold than in any other single country; though much of this was due to the help of a quite exceptional publisher, Luis Sczwarcz.

In this way the professional career of one author during and after the rise, slackening and fall of governments of the hard-line right in the west may throw light on the wider intellectual history of the 'free world' in the second half of the twentieth century, that is to say on the rise of the new generations of educated elites since the 1960s, brought up in the spirit of rebellion, even when they were soon to be 'co-opted' by (as the phrase then went), or co-opt themselves into the 'Establishment'. That is not to overestimate the significance of reading these authors. Some were merely badges of temporary political or ideological fashion. For instance, in the years of the great student revolts of the late sixties the writings of the political philosopher Herbert Marcuse were displayed in every university bookshop of the western world – at least I saw them on the East and West coasts of the USA, in Paris, Stockholm, Mexico City and Buenos Aires. (Marcuse himself, a tanned outdoor type who might have been a retired ski instructor, did not look the part when I met him in the house of friends in Cambridge, Massachusetts at the time.) Yet within a few years his writings had returned to the underworld in which aspiring Ph.D. candidates desperately seek thesis subjects.

Whether the authors who thus became political badges in a country were aware of what was happening to their names was largely irrelevant. There are countries in which I did not even know I had readers until I discovered, as on visiting South Korea in 1987, that five of my titles were in print in (pirated) local translations. But for an Iranian friend at the New School, I would not know at all that one Ali-Akbar Mehdian, not otherwise known, had translated and published *The Age of Revolution* in Tehran in the spring of 1995 adding 'Europe' to 1789–1848, 'probably to be able to get permission for publication'. In Brazil and to a lesser extent in Argentina, countries I knew and where I had friends, I had a shrewd idea of how such names could become familiar, though, until much later, not of the extent of this potential readership.

This takes a Marxist autobiographer into the welcome territory of technology and culture, namely the explosion of photocopiers that accompanied the enormous expansion of higher education in the West since the 1960s. This gave the new masses of teachers and students access, mostly unpaid, to fiendishly expensive imported academic texts otherwise far beyond their modest budgets and the sparse resources of their libraries. It was the Buenos Aires office of my admirable Spanish publisher, Gonzalo Ponton of Critica, which consequently guessed that there was scope for a special local edition of my work, and I discovered the extent of my youthful readership, or at least of those who had a positive reaction to my name, on a 1998 visit to Buenos Aires to promote it. Conversely, it was the systematic absence of such devices in the communist world that long limited its dissident literature to what could be laboriously typed and copied with carbon paper, or learned by heart.

No doubt there are authors – I am plainly not among them – who may trace the intellectual dimensions of the decline and collapse of communism and its consequences in a similar manner, through the fortunes of their works. It is obviously far harder to do so for two reasons. Before the fall of these regimes dissident or even heterodox literature was barely allowed above ground. There is no way to measure the impact of writings which were inaccessible in print to most readers, though this does not mean that such works might not become known in other ways. Since the end of communism the publication of serious writing about history and politics has depended on the subsidies of well-wishers such as the admirable George Soros. This tells the author little about his or her intended, potential or actual readers. Thanks to Soros, whose foundations and other benefactions have almost single-handedly kept intellectual and scientific activities in the ex-USSR and much of Eastern Europe from being swept away by the forest fire of the so-called 'free market', at least two of my books, *The Age of Extremes* and *Nations and Nationalism*, have been published in a variety of the lesser East European languages, whose tiny public could never possibly have justified the enormous costs of translation. Moreover, one of them (*Nations and Nationalism*) is a critique of the very ethno-linguistic nationalism on which the small successor states are based, so that it is extremely unlikely that there was much pent-up demand for such critiques in the relevant bookshops of Tirana, Priština and Skopje. However, since the world still lives in the shadow of the tower of Babel, how could I tell?

Nevertheless I have probably coped better with the Babel problem than most of my English-speaking colleagues, not least because my professional life has not only been peripatetic but multilingual. Historians, of course, need languages more than any scholars other than linguists and students of comparative literature, as very little except purely local history can be seriously studied entirely in a single language, even within most single states. Thanks to the advantage of a bilingual upbringing, a certain gift for picking up languages by talking rather than formal instruction, and the ancestral Jewish experience of moving from place to place among strangers, I have conducted my teaching, and to a modest extent my writing and radio or TV work, in various, not always well-mastered, languages. This has given my professional career a more cosmopolitan tinge than is common, not to mention a more recognized presence in countries whose radio and TV journalists can rely on a few words in their public's language spoken into their outstretched microphone, or even a public lecture or TV conversation. Over the years the departmental office in Birkbeck grew accustomed to the multiple accents of foreigners asking for Professor Hobsbawm's room, the non-Anglo-Saxon sounds round my table in the cafeteria, and the gradual adjustment of Peruvian, Mexican, Uruguayan, Bengali or Middle Eastern research students to London life. Not all these students were bona fide academics. In the past forty years English has become so much the universal idiom of global communication, and knowledge of French, the other international language, has declined so fast, that scholars like myself have lost much of their earlier function as interpreters and intellectual brokers. Yet that role remained important in Europe, at least during the lifetime of the generation of great monoglot French intellectuals who (with the rarest exceptions such as the brilliant and unhappy Raymond Aron) could neither speak nor understand English. I acted as translator for the great historian Ernest Labrousse at the early postwar conferences of the Economic History Society. (He warned me firmly against having anything to do with *white* Bordeaux, unworthy, he thought, of any self-respecting French drinker.) Except in French, I could not have established any relationship with Fernand Braudel. Even in the mid-1960s, when the next, less monoglot, generation reached maturity, it was far from fluent, as France's premier historian, Emmanuel Le Roy Ladurie, will confirm, if he recalls his first visit to London. Scholars from Eastern Europe once relied on French; in the 1990s their pupils at the New School had no difficulty in writing their term papers in English. And yet, even today the global village in which academics live must continue to rely on multilinguality, as any western intellectual can verify if he or she finds him or herself guideless on a street in Nanjing, Nagoya or Seoul – that is to say functionally deaf, dumb and illiterate. Someone there has to speak at least two languages.

Nevertheless, the global village is real, and since the limits of time and space have been virtually eliminated, the academic profession, having once again become what it was in the European Middle Ages, namely one of wandering, or rather nowadays airborne, scholars, lives in it. I suppose I have now lived in it for something like forty years. It is at this point that the line between professional career and private life becomes hazy, or disappears altogether. In memory the dinners for some visitor from abroad in the seasons of academic migration (as after the end of the summer term) merge with the memories of the Christmas dinners where the family was usually joined by friends, local or foreign, temporarily unattached or hostile to the seasonal spirit: Francis and Larissa Haskell, Arnaldo Momigliano, Yolanda Sonabend. Not that professors have friends only among other academics, though in the nature of things many of their friends are. Indeed one reason why Marlene and I have chosen to live in metropolitan milieus is that no university community is big enough in London or New York to dominate social life there. On the other hand, whether among academics, media people or in business, the global village is a place not so much of lives as of encounters. Each of its inhabitants has roots and most have permanence – either 'here' (wherever this may be, London, Cambridge, Manhattan) or elsewhere. Often, and this is new, they have multiple roots or at least multiple attachments, domestic or professional – my seasonal commute from London to Manhattan, the professional couples whose working weeks are separated by continents and oceans, united only at weekends or even more rarely.

The global village is the set of points of encounter of these entities in constant Brownian movement across the contemporary globe, expected, as in conferences and symposia, or casual and unexpected, at work or on holiday. It is the question 'What are you doing here?' which has punctuated my life in Santiago de Chile, Seoul and Mysore. But this is only one kind of encounter in the global village. Impermanence, isolation, unforeseen contingency in rental car, bar and hotel room with CNN are its dimensions. Even the highly organized circuits of what might be called business or professional tourism – the academic symposia in beautiful places, the Villa Serbelloni on Lake Como, the Fondazione Cini in the waters of Venice, the luxury business get-togethers within reach of beach and golf – are not the real locus of the global village. It really takes shape in the local network of human communications which fits together indigenous families, peripatetics and foreigners, arrivals, projects and departures. In short, it operates primarily through global circuits of domestic hospitality. For that is the basic pattern of life of most married academics, as of other settled professionals. The men and women who come into our houses are not 'family' but they are as familiar as if they were, whether they happen to come from New Delhi or Florence or whether they do so in Helsinki or Manhattan. They are part of our small everyday world. Very likely we have heard about them, they about us, even when friends bring us together for the first time, which will generally not be the last. We have the same points of reference and share the same news and gossip. We may well arrive with them from somewhere else to establish a new, permanent or semi-permanent existence in a new environment, as happened to us in my early years in the New School in the 1980s. We live among them, they among us, as neighbours.

In my case it has been an extraordinarily enjoyable life, comfortable, varied by travels, increasingly accompanied by Marlene, combining work, discovery and holiday, novelty and old friendships. Only the knowledge that people who live in poverty, the constant presence of disaster and death can also laugh, or at least tell good jokes, gives me the courage to say: it has been a lot of fun. It has not been a professional life of dramatic action, hardship or (except in the mind) of danger and fear. Like others in the small favoured minority to which I belong, I am amazed at the 'patent contradiction between one's own life experience . . . and the facts of the twentieth century . . . the terrible events which humanity has lived through'.[3] By the criteria of professional success, it has not been unsatisfactory. It has given me more private happiness than I ever expected.

Has it been the life I had in mind when I was young? No. It would be pointless, even stupid, to regret that it has turned out this way, but somewhere inside me there is a small ghost who whispers: 'One should not be at ease in a world such as ours.' As the man said when I read him in my youth: 'The point is to change it.'

19

Marseillaise

I have gone to France almost every year since 1933, except during the Second World War. The country has been part of my life for almost seventy years, indeed for longer, because my mother had begun to teach her children French at home from the elder Dumas's *Les Trois Mousquetaires*, an enormous stiff-bound volume which we never finished. She and her sisters had been sent as teenagers to perfect their French at a *pensionnat* in Belgium. I belong to the last European generation for which French was still the universal second language. Even after a long travelling life, I have probably gone to Paris more often than to any other foreign city: and for all of us Paris was and remained the core of our experience of France.

I had first encountered it physically during a brief stopover on the way from Berlin to England in the spring of 1933. I travelled with my uncle, who presumably still had some final arrangements to make in Berlin, and must have had some business in Paris, for that city was certainly a detour from the direct route to London. I assume it must have been film business, for his later activities in Paris were based on an extensive network in the French movie scene, no doubt derived from his days at Universal, reinforced by his acquaintance with the emigrant film technicians he had known in Berlin.

As boys from families such as mine expected to go to Paris sooner or later, I was excited, but not surprised. Indeed, excited not only by Paris but also by the prospect of passing Nazi frontier controls in the company of a young and well-dressed middle-class communist called, I think, Hirsch, also going to France for undisclosed reasons, with whom I struck up an acquaintance in the train corridor and who taught me my first phrase of colloquial French ('*merde alors*'). My uncle had booked us into the Hotel Montpensier in the rue de Richelieu, between the Comédie Française and the Bibliothèque Nationale, of whose existence I was then unaware; a building which introduced me to the basic pattern of French lifts in the 1930s, apparently unchanged since the early days of the Third Republic. (On his later business trips to Paris my uncle stayed in somewhat less basic establishments – during his most sanguine era, the Georges Cinq.) That evening, and perhaps the next, he took me for a stroll along the Grands Boulevards, the long stretch of café-lined avenues from the République in the east to the Madeleine in the west, which in those days were still the main promenade of Paris, as they had been from the days of Haussmann, pointing out the whores, who were then called *grues* (cranes) and the red-light district around the boulevard Sébastopol, one of whose brothels is now being preserved as a historic monument from the ravages of property development. However, I did not enter any of them until some years later, when, in the course of a night on the town with a Hungarian communist, I lost my virginity in an establishment – I can no longer recall its address – with an orchestra of naked ladies, and in a bed surrounded on all sides by mirrors. The Hungarian, Gyorgy Adam, strongly urged me to visit Hungary, where the married middle-class ladies summering on Lake Balaton were, he assured me, only waiting for fellows like us. He was subsequently jailed in the days of the Stalinist purges, but remained a convinced Marxist. The only married lady with whom I ever tested his hypothesis on Lake Balaton, many years later, was my wife with whom I spent a short vacation there in the guest-house of the Hungarian Academy of Sciences, a rather charming family-type establishment in which visitors kept their own bottle of wine from one meal to the next.

The next day, alone, I went to the nearby Louvre, then still flanked by the gigantic wedding-cake of the monument to Gambetta, which did not survive the holocaust of (mainly Republican) statuary during the German occupation and since the war. I was impressed by the size of the *Venus de Milo* and, more sincerely, by the *Victory of Samothrace* and doubtless stopped before the *Mona Lisa*. But she did not speak my language. Another picture did, Manet's *Olympia*. Perhaps it was natural that a virgin boy of fifteen should be transfixed by the cool, adult gaze of that astonishing image of a naked woman, glorying in *luxe* and *calme*, and for the moment visibly uninterested in *volupté*. And yet, what made my first encounter with this masterpiece so unforgettable was not the sensuality – after all, the Louvre is full of sexy nudes – but the sense that this wonderful painter was not interested in the incidental emotion but in 'the truth'; in the stumbling words of a later generation of adolescents in 'telling it like it is'. The *Olympia* is what I remember from my first visit to Paris. If I needed converting to France, Manet was the right missionary.

I was in need of information rather than conversion. For the next three years, obliged to pass examinations in French for the first time, it came from books and schoolmasters, including a French intellectual preparing *agrégation* or *thèse*, who naturally assumed he was at the cutting edge of French culture. He assured me that there were only three *serious* contemporary writers, namely the three Gs – André Gide, Jean Giono and Jean Giraudoux. I do not know why he favoured this selection rather than, say, Gide, Céline and Malraux. I tried them all conscientiously, and found Gide boring as, I confess, I still do. I already knew about Jean Giono, from the *Vossische Zeitung* in Berlin, which had published in instalments a translation of one of his rhapsodies of peasant life in upper Provence. I was so deeply moved by his *casserole* of sun, soil, passion and rural brutalism, that some years later on a hitchhike to the Mediterranean I made a special detour to visit Manosque in the Basses Alpes, where he lived, to pay my homage to the author – he was not there – and to dip briefly into the rushing icy waters of the river Durance, witness to his human dramas. I found that at least one other admirer had made the same pilgrimage, a not very attractive young woman of Polish immigrant parents, equally knocked out by his searing eloquence, and we compared notes chastely in the Provençal night. I still have the cheap editions of his novels of the period, but I have not had the courage to re-read them since.

On the other hand, even today I find myself from time to time re-reading the elegant Jean Giraudoux, who was then known to a wider French public chiefly as a very successful playwright of intellectual inclinations, performed by the great actor-manager Louis Jouvet. His *La Guerre de Troie n'aura pas lieu* (The Trojan War will not take place), which demonstrated a melancholy conviction that another world war was utterly inevitable, remains a major text for students of the French establishment in the 1930s. I admired him for his soliloquies in the form of novels, especially the wonderful fireworks display of *Siegfried et le Limousin*, written shortly after the First World War and devoted to demonstrating both the utter incompatibility between what France meant to the French and Germany to the Germans and the complementarity of the two civilizations. Perhaps this explains why its author disappeared from French intellectual sight after Liberation, though not an unduly prominent Vichyite or collaborator. Suspended between languages and cultures like a lover between the competing objects of desire, I warmed to Giraudoux's ability to be passionately, viscerally and intellectually French while loving Germany, especially as he made fun of both.

I did not need him to tell me about the Germans, but in Giraudoux I encountered and recognized for the first time the kind of France of which my friend the historian Richard Cobb has written better than anyone: the France of the Third Republic in which Giraudoux was rooted. The France to which I was introduced through the implausible medium of his novels was not the France of high intellectuals, confident in their superiority as only Etonians are in Britain – although as a product of the Paris Ecole Normale Supérieure he was himself a very good specimen. It was the Jacobin France I shortly discovered for myself through its very own mouthpiece, and which became the France of my 1930s, the Republic of the *Canard Enchaîné*.

That grey four- or exceptionally six-page broadsheet of comments, jokes and cartoons, unsponsored, unsubsidized, refusing all advertisements, describing itself simply as 'a satirical journal appearing on Wednesday' and bought weekly by half a million frequenters of the Cafés du Sport and the Cafés du Commerce from Dunkirk to Perpignan, was perhaps the only national expression of the Third Republic. Indeed, its language, conventions, terms of reference and assumptions were so esoteric as to be largely incomprehensible to anyone not born and bred within it, at least without extensive commentary. Since General de Gaulle, whom it was to send up in a weekly 'court bulletin' in the classical style of the Duke of Saint-Simon's Memoirs of Louis XIV, it has perhaps appealed more to graduates and the political in-groupies than to its original readers, the radical-socialist, socialist or even communist electors of Clochemerle (the archetypical community of the Third Republic, no longer recognizable in a country which is to abolish rural public telephones because of the spread of mobile phones in *la France profonde*).* For it was an article of its and their basic faith that the Republic had no enemies on the left. (The other articles were a belief in Liberty, Equality, Fraternity and Reason, anti-clericalism, an abhorrence of war and militarism, and in the virtues of good wine.) It was utterly sceptical of governments. Its readers in the 1930s liked to think they had no illusions about the rich, who exploited them and corrupted both the government, which overtaxed them, and most of the politicians and the journalists who tried to 'stuff our brains' (*bourrage de crânes*). The *Canard* confirmed their convictions, though, like its readers, it did not actually *denounce* the system. As in Marcel Pagnol's then famous comedy *Topaze*, in which an idealistic schoolmaster learns that careers and wealth are not achieved by republican virtue – not even the state's recognition of educational merit, the order of the Palmes Académiques for which he thirsts† – corruption was not for crusading but for disenchanted laughs.

Nothing could have been further from the world of the *Canard* than my instructor in the ways of another France, Madame Humbline Croissant, in whose apartment by the Porte de Versailles I lived during the summer of 1936. I was on a grant from the London County Council while waiting to go up to Cambridge. Madame Croissant, a grey-haired lady of Norman origin, played the harp, took the ancient and conservative *Revue des Deux Mondes*, and disapproved, among many other matters, of my reading of Proust, whom I brought into her salon from the Gallimard lending library on the boulevard Raspail which I visited almost as regularly as the Dôme in Montparnasse. (The Gallimard bookshop is still on the same block today.) In her view Proust wrote bad French. On the other hand, she taught me the firm truths of the French table such as that meat and vegetables must not be placed hugger-mugger on the same plate but eaten separately, and that fish requires wine (*'le poisson sans boisson est poison'*). Her social life was restricted and formal. Marvellous though her cuisine was, I fear each of us was a disappointment to the other. Her France was not mine.

* The politics of this Burgundian town, immortalized in an interwar novel of that name by Gabriel Chevallier, turned on the proposed location of a public urinal – another characteristic feature of life in the Third Republic – disputed between right and left.
† *Topaze* was inevitably in my mind, and made it difficult to keep a straight face when, many years later, the French government awarded me the 'Palmes Académiques'.

Young intellectual males of my generation were lucky to encounter France in the 1930s. (The scope it provided for young women of that generation was distinctly narrower.) Historians are unenthusiastic about the France on which I first set foot in the spring of 1933 and in which I passed most of my summers between then and the Second World War. Politically, the Third Republic was on its way to the grave. Culturally, France lived on capital accumulated before the Great War, to which Frenchmen added little after 1918. Most of the great names of the interwar *Ecole de Paris*, native or immigrant, belonged to artists who had reached maturity and established their reputation before 1914. As A. J. Liebling, the finest American writer on boxing, New Orleans, politics and gastrononomy, has pointed out, between the wars even French *haute cuisine*, like Paris courtesans, was past its golden age.

And yet, this is not how it looked to us. After all, Matisse and Picasso were still in full spate, and Renoir's son, the finest talent in French movies, was producing a masterpiece every other year. What we saw was not a country in decline, let alone on the verge of the miserable and shameful episode of the Second World War, with which the French have difficulty coming to terms even half a century later, but the France whose image had been imprinted on the educated western world since the eighteenth-century Enlightenment as the quintessence of civilization and the good life. The famous joke that when good Americans die they go to Paris – it first occurs in print in the extraordinary compendium of French intellectual distinction, the *Paris Guide* of 1867 – still carried full conviction; indeed, Americans (North, Central and South) were to maintain their belief in Paris as paradise longer than most other foreigners. Even Nazi Germany could not free itself from this belief. The wartime memoirs of German sophisticates, civil and military, in occupied France, however convinced of the inferior moral fibre of the defeated, suggest that the conquerors still saw themselves in some ways as Romans among Athenians. Francophile foreigners accepted the patent and still unshaken conviction of the French that their country was indeed the centre of world civilization, a 'middle kingdom' of the mind like China, the only other culture which shared this conviction of its own unquestioned superiority.

What was it that made us take France at its own valuation? What

319

made us think that Paris was still in some sense the 'capital of the twentieth century', as it had patently been that of the nineteenth? Except for painting and sculpture, and the extraordinary tradition of the French novel, nothing in French high culture and intellectual life was, or seemed, *obviously* 'the best in the world'. The literatures of other leading European languages did not feel inferior to the French. Even passionate Francophiles did not argue the superiority of Rabelais or Racine to Shakespeare, Goethe, Dante or Pushkin. French music, however original, ran second to the Austrians'. French philosophy plainly seemed inferior to German (for young people of central European background), contemporary French science lacked the sheer mass of top-class achievement of Britain and pre-1933 Germany, French technology seemed to be stuck in the era of the Eiffel Tower and the *art nouveau* Metro, and as for the modern conveniences of life, apart from the bidet, as yet unknown to Anglo-Saxon culture, it was surely not the state of French toilet facilities that attracted young Americans and Britons to the sort of hotels most of them could afford to live in.

At a somewhat less rarefied level, the superiority of French civilization was taken for granted. Ever since Voltaire French wit had been the model for the western world. Nobody doubted that French women's *couture* and cosmetics, French wine and food, were the best in the world, French (heterosexual) sex was considered the most sophisticated and adventurous, French style and taste in all these and other matters was something to which my generation inclined to defer. Even this rested on the long-established habit of turning selected superiorities of France into a general superiority supposed to be inherent in that country. We knew very well that there were a lot of things in which France was not superior. Yet our admiration for France was quite unaffected by the fact, which young men and women of my generation from North America, central and northern Europe could hardly fail to notice, that the French way of life between the wars as yet had virtually nothing to say about outdoor activities. It was not much into communing with nature. It showed no great interest in hiking, singly or in groups, mountaineering, skiing, practising, or even watching, team games; not even football. In the 1930s an ideological interest in the open air still seemed to be confined to conservatives, ranging from social Catholics to the frankly reactionary. In return, its only national grassroots sporting passion, the Tour de France of the cyclists, aroused no interest outside France except in a few bordering countries.*

On the other hand, France had one major asset. It appeared to offer its civilization to any foreigner who wanted it. It was ours to share, and we accepted it, and this not just because Mussolini and Hitler had soiled German and Italian culture – my generation would not have dreamed of vacations in fascist Venice or Rome – because British culture was too insular, and US culture visibly belonged to a different tribe from ours. The French Revolution, the starting-point of modern world history for every person on the globe with a western education, had democratized the most prestigious and exclusive of the great court cultures, and had opened the gates of a notoriously chauvinist nation to all who accepted the principles of liberty, equality and fraternity and the French language one and indivisible. In the nineteenth-century France became not only the major immigrant-absorbing country in Europe, but also – especially between the 1830 and 1848 revolutions – the welcoming refuge for international political and cultural dissidents from all of Europe. Paris was the centre of international culture, the place to be or to have been. How else could the *Ecole de Paris* of the early twentieth century have become possible, in which Spanish, Bulgarian, German, Dutch, Italian and Russian artists rubbed shoulders with Latin Americans, Norwegians and, of course, the native French? In no other country was the wartime Resistance movement to rely so heavily on resident foreigners – refugee Spanish Republicans, assorted Poles, Italians, central Europeans, Armenians and Jews of the Communist Party's MOI (*main d'oeuvre immigrée* – immigrant labour). My own memories of Paris before going to Cambridge are of Americans in Left Bank art galleries, German surrealists in attics, the tables of the Dôme café in Montparnasse crowded with impecunious artistic geniuses from Russia and central Europe waiting for recognition. My memories after I went to Cambridge and joined the Communist Party are of meetings with anti-fascist central Europeans in the

---

* However, for a few years before the rise of American and Australian tennis in the 1930s, France played a prominent role on the international tennis scene, through the 'Four Musketeers' – Cochet, Lacoste, Brugnon and Borotra – and one of the rare prominent sportswomen of the time, Suzanne Lenglen.

Restaurant des Balkans in the rue de la Harpe, of the international conferences, filled with Italian, German and eventually Spanish refugees, persecuted Yugoslavs, Hungarians and assorted Asian revolutionaries, for which James Klugmann mobilized his young Cambridge loyalists.

For Hitler not only made France more than ever into an international centre, but, between 1933 and 1939, into the last major refuge for European civilization and, as fascism advanced, the only surviving headquarters of the European left. Though it did not welcome refugees and asylum seekers, being used to mass immigration unlike Britain before Munich, France made no systematic effort to keep them out. There were other places of refuge – the little Benelux countries, Czechoslovakia (until Munich), reluctant Switzerland, Denmark, where Brecht went, even, for very non-political Jews, Italy, until Mussolini introduced racism in 1938. (But not, from the time of the Great Terror, Stalin's Russia.) They were only boltholes for the persecuted. France was different. In better times even the exiles would have gone there voluntarily. It seemed, and still seems, natural that the last great occasion before the descent into hell, when the entirety of a riven Europe still went on show, the International Exposition of 1937, should have been held in Paris. Where else? Almost certainly I am not alone in remembering it as both international and French: not only for Picasso's *Guernica* and the giant German and Soviet pavilions glowering at each other, but also for the wonderful and luminous exhibition of French art, the finest I have ever seen.

And then, for a brief moment, France became not only the refuge of civilization, but the place of hope. In 1934 the native instincts of popular republican politics (union in defence of the Republic, no enemies on the left) combined with the unusually realistic sense of the passionately Francophile central European Comintern representative with the French CP, 'Comrade Clément', to devise the best strategy for fighting the apparently irresistible advance of fascism, the 'Popular Front'.[1] A Popular Front won the elections in Spain in February 1936. In May it won the elections in France. It brought into office the first government in French history to be headed by a socialist – the communists could not bring themselves actually to enter the Cabinet – and an extraordinary, spontaneous outburst of working-class hope and joy, the wave of sit-in strikes, or more exactly factory occupations, of June 1936. I arrived in Paris at the tail-end of this extraordinary and remarkably good-tempered victory celebration, but enough was still there a few weeks later to make that year's Fourteenth of July unforgettable. I was lucky to see it in the best possible way: driving round Paris on a truck with a newsreel team of the French Socialist Party, photographing the great day, doubtless on film-stock sold to them by my uncle.

For young revolutionaries of my generation mass demonstrations were the equivalent of papal masses for devout Catholics. But in 1936 the anniversary of the taking of the Bastille, east of the Place de la République, was more than the greatest of mass demonstrations of the French left. (Nobody that year paid much attention to the military parade and other official government celebrations of the national holiday in the bourgeois part of the city.) The whole of popular Paris was on the street to march – or rather to perambulate between endless waits – or to watch and cheer the march, as families might cheer departing newlyweds after the marriage ceremony. The red flags and tricolours, the leaders, the contingents of workers from the victorious male strikers of Renault and the female strikers of Printemps and Galeries Lafayette, the Emancipated Bretons marching under their banners, the green flags of the Star of North Africa passed before the serried masses on the pavement, the crowded windows, the hospitably waving café proprietors, waiters and clients, the even more hospitable enthusiasm of the assembled and applauding brothel staffs.

It was one of the rare days when my mind was on autopilot. I only felt and experienced. That night we watched the fireworks over the city from Montmartre and, after I left the party, I walked back slowly across Paris as though floating on clouds, stopping to drink and dance at I do not know how many street-corner *bals*. I reached my lodgings at dawn.

Indeed, the Popular Front was almost designed for the young, for (through the agency of a new law under a new undersecretary 'of sport and leisure', Léo Lagrange) it introduced both the first national paid holidays and cheap rail fares. On the strength of the only money I was ever to win in the national lottery, 165 Francs (or about £2–3 at the 1936 rate of exchange) I bought myself a fortnight's backpacking in the Pyrenees and Languedoc, joining the first beneficiaries of the Loi Lagrange on the night train from the Gare d'Orsay to Luchon. The trip was to bring my first and only direct contact with the weeks-old Spanish Civil War, which is described elsewhere (chapter 20). It also introduced me (through a young Czech I met on the road) to hitchhiking, a practice then still virtually unknown in Europe, except to a minority of young footloose central European *Tippler* (hitchhiker). It was therefore very easy, especially after I discovered that middle-class French car drivers could be kept from expressing their detestation of Léon Blum and the communists by well-timed enquiries about what they thought about Napoleon – a subject which kept them talking for up to 200 kilometres. From then on I extended my knowledge of France every year through long backpacking hitchhikes.

By the time the war broke out I, like so many others of my generation, thought I knew Paris pretty well; in some ways better than London. I was probably more at ease between Montparnasse, the Panthéon, the Pont Saint-Michel and the long stretch of the boulevard Raspail and the rue de Rennes than in any equally large chunk of central London. I could speak French sufficiently well to be beyond the stage when Frenchmen politely congratulate one on how well one speaks their language. I knew, or thought I knew, as much about the politics of France as about those of Britain, knew who were supposed to be the 'in' theatrical companies (Jouvet, Dullin, the Pitoëffs), had seen Renoir's *La règle du jeu* when it first came out, smoked Gauloises at the corner of my mouth like Jean Gabin, and had bought both the works of Saint-Just and the speeches of Robespierre. In fact, we knew and understood very much less than we thought we did, but considering that most of us had no special academic, professional or family interest in French affairs, we felt at home in Paris. We were comfortable in France and with France.

However, there was one curious thing about the relationship with France. French people, the indigenous French rather than immigrants and more or less permanently resident foreigners, were virtually absent from it. For most of the foreigners in the 1930s, the French were physically present mainly as service-providers or extras on the permanent film-set of their country. It was not till the 1950s that my

Paris became a city in which I had French friends and habitually spent my time with French people, as well as with the usual cosmopolitan community of visiting foreigners or immigrants.

The French were – indeed they still are – a remarkably formal people and their society a theatre with clearly prescribed roles and procedures. I cannot think of another country in which a notoriously womanizing, admittedly middle-aged philosopher in the 1950s still had as his stock-in-trade falling on his knees and presenting the lady with a rose. Unless officially committed to intimacy, Frenchmen still tend to sign everyday correspondence in the carefully graded flourishes of traditional deference ('Kindly accept, Monsieur, the expression of my distinguished/most distinguished/most devoted sentiments'). To be elected to the French Academy or the Collège de France, which still requires the formal declaration of one's candidature, followed by the candidate's ritual canvassing visits to all the electors, is a far more ceremonious affair than elsewhere; it is an honour and a recognized social obligation for those who have contributed to the successful academician's outfit to attend the occasion when they are summoned to admire his ceremonial sword. Even informality is not without its obligations. When intellectuals were on the left, they believed that their status as such committed them to talking to each other in the vocabulary of Belleville. Nevertheless, it was then – perhaps it still is – difficult to enter their lives without some form of presentation. Only in France would one, calling on the great historian Ernest Labrousse at home – we knew each other quite well from economic history conferences in Britain – be kept waiting in the vestibule for the statutory ten minutes before being asked into his study and greeted affably as *cher ami, cher collègue*. A Professor at the Sorbonne and former Chef-de-Cabinet to Léon Blum knew what was his due. Jean-Paul Sartre was the only *ex-officio* 'great French intellectual' I ever met who seemed totally lacking in this sense of public status.

Equality itself was formalized. I knew I was accepted as an intellectual who belonged when somewhat younger French colleagues automatically addressed me as *tu*, as one does old boys and fellow-graduates of the Ecole Normale Supérieure or similar elite educational establishments. (Of course communists of whatever status and country, except perhaps from the German Democratic

Republic, also did so automatically, but most formerly communist French historians had ceased to be in the Party by the time I got to know them well.) Not that this implied personal intimacy. Because I could not detach it from intimacy, my personal relations with Fernand Braudel were crippled for ever after the great man, very much my senior in age as well as eminence, formally suggested that we should say *tu* to one another. Conversation became too difficult – rather like writing a novel without the letter *e*, in the manner of Georges Perec – if one could use neither the old formal *vous* nor the *tu* which resisted crossing one's lips. I simply could not bring myself to treat him as an ordinary informal friend, rather than a graciously condescending patron, which was the role in which I had learned to admire and like him. (He played it to perfection.)

In such a country, however easy the entry to the geographical space, entry to the human space was difficult without personal introductions, or tacit recognition signals rather like those codes which – now that the traditional *concierge* no longer watches over the comings and goings after dark and at weekends – are necessary to visit Parisian friends in their apartment buildings. My own codes of entry were the Communist Party and association with one clan of French historians. The doors opened for me at, and through, the Paris International Congress of Historical Sciences in 1950. At this congress, described in chapter 17, I met the sort of people out of whom Braudel, the great academic entrepreneur, with his wonderful chief-of-staff, Clemens Heller, was soon to fashion the counter-establishment to the Sorbonne, the 'Sixth Section' of the Ecole Pratique des Hautes Etudes. Today it operates as the 'High School for Social Sciences' in the black glass building of the Maison des Sciences de l'Homme, which Braudel and Heller managed to erect on the site of the former Cherche-Midi prison, facing the comforts of the Hôtel Lutetia, where the Gestapo had tortured its prisoner not long before. And the great innovation of the Maison as an official institution was not only that, thanks to Braudel, but particularly to Heller, it systematically tried to bring French and foreigners together, but above all that it recognized the importance of informality and personal talk.

It naturally helped personal relations to be on easy terms with the group of historians round Braudel and the *Annales*, all the more so as with the exception of the great chieftain himself, whom I got to know in the middle fifties, they were not yet great, or even significant, names with major works to their credit. In a sense our careers advanced together, and so did our social relations – at least until the curious posthumous reversion to Cold War anti-communism among French intellectuals in the 1990s. However, the academically mediated friendships did not develop fully until the 1960s, and my closer connections with the Maison, the Ecole (where I later taught for a month a year) and the Collège de France not until the 1970s. This was primarily due to the remarkable Clemens Heller.

Clemens, a large, shambling, distracted-looking man who disliked phone conversations of more than fifty seconds, apt to lapse into a macaronic mixture of languages, may best be described as the most original intellectual impresario of postwar Europe. The theatrical metaphor is suitable. Son of Hugo Heller, a Viennese bookseller and cultural entrepreneur who had the bad luck to attract the sarcasm of Karl Kraus, he began his career as a pupil in the Max Reinhardt Theatre School, before being sent to the USA after Hitler came to Austria. He returned as a US officer to launch the celebrated Salzburg Seminars, was extruded from them by the US witch-hunt, and established himself in Paris. There he and Braudel formed their extraordinarily successful partnership, to which Heller brought the profoundly cosmopolitan culture of expatriate central Europe, a smell for intellectually interesting and promising people and ideas, an international network and the ability to mobilize American foundation money for his academic projects. France being what it is, this led him to be denounced as an agent of the CIA in due course, fortunately in vain. Music and the intellect were the guiding passions of this man of extraordinary warmth and generosity. One of the rewards of a long life has been to be his friend.

Although my friendships in the 1950s came through the Historical Congress, they were mediated through the politics of intellectuals. They did not actually come through the Communist Party, although most of the people I met were at that time still in the Party. The French CP, an organization apparently run by political sergeant-majors, had a quite extraordinary knack of bullying and then antagonizing the intellectuals its Resistance record had attracted in such quantities, which astonished those of us used to the more relaxed ways of the

British and Italian Communist Parties; but then, as my friend Antonin Liehm has pointed out, being a genuine mass party between the wars, it had, like the Czech CP, stalinized itself, rather than had 'bolshevization' imposed on it from outside. On the defensive after 1947 it retreated into a private cultural and political universe, fortified against the temptations of the outside world in a manner which reminded me of Roman Catholic minorities in the era of Vatican One, at all events in Britain. (Having been brought up in a Catholic country, French communist intellectuals were, of course, keenly aware of the structural similarities between the Party and the Church.) It had a proletarian distrust of intellectuals. When the British Communist Historians' Group looked for opposite numbers in France, we got no help from the PCF. The pre-war party wanted militants, not academics. Hence the 1950 Historical Congress, though attracting young Marxists, was not attended by several of the subsequently eminent and eventually anti-communist historians who were hard-line young CP activists at the time – François Furet, Annie Kriegel, Alain Besançon, Le Roy Ladurie. I did not get to know them until their post-communist days.

In fact, looking back, it now seems clear to me that the foundation of my network of friends was not so much communism as the common experience of and identification with the Resistance.

For all this decade and until the tragic break-up of their marriage, my Paris base was to be the rather basic working-class flat on the boulevard Kellerman of Henri Raymond and the enchanting Helène Berghauer. To the Raymonds I went most of my vacations, and with them I spent most of my free time. For some years after the break-up of my first marriage they were the closest thing to a family I had. When they left Paris I would travel with them in their small car to wherever we agreed to go – to the Loire valley, to Italy, wherever. When they were in town I shared it with them, going round in their company, observing the passing scene from the approved cafés such as the Flore or the Rhumerie, watching out for, and passing the time of day with, acquaintances among the intelligentsia – Lucien Goldmann, Roland Barthes, Edgar Morin. When they were absent, I stayed there alone, using it as a private desert island. The flat made up for the austerity of its equipment by the sheer sparkling high spirits of Helène, and a spectacular Lurçat tapestry that had later to be sold at a moment of financial stringency. Like Henri's friendship with the libertine novelist Roger Vailland and the Marxist philosopher and sociologist Henri Lefebvre, it was a relic of the Resistance, which he had joined as a very young man. (It was to get an introduction to Lefebvre that I had first been brought to the Raymonds' flat by a young woman, also of Resistance background, whom I had met at the congress.)

A few years my junior, Henri came from what he described as a peasant family in the Orléanais, published his own and his friends' poetry in small *plaquettes* or pamphlets with drawings by Helène, for which he also made me write a piece on jazz, and at that time worked for the nationalized railways. He followed Lefebvre in studying sociology and urbanism and eventually taught at the Beaux Arts, thus catching up to some extent with his older brother André, a bona fide thesis-producing academic from the start who was to become the world expert on Islamic guilds and a pillar of French oriental scholarship. Helène, both more cosmopolitan and dramatically Parisian, who had spent the war with her family in Brazil, worked hard to make herself a painter. Frankly, she was never much good, but although people did not like to say so to a charming and extremely attractive young woman, I suspect that she was too intelligent not to be aware of her limitations, and suffered accordingly. Meanwhile she earned her living by working at the Brazilian consulate. Her Polish father, with whom relations were tense, was in business, her brother was something in *couture*, or at least the friend of one of the first of the beautiful Japanese models who anticipated erotic multiculturalism. Perhaps this helps to explain how she managed to wear Balmain at a time when *haute couture* labels had not yet been licensed to every department store. Like Henri she was a communist, in a *cellule* in the proletarian 13th *arrondissement*, but she had begun on the periphery of the Palestine Jewish terrorist organization known as the Stern Gang, or at least the extreme left-wing part of it. She retained an affinity for direct action. During the period of Algerian OAS terrorism she visited me in London, while she was making purchases of timers on behalf of what she said was a left-wing anti-OAS bombing campaign. I asked where she would get them. 'At Harrods, naturally,' she said. Of course, where else?

Though some of the people in the Raymonds' network were to become well known in their fields, essentially it operated on the lower slopes of the Parisian left-wing intelligentsia, although Helène plausibly claimed to be *au fait* with the scandals on the more elevated peaks, the gossip about literary prizes and who was on the skids in the CP leadership. It read *Le Monde* and sometimes still *L'Humanité*, but most of the people we knew (as distinct from gossiping about them) were not likely to be asked to sign those manifestos of intellectuals on public issues which were so characteristic of the times before the eminent 'media intellectuals' had their own regular columns in the dailies and weeklies. It was very much a pre-1968 milieu and the 1950s and 1960s saw it gradually crumble as the old left splintered and shifted over Stalin and Algeria, and the old guard of the French CP increasingly found anyone suggesting change uncongenial, especially intellectuals. My communist friends tended to move from the Party to a smaller body, the Party of Socialist Unity (PSU) and when that proved unviable, into full-time research, writing or, if they wanted to remain in politics, the old Socialist Party. Since I did not then know some of the ex-communists who were to move directly into a passionate anti-communism, or had met them only casually, I was unable to follow the tracks of their political travels.

Inevitably the breakdown of the Raymonds' marriage changed the pattern of my visits to Paris. In any case from 1961 on my life was transformed by the partnership of Marlene. However permanent the passion, like jazz, Paris could no longer be the same for a then middle-aged man with wife and, eventually, children. And in any case she had, and made, her own friends in France, quite apart from the ones we had, or from then on acquired together. Moreover, since 1957 I had acquired another couple of close Parisian friends who remain our friends to this day: Richard and Elise Marienstras. The Raymonds and I had decided to travel to a small seaside town in the Gargano peninsula of Italy – the 'spur' that sticks out of the 'boot' of Italy into the Adriatic – on the strength of a novel set there, *La Loi*, recently published by the then still communist or recently communist writer Roger Vailland, whom Henri had known since Resistance days. There on the beach were the Marienstrases, he a tall broad-chested blond, she tiny, thin and dark, en route for a spell as secondary-school teachers in Tunisia, by then independent but still educationally linked with the French schools system. Never were French intellectuals more involved in North Africa than in the 1950s, when Tunisia and Morocco won their freedom and the Algerians were fighting for theirs. So we had plenty to talk about. In any case, ever since the early nineteenth century the Maghreb has played a major role in the imagination of French painters and writers, but equally so as an intellectual stimulus to the young *agrégés* who went there as teachers, that is to say as future academics: Fernand Braudel among historians and Pierre Bourdieu among sociologists, to name but two. The Marienstrases' academic interests were not Mediterranean or Oriental, but Anglo-Saxon, which provided another link. Richard was to become the major French authority on Shakespeare, and Elise was to establish a reputation as a historian of the USA.

Both were from Polish-Jewish families, fortunate to survive in the unoccupied zone of wartime France. Richard had joined the armed Resistance in the south-eastern hills at the age of sixteen, an experience he recalled as the only time in his life when nobody cared, or even asked, whether he was Jewish. Many years later he was deeply moved when, being the only intellectual among his surviving and now ageing Resistance comrades, he was asked to make the commemorative speech at their fiftieth anniversary dinner somewhere in the Rhône valley. Though they were naturally on the left, Marxism did not attract the Marienstrases, but proud of secular, emancipated, diaspora Judaism, neither did Zionism. Theirs was, or perhaps increasingly became, a minority position among French Jewry which in their lifetime, thanks mainly to the massive exodus from formerly French North Africa, became the largest Jewish community in Europe and, since the end of the USSR, in any country of the old world.

There was a third, more academic, reason why my relationship with Paris changed in the 1960s. The convergence between what the French historians were doing in *Annales* and we in *Past & Present* was becoming obvious. From about 1960 I was increasingly drawn into Parisian academic life, and especially towards the new academic empire of Fernand Braudel. Indeed, in the 1970s I joined it for a while officially as an associate *directeur de recherche* for part of the year at the new Ecole des Hautes Etudes en Sciences Sociales. In short, from 1960 on academic engagements increasingly set the rhythm of my, or rather our, visits to Paris.

In a way these changes went together. When I first went to Paris after marrying Marlene, whose knowledge of the academic world was negligible, the Braudels, justifiably charmed by her, invited us to lunch at their apartment and Fernand won her permanent goodwill by assuring her that being a good husband was an essential element of being a good historian. On such occasions grandees of French intellectual life are not on oath, but since they know how to make the statements proper to the occasion in a manner suggesting sincerity without condescension, all of us were satisfied. Conversely, she was the hostess in London both to Emmanuel Le Roy Ladurie when he stayed with us after I had invited him to a seminar in London and, many years later, to the philosopher Louis Althusser in one of his manic phases, not long before he killed his wife in one of the subsequent depressions. As in other academic households, personal and professional relations were not clearly separable.

Unlike in the France of the Third and even the Fourth Republics, I no longer felt at ease in the France of de Gaulle and his Gaullist successors, or in the France of Mitterrand, the France that developed a new kind of public rhetorical jargon where politicians called their country the '*Hexagone*', talked of '*la France profonde*' and showed their energy by forging ahead '*tous azimuts*', in which Paris became one gigantic gentrified bourgeois ghetto, the largest in Europe, where the street-corner bars were shut at weekends because the old people of Paris could no longer afford to live there, although they worked there on weekdays. Except for the great hole in the centre left by the emigration of the markets and filled by Richard Rogers's Beaubourg, the city remained more or less recognizable until President Mitterrand filled and surrounded it with his architectural dinosaurs. (The General, knowing that his place in history was secure, had disdained trying to preserve his memory by monumental architecture.) Paris remains as wonderful a city as ever for the tourist, but it is hard for a historian to get used to the fact that the left can no longer elect more than the odd councillor in the home of the Paris Commune, unless the corruption of the right-wing municipal administrations has temporarily become too scandalous. On the other hand, nobody living in Britain could fail to appreciate the advantages of French postwar modernization, which supplemented the unchanging quality and variety of French food-markets and cooking with the TGV and a superb system of public urban and suburban transport.

I learned, at first reluctantly, to appreciate the greatness of the General and to develop a taste for his style. I learned, with even greater reluctance, to respect Mitterrand. Neither could have flourished in the Third Republic. Both came out of the milieu of what the Third Republic would have (rightly) called 'reaction'. De Gaulle was a man of the right, but one for whom the Republic, including its left, was an essential part of that 'certain idea of France' which he recreated after the war. He was the first French politician since 1793 whose France had a place both for the monarchy and the Revolution. Indeed, he was presumably not entirely displeased to be compared with Louis XIV, who would have addressed his servants much as de Gaulle addressed the publisher who edited his memoirs, when the man admitted to a rather un-Gaullist past between 1940 and 1944. 'I take it,' said the great man (who may well have had the relevant files looked up), 'that you have been inside one of my prisons.' Both the personal pronoun and the plural are very much de Gaulle.*

Since his death there has been much criticism of the ambiguities and complexities of François Mitterrand's career. Yet it cannot be denied that it moved leftwards with surprisingly little discontinuity, from the pre-war ultra-right through Vichy and the Resistance to a political progress that turned him into the builder and chief of a reconstructed Socialist Party which recaptured control of the left not by isolating the communists in the usual Cold War manner, but by bringing him to power in alliance with them. In both Third and Fourth Republics politicians would have moved in the opposite direction. He and de Gaulle belong to an era – no, both were architects of the era – when French politics ceased to be essentially a battle about the great Revolution whose memory divided the left from the right, though both men knew in their bones that the Revolution was as central to the France they ruled as the American

* *'Alors, vous avez bien connu mes prisons.'* The anecdote was told me by the publisher himself.

Constitution was to the USA. In this they were more realistic than the ideologists of moderate liberalism, immoderate anti-communism and market society, always an untypical minority in France, who came to dominate Parisian intellectual fashions in the late 1980s and early 1990s.

And yet, if I did not feel at ease in Gaullist and Mitterrandist France, I could understand its continuity with my own France, the blue-white-and-red tricoloured 'remembered hills' of the past. In one way or another, the France of the *Canard Enchaîné* was not yet dead. Indeed, the scandals and the growing corruption in the later Gaullist and the later Mitterrand eras revived the fortunes of this publication.

Nor did I feel at ease with the intellectual mood of the time. Like everyone on the global left, I was excited by the rebellion of 1968 but I remained sceptical. True, I was in much closer touch with French historians, who formed the core discipline of the French social sciences until the 1970s, and who supplied so many of Hamon and Rotman's Parisian 'intellocrats'.[2] Nevertheless, in some ways I had lost touch with many of the currents of French culture and theoretical discussion after the 1960s, and, although any admirer of Queneau and Perec cannot but be sympathetic to the French intellectual tradition of playing games with language, as French thinkers increasingly moved into the territory of 'postmodernism' I found them uninteresting, incomprehensible, and in any case of not much use to historians. Even their puns failed to grip.

After the brief 1968 surge, in the 1970s and 1980s the left, both old and new, was clearly on the retreat in France. My opinion of the French Communist Party since 1945 had never been high, and I had long regarded its leadership under George Marchais as a disaster, yet it would be dishonest of me not to admit that its decline from the great mass Party of the French working class to a rump of less than 4 per cent of voters caused an old communist pain. And it would be equally dishonest not to admit that most of what has remained under the label 'Marxism' in France is unimpressive. On the other hand, particularly in the 1980s and 1990s, the increasingly militant and ill-tempered anti-communism of so many of the formerly left-wing 'intellocrats' began to complicate my relations with some of them. Though we respected and sometimes liked each other, some of those with whom I had dealings in Paris, intellectual or social, were politically uneasy in my company, and I in theirs. Since I remained what I had been since 1956, a known, though heterodox communist whose work had never been published in the USSR, some, who might have been more Stalinist or even Maoist in their youth than I ever was, resented what they regarded as a wilful refusal to take the same road. I, in turn, found myself more repelled by the Cold War rhetoric and free market liberalism to which some of the ablest and most prestigious were drawn in the 1980s than by the straightforward return of a man like Le Roy Ladurie (a major historian by any standards) to the traditional conservatism of his Norman ancestry. Paradoxically, as Communist Parties declined, the Cold War ended and the Soviet Union and its empire collapsed, the tone of anti-communist and anti-Marxist polemic became more embittered, not to say hysterical. The late François Furet, a historian and publicist of great intelligence and influence – perhaps the nearest thing to a *chef d'école* of the tendency – did his best to turn the second centenary of the French Revolution into an intellectual assault on it. A few years later his *Le passé d'une illusion* presented the history of the twentieth century as that of the process of liberation from the dangerous dream of communism. Not surprisingly, I criticized his views.[3] As a by now quite well-known Marxist historian, I found myself for a while a champion of the embattled and besieged French intellectual left.

This complicated relations further, especially since, by chance, my own history of the twentieth century, *The Age of Extremes*, appeared just before Furet's book. While it was accepted on its merits and received calmly even by notably conservative reviewers in other countries, in France it was seen – at least by an influential part of the intellocrats – essentially as a work of political ideological polemics directed against anti-communist liberals. Though discussed (in its English version) in intellectual journals, it was not translated, on the ostensible grounds that it was too expensive to translate for its necessarily small market. The argument was implausible, since the book had already sold well in every other western language. Indeed, such was the curious self-absorption of the French intellectual scene in those years that French was for several years the *only* language of the member-states of the European

Union, and indeed the only global culture-language (including Chinese and Arabic) in which the book was not published or contracted to be published. It finally came out in France in 1999, thanks to the initiative of a Belgian publisher and the active help of one of the few unrepentant publications of the left, *Le Monde Diplomatique*. Perhaps the ideological mood had changed since Lionel Jospin, who put less strain on the conscience of the French left than the dying Mitterrand, took over as prime minister in 1997. It was received well enough by the critics. The potential reviewers of the early nineties kept silent or had buried their hatchets. It sold rather satisfactorily, at least for a while. It brought me more personal letters from unknown readers scattered across the map of France than any of the other translations of this much-translated work. And it enabled an ancient Francophile, whose love affair with the tradition of the French left began on a newsreel truck on Bastille Day 1936, to round it off sixty-three years later with another suitably symbolic experience in the Grand Amphitheatre of the Sorbonne, once the only university of Paris, now the parent of a family, packed with Parisians who had been invited to listen to a debate on my newly published book. Very few of the people who came in sufficient numbers to crowd the enormous auditorium had read any of my books which, as the publishers who refused me always reminded me, had only had a *succès d'estime* in the hexagonal market. What brought them there was the fact that someone – it happened to be me – spoke frankly, critically, sceptically, but impenitently, and not without pride for those who stood for a left in which the old distinctions of party and orthodoxy no longer counted. I like to think that on this occasion I was present at a sort of re-emergence, however brief, of a Parisian intellectual left from a period of siege.

It is a suitable episode with which to end this chapter of a lifetime affair. For my generation France remains special. I can sympathize with the French sense of loss at the defeat of the language of Voltaire by the world triumph of the language of Benjamin Franklin. It is not only a linguistic but a cultural transformation, for it marks the end of the minority cultures in which only the elites needed international communication, and it hardly mattered that the idiom in which it took place was not widely spoken on the globe, or even – as in the classical dead languages – that it was not spoken at all. I can understand the retreat of a once hegemonic French culture into an hexagonal ghetto, only slightly mitigated by the popularity of 'postmodern' French ideologues among American graduate students, who do not always understand them. It is not that this is what Paris wants, but simply that it cannot get used to a state of affairs in which the rest of the world no longer looks to Paris and follows its lead. It is a hard fate to go from global hegemony to regionalism in two generations. It is hardest of all to discover that for most of the world none of this matters. But it matters for my generation of Europeans, Latin Americans and Middle Easterners. And it should matter to younger generations. The stubborn rearguard action of France in defence of the global role of her language and culture may be doomed, but it is also a necessary defence, by no means predestined to failure, of every language, and national and cultural specificity against the homogenization of an essentially plural humanity by the processes of globalization.

20

From Franco to Berlusconi

Aspiring novelists are never short of a subject. When all else fails, there's family and autobiography. Aspiring professional historians have no built-in guide to what part of the past they want to explore, and therefore in most cases what their reputation will rest on – the Tudors, the English Revolution, seventeenth-century Spain or whatever. Usually they acquire a subject at university, give it a title to get a doctorate (or, in my day, when Oxbridge looked down on such titles, a fellowship dissertation) and in most cases stick to their 'field' or 'period' thereafter. The war had blocked my own attempts to follow this path. So it happened that my first book as a historian, *Primitive Rebels*, was in a field I had not previously thought much about, and indeed a field nobody else had thought about at all.[1] Essentially, it is a book based on my frequent travels in Spain and Italy in the 1950s, two countries to which my life and the fortunes of my writings have been linked ever since.

Unlike Italy – what antifascist would go there? – Spain, where I began to travel in 1951, had been part of my life for a long time – even before the Spanish Civil War, which made it part of everyone's life in my generation. In spite of everything, after 1945 it was still a strange country for other Europeans. In the minds of most of us it still belonged to a curious realm where the images of revolution, war and defeat in arid landscapes were superimposed on the images of exoticism – flamenco, castanets, bullfights, Carmen, Don José, Escamillo – and those of a generic 'Spanishness' – Don Quixote, honour, pride and silence. My uncle had been there and had got to know people there in his time with Universal Films. The relics of his visits filled odd corners of our house: a *banderilla* soaked in dry blood, a book on bullfighting, a signed photo of an elderly, military-looking Catalan autonomist leader and the like. After the

1934 insurrection in Asturias, a friend sent him copies of the Spanish illustrated papers, I imagine the monarchist *ABC* with dramatic pictures. And then, in the summer of 1936, in the first weeks after the generals' rising, thanks to a curious combination of historical circumstances, for a brief moment I saw it myself.

I was then living in Paris for three months before going up to Cambridge, on a grant from the London County Council to improve my French. One day at the end of July I discovered to my agreeable surprise that I had bought a winning lottery ticket. It did not amount to much – I remember it as 165 Francs or about £2–3. Fortunately the new Popular Front government of France had shortly before introduced one of its rare lasting innovations, *les congés payés* (holidays with pay) and – thanks to another innovation, an under-secretaryship of sports and leisure – ultra-cheap rail travel to enable the population to enjoy them. I therefore used my lottery winnings to take the train from Orsay station – still half a century away from being turned into a museum of nineteenth-century French art – to the Pyrenees for a fortnight of walking, youth hostelling and camping. Halfway through this superb excursion I was introduced to a more expeditious form of cheap movement by one of those peripatetic young central Europeans who in those days pioneered hitchhiking (*'Tippeln'*, *'Autostop'*) on this side of the Atlantic. And so I found myself, carried from the Atlantic to the Mediterranean side of the Pyrenees, in a youth hostel close to the Spanish border near the town of Puigcerda. The occasion was too tempting. I went to the frontier, and was turned back by the young militia man who guarded it. I did not have the right papers. I walked a mile or so to the next crossing, where they let me pass without problems and I spent the day looking round Puigcerda, then for all practical purposes an independent revolutionary commune, dominated by the anarchists, with an admixture of members of POUM (Workers Party of Marxist Unification). (I could see no sign of the communists or the socialists, merged by then into a single party, the PSUC [Unified Socialist Party of Catalonia].) I don't remember how exactly I communicated with the locals, who were naturally interested in an unannounced, indeed in any, stranger, but this is a corner where Spain and France are very mixed up, and Catalan is in any case as close to one language as to the other. I recall no problems. My most lasting image of this memorable day is of a few trucks parked on the main square. Whenever someone felt like going to the war, he went to the trucks, and whenever one filled up with enough volunteers, I was told, it went off to the front. As I wrote about this experience many years later:

> The phrase *c'est magnifique, mais ce n'est pas la guerre* should have been invented for such a situation. It *was* marvellous, but the main effect of this experience on me was, that it took me twenty years before I was prepared to see Spanish anarchism as anything but a tragic farce.[2]

In fact, Puigcerda did not give the impression of a community geared for war, nor do I recall it as a place full of armed young men in militia outfits, in the manner of later revolutions. (No sign in the Spanish provinces of 1936, for example, of uniformed young women.) If anything, it seemed a town full of politics, talk and arguments, of people standing in groups or sitting at café tables with newspapers.

Unfortunately, the day ended badly. The young anarchist frontier-guard who had turned me back at my first crossing-point came off duty that evening, saw me eating and chatting on the plaza, and immediately reported me to his commissar. I was interrogated, politely enough but firmly, by an unsmiling man in something like military gear. I am sure that he did not know what to make of my presence there – I did not know what to make of it myself – but clearly, the power of the workers could not be treated so lightly, even if the young Englishman who crossed the frontier not only irregularly, but in flat defiance of the decision to keep him out, had shown no signs of wanting to be a danger to the revolution. To be grilled by trigger-happy amateurs on the lookout for counter-revolutionaries is never relaxing. I confess that I was nervous, late that evening, when I was told to walk along the dark road back to the French frontier, the gun-barrel of an armed militiaman aimed at my back. So my fleeting contact with the Spanish Civil War ended with expulsion from the Spanish Republic.

What was I doing that day in Puigcerda? This is where the historian throws up his hands, faced with the autobiographer. It is not simply that my memory of that day has almost certainly been corrupted by sixty-odd years of mental redrafting, but that even on the day itself my purpose, if that is the right word, in crossing the frontier, cannot have been clear. What would I have done, if my stay there had not been cut short so suddenly? Given the common memory of the Spanish Civil War I should have been considering joining the forces of the Republic in the war against fascism, as several other young English people did in the first weeks of the Civil War. Almost certainly nothing like this was in my mind as I went to have a look at what a revolution was like, in spite of the passionate identification I, like others of my generation on the left, immediately felt with the fight of the Spanish Popular Front government. Did it enter my mind during that day? I cannot say, or if I could reconstruct my feelings perhaps I would want to take refuge behind the 5th Amendment of the US Constitution, because in the light of the subsequent establishment of International Brigades* any answer might be discreditable. If I did not consider it, then why not? And if I did, why did I nevertheless not join up? Supposing there were any sources other than my personal memory, what conclusion might another historian, less personally biased in the matter, come to about the strange case of young EJH in the Spanish revolution? Such are the problems of writing history as biography, or perhaps the wider problems of understanding human nature. At all events, my day in Puigcerda demonstrates the pointlessness of the 'what if' exercises in history which now carry the jargon title of 'counterfactuals'. There is no way we can choose between the countless hypotheses about how my subsequent life might or might not have been affected, if that young anarchist border guard had not refused me entry at that first frontier crossing. And it also demonstrates that nothing serves the historian better than keeping his eyes and ears open, especially

---

* The first units formally recruited and organized for international volunteers, by the Italian *Giustizia e Libertà* group, date to the end of August; the Comintern's International Brigades were set up rather later. Most of the original foreign units were composed of foreigners who were in Barcelona for a 'People's Olympiad' at the moment of the generals' insurrection. John Cornford (see chapter 8), who must have arrived in Barcelona at about the time I reached the frontier, decided to enlist 'quite impulsively' (Peter Stansky and William Abraham, *Journey to the Frontier*, London, 1966, p. 328) about a week later.

if he or she has the luck to be in the right place at the right time. Puigcerda gave me my first introduction to, and a permanent fascination with, that quintessential breeding ground for 'Primitive Rebels', namely Spanish anarchism. In the 1950s I found myself pursuing it 'in the field', largely inspired by that remarkable work of Gerald Brenan, *The Spanish Labyrinth*, which I must have read soon after its second edition came out in 1950. I can no longer remember whether I read it before or, more likely, after my first real acquaintance with Spain, which left behind 'the deep and lasting impression which Spain makes on those who know her'.[3] At least two of my visits to Spain were essentially explorations of the anarchist tradition: in 1956, when I found my way to Casas Viejas, the village which had once upon a time (in 1933) tried to make the world revolution on its own, and in 1960, when, deeply moved, I followed the traces of a recently fallen anarchist *guerrillero* Francisco Sabaté.[4]

I am no longer sure why I decided in the Easter vacation of 1951 to travel to Spain. It was a country of whose language I was ignorant, give or take the texts of Civil War slogans and songs and the ideological vocabulary which was international anyway. As later in Italy, I had to pick it up in conversation, with occasional reference to a small pocket dictionary – easier in Italy, where talk was mainly in educated Italian, than in Spain, where my informants were hardly ever intellectuals. (If they had been, we would probably have communicated in French.) One way or another, I was to pick up some spoken if ungrammatical fluency in both languages fairly quickly, beginning immediately after my arrival in Barcelona with an evening at the Café Nuevo on the Paralelo (coffee and show, five pesetas) where my neighbour, a mason just arrived from Murcia looking for work, taught me the words for 'beautiful', 'ugly', 'fat', 'thin', 'blonde', 'brunette', and other relevant terms by pointing to the corresponding features of the (mediocre) artistes on the tiny stage.

My contemporary notes[5] suggest I was attracted by the news of the great and successful tramway boycott against higher fares of early March in Barcelona, followed by a general strike, about which I wrote a piece when I returned. I thought, with excessive anticipation, that it 'broke that crust of passivity and *attentisme* which (with the lack of effective illegal organisations) is Franco's greatest asset today . . .'⁶ This was an overoptimistic assessment, although the first cracks in the regime appeared in the second half of that decade. The anti-Franco exiles I came to know then were not only from Republican backgrounds, such as the historian (and eventual head of the post-Franco Spanish cultural services) Nicolas Sanchez Albornoz, son of the man still recognized by the émigrés as the nominal president of a ghost-republic, but children from the families that made up the Franco establishment. One of them, my dear friend Vicente Girbau León, had gone to a Franco jail directly from a post in the general's foreign service. He later shared my flat in Bloomsbury, before helping to establish the publishing house Ruedo Ibérico in Paris, whose contraband titles, including Hugh Thomas's pioneering book on the Civil War, were to be influential inside Spain in the sixties among the rapidly growing movement of young dissidents. It was he who later put me in touch with the anarchists.

At all events in 1951 I had my first experience of a Barcelona still filled with 'the field-grey teams of the armed police, with rifles and sub-machine guns sticking out like bristles, every hundred-odd yards in the town-centre, and by the factory gates' and guarding the characteristically palatial banks, symbol of the downtown street scene of Franco Spain, like fortresses of the rulers who dominated a hungry people. After a few days in Barcelona I made my way by a mixture of trains and hitchhiking down the coast to Valencia, then to Murcia, Madrid, Guadalajara, Zaragoza and back to Barcelona.

Spain was poor and hungry in the early 1950s, perhaps hungrier than at any time in living memory. People seemed to live on potatoes, cauliflower and oranges. Had Tarragona ever been so badly off in its entire history, I asked myself as I looked at that wonderful gold-blond cathedral among the ruins of the Roman Empire. Spain had no public voices. The news from Barcelona reached the rest of Spain through rumour, travellers such as myself, hawkers, truck-drivers, occasional listeners to foreign radio. There were only obscure allusions in the press. Intellectually, the country, most of its talent in emigration, seemed strangled ('few Spanish works in the "serious" bookshop' – translations and even Spanish classics mainly in Latin American editions).

Spain was unhappy. Time and again, in cafés, in the cabs of trucks, or on the unspeakably awful *correos*, the slow but cheap trains stopping at all stations, people would say things like: 'This is the worst country in the world' or 'People in this country are poorer than anywhere else.' 'Everything in this country has gone to pot since Primo de Rivera [1923–30],' said the matriarch of a family of cheapjack traders from Madrid who took me under their wing. Spain had not forgotten the Civil War and the vanquished, though powerless and hopeless, had not changed their mind about it. And yet, time and again, when the subject came up, someone would say: 'Civil War – nothing is worse. Father against son, brother against brother.' Franco Spain in the early 1950s was a regime sustained by the argument of Thomas Hobbes that any effective political order is better than no order. The regime survived, in spite of its perceived injustice and massive unpopularity – at all events in the eastern parts of the country, where I travelled – not so much because of its power and readiness to terrorize, but because nobody wanted another Civil War. Perhaps Franco might not have survived if, at the end of the Second World War, the Americans and British had decided that he should not, and allowed the armed resistance units from southern France, largely composed of Spanish Republicans, to invade the country. But they did not.

Above all, Spain was isolated. Its blood-soaked regime was still enclosed in the carapace of anti-modernity, traditionalist Catholicism and self-contained autarchy. The extraordinary industrialization of the country, which was to make it unrecognizable, and even to change the very physical appearance of Spaniards in the next thirty or forty years, had hardly begun. Where else in Europe, except the equally self-sealed Portugal, could one still have found a place like Murcia, indistinguishable from a Habsburg provincial city before 1914: nannies in black-and-white uniforms by the dozen supervising their children along the river promenade, eyed by soldiers from the local barracks; middle-class young women with chaperones; farmers and pig-dealers settling bargains in market cafés? Tourists were counted in hundreds, not in tens of millions. The Mediterranean coasts were still empty. When I recall the *costas* of Andalusia in the early 1950s, what comes into my mind is a dusty, white-hot, empty road between stones and sea with a view of vultures descending from all parts of the sky to join the mob already eviscerating the cadaver of a mule or donkey. Perhaps it was the absence of that great corrupter of morals, the mass tourism of the rich in the territories of the poor, which allowed the Spaniards of the time to keep their traditional pride. Nothing struck me more in those days than the insistence of poor men and women on maintaining relations of reciprocity: not accepting a cigarette without offering one in return, or refusing a brandy from an evidently better-off Englishman, which was not compatible with equivalence, but accepting a coffee, which was. In my experience foreigners had not yet become essentially sources of income for poor natives, not even when – as in 1952 – they arrived in Seville, as I did with some student friends, in an evidently British yacht and moored in town, just opposite the as yet ungentrified bars of Triana.

Because Spain seemed to be, and likely to remain, frozen in its history, it was unusually dangerous ground for outside observers and analysts. The overpowering presence of an apparently unchanging past – including the recent past – concealed the forces, internal and external, that were about to transform the country more dramatically and irreversibly than almost any other in Europe within the next few decades. I tried to understand its history, but apart from recognizing that Francoism would not last, I clearly had no clue where it was going. As late as 1966 I found myself writing: 'capitalism has persistently failed in that country and so has social revolution, in spite of its constant imminence and occasional eruption'. It was not yet obvious to me how anachronistic that sentence had by then become. Would closer contact with the anti-Franco opposition or Spanish intellectuals in the 1950s have given me a greater sense of realities? I doubt it, for the only effective opposition party, the Communist Party, was then still resisting the information brought out of the country by its illegal cadres, that there was no prospect of a sudden overthrow of the regime. The anarchists, once so powerful in the Spanish labour movement, had not survived the Civil War as a serious force. Nevertheless, on looking back, I am astonished at how little contact I had in the 1950s with intellectual and politically hip persons in Spain, or, before the 1960s, with the new generation of younger Spanish students and ex-students who came to me in London as someone they had heard of on the left, or as readers of my books, which began to be issued by publishers unknown to me, sometimes in rather bad translations, from 1964 on

– a symptom of the slow weakening of the regime faced with the massive cultural and political dissidence of its educated young. The 1960s in Spain were the first of several historic moments when the fading of authoritarian regimes proved beneficial to this author.

II

My discovery of Italy in 1952 differed from that of Spain in almost every respect. For one thing, Italy was neither hungry nor stagnant. Even getting around cheaply – and in the 1950s I usually budgeted for the equivalent of £1 a day all in – I would not expect to find, as in Spain, would-be middle-class travellers with patched clothes. Though the days of the economic miracle did not transform the lives of ordinary Italians until the 1960s, even in the north, the early signs of dynamism were already visible: colourful modern roadside-stations, already more than mere dispensers of petrol, the universal high-tech espresso machines which were about to conquer the world, the crowds of motor-scooters anticipating the eruption of cheap cars. Not that Italy was entirely on the way to western 'modernity', especially not in the south and the islands. Indeed, if *Primitive Rebels* has any single origin it lies in a dinner in the house of Professor Ambrogio Donini in Rome in 1952, or rather conversations after dinner, since, by the egalitarian convictions of the Doninis, family, servants and guests took their meals together. My host 'told me something about the Tuscan Lazzarettists and the sectarians of Southern Italy'.[7] For he was both a member of the Italian Communist Party's Central Committee – indeed a rather hard-line Stalinist – and an expert in the history of religions. He therefore noted with approval that the followers of a Tuscan rural Messiah killed in 1878 had quietly survived to have another try at the millennium by rising in 1948 after the attempted assassination of the Italian CP leader, Palmiro Togliatti. He also told me about the problems arising for the Party leadership from the insistence of several rural Party branches – 1949–50 was a great era of radicalization in the south – on electing as branch secretaries members of the Seventh Day Adventists or similar sects, who would not normally have been regarded as obvious material for the cadres of a Marxist party. Who were these people, who brought ways of thinking which would have been quite usual in the Middle Ages into mid-twentieth-century political movements? Who treated the era of Lenin and Stalin as though it were also the era of Martin Luther? What went on in their minds? How did they, as distinct from the political movements which drew strength from their support, see the world? Why was so little attention paid to them, except by Italian thinkers such as the extraordinary Antonio Gramsci? Italy, it seemed, was full of their traces. Fascinated and moved, I tried to discover them by travelling along Mediterranean back roads for the next few years. Luckily some anthropologists were developing an interest in similar problems they encountered in their enquiries into the anti-colonial movements in Africa. Max Gluckman of Manchester, a man of great originality and a formidable academic chieftain who took his department every week to support Manchester United in the proper anthropological manner, arranged for me to give three lecture-seminars, in the course of which (also followed by his tribe) he gave me my first sight of Marilyn Monroe in *The Seven Year Itch* and decided I should expand my lectures into a book.

I recall my first visit to Sicily in 1953, where I was taken under the wing of Michele Sala, mayor and deputy of Piana degli Albanesi, a red stronghold since 1893 when the noble Dr Nicola Barbato had preached the gospel of socialism to the inhabitants of what was then Piana dei Greci from the rock in the remote mountain pass of Portella della Ginestra, still known as the Barbato Stone. (In his youth Michele Sala, born in the neighbourhood, had himself heard the good word from the apostle's lips.)[8] Rain or shine, war, peace or fascism, some Pianesi had never since then failed on the first of May to send a demonstration to this place. The occasion in 1947 when the bandit Giuliano massacred this May Day meeting has been wonderfully reconstructed in Francesco Rosi's superb film *Salvatore Giuliano*. Shortly after this the Party had sent Sala to take charge of this complicated part of Sicily. He had the Sicilian sense of realism. In his youth he had signed up, among others, Giuseppe Berti, a leading communist in the Comintern era, and then a student in Palermo, because having carefully situated the socialist office strategically in an apartment facing the exit to a brothel, he could rely on meeting potential recruits ready for red propaganda in a relaxed mood. He had combined this with the hard-nosed political experience of Brooklyn, where he spent twenty years of political emigration and learned enough English to show me the masses of masonry with which he was filling the outskirts of town ('lotta guys need jobs'), as we criss-crossed it in his mayoral car, greeting citizens to the right and left ('In this town I know who I gotta say hello to!').

I was shown the cemetery, or rather the necropolis of the Matrangas, Schiròs, Barbatos, Loyacanos and the rest of the Albanian Christian families who had emigrated to southern Italy and Sicily in the fifteenth and sixteenth centuries. Every modern gravestone, large or small, had the photograph of the departed. Death, respected and unforgotten, was always present in Piana. I saw what was still taken for granted, the silent black-clad women sitting in the street, but always facing indoors. We were walking along one side of the piazza – the anti-communists and Mafiosi walked on the other side – when he stopped me for a moment. 'Don't tell anyone here you are English,' he warned. 'There are people here, they don't like it if they see you with me. I tell them you are from Bologna.' It was logical enough: even in Sicily they knew that Bologna was red, and it was therefore natural that one communist should visit another. There was only one flaw. We had been together all day audibly speaking English. Sala, who knew his people, dismissed this problem. 'What do these guys know how they talk in Bologna?' Indeed, ninety-odd years before, shortly after the unification of Italy, this had been literally true. In 1865 the first schoolmasters sent by the new kingdom to teach the Sicilian children Dante's Italian language were taken for Englishmen. In this respect nothing fundamental changed in inland Sicily until national television programming. But even less backward parts of Italy still had something of the Third World about them. For the bulk of its inhabitants – even the bilingual ones who spoke it instead of Sicilian, Calabrian or Piedmontese – Italian consisted of two languages: the spoken daily language and the formal language still rooted in baroque usage, in which newspapers and books were written and official speeches were made. It remained a relic of the past even in its public respect for, and reliance on, intellectuals as such. I cannot think of another European country in which an unconcealed intellectual such as Bruno Trentin, child of a family of anti-fascist academic emigrants, would have been acceptable as the leader of a major industrial trade union, and later of the major national organization of labour unions.

Learning about Italy was different in another respect. After 1945 tourism without a bad conscience once again became possible, for art and fun, in a country that had so clamorously broken with its fascist past. I was lucky to have the best possible guides: Francis Haskell, who planned, and Enzo Crea, with his encyclopedic knowledge of all the arts, who revealed the remotest corners and the most celebrated treasures of Italy to his friends with equal enthusiasm. What is more, I rarely went to Italy alone, or, when I arrived there, I was rarely without Italian friends, After I married again, they included the friends of Marlene, who had lived in Rome for several years before we met. Moreover, I had the enormous advantage of introductions by a man whose name opened all doors on the Italian left and a good many others besides, Piero Sraffa. Long established in Cambridge in a wonderful set of rooms in Trinity, opposite the rooms of Maurice Dobb, with whom he was producing a monumental edition of the works of the economist David Ricardo, this small, courteous and grizzled man who avoided loquacity and wrote little, was known as an intellect of formidable critical power. His natural habitat was behind the scenes. Though he was taciturn about his political views, as about everything else, it was known that he had been a close friend of Antonio Gramsci and from 1926 until Gramsci's death in 1937 the chief contact of the jailed communist leader with the outside world. He had been the conduit through which Gramsci's prison writings were preserved after his death, with the help of another influential friend in banking. What was not known was the fact that without him Gramsci's remarkable manuscripts could probably not have been written at all, for, after the arrest, Sraffa (from a well-to-do Turinese family) had immediately opened an unlimited account for the prisoner at a Milanese bookshop. He had been a trusted friend of the current leader of the Party, Togliatti, since their university days. It is said that he had considered returning to Italy after the war, but abandoned the idea after the result of the 1948 election, disastrous for the socialist–communist alliance.

As he knew everybody on the anti-fascist scene – after all, Turin had been the capital of both liberal and communist anti-fascism – Sraffa's name made me immediately accepted among the Party's intellectuals. In those days a foreign communist was automatically a member of the brotherhood, a '*compagno*' addressed as '*tu*' and not '*lei*'. Indeed the first name on Sraffa's list I telephoned in Rome, the most senior communist historian at the time, Delio Cantimori, a slow-moving, stout expert on the heretics of the sixteenth century, who had a wicked wit and looked older than his age, immediately invited me to stay with him and his Marx-translating wife, Emma, in their apartment in Trastevere. From there, with his help, I made contact with the Rome-based anti-fascist intellectuals, at that time overwhelmingly communist or Party-sympathizing. One way or another, most of what I learned about Italy – landscape and art history apart – came to me via Italian communists or those Italians still close to them in the early 1950s. It was my luck that my friends among Italian left-wing intellectuals, and especially historians, combining practice with theory, often doubled as observant and analytical journalists.

However, almost anyone who travelled in the remoter rural parts of Italy in the 1950s found people ready to ask and answer questions from foreigners. This was, after all, still a country of oral communication, face to face. In places like Spezzano Albanese (Cosenza, Calabria) such few papers as reached the place still had to be read aloud to the illiterates in cafés, artisan workshops and the PCI 'Sezione'. In 1955 the telephone had reached San Giovanni in Fiore, the home of the great medieval millennial theorist, Abbot Joachim of Flora, only a few months ago. Strangers, Italian or foreign, brought news – even to people who whether they liked it or not knew that new times were inevitably coming. 'Things are changing,' I was told more than once in 1955 Sicily. 'Our customs are getting like those of the North, for instance women going out. In the end I expect we'll be like the Northerners.'

At that time the PCI seemed the main gateway into these new times. It had a membership of about two million – about one quarter of the national electorate – which continued to rise with every election until at its peak in the later 1970s it more or less equalled – enthusiasts claimed it was about to pass – the 34 per cent of the party of permanent government, the Christian Democrats. Socially the PCI was a cross-section of Italian society as much as a class party, especially in its massive strongholds in north–central Italy: Emilia-Romagna, Tuscany, Umbria – regions of culture, prosperity, technological and business dynamism, and honest administration. Italian communism was not the whole of Italy, but a central and a wonderfully civilizing element of it. But, like nonconformity in Britain, it was and remained a minority.

Nevertheless, it was a huge and deeply rooted movement. The *popolo comunista* (communist people), as the cadres called it, was more than merely a collection of crosses on ballot-papers or annually renewed membership cards. Its major regular manifestation, nominally a way of organizing financial support for the Party's daily newspaper, *L'Unità* (which the vast majority of communists read no more than most Italians read any daily paper), was a pyramid of regular popular festivals with its base in every village or city district, which culminated in the annual *Festa Nazionale de l'Unità* in some major centre. My connection with Italian politics began when I was described as a 'fraternal delegate' and had to address such an occasion, God knows how, in 1953 in a village near the Po. The *Festa* was essentially a collective national *family* holiday excursion to spend money for the cause and to have a collective good time with wives, children, friends and trusted leaders. It is said that, on the first occasion it was held in Naples, the population of that great city, conscious that the influx of visitors was not tourists to be fleeced, but plain folks and *compagni*, listened to the appeal of its leaders and for twenty-four hours abstained from its proverbial activities. The *Festa* was, of course, also a political rally, for in the days before television, political oratory by a visiting star, its merit proportionate to its length, and its technique based on that of open-air thespians, was also the biggest public entertainment likely to be seen by the faithful. Since the 'communist people' were also the only part of non-middle-class Italy given to self-improvement and *reading*, progressive publishers relied on these occasions, especially the national *Festa*, for a major part of their annual sales, particularly for the multi-volume series of encyclopedias, histories and other intellectual consumer durables. With his usual sense of the national market, my publisher Giulio Einaudi chose to launch the multi-volume *Storia del Marxismo* (which I co-edited with others) at what was both the peak of the PCI under Enrico Berlinguer and the start of its (unforeseen) decline, the great Genoa *Festa* of 1978. Unfortunately, like the PCI, the popular interest in Marxism was also about to dwindle, though the first volume of the *Storia* still sold well. It was the only one translated into English. Nevertheless, this was an unforgettable occasion of oratory in the vast amphitheatre above the blue sea, food-loaded tables in great marquees full of family parties and the greetings of friends, and hopeful communist leaders (except for the quiet Berlinguer), chatting and joking in the hotel lounge.

I was lucky to be guided into Italy by a strikingly impressive group of pre-war and Resistance communists. The full-time politicians among those I knew tended to maintain their standing as intellectuals and writers – Giorgio Napolitano, Bruno Trentin, the large Giorgio Amendola and the small, chubby and universally erudite Emilio Sereni, from one of the most ancient Jewish families of Rome, jailed by the Germans in wartime Rome, who wrote with equal originality about the history of the Italian landscape and the prehistory of Liguria. The academics among them tended also to double as politicians. Several were on the Central Committee. Renato Zangheri, an economic historian, was brilliantly successful as mayor of the wonderfully preserved yet modern medieval city of Bologna, Italy's greatest 'red' metropolis; Giuliano Procacci and Rosario Villari (with his wife, Anna Rosa, our closest friends) had spells in the Italian Parliament.

From the start I found myself getting on exceptionally well with Italian communists, possibly because so many were intellectuals, but also because they were disarmingly kind. Not every national leader would have quietly visited Cambridge, as Giorgio Napolitano did, simply to hold hands with the dying Piero Sraffa, desperately fighting senility; or, for that matter, would have interrupted his work as the country's Minister of the Interior for a few hours, to take part in a public celebration of my eightieth birthday in Genoa. Within a few years of first arriving I found myself drawn into the penumbra of the PCI establishment as an official patron of, and the only person from Britain present at, the Congress of Gramsci Studies in January 1958, the occasion for the first formal recognition of the Italian communists' theorist by the watchdogs of ideological orthodoxy in Moscow. It was also the only occasion on which I met the Party's leader, Palmiro Togliatti, himself. In turn, I took to Italian communism, found its dead guru Gramsci marvellously stimulating, and after 1956 its political position welcome. Unlike in Britain, in Italy it was still worth joining the Party after 1956.

Why was it so easy to get on with the Italians? Unlike the French or the English, Italians are charmed, flattered, and even encouraged by foreigners' interest in their affairs, even or perhaps especially when these outsiders are visibly unlike themselves, or – as in my case – when their knowledge of the Italian language is shaky and that of the country superficial. It is, I think, partly due to a lengthy history of belonging to a country treated by the outside world as enchanting but not totally serious, a country united since 1860 but underperforming in peace and war. I think this led to an ingrained feeling of marginality and provincialism. Italians had reconciled themselves to the belief that the real historical action, the centres of civilization and intellectual authorities were elsewhere. Since the seventeenth century nobody had actually looked to Italy for models of cultural and intellectual achievement and example outside music; since the nineteenth century not even in opera. Fascism, though in some sense strengthening a feeling of national identity, had tried and failed to cure the Italian sense of political and military inferiority, and certainly did nothing to deprovincialize Italian culture. Post-fascist Italy, it was felt, had an enormous amount of cultural catching-up to do, and, one way or another, the place to look for it was abroad. Translations of foreign authors still remain more prominent on the Italian book market than in any other country of comparable size. And almost any foreign recognition of Italian achievement was welcomed. Giulio Einaudi knew very well what he was doing even as late as 1979, when he launched the publication of Gerratana's superb critical edition of Gramsci's *Prison Notebooks*, not in Rome but in Paris, as he had launched his great multi-volume *Storia d'Italia* (History of Italy) in Oxford. The stamp of Paris approval or Oxford prestige was still the way to market them in Italy. And of course after the eighteenth century Italian culture was largely provincial, as is evident from Gramsci's own reading and writing. Even at its best, leaving aside mathematics, opera and a temporary interest in futurism, nobody had taken much notice of Italian productions outside.

Perhaps the most impressive and unexpected achievement of the Italian Republic born of the anti-fascist Resistance was to change all this, and in doing so to demonstrate what was always evident to any unprejudiced foreigner, namely that Italians had not lost any of the intellectual, artistic and entrepreneurial gifts that had produced such amazing and universally admired achievements between the fourteenth and seventeenth centuries. In some ways the postwar paths of French and Italian culture have followed opposite directions. While France after 1945 lost the cultural hegemony it had so long taken for granted, and retreated into what was, in effect, a francophone ghetto, the prestige of Italian art, science, industry, design and lifestyle was rising, the image of Italy was moving from the margins to the centre of western culture. Even the talents that had flourished or been tolerated under fascism – such major figures of Italian cinema as Rossellini, Visconti and de Sica were in action well before Mussolini fell – were liberated by Resistance. In the 1950s it would have been inconceivable that the international high-fashion industry would one day look to Milan and Florence rather than to Paris.

Nevertheless, except in completely transnational fields such as the mathematical and natural sciences, Italian thinking found it hard to shake off the provincialism of the past; not least because of the long resistance of the Italian university system, with its deeply ingrained combination of control by national bureaucrats and politicians and the manoeuvres of its own 'barons' with their powerful patronage system. Hence the exceptional importance in the Italian intellectual life of the first three or four postwar decades of commercial publishing houses such as Laterza, Einaudi and Feltrinelli. In fact, as in postwar Federal Germany, they largely substituted for the unreconstructed universities as intellectual and cultural powerhouses or, if one prefers the fashionable post-1989 jargon, organs of 'civil society'.

The prince of these cultural architects of post-fascist Italy was Giulio Einaudi (1912–99), my friend and publisher, son of Italy's most eminent free market economist and later the country's first President, who had founded his publishing house at the age of twenty-one in 1933 and led it for fifty years thereafter. Paradoxically, he was not himself a very intellectual figure, but he headed a team of advisers that combined exceptional intelligence, learning, wit, cosmopolitan culture and literary creativity. All were united by anti-fascism and the active Resistance – either in the communist or the liberal-socialist tradition of Giustizia e Libertà – most by the severe and independent intellectual milieu of Turin and they created what was almost certainly the finest publishing house in the world in the fifteen years after 1945.

The word 'prince' is chosen deliberately, for in spite of his communist sympathies, Giulio's style, his magnificent *bella figura* in town or country, was royal, or at least feudal. Even as a guest in a Hampstead sitting-room, he radiated a seigneurial affability. Even in bathing trunks on a Havana beach, he was recognizable as a patron. The feudal spirit extended to his approach to business debts, including those to his authors, which eventually bankrupted him. (On the other hand, authors were likely to receive as a New Year's gift cases of Barolo wine from the Einaudi vineyards, a wine so serious that the Einaudi cellars recommended letting it breathe for at least eight hours before drinking.) Like absolute monarchs, he thought of his kingdom as an extension of himself, and in the end it was his refusal to listen to financial advice, or even to consider the post-Giulio future of the house, that broke him. Such was the prestige of the firm that he was more than once saved from bankruptcy as a national treasure by a conjunction of the Italian anti-fascist establishment, co-ordinated by the great banker Raffaele Mattioli (the one who, in 1937, had hidden the dead Gramsci's manuscripts in the bank safe until they could be passed, via Piero Sraffa, to the foreign HQ of the PCI). In the eighties he finally lost control, and in 1991 Giulio Einaudi Editore was sold to Silvio Berlusconi's media empire. I cannot remember when I saw Giulio last. Probably at the eightieth birthday party which was organized for me in 1997 by the City of Genoa, old, sad and no longer quite upright, in an Italy very different from the one of his days of glory. Once he and Italo Calvino had formed part of the guard of honour at the coffin of Togliatti, who had recognized both his prestige and his political sympathies by granting to the house of Einaudi the rights to publish the works of Antonio Gramsci himself. Alas, by then what had once been Togliatti's PCI was also in decline.

Italy between 1952 and 1997 combined dramatic social and cultural change with frozen politics. By the end of the Cold War the inhabitants of a traditionally poor country owned more cars per head of population than practically any other state in the world. The Pope's country legalized birth control and divorce, taking to the first with enthusiasm, though notably abstaining from the second. It was a different country. But from the start of the East–West confrontation in 1947 it was clear that the USA would under no circumstances allow the communists to come to power in Italy, or even to elected government office. This remained Washington's basic principle, one might say its 'default position', so long as there was a USSR and a PCI, and for a few years thereafter. But it also became equally clear that a mass Communist Party could not be eliminated either by police repression or by constitutional finagling, although the great rural revolt in the Italian south, whose by-products attracted my attention to 'primitive rebellion', faded away by the mid-1950s. As realists Christian Democrats accepted this, allowing the PCI political space in its regions, in culture and the media. After all, they had founded the Republic jointly with the communists. Inside Italy the Cold War was not a zero-sum game.

The Italy into which I came had therefore begun to settle down for the foreseeable future, rather like Japan, as a spectacularly corrupt political dependency of the USA, under a single party, the Christian Democrats, maintained in permanent government power by the US veto. When I first arrived in Italy I noted that the modest postwar Sicilian Mafia was still virtually undocumented and undescribed, while the Neapolitan Camorra, perhaps even more powerful today, then appeared to be extinct.[9] Both are products of the Cold War political system. In the course of the decades after 1950 the Italian Republic became a strange, labyrinthine, often absurd and sometimes dangerous institution, increasingly distant from the actual reality of life of its inhabitants. The joke that Italy showed a country could do without a state, thus proving Bakunin right against Marx, is not strictly true, since Italians spent much of their time sidestepping what was on paper a strong, all-embracing and interventionist state. Italians were and had to be good at this game, since the massive transformation of public power, resources and employment into a nationwide patronage system and protection racket made it increasingly necessary to find ways of circulating the blood of the body politic by a million capillaries bypassing its increasingly clogged arteries. 'Fixing it' – by relations rather than simple bribery – became the Italian national motto.

Somewhere between a thriving and ever more confident civil society and the esoteric activities of the state, and covered by layers of silence and obfuscation, lay the field of *power*. It had no constitution and no formal structure. It was an acephalous complex of power centres which had to come to terms with each other locally or nationally: private, public, legal, clandestine, formal, informal. Everyone knew, for instance, that the '*avvocato*' – Gianni Agnelli, head of the family that owned FIAT and a lot else – was a national power centre, just as he knew that, while no Italian government could fail to come to terms with him, he in turn had to deal with whoever pushed the buttons in Rome. Part of this field of power was subterranean and secret, half-emerging only in periods of crisis such as the 1970s and 1980s. In those periods Italian politics returned to the operatic or Borgia mode, amid endless arguments not so much about who the assassins of the '*cadaveri eccellenti*'* or illustrious corpses were, but who was behind them, how they were linked to discreet but influential masonic lodges and the obscure projects to prevent the PCI from entering the ring of political power, if need be by military coups.

In the 1990s this system collapsed. The end of the Cold War deprived the Italian regime of its only justification and a genuine revolt of public opinion against the really spectacular greed of the socialist prime minister and his party broke its back. All the parties of postwar Italy were wiped out at the 1994 elections except the PCI, whose relatively deserved reputation for honesty saved them, and the Neofascists, who had also been in permanent opposition. Alas, there as elsewhere the 1990s proved that destroying a bad old regime was possible, but did not necessarily produce the conditions for creating a better one.

---

* The name of Francesco Rosi's 1976 film, based on a novel by the superb Sicilian writer Leonardo Sciascia.

III

What is the autobiographer to say about a country that has been part of his and his wife's life for half a century? Some of the people closest to us are or were Italians. We spoke Italian at home when we did not want the children to understand. Italy has been good to us, giving us friendship in beautiful places, the endless discovery of its capacity for creation, past and present, and more of those rare moments of pure satisfaction at being alive than human beings can reasonably expect past their youth. It has given me my themes as a historian. Its readers have been generous to me as a writer.

Yet as I believe that being a historian helps to understand a country, I must ask myself why the Italy of Signor Berlusconi in 2002 is not one I expected fifty years ago. How far did I fail to see where Italy was going because my observation was deficient, or biased, how far because twists in the road were not yet visible? Was it the democratization of consumer society that widened the gap between the minority of the educated and intellectual whose company elderly historians keep, and the rest of a people who read few newspapers and spent less money on books per head than all but the two poorest members of the European Union? Did the sheer speed of economic and hence social and cultural transformation defeat foresight, in Italy as elsewhere?

Certainly few read the signs right in that coup-threatened period of fear and tension, the 1970s, the peak of the PCI's electoral support nationally and in the big cities. We did not see that dramatic industrial transformation was fatally weakening the PCI's political influence in the economic core of Italy, the north: the FIAT assembly-line building in Turin now houses the annual Book Fair. The Party did not recognize that after 1968 it had lost its major political asset, namely the accepted hegemony over the Italian left, and indeed over all forces of opposition other than the remainders of fascism. The small instant book I did at the time with Giorgio Napolitano, then on the Secretariat of the PCI, shows no sign of having been written in the decade that culminated in the kidnapping and murder of the Italian Premier Aldo Moro by the Red Brigades, the most formidable European terrorist movement of the left.[10]

Perhaps, worst of all, the Party, like working-class movements elsewhere, was beginning to lose touch with its *popolo comunista*, for whom it had been the party of resistance, liberation and social hope, the defender of the poor. As early as the seventies friends from Turin told me: 'We are no longer a movement; we are becoming a "party of opinion" like the others.' How could one talk politics in the same way to the sharp, media-wise youngish journalists who telephoned from the (now struggling) Party daily *L'Unità* as to the journalist generation of partisans and liberation? Rejuvenating its cadres, the Party found it had changed their character. As it slowly declined, abandoning too much of a great tradition with its name, it prepared to make its way through the 1990s in the uncertain shadow of its newly improvised botanical logos – the oak and the olive tree.

Within five years of Berlinguer's death the Berlin Wall had fallen, and the PCI, dropping its symbols and traditions, reconstructed and renamed itself vaguely as the Democratic Left (the usual fall-back label of the old Moscow Communist Parties), against bitter internal opposition and the secession of a new Party of Refounded Communism.

So in the long run enjoying Italy proved easier than understanding it. Paradoxically, that was easier to do in the era of the Republic's crisis. Seen from the private watchtower, Italy in the 1980s was a succession of public occasions and academic conversations in places whose familiarity did not diminish their beauty, of days with friends mostly in or around Rosario and Anna Rosa Villari's farmhouse in Tuscany. It was an unreal country, in which one stretched out with friends on the terrace overlooking the Val d'Orcia after lunch, listening to the voice of Callas singing 'Casta Diva' from a record-player in an upstairs room.

Meanwhile, the collective Italy of the 1980s was a sort of *reductio ad absurdum* of public life, an era of moderately bloodstained Marx Brothers politics. While Craxi's men bought up former 'progressive intellectuals', high-living socialist ministers stepped out with starlets in nightclubs, their bills paid by managements anxious to attract their entourage, enormous government grants after enormous earthquakes disappeared into thin air, the Vatican's finances were in disarray because of financial speculations by Mafia-connected bankers, one of them recently discovered hanged under London's Blackfriars

Bridge, and a Neapolitan professor succeeded in building himself an academic empire in a municipal palace on the strength of his research, refereed by eminent colleagues who failed to notice that every one of his books had been carefully translated word for word from German Ph.D. theses.

My most vivid memory of those years is of a brief overnight trip to Rome, Marxian in both senses. Italian television invited me to take part in a programme on the great man's centenary under the title *An Evening with Karl Marx*.

The occasion was surreal, though I unfortunately never saw the programme, thus missing the performance of the 'Internationale' by the celebrated classical avant-garde singer Cathy Berberian. Inside a vast RAI (Italian television) hangar an elaborate set had been constructed round a giant papier-mâché head of Karl Marx, the top of which was removable. From it the presenter, a well-known comedian, would from time to time withdraw large cards marked CLASS STRUGGLE, DIALECTICS and the like. Something looking like a dacha on some Chekhovian country estate had also been constructed, on whose veranda I sat with the late Lucio Colletti, a brilliant ex-communist academic, with whom I was supposed to expound THE LABOUR THEORY OF VALUE for not more than five minutes, when it emerged from Marx's head. He subsequently supported Silvio Berlusconi, but even he could not yet have known or perhaps imagined this in 1983.

I do not know what happened on the rest of that *Evening with Karl Marx*, but I left to collect my fee, offered in cash, from a young representative of the Italian state's public service. She gave me the following advice: 'You know, you're not supposed to take so much money out of the country. The best thing, I suggest, is that you pack it between the shirts in your suitcase. They'll never bother to look.'

I should recall the 1990s with pleasure. *Il Secolo Breve* (*The Age of Extremes*) was a considerable success in Italy. In its public mode the Italian people threw out the most corrupt regime in Europe, utterly destroying the parties of the Cold War Republic. We were in Italy ourselves at the time of the elections of 1994 which reduced those fighting it under the name Christian Democrats and Socialists to thirty-two and fifteen seats respectively in a Chamber of Deputies of 630, a triumph already tarnished by the victory, shaky as it then was, of Berlusconi's right-wing coalition. And yet, what was particularly disappointing for its old admirers, though no longer unexpected, was the failure of what had once been the PCI. Finally in a position to take its place at the head of a progressive democratic government, it was unequal to the task. As Britain, France and Germany were ruled by governments of the left, Italy entered the new millennium by getting ready for the first government clearly of the right since the fall of fascism.

For most Italians life went on, probably more satisfactorily than ever after the most miraculous half-century of improvement in their history. And yet, would one guess so from what is (at least in my opinion) perhaps the greatest book produced by an Italian in my lifetime, Italo Calvino's wonderful *Invisible Cities*? (I recall him still, shortly before his untimely death, on his green roof terrace above the Campo Marzio in Rome, with a sceptical half-smile on his dark face, full of wit and tactful learning.) It is about the stories told to Kublai Khan, the Emperor of China, of cities, real, imagined or both, encountered by Marco Polo on his travels. It is about Irene, the city which can be seen only from outside. What is it like seen from within? It does not matter. 'Irene is the name of a distant city. Once you get closer, it is no longer the same.' It is also about the promised but undiscovered cities whose names are already in Kubla's atlas: Utopia, the City of the Sun. But we do not know how to reach or enter them. And what, asks the Emperor at the end, of the nightmare cities, whose names we also know?

Polo: The inferno of the living is not something that will be; if it exists, it is already here, the hell of our daily life, formed by living together. There are two ways of enduring it. The first is what many find easy: accept hell and become part of it, until you no longer see that it is there. The second is risky and needs constant attention and learning: in the midst of hell to look for, and to know how to recognize what is not hell, to make it last, to give it space.

That was not the spirit in which my generation, including Calvino, saw the Italy that had just liberated itself from fascism.

21

Third World

I

In 1962 I persuaded the Rockefeller Foundation to give me a travel grant to South America, in order to enquire into the subject-matter of my recent book, *Primitive Rebels*, in a continent where it could be expected to play a more prominent part in contemporary history than in mid-twentieth-century Europe. Those were the days when foundations still sent their air travellers by first class, by airlines whose names record a vanished past – Panamerican, Panair do Brasil, Panagra, TWA, though, except for Peru, the old national flag carriers still seem to survive. For about three months in 1962–3 I made the circuit of South America – Brazil, Argentina, Chile, Peru, Bolivia, Colombia – in this luxurious style, implausible for an enquirer into peasant rebellion. It was the first of numerous visits to continental Latin America in subsequent years, both to Mexico and to various parts of South America, indeed to all countries in that continent bar the Guyanas and Venezuela. Probably the longest unbroken period I have ever spent outside the United Kingdom since 1933 is the half-year or so I spent with my family teaching, researching and writing from Mexico to Peru in 1971. It is a continent on which I have many friends and pupils, with which I have been associated for forty years, and which, I do not quite know why, has been remarkably good to me. It is the only part of the world where I have found myself not surprised to meet presidents, past, present and future. Indeed, the first one I met in office, the canny Víctor Paz Estenssoro of Bolivia, showed me the lamp-post on the square outside his balcony in La Paz from which his predecessor Gualberto Villaroel had been hanged by a rioting crowd of Indians in 1946.

After the triumph of Fidel Castro, and even more after the defeat of the US attempt to overthrow him at the Bay of Pigs in 1961, there was not an intellectual in Europe or the USA who was not under the spell of Latin America, a continent apparently bubbling with the lava of social revolutions. Though this also drew me there, my chief reason was practical, namely linguistic. Historians who deal with the activities of ordinary people must be able to communicate with them by mouth, and Latin America was the only part of what was known as the Third World where large numbers of them spoke languages within my reach. For I was not concerned simply with a geographical region, but with a much larger unknown, that is to say the 80 per cent of men, women and children who live outside the zone inhabited until the last third of the twentieth century primarily by people with (notionally) white skin.

For the first half of my life these 80 per cent knew nothing of the world and, give or take a few thousand individuals, the world knew practically nothing about them. Nothing is more impressive to someone of my age than the extraordinary discovery, since 1970, of the First World by the peoples of the Third World or – since these terms themselves belong to the era of the Cold War – of the possibility that poor people from anywhere can change their lives for the better by moving to the rich countries. Of course, with the rarest exceptions, such as the USA since the 1960s, we do not want them to come, even when we need them. A world dedicated to the free global movement of all profit-making factors of production is also a world dedicated to stop the one form of globalization that is unquestionably desired by the poor, namely finding better-paid work in rich countries. We have come to be so familiar with the century's inhumanity that we no longer distinguish between refugees and the Afghan and Kurd emigrants transported in coffin-ships by emigration contractors, like the Italians and Russian Jews of the 1880s, who had just discovered that they did not have to live and die in the *paesi* and *shtetls* of their birth.

For the first forty years of my life it was simply not so. Language – not the 'national' languages but what illiterates really spoke, the dense localized dialects or *patois* almost incomprehensible fifty kilometres away – isolated people from each other. Illiteracy, but even more, the absence of accessible radio and television, isolated them from what we think of as 'news', though not from one or two major world events. 'Where is England?' a Mexican farmer asked me, even in the 1970s, when I told him that was where I came from.

(The first question to strangers in all societies that live by oral communication, including armies, is always 'Where are you from?') My explanations did not help. He had probably never thought about the Atlantic either. Finally he narrowed me down to something he had heard of: 'Is it near Russia?' I said, not too far. That satisfied him.

Then non-white skins were exceptionally rare in 'Caucasian' countries, except for the anomaly of the African-Americans in the USA. Latin American immigration was so small that before 1960 the US census counted South and Central Americans together, without distinguishing between separate countries of origin. So, apart from European settlers such as the French-Algerians (actually largely of Spanish stock) and the Jewish colonists in Palestine, were whites who lived in countries with large indigenous populations. Ordinary whites were very unlikely in the course of normal life to encounter the pluri-racial street-scene of today's large western cities. Except for small and untypical minorities very few whites not resident overseas were likely to know, and even fewer to be on terms of friendship with, people of other skin colours. Before the 1960s they belonged primarily to two groups: Christians (assuming the label stretches to include Quakers) and communists, both committed, in different ways, to a general emancipatory and egalitarian hatred for racism. And both, but especially the Marxists, on grounds both of practical anti-imperialism and the potential of eastern revolution, had a special interest in the history of non-white humanity. That is what had brought me into the 'colonial group' of the Party as a student and drew me into exploring North Africa, and eventually Latin America. And our 'colonial' friends, in my case mostly from South Asia, were our first windows into these worlds.

Until much later I did not realize how untypical they were of their societies. Those who got to Cambridge, Oxford and the London School of Economics were the elite of elites of the 'native' colonial populations, as soon became evident after decolonization. They also tended to be rather better heeled than us. They were family friends of the Nehrus, like P. N. Haksar of the LSE, who provided cover in Primrose Hill for the courtship of Indira Nehru with Feroze Gandhi and, as civil servant, was the most powerful man in independent India when I visited him in New Delhi in 1968. The man who came to meet my plane on the tarmac was my old friend from King's Mohan Kumaramangalam, until recently a communist, then in charge of Indian Airlines, soon to be the minister perhaps closest of all to Mrs Gandhi until he died tragically in an air crash in 1973. His younger sister, Parvati, who visited Mohan in Cambridge, had now let her hair grow again, had married the General Secretary of the Communist Party and sat in Parliament. Another brother, an Etonian like his siblings but this time non-communist, had become the commander-in-chief of the Indian army. The Kumaramangalams of Madras were that sort of family. So, in a different way, were the Sarabhais of Ahmedabad, strict Jains who abstained from killing any animal however tiny, whom I came to know through Manorama, a close friend from L S E days of my first wife, who had Le Corbusier build her a house. They were one of the great Congress-supporting Gujarati business dynasties, textiles diversifying into higher technologies. Culture was probably their most visible public activity, but a Sarabhai was to be in charge of the Indian nuclear programme. For the first generation of independence, the affairs of an India of several hundred millions – public and private, government and opposition – were run by an extraordinary anglicized, modern-minded 'Establishment' of perhaps 100,000 people drawn from highly educated (that is, mainly wealthy) families, those who had served the Raj as well as those who had built the freedom movement. The bizarrerie of this combination came out at a Christmas dinner in the house of the doe-eyed Renu Chakravarty, by then a communist MP – the Communist Party had not yet split – and powerhouse in Calcutta. After ham and turkey, provided by Renu's cousin, secretary of the Calcutta Club, which clearly had not abandoned the menu of the days when no Indian would have been allowed into the building except as a servant, came biryani and finally Christmas pudding, also provided by the Club and chewing *pan* (betel nut). They were anglicized even in the language some of them spoke at home and wrote or read most easily, for I had the impression that only the Bengalis among them, and perhaps some of the more traditional Muslim families whose radical young read the progressive poets in Urdu (admired by my old friends and comrades Victor Kiernan and Ralph Russell) lived their mental lives fully in a vernacular.

There is only so much – actually not very much – that one can learn about a society through personal friendship. Friends may be too deeply rooted in it to recognize its peculiarities, and in any case class is at least as great a segregator of experiences as distance, culture or language. When the Party put him in charge of leading the tramwaymen's union in Calcutta, and later the juteworkers of (West) Bengal my admirable friend and comrade from King's, the late Indrajit ('Sonny') Gupta, subsequently General Secretary of the Communist Party and briefly Minister of the Interior, had as much to learn about the Calcutta working class as any foreigner. What I hope I owe to such friendships, based on the anti-racist comradeship of student communism, is the separation of the sense of equality from the consciousness of skin- or hair-colour, physical appearance and culture. The global village of business, science, technology and universities of the twenty-first century is so multi-coloured that this may no longer be a problem, although I suspect it is. Before 1960 or so the sense of racial superiority among western whites was reinforced by the sheer weight of western power and achievement in all fields except some of the arts, and the sheer bodily superiority of races commonly regarded as inferior, and so psychologically resented, repressed and overcompensated, especially by white males. The Israeli Jews made no secret of their contempt for 'the Arabs', especially before 1987, when their *intifadas* had not yet broken the passive acceptance of Israeli occupation of the Palestinians' territories. It was a strange but instructive experience to be treated as one of them on my visit to the West Bank in 1984, the only time I have found myself living under the rule of a foreign military.

The enormous advantage of communism, especially when reinforced by friendship, was that one could simply not treat a comrade other than as an equal. The patent self-confidence of the favoured few from the coloured 'colonial' elites who made it into pre-war British universities helped. Just as horses sense fear in their riders, so humans sense the expectation of being treated as inferiors in their respondents. Ruling classes and conquerors have always exploited this expectation of superiority. My pre-war 'colonial' friends did not expect to be treated as inferiors.

Nevertheless, until I was awarded a travelling grant from the university to go to French North Africa in 1938, I had not been to what was not yet known as the Third World since I left Egypt as a baby. I travelled in Tunisia and east-central Algeria, from sea to Sahara, but never got to western Algeria and Morocco, and I acquired a lifelong scepticism about rural statistics in such places from a lonely French administrator in the field, ready to talk to any educated visitor. ('When the government asks me for a livestock census, I make very casual enquiries, because the flocks would vanish into the hills otherwise. Then I look up what we said last time round, and put in a figure that looks plausible.') I also acquired respect for the mountains and people of Kabylia and for the intelligence and erudition of the French Maghrebists and Islamic experts, even though most of them, like British African anthropology in those days, served the relevant empire. I met the leader of the small Algerian Communist Party, exiled into the Sahara after 1939 and killed, but not the then most important revolutionary, Messali Hadj. I have sometimes wondered whether I would have become a better historian if, after the war, I had returned to the research theme of 'The Agrarian Problem in French North Africa' which I brought back from my travels. People I admire – the great historian Braudel, my friend Pierre Bourdieu and the late Ernest Gellner – have been inspired by working in the Maghreb, and I can understand why. However, if I had, few would have noticed. Except, curiously enough, in sub-Saharan Africa, the end of empires led to a generation of amnesia about their history. Besides, the bloody Algerian war of the 1950s and the bitterly disappointing record of independent Algeria since would have rather marginalized the field. I note in passing that, while the future of Tunisia under its eventual president Habib Bourguiba was already identifiable in 1938, absolutely nothing discoverable about Algeria in that year would have led anyone to predict, or even to envisage, the force that eventually liberated the country, the FLN (National Liberation Front).

II

Fidel Castro's revolution in 1959 led to a sudden upsurge of interest in everything to do with Latin America, a region about which there was much rumour, but at that time little knowledge outside the Americas. With rare exceptions the locally resident Europeans, other than the Spanish war refugees and North Americans, lived in their own worlds like my non-intermarrying Chilean relatives, who still saw themselves as English expatriates or at least European refugees. (I think all my five cousins spent the Second World War serving their country in British uniforms.) Since the continent had been decolonized, it lacked the large, intelligent and documented literature provided by imperial administrators whose business it was to understand countries in order to rule them efficiently. Communities of expatriate businessmen, as the record shows, are almost completely useless as sources of information about the countries they operate in, although the British ones in their time founded the football clubs in which South American patriotism has found its most intense expression.

Latin America was then remoter from the Old World than any other part of the globe – though not, of course, from the imperial power in the north, overseeing its technically independent satellites. It experienced the two world wars only as bringers of prosperity. It passed through the most murderous of centuries without more than a single brief international war on its territory (the Chaco War of 1932–5 between Bolivia and Paraguay), though not, alas, without considerable domestic bloodshed. A continent of a single religion, it has so far escaped the world epidemic of linguistic, ethnic and confessional nationalism.

Latin America was not easy to come to grips with. When I first went there in 1962, the continent was in one of its periodic moods of expansive economic confidence, articulated by the Economic Commission for Latin America of the UN, an all-continental brains trust located in Santiago de Chile under an Argentine banker, which recommended a policy of planned, state-sponsored and largely state-owned industrialization and economic growth through import substitution. It seemed to work, at least for giant, inflation-plagued but booming Brazil. This was the time when Juscelino Kubitschek, a president of Czech origin, launched the conquest of Brazil's vast interior by building a new capital in it, designed largely by the country's most eminent architect, Oscar Niemeyer, a known member of the powerful but illegal Communist Party who, he told me, designed it with Engels in mind.

Its main countries were also in one of the continent's occasional phases of constitutional civilian government which was soon to end. However, the *caudillo* or personal chieftain of the old type was already on the way out – at least outside the Caribbean. The regimes of the torturers were to be collectives of faceless and mostly colourless officers. In South America the only country under military dictatorship at that time was the unusually old-fashioned Paraguay under the eternal General Stroessner, a nasty regime, kind to expatriate Nazis, in a disarmingly attractive and charming country, which lived largely by smuggling. Graham Greene's touching *The Honorary Consul* is an excellent introduction to it. I am, perhaps, inclined to excessive kindness, for it was the only Latin state officially recognizing an Indian language, Guaraní, and, when I visited it some years later, I discovered that my name was familiar to the editor of the somewhat unexpected *Revista Paraguaya de Sociologia* published there, as the author of *Rebeldes Primitivos*. What scholar can resist fame in Paraguay?

Nobody who discovers South America can resist the region, least of all if one's first contact is with the Brazilians. Nevertheless, what was most immediately obvious about its countries was not so much its spectacular economic inequality, which has not ceased to increase since, as the enormous gap between its ruling and intellectual classes with which visiting academics had contact, and the common people. The intellectuals, mostly from comfortable or 'good' – overwhelmingly white – families, were sophisticated, widely travelled, and spoke English and (still) French. As so often in the Third World (to which the Argentines vociferously refused to belong), they formed the thinnest continent-wide social layer, for in their minds, unlike the artificial concept of 'Europe' in the minds of the old continent, Latin America was a constant reality. If they were in politics, they almost certainly had a spell as exiles in another Latin American country or a common trip to Castro's Cuba; if academics, a spell as members of some multinational establishment in Santiago, Rio or Mexico City. Since they were thin on the ground, they knew each other or knew about each other. That is how in 1962, from the start, being passed from one contact to another, a visitor like myself could quickly find his bearings from people whose names meant nothing in Europe, but who turned out to be key intellectual or public figures. But the very fact that such people moved in a world equally familiar with Paris, New York and five or six Latin capitals separated them from the world in which most darker-skinned and less well-connected Latin Americans lived.

Outside the already urbanized 'southern cone' (Argentina, Uruguay and Chile) these people were flooding from the countryside into the shanty-towns of the exploding cities, bringing their rural ways with them. São Paulo had doubled in size in the ten years before I got there. They squatted on city hillsides as in the country they had dug up unoccupied corners of the big estates and built shelters and shacks, eventually to become proper houses, the way it was done in the village, by mutual help of neighbours and kin, rewarded with a party. On the street markets of São Paulo, overshadowed by the new high-rise buildings, the masses from the parched hinterlands of the northeast bought shirts and jeans on instalment payments and the cheap illustrated booklets of verse ballads about the great bandits of their region. I still have the copies I bought then. In Lima, Peru, there were already radio stations broadcasting in Quechua – in the early morning hours when the whites were still in bed – to the Indian immigrants from the mountains, now numerous enough to constitute a market, in spite of their poverty. The great writer, folklorist and Indianist José Maria Arguedas took me to one of the music halls where, on Sunday mornings, the highland people came to listen to songs and jokes about 'down home'. ('Anyone here from Ancash? Let's hear it for the lads and lasses from Huanuco!') In 1962 it seemed almost unthinkable that thirty years later I would supervise the son of one of them for a doctorate at the New School in New York. It is an extraordinary experience to have lived with the first generation in recorded history in which a poor boy with an illiterate wife from a Quechua-speaking village in the high Andes could become a unionized hospital driver by picking up the skills of driving a truck and thus open the globe to his children. I have his long letter still, written in the deliberate handwriting and careful Castilian orthography of the autodidact. Though his life was hard by our standards, by those of the masses of day-labourers, street-sellers, casual and miscellaneous poor he was at the top.

The people who came to the city were at least visible on the streets. The people in the countryside were doubly remote from the middle classes, including their revolutionaries such as Che Guevara, by geographical and social distance. Even those with the greatest interest in having the closest contacts with them found the differences in lifestyle, not to mention expected living standards, a forbidding obstacle. Few outside experts actually lived among the peasantry, though many had fairly good contacts in the countryside, including, as usual, the omnipresent researchers of various international organizations connected with the United Nations.

Most remote of all were those foreigners who relied for their knowledge of the Latin American countryside on the local intellectual left or the international press. The one, as so often, tended to confuse political agitation and Fidelista hope with information, the other relied on what reached its bureau chiefs in the capital city. Thus, when I first went to South America the major 'peasant' story, insofar as there was one, was about the Peasant Leagues in Brazil, a movement established in 1955 under the leadership of Francisco Julião, a lawyer and local politician from the northeast, who had attracted the attention of US journalists by expressions of support for Fidel Castro and Mao. (I met him ten years later, a small, sad, disoriented exile from the Brazilian military regime, living under the protection of the dramatic central European ideologue Ivan Illich in Cuernavaca, Mexico.) A few hours at their offices in Rio in late 1962 showed that the movement had little national presence, and that it was clearly already past its peak. On the other hand, the two major South American peasant or rural upheavals which no observer with open eyes could fail to discover within a few days of arriving in their countries were virtually undocumented, and indeed virtually unknown to the outside world at the end of 1962. These were the great peasant movements in highland and frontier Peru and the 'state of disorganization, civil war and local anarchy' into which Colombia had fallen since the implosion of what had been, in effect, a potential social revolution by spontaneous combustion set off, in 1948, by the assassination of a nationally famous tribune of the people, Jorge Eliezer Gaitan.[1]

And yet, these things were not always utterly remote from the outside world. The vast movement of peasant land occupations was at its height in Cuzco, where even tourists who did not read local newspapers could, when walking round the Inca blocks in the cold thin air of the highland evenings, observe the endless, silent columns of Indian men and women outside the offices of the Peasant Federation. The most dramatic case of a successful peasant revolt at the time, in the valleys of La Convención, occurred downriver from the marvels of Macchu Picchu, known to all tourists in South America even then. Only a few dozen kilometres' train ride from the great Inca site to the end of the railway line and a few more hours on the back of a truck took one to the provincial capital, Quillabamba. I wrote one of the first outside accounts of it. For a historian who kept his eyes open, especially a social historian, even these first, almost casual impressions were a sudden revelation, rather like the sight of the treasure-room in the Bogotá Gold Museum for my eight-year-old son, when I took him there several years later. How could one not explore this unknown but historically familiar planet? My conversion was completed, a week or two later, among the endless slopes of stalls manned by squat, heavy-braided, bowler-hatted Aymara peasant women in the enormous street-markets of Bolivia. Unable to go to Potosí, I spent Christmas with another temporary loner, a French UN expert on village development, mainly in a hotel bar in La Paz. We drank and he talked, endlessly, passionately, the way a man back from a spell in the cold villages of the Altiplano unloads his experience on the only available willing listener. It was an intellectually and alcoholically rewarding Christmas, though otherwise short on the holiday spirit.

The New Year of 1963 after that Christmas I spent in Bogotá. Colombia was a country of whose very existence hardly anyone outside Latin America seemed to be aware. This was my second great discovery. On paper a model of representative two-party constitutional democracy, almost completely immune to military coups and dictatorship in practice, after 1948 it became the killing field of South America. At this period Colombia reached a crude rate of homicide of over fifty per 100,000, although even this pales beside the Colombian zeal for killing at the end of the twentieth century.[2] The browning press cuttings I collected from the local newspapers then are before me as I write. They familiarized me with the term *genocidio* (genocide), which Colombian journalists used to describe the small massacres in farm settlements and of bus passengers – sixteen dead here, eighteen there, twenty-four somewhere else. Who were the killers and the killed? 'A spokesman of the war ministry said . . . no categorical information about the perpetrators could be given, because the districts (*veredas*) of that zone [of Santander] were pretty regularly affected by a series of "vendettas" between the partisans of traditional political affiliations,' namely the Liberal and Conservative parties into one of which, as readers of García Márquez know, every Colombian baby belonged by family and local loyalty. The wave of civil war known as *La Violencia* that had begun in 1948, long officially ended, had still killed almost 19,000 persons in that 'quiet year'. Colombia was, and continues to be, proof that gradual reform in the framework of liberal democracy is not the only, or even the most plausible, alternative to social and political revolutions, including the ones that fail or are aborted. I discovered a country in which the failure to make a social revolution had made violence the constant, universal, omnipresent core of public life.

What exactly the *Violencia* was or had been about was far from clear, although I was lucky enough to arrive just at the time when the first major study of it was coming out, to one of whose authors, my friend the sociologist Orlando Fals Borda, I owe my first introduction to Colombian problems.[3] I might have paid more attention at the time to the fact that the chief student of the *Violencia* was a Catholic Monsignor, and that some pioneer research on its social fallout had just been published by a spectacularly handsome young priest from one of the country's founding clans, a great breaker of hearts, it was said, among young women of the oligarchy, Father Camilo Torres. It was not an accident that the conference of Latin American bishops which initiated the socially radical Theology of Liberation a few years later was held in the hilly Colombian city of Medellín, then still known for entrepreneurs in textiles and not yet in drugs. I had some conversations with Camilo and, to judge by my notes at the time, took his arguments very seriously, but he was still a long way from the social radicalism that led him three years later to join the new Fidelista guerrillas of the Army of National Liberation which still survives.

Amid the *Violencia* the Communist Party had formed 'armed self-defence' zones or 'independent republics', as places of refuge for peasants who wanted or had to stay out of the way of the Conservative, or sometimes also the Liberal bands of killers.

Eventually they became the bases of the formidable guerrilla movement of the FARC (Armed Forces of the Colombian Revolution).
The best-known 'liberated' areas of this kind, Tequendama and
Sumapaz, were surprisingly close to Bogotá as the crow flies, but,
being mountain country, a long and difficult way by horse and mule.
Viotà, a district of coffee haciendas expropriated by the peasants in
the reforming 1930s, and from which the landowners had withdrawn,
did not need to fight at all. Even the soldiers kept away, while it ran
all its affairs under the eye of the political cadre sent there by the
Party, a former brewery worker, and sold its coffee peacefully
on the world market through the usual traders. The mountains of
Sumapaz, frontier terrain for free men and women, were under the
rule of a home-grown rural leader, one of those rare peasant talents
who escaped the fate patronized by the poet Gray in his famous
elegy, that of being 'some mute inglorious Milton . . . some Crom-
well guiltless of his country's blood'. For Juan de la Cruz Varela
was far from mute or peaceable. In the course of his varied career
as chief of Sumapaz, he was prominent as a Liberal, follower
of Gaitan, communist, head of his own agrarian movement and
Revolutionary Liberal, but always firmly on the side of the people.
Discovered by one of those wonderful village teachers who were
the real agents of emancipation for most of the human race in the
nineteenth and twentieth centuries, he had become both a reader and
practical thinker. He acquired his political education from Victor
Hugo's *Les Misérables*, which he carried with him everywhere,
marking the passages which seemed to him particularly apposite to
his own or the political situation of the time. My friend Rocío
Londoño, who worked on his biography during her spell of research
at Birkbeck College, inherited his copy of the book from him with
the rest of his papers. He acquired his Marxism, or what there was
of it, rather later via the writings of a now forgotten English clerical
enthusiast for the USSR, the late Hewlett Johnson, Dean of Canter-
bury (inevitably confused by everyone abroad with the Archbishop),
which he appears to have got from Colombian communists, whose
belief in agrarian revolution appealed to him. Long accepted as a
person of power and influence, whose region was beyond the reach
of government troops, he sat for it in Congress. Sumapaz remained
beyond the reach of the capital even after his death, honoured –

according to Rocío who attended the funeral – by a display of his armed horsemen. The first negotiations for an armistice between the Colombian government and the FARC were to be held on the hinterland of his territory.

The FARC itself, which was to become the most formidable and long-lasting of the Latin American guerrilla movements, had not yet been founded when I first came to Colombia, although its long-time military leader Pedro Antonio Marin ('Manuel Marulanda'), another home-grown countryman, was already active in the mountains adjoining the old stronghold of communist agrarian agitation and self-defence in South Tolima.[4] It was only born when the Colombian government, trying out against the communists the new anti-guerrilla techniques pioneered by the US military experts, drove the fighters out of their stronghold in Marquetalia. Several years later, in the mid-eighties, I was to spend some days in the birthplace of communist guerrilla activity in the coffee-growing *municipio* of Chaparral, in the house of my friend Pierre Gilhodès, who had married into the locality. The FARC, stronger than ever, were still in the mountains above the township, which was now easily accessible by car from Bogotá and sufficiently in touch with the outside world and prosperous to sell *Vogue* in the news-kiosk on the main *plaza*. The mule-tracks and footpaths still led into the mountains up steep gullies. It was a quiet landscape, in which not surprisingly discretion was the golden rule. Chaparral farmers were about to discover the potential of poppy cultivation, but had not, I think, yet done so.

Colombia, as I wrote after my return, was experiencing 'the greatest mobilisation of armed peasants (whether as guerrillas, bandits or self-defence groups) in the contemporary history of the western hemisphere, except, possibly, for some moments of the Mexican Revolution'.[5] Curiously, this fact was either unnoticed or played down by the contemporary ultra left in and outside South America (all of whose Guevarist attempts at guerrilla insurrection were spectacular failures) on the ostensible grounds that it was linked to an orthodox Communist Party, but in fact because those inspired by the Cuban Revolution neither understood nor wanted to understand what actually might move Latin American peasants to take up arms.

III

It was not hard to become a Latin American expert in the early 1960s. Fidel's triumph created enormous interest in the region, which was poorly covered by press and universities outside the USA. I had not intended to take a specialist interest in the region, although I also found myself lecturing and writing about it in the 1960s and early 1970s in the *New York Review of Books* and elsewhere, adding appendices on the Peruvian peasant movement and the Colombian *Violencia* to the (first) Spanish edition of *Primitive Rebels*, and in 1971 spending a sabbatical *en famille* doing more serious research on peasants in Mexico and Peru. I continued to go there several times in each decade, mainly to Peru, Mexico and Colombia, but also on occasion to Chile, before and during the Allende period and after the end of the Pinochet era. And, of course, I did not even try to resist the sheer drama and colour of the more glamorous parts of that continent, even though it also contains some of the most anti-human environments on the globe – the high Andean Altiplano on the limits of cultivability, the cactus-spiked semi-desert of northern Mexico – and some of the world's most uninhabitable giant cities – Mexico City and São Paulo. Over the years, I acquired dear friends such as the Gasparians in Brazil, Pablo Macera in Peru and Carlos Fuentes in Mexico, and students or colleagues who became friends. In short, I was permanently converted to Latin America.

Nevertheless, I never tried to become or saw myself as a Latin Americanist. As for the biologist Darwin, for me as a historian the revelation of Latin America was not regional but general. It was a laboratory of historical change, mostly different from what might have been expected, a continent made to undermine conventional truths. It was a region where historical evolution occurred at express speed and could actually be observed happening within half a lifetime of a single person, from the first clearing of forests for farm or ranch to the death of the peasantry, from the rise and fall of export crops for the world market to the explosion of giant super-cities such as the megalopolis of São Paulo, where one could find a mixture of immigrant populations more implausible even than in New York

– Japanese and Okinawans, Calabrians, Syrians, Argentine psycho-analysts and a restaurant proudly labelled 'CHURRASCO TIPICO NORCOREANO' (Typical North Korean Barbecue). It was a place where ten years doubled the size of Mexico City, and transformed the street-scene of Cuzco from one dominated by Indians in traditional costume to people wearing modern ('*cholo*') clothes.

Inevitably it changed my perspective on the history of the rest of the globe, if only by dissolving the border between the 'developed' and the 'Third' worlds, the present and the historic past. As in García Márquez's great *One Hundred Years of Solitude*, in which everyone who knows Colombia recognizes both the magic and the realism, it forced one to make sense of what was at first sight implausible. It provided what 'counterfactual' speculations can never do, namely a genuine range of alternative outcomes to historical situations: right-wing chieftains who become the inspiration of labour move-ments (Argentina, Brazil), fascist ideologists who join with a left-wing miners' union to make a revolution that gives the land to the peasants (Bolivia), the only state in the world that has actually abolished its army (Costa Rica), a single-party state of notorious corruption whose Institutional Party of the Revolution recruits its personnel systematically from the most revolutionary among its university students (Mexico), a region where first-generation immi-grants from the Third World can become presidents and Arabs ('*Turcos*') tended to be more successful than Jews.

What made this extraordinary continent so much more accessible for Europeans was an unexpected air of familiarity, like the wild strawberries to be found on the path behind Macchu Picchu. It was not simply that anyone of my age who knew the Mediterranean could recognize the populations round the limitless dun-coloured surface of the River Plate estuary as Italians fed for two or three generations on huge pieces of beef, and was familiar from Europe with the prevailing creole values of macho honour, shame, courage and loyalty to friends, as well as with oligarchic societies. (Not until the battles between young elite revolutionaries and military governments in the 1970s was the basic social distinction, so clearly formulated in Graham Greene's *Our Man in Havana*, abandoned, at least in several countries, namely that between the 'torturable' lower and the 'non-torturable' upper classes.) For Europeans those aspects of the continent most remote from our own experience were embedded in, and interwoven with, institutions familiar to historians, such as the Catholic Church, the Spanish colonial system or such nineteenth-century ideologies as utopian socialism and Auguste Comte's Religion of Humanity. This somehow emphasized, even dramatized, both the peculiarity of their Latin American transmutations and what they had in common with other parts of the world. Latin America was a dream for comparative historians.

When I first discovered the continent, it was about to enter the darkest period of its twentieth-century history, the era of military dictatorship, state terror and torture. In the 1970s there was more of it in what was described as 'the free world' than there had ever been since Hitler occupied Europe. The generals took over in Brazil in 1964 and by the mid-seventies the military ruled all over South America, except for the states bordering the Caribbean. The Central American republics, apart from Mexico and Cuba, had been kept safe from democracy by the CIA and the threat or reality of US intervention ever since the 1950s. A diaspora of Latin American political refugees concentrated in the few countries of the hemisphere providing refuge – Mexico and, until 1973, Chile – and scattered across North America and Europe: the Brazilians to France and Britain, the Argentinians to Spain, the Chileans everywhere. (Although many Latin American intellectuals continued to visit Cuba, very few actually chose it as their place of exile.) Essentially the 'era of the gorillas' (to use the Argentine phrase) was the product of a triple encounter. The local ruling oligarchies did not know what to do about the threat from their increasingly mobilized lower orders in town and country and the populist radical politicians who appealed to them with evident success. The young middle-class left, inspired by the example of Fidel Castro, thought the continent was ripe for revolution precipitated by armed guerrilla action. And Washington's obsessive fear of communism, confirmed by the Cuban Revolution, was intensified by the international setbacks of the USA in the seventies: the Vietnam defeat, the oil crises, the African revolutions that turned towards the USSR.

I found myself involved in these affairs as an intermittent Marxist visitor to the continent, sympathetic to its revolutionaries – after all, unlike in Europe, revolutions were both needed and possible – but critical of much of its ultra left. Utterly critical of the hopeless Cuban-inspired guerrilla dreams of 1960–67,[6] I found myself defending the second-best against the criticisms of campus insurrectionaries. As I wrote at the time:

The history of Latin America is full of substitutes for the genuinely popular social revolutionary left that has so rarely been strong enough to determine the shape of its countries' histories. The history of the Latin American left is, with rare exceptions . . . one of having to choose between an ineffective sectarian purity and making the best of various kinds of bad jobs, civilian or military populists, national bourgeoisies or whatever else. It is also, quite often, the history of the left regretting its failure to come to terms with such governments and movements before they were replaced by something worse.

I was thinking of the junta of reformist militarists under General Velasco Alvarado in Peru (1969–76) who proclaimed the 'Peruvian Revolution' on which I reported sympathetically but sceptically.[7] It nationalized the country's great *haciendas* and was also the first Peruvian regime to recognize the mass of Peruvians, the Quechua-speaking Indians from the high Andes now flooding into coast, city and modernity, as potential citizens. Everyone else in that pitifully poor and helpless country had failed, not least the peasants themselves, whose massive land occupation in 1958–63 had dug the grave of the oligarchy of landowners. They had not known how to bury them. The Peruvian generals acted because nobody else wanted to or could. (I am bound to add, they also failed, though their successors have been worse.)

It was not a popular note to strike, inside or outside Latin America, at a time when the suicidal Guevara dream of bringing about the revolution by the action of small groups in tropical frontier areas was still very much alive. It may help to explain why my appearance before the students of San Marcos University in Lima – 'Horrible Lima' as the poet rightly calls it – did not go down at all well. For Maoism in one or other of its numerous subvarieties was the ideology of the sons and daughters of the new *cholo* (hispanized Indian) middle class of highland immigrants, at least until they graduated.

Their Maoism, like military service for the peasants, and the 'gap year' of European students, was a social rite of passage.

But was there not hope in Chile, the country with the strongest Communist Party and with which I had both personal and political connections? Indeed, my father's brother Berk (Ike or Don Isidro), a mining expert based in Chile since the First World War, and founder with his wife, a Miss Bridget George from Llanwrthwl in Powys, of the largest extant branch of the family bearing the name Hobsbawn, had had a connection with the ephemeral Chilean Socialist Republic of 1932, led by the splendidly named Colonel Marmaduke Grove. More recently, through Claudio Veliz, then at Chatham House in London, who gave me most of my original introductions for the continent, I had met a patently very intelligent as well as good-looking lady, wife of a prominent Chilean socialist, whom I took round Cambridge, England: Hortensia Allende. On my first visit to Santiago I had lunch at the Allende house, coming to the conclusion that her unsparkling husband Salvador was the less impressive partner of the couple. That, as it turned out, was to underestimate the stature and the sense of democracy of a brave and honourable man who died defending his office. Others remember where they were when President Kennedy died. I remember where I was when I was rung up by some radio programme with the news that President Allende was dead – at an international conference on labour history, looking down on Linz and the Danube. I had last been in Chile in 1971, on a side trip from Peru to report on the first year of the first socialist government democratically elected to everyone's surprise, including Allende's.[8] Nevertheless, in spite of my passionate wish that it might succeed, I had not been able to conceal from myself that the odds were against it. Keeping my 'sympathies entirely out of the transaction' I had put them at two to one against. I did not visit Chile again until 1998 when I shared with Tencha Allende and other friends and comrades watching Santiago television the wonderful moment when the British Law Lords announced their epoch-making judgment against the former Chilean dictator General Pinochet on Santiago television. I did not share this joy with my Chilean relatives, who – at least those continuing to live in Santiago – had been supporters of his regime.

Debates about the Latin American left became academic in the

1970s with the triumph of the torturers, even more academic in the 1980s with the era of US-backed civil war in Central America and the retreat of army rule in South America and entirely unrealistic with the decline of the Communist Parties and the end of the USSR. Probably the only significant attempt at old-style armed guerrilla revolution was the 'Shining Path', brainchild of a fringe Maoist lecturer at the University of Ayacucho, who had not yet taken to arms when I visited that city in the late 1970s. It demonstrated what the Cuban dreamers of the 1960s had spectacularly failed to show, namely that serious armed politics were possible in the Peruvian countryside, but also – at least to some of us – that this was a cause that ought not to succeed. In fact, it was suppressed by the army in the usual brutal fashion, with the help of those parts of the peasantry whom the *Senderistas* had antagonized.

However, the most formidable and indestructible of the rural guerrillas, the Colombian FARC, flourished and grew, though in that blood-soaked country it had to deal not only with the official forces of the state but with the well-armed gunmen of the drugs industry and the landlords' savage 'paramilitaries'. President Belisario Betancur (1982–6), a socially minded and civilized Conservative intellectual not in the pockets of the USA – at least in conversation he gave me that impression – initiated the policy of negotiating peace with the guerrillas, which has continued at intervals ever since. His intentions were good, and he succeeded in pacifying at least one of the guerrilla movements, the so-called M19, favourite of the intellectuals. (There was a time when every party in Bogotá was likely to contain one or two young professionals who had spent a season in the hills with them.) Indeed, the FARC itself was prepared to play the constitutional game by creating a 'Patriotic Union' intended to function as that electoral party of the left which had never quite managed to emerge in the space between the Liberals and the Conservatives. It had little success in the big cities, and after about 2,500 of its local mayors, councillors and activists, having laid aside their arms, had been murdered in the countryside, the FARC developed an understandable reluctance to exchange the gun for the ballot-box. I was host to one of the militants, en route to or from an international gathering, in the cafeteria of Birkbeck College, far from the wild frontier of banana plantations, battles between FARC and Maoist guerrillas and the local paramilitaries in Urabà, near the isthmus of Panama, where he practised his legal politics. When I next asked friends for news of him, he was already dead.

IV

What has happened to Latin America in the forty or so years since I first landed on its airfields? The expected and in so many countries necessary revolution has not happened, strangled by the indigenous military and the USA, but not least by domestic weakness, division and incapacity. It will not happen now. None of the political experiments I have watched from near or far since the Cuban Revolution has made much lasting difference.

Only two have looked as though they might, but both are too recent for judgement. The first, which must warm the cockles of all old red hearts, is the national rise, since its foundation in 1980, of the Workers' Party (Partido dos Trabalhadores or PT) in Brazil, whose leader and presidential candidate 'Lula' (Luis Inácio da Silva) is probably the only industrial worker at the head of any Labour Party anywhere. It is a late example of a classic mass socialist Labour Party and movement, such as emerged in Europe before 1914. I carry its plaque on my key-ring to remind me of ancient and contemporary sympathies, and memories of my times with the PT and with Lula, often touching, sometimes moving, like the stories of the party's grassroots activists from the São Paulo car factories and the remote inland townships. And as tribute to the democratic and educational zeal of the PT's prize city, Porto Alegre (Rio Grande do Sul), honest, prosperous and anti-globalist, which moved its council to organize and its mayor to preside over an open-air question-and-answer session for the citizenry with a visiting British historian on the main square, amid the noise of the municipality's efficient trams.

The other, more dramatic, landmark was the end in 2000 of Mexico's seventy years of unshakeable one-party rule by the PRI (the Institutional Revolutionary Party). Alas, one doubts whether this will produce a better political alternative, any more than the revolt of the Italian and Japanese voters in the early 1990s against the frozen Cold War regimes of their countries.

So the politics of Latin America remain recognizably what they have long been, as does its cultural life (except for the vast global explosion in higher education in which its republics have shared). On the world economic scene, even when not shaken by the great crises of the past twenty years, Latin America plays only a bit part. Politically, it has remained as far from God and as near to the USA as ever, and consequently less inclined than any other part of the globe to believe that the USA is liked because 'it does a lot of good round the world'.[9] For half a century journalists and academics have read secular transformations into temporary political trends, but the region remains what it has been for most of a century, full of constitutions and jurists but unstable in its political practice. Historically its national governments have found it hard to control what happens on their territory, and still do. Its rulers have tried to avoid the logic of electoral democracy among populations which cannot be guaranteed to vote the way their betters would want them to, by a variety of methods ranging from control by local grandees, patronage, general corruption and occasional demagogic 'fathers of the people' to military rule. All of these still remain available.

And yet, during these past forty years I have observed a society being utterly transformed. The population of Latin America has just about tripled, an essentially agrarian and still largely empty continent has lost most of its peasants, who have moved into giant cities and from Central America to the USA, on a scale comparable only with the Irish and Scandinavian migrations in the nineteenth century, or even, like the Ecuadoreans working on the Andalusian harvests, across the ocean. Emigrant remittances have replaced the great hopes of modernization. Cheap air travel and phone communication have abolished localization. Life-patterns I observed in the 1990s were unimagined in 1960: the New York taxi-driver from Guayaquil who lived half in the USA and half in Ecuador, where his wife ran a local print-shop; the loaded pick-up trucks of immigrant Mexicans (legal or clandestine) returning from California or Texas for the holiday to Jalisco or Oaxaca; Los Angeles turning into a town of Central American immigrant *politicos* and union leaders. True, most Latin Americans remain poor. In fact, in 2001 they were almost certainly relatively poorer than in the early 1960s, even if we set aside the ravages of the economic crises of the past twenty years, for not only has inequality within these countries soared, but the continent itself has lost ground internationally. Brazil may be the eighth economy of the world by the size of its GDP, Mexico the sixteenth, but *per capita* they rank respectively fifty-second and sixtieth. In the world's league table of social injustice Brazil remains at the top. And yet, if one were to ask the Latin American poor to compare their life at the start of the new millennium with their parents', let alone their grandparents', outside a few black spots most would probably say: it is better. But in most countries they might also say: it is more unpredictable and more dangerous.

It is not for me to agree or disagree with them. After all, they are the Latin America that I went to look for, and discovered, forty years ago, the one Pablo Neruda wrote about in the marvellous baroque poem of poems about his continent, the section 'The heights of Macchu Picchu' in his *Canto General*. It ends with the invocation of the unknown builders of that dead green Inca city, through whose dead mouth the poet wants to speak:

> Juan Cortapiedras, hijo de Wiracocha
> Juan Comefrio, hijo de la estrella verde
> Juan Piedescalzos, nieto de la turquesa

(John Stonecutter, son of Wiracocha, John Coldmeals, son of the green star, John Barefoot, grandson of the turquoise.)

'If you want to understand South America,' they told me before I left Britain, 'you must go to Macchu Picchu and read the poem there.' I had not met the great poet then, a plump man whose natural element was not the mountains but the sea, on which his wonderful house still looks out, and who, asked what he wanted to see in London, had only one wish: the *Cutty Sark* sailing ship at Greenwich. He died of a broken heart a few days after the overthrow of Salvador Allende. I did read his poem in Macchu Picchu in 1962, on one of the steep stepped hills, as the sun went down, in an Argentine paperback bought in a Chilean bookshop. Whether it helped me to understand it as a historian, I do not know, but I know what the poet wanted to say and the big-chested, coca-chewing, brown, quiet men and women whom he had in mind, who scrabbled a living in the thin air of the Andean high country where it is harder to be a human being than almost anywhere else between Arctic and Antarctic. When I think of Latin America these are the people who come into my mind. Not only the poet but the historian should give them their due.

22

From FDR to Bush

I

If all intellectuals of my generation had two countries, their own and France, then in the twentieth century all inhabitants of the western world, and eventually all city dwellers anywhere on the globe, lived mentally in two countries, their own and the USA. After the First World War no literate person anywhere failed to recognize the words 'Hollywood' and 'Coca-Cola', and very few illiterates could fail to make some contact with their products. America did not have to be discovered: it was part of our existence.

And yet, what most people knew of America was not the country itself, but a set of images mediated essentially by its arts. Until well after the Second World War relatively few people from outside the USA actually travelled there, unless as immigrants, and from the early 1920s to the 1970s US government policy made immigration extremely difficult. I did not step on its shores myself until 1960. We met North Americans elsewhere. I suppose my first real contact with what was not yet called 'Middle America' was when the Rotarians chose to hold their international convention in Vienna in 1928 and I, as a bilingual boy, was mobilized as an interpreter. I remember nothing about it, except the lobby of a hotel on the Ring containing herds of men dressed in brighter shirts than Vienna was used to, a kind anaesthetist from somewhere in the Midwest who subsequently sent me stamps for my collection, and puzzling about what exactly Rotary was supposed to be for. The official explanation ('Service') seemed to me to be short of content.

I find it hard to reconstruct the image of the USA formed by an anglophone continental boy before the 1930s. Oddly enough – for my uncle actually worked for a Hollywood company – for me it did not come from Hollywood films. The sort of Tom Mix Westerns we saw hardly counted, since it seemed obvious even to children that life in America was not quite like that. (This showed that we knew little of the US.) The Hollywood films set in America were not intended to be about life stateside but about a never-never land of moviegoers' dreams. If our view of America came from anywhere, it was from technology and music: the one as an idea, the other as an experience. For we also got the technology at second hand. Most of us were unlikely ever to see an assembly line, but we knew that is how Ford cars were made.

On the other hand, the arts reached us directly. My mother and aunts shimmied and foxtrotted, and we listened to recognizably American music even when produced by English bands and vocalists. Radio and gramophone brought us Jerome Kern and Gershwin. 'Jazz', as then commonly understood – syncopated rhythmic music with saxophones and lacking bowed strings – was already the sound of urban middle-class leisure in the twenties. It meant America, and because of what the USA symbolized, it meant modernity, short hair for women and the age of machines. The staff of the *Bauhaus* had itself photographed with a saxophone. And so, when I came to England and was converted to jazz by my cousin Denis, this time to the real thing, the gates opened not only on a new aesthetic experience, but on a new world. Like Alistair Cooke, one of my predecessors as editor of *Granta*, who was then beginning his career as a lifetime commentator on the US with a radio series *I Hear America Singing*, I also discovered America by ear.

Jazz was as good an introduction to the USA as any, because in Britain at least the sound and its social significance – a very 1930s phrase – went together. To be a jazz-fan was not only, and for obvious reasons, to be against racism and for the Negroes (this was the era before they wanted to be described as Black and then African-American), but to gobble up all information about the USA even faintly relevant to jazz: and very little about the country was not relevant in some way. So all fans collected an endlessly fascinating bric-a-brac of facts about the USA, from the names of American cities, rivers and railroads (Milwaukee, the wide Missouri, the Aitchison, Topeka and Santa Fe) to the names of gangsters and senators. In the 1930s reputations could be made simply by *knowing facts* about the USA. Denis Brogan, a hard-drinking and eventually not quite so hard-working Glaswegian, teaching politics in

Cambridge, was an expert on two countries, but he made his radio reputation – and he was one of the first media dons in Europe – not as a very knowledgeable historian and observer of France, but as the sort of man who could name all the state capitals of the United States and the title of every song by Irving Berlin.

The image of America is so powerful and all-embracing that it is easy to suppose that it has barely changed over what we now know to have been 'the American century'. But for those of us who became conscious of it in the 1930s, especially if we were on the left, it was in some respects quite different. For one thing, it was not dominated by envy. We began thinking about America at the only moment when the US economy was not a triumphant model of wealth and productive potential for the rest of the world. In the decade of the Great Depression we no longer saw the world of *Gatsby* but that of *The Grapes of Wrath*. In the 1920s and early 1930s America was a by-word for the hard-faced pursuit of profit, for injustice, for ruthless, unscrupulous and brutal repression. But F. D. Roosevelt's USA not only disclaimed this reputation; it turned it sharply to the left. It visibly became a government for the poor and the unions. What is more, Roosevelt was passionately loathed and denounced by American big business, that is to say by the very people who more than any others represented the evils of capitalism to us. It is true that, as usual, the Communist International, stuck in its ultra-sectarian phase, took its time to recognize what was obvious to everyone else and denounced the New Deal, but by 1935 even it had come round. In short, in the 1930s it was possible to approve of both the USA and the USSR, and most youthful communists did both, as did a very large number of socialists and liberals. Franklin D. Roosevelt was certainly not Comrade Stalin, and yet, if we had been Americans, we would have voted for him with genuine enthusiasm. I cannot think of any other 'bourgeois' politician in any country about whom we felt that way. During the more than sixty years since I got to know Arthur Schlesinger Jr in Cambridge, England, we have probably never agreed on any political issue except this one. I shared, and still share, his admiration for FDR.

Although crossing the Atlantic from Cambridge was common enough, I never had the chance to do so before the war – and after 1945 the Cold War seemed to make it impossible. For the United

States did not want communists on its soil. It certainly wanted no foreign ones. As a Party member I was automatically debarred from a visa, except by a special waiver of my ineligibility, which I was unlikely to get, unless by meeting the indispensable condition for being received, however temporarily, into the community of the free: confessing and abjuring sin in public, although I do not think denouncing other communists was mandatory for foreigners. These were not formalities. I recall a long talk with Joe Losey, the film director, a victim of the Hollywood witch-hunt, with whom I had struck up a friendship – which did not survive this conversation – on the basis of a common passion for Billie Holiday. For several years he had scuffled round Europe, making movies under pseudonyms or as best he could. At last, in the 1960s, he had broken through. Not only his talent, but his box-office value were about to be recognized. The notorious question ('Are you now or have you ever been?') stood in his way. Friends and entrepreneurs suggested that no harm would now be done if he answered it. Should he? he asked me, a question which I took to mean that he was close to doing so. I could not blame him, but was too honest, or too sanctimonious, simply to give him the answer he wanted. Probably I should have. It is not a small thing for a man to consider whether the chance to realize a great talent is worth the sacrifice of his pride and self-esteem. I can still feel the anguish behind his question.

Fortunately I myself did not face any such dilemma. If the US asked me the question and would not admit me when I answered it honestly, then I would just not go there. Of course I wanted to. What is more, the reasons for going there multiplied, if only because the American academic community was even then far quicker to recognize the heterodox than the rather hidebound British.

Just then the opportunity arose to visit the country I had hitherto known only, as it were, as a virtual reality. At one of the early postwar International Congresses of Sociology – in Amsterdam in 1956 or, more likely, Stresa in 1959 – I had got to know the economist Paul Baran, a 1930s refugee from Germany, who claimed to be the only overt Marxist with academic tenure in the USA.[1] I must have got on well with this big, passionate, shambling, soft-eyed man, because he invited me to stay with him and teach for a summer quarter at Stanford University in 1960. We planned to write a paper together attacking Walt Rostow's recently published *The Stages of Economic Growth*, a self-described 'anti-Communist Manifesto' which was then much talked about. We did so later in a cabin on Lake Tahoe.[2]

On this occasion the problem of my visa was finessed, thanks to the lack of bureaucratic experience of the US Consulate in London. They forgot to ask me the question. My status as a visitor to the USA was not permanently settled until 1967, when I was invited to take a visiting chair at the Massachusetts Institute of Technology. Fortunately MIT was used both to dealing with visa applications from backgrounds suspect to FBI and CIA, and to the political operations of Washington. The prestige of the institution and its president, as also the knowledge that it was doing the state substantial service, gave it enough leverage to insist that it must be allowed to judge what foreigners were or were not worth inviting. The office politics of power thus drove MIT to mobilize all its resources to get a visa waiver for an otherwise unimportant British communist academic. I got my waiver, although on condition that I reported to the friendly but determined lady who 'looked after' foreigners at MIT every time I proposed to leave the Boston area. 'You mean I can't spend the night in New York without your OK?' I asked. She recognized the absurdity of the situation and did not insist. Nobody subsequently interfered with my freedom of movement in the USA.

I did not realize until very late just how difficult the US authorities must have found the problem of my visa. Like all bureaucracies they reacted in the first instance by silence and evasion. However, in the course of a series of increasingly frantic transatlantic telephone conversations I discovered some of what made my case so tricky. 'Do you mind,' said my sponsor in the course of one of them, 'if I ask you a question, which, I can assure you, does not affect our invitation to you? Are you or have you ever been the chairman of the British Communist Party?' It was a typical intelligence file entry, combining laziness (for the names of all the Party's chairmen were certainly within easy reach of the spooks) and confusion. Since 1939 I had, as far as I can recall, *never* occupied any political function in the Party, not even at branch level. Someone had clearly been unable to distinguish the only thing I had ever been chairman of, in or outside the Party, namely the Historians' Group of the CP (see chapter 12) from the chairmanship of the Communist Party. Anyway, MIT won out against Immigration. I got my waiver.

From that moment my troubles were almost over. Once there is a precedent, bureaucracies know what to do: the same as last time. From then on I went to the States without real trouble, though initially I was interviewed once or twice by the consular officer in charge of waivers, who might look at my file, say casually, 'I see you've been to Cuba again,' to prove that Uncle Sam had his eye on me, and arrange for the waiver. I still could not, of course, land in America without a visa, even in air transit, but eventually my applications were routinely made and granted within days, until the *a priori* ineligibility of communists was finally abolished and British visitors no longer neded visas.

II

So in 1960 the USA as virtual reality turned into the USA as a real country. How? Here, at least initially, my jazz identity proved far more relevant than either my Marxist or my academic contacts. For the truth is that by 1960 the American Marxists of my generation were largely isolated from the world in which they lived and the American academic historians I knew did not know a lot about it in the first place. In New York I could discuss the problems of capital accumulation and the transition from feudalism to capitalism with my friends from *Science and Society*, the oldest anglophone journal of intellectual Marxism, for which I wrote, but they taught me no more about New York than any other Manhattan lower-middle-class Jews would have taught a visitor from outer space: where the good dairy delicatessens and second-hand bookshops were (not yet reduced to the Strand Bookshop on Broadway and Twelfth), what Dr Brown's Celery Tonic was and that in the USA pastrami was not what Englishmen called salt beef.

I got rather more through Paul Baran on the West Coast, chiefly because (I think via his then lover, a Californian Japanese lady) he knew the intellectuals who worked with Harry Bridges' International Longshore and Warehousemen's Union, foundation-stone of the Bay Area left. It organized all Pacific ports from Portland to San

Diego and, for good measure, everything that could be organized in Hawaii. To my intense satisfaction I was introduced to Bridges himself, a lanky hook-nosed hero, who had imposed exclusive job hire through the union at Californian conditions on the Pacific Coast employers, no lambs by nature, by means of two general strikes and a sound sense of power and bargaining strategy. He had also fought off several attempts by the American government to deport him as an alien subversive. He was then in the process of reluctantly supervising the euthanasia of the Pacific waterside workers by negotiating the substitution of container and tanker technology for manpower, against ample lifetime pensions for the union members whose jobs disappeared. The union was still strong, and Bridges' revolutionary convictions, expressed in an Australian accent that made few concessions to half a lifetime as an American union leader, were undimmed. He still dreamed of a general strike of the world's dockers that would bring the capitalist system to its knees, for in the minds of watersiders the great oceans are bridges between continents, not barriers. Not that he had much time for seamen, all of whom, he thought, were 'bums', because they lacked the staying-power of a union on *terra firma* like the longshoremen, held together by families and regular communities. Nor, as a good Australian, had he much use for pommies. In his youth as a seaman he had once, he told me, kept company with a docker's daughter in the port of London. This had given him a permanent contempt for the forelock-tugging acceptance of their social inferiority by British workers.

As it was 1960, we discussed the presidential election. Jimmy Hoffa of the teamsters (truck-drivers), the target of Bobby Kennedy and the FBI, was thinking of throwing his union's vote behind Nixon rather than Kennedy. The teamsters' goodwill was essential to both labour and capital in California, but Hoffa's reputation was bad. Bridges, who felt no loyalty to either 'bourgeois party', saw this as a purely pragmatic choice. Was Hoffa not, I asked, in the hands of the mob? 'He may work with the hoods,' said Bridges sternly and from experience, 'but he is a stand-up guy and so far as I know he has *never* sold out his members. What he skims off comes from the bosses, not the workers.' Nobody ever accused Bridges of either becoming rich or selling out his members. He died not long after I met him, as San Francisco was moving far away from the city of Bridges and Sam Spade. I recall him with admiration and emotion. His union certainly knew about the mob. One afternoon its organizer, who later moved into the academic sphere, gave me what amounted to a seminar on negotiating with the Mafia, with which the ILWU had to coordinate its activities, since, though the Pacific port unions were clean, the mob controlled the unions on the Atlantic and Gulf coasts. Dealing with the Mafia, it seemed, rested on two basic assumptions and a knowledge of its limitations. The first, mutual respect, could be taken for granted. Both parties operated on the waterside, which was not a children's playground. They knew its rules, the most important of which was that you didn't snitch. Stand-up guys didn't have to trust one another, but they could talk. The second was that no favours, however minor or symbolic, must be accepted from the Mafia, because that would automatically be interpreted as establishing dependence. So, there were always polite but firm refusals to suggestions that the two unions might get together to decide questions of common interest – say, a single date for ending contracts – in an agreeable location such as Vegas.

On the other hand, the knowledge of the Mafia's limitations gave a politically hip organization like a red union the possibility of demonstrating what to the mob must have looked like power worthy of serious respect. Of course the ILWU had no power, even though, one suspects, the Representatives and Senators from Hawaii treated its views very seriously. It merely had strategies, national political horizons, committed and knowledgeable intellectuals, and it knew how to operate on Capitol Hill. On the other hand, in the experience of the ILWU, the mob's economic perspectives were short, its political horizons local. 'They talked to city aldermen and mayors' offices. We took them round Congress in Washington once,' the organizer told me. 'They could see our people, said hello to Representatives and Senators from all parts, we asked them would they like to meet Jimmy Roosevelt Jr, the son of FDR. That impressed them. After that negotiations became a lot easier.' All this helped to inoculate me against the tendency of US laymen and political campaigners to exaggerate the power and reach of the Mafia. Or even its wealth, although the actual net worth of a Mafia family, rather modest by the standards of real money in New York, was only recorded in the early 1970s, the decade when Italo-Americans came into their own and America conducted its love-affair (via Hollywood) with the godfathers.[3] It also gave me a realistic introduction to American politics.

How far did this change my view of the USA? Like all transatlantic US watchers and, as I discovered, a subculture of American intellectuals, I had been fascinated by gangsters. Fortunately in the 1950s a mass of material became available for the first time about the development of organized crime in the USA, which naturally paid attention to the interactions between the mob and labour. (This had not been stressed in the young leftwingers' image of American labour history.) My studies of the Sicilian Mafia had in any case given me a professional interest in the American side of its operations. So I was sufficiently familiar with it to write a small study on 'The political economy of the gangster' as a subvariety of the market economy, that passed completely unperceived, perhaps in part because, for a joke, I sent it to the most ancient, indeed almost prehistoric and unread, Tory journal, The Quarterly Review, which published it without a murmur.[4] By the time I arrived in the USA I was therefore well clued up on such topics (but, for obvious reasons, not on the Kennedy family's impending projects to use their mob connections to kill off Fidel Castro). And yet, in some ways I still shared the basic view of primary school or Hollywood morality, in which goodies (honest people) behave as goodies and are therefore better than, and have nothing to do with, the baddies (crooks), even when they have to coexist with them. Even after living a long time in a very imperfect world, I would still prefer to believe this. In the law-abiding and state-governed British Isles of the 1950s, it still seemed not only an aspiration, but a sort of reality. But the USA was neither law-abiding, though it had more lawyers than the rest of the world put together, nor a society that recognized the rule of the state, though to my surprise I discovered it to be much more enthusiastically bureaucratic at all levels.

Politics and professors took me to America, but once again it was jazz which made me feel that I had some understanding of the reality of this extraordinary country. I could hardly have chosen a better moment to visit the USA as a jazz-lover than 1960. At no time before or after was it possible to enjoy the entire range of the music live, from the survivors of the 1920s to the anarchist sonorities of Ornette Coleman and Don Cherry which could already be heard by a determined avant-garde on the eastern outskirts of Greenwich Village. Indeed, in spite of the suicidal lifestyle of jazz people, with some notable exceptions the great names on which my generation had been raised were still in operational form. What is more, as we listened to the unique originality of Monk and the absolutely extraordinary Miles Davis Quintet of *Milestones* and *Kind of Blue*, we could not help noticing that the second half of the fifties was a golden age of the music, the last as it turned out. Bliss was it in those New York and San Francisco nights to be alive, even if it was too late for a historian in his forties to enjoy the very heaven of Wordsworth's youth.

Not that jazz was separable from the politics of the left, although in 1960 its place in the professional academy was rather like homosexuality: it was a private taste of some teachers, but not part of their academic activity. That is why New York, notoriously so much less typical of middle America than, say, Green Bay, Wisconsin, was probably the best place to convince someone like myself that it was actually possible to understand, perhaps even to love, that extraordinary country. *Le tout* Manhattan despised the witch-hunt and, being a city of immigrant Jews and the centre of intellectual publishing, theatre and the popular music and recording business, took for granted the existence among some of its denizens of revolutionary Marxism, past or present. In the Big Apple only the FBI really worried about the precise nature of someone's political commitment, for by the time I got there it was a city in which even the billionaires were, as likely as not, to be Democrats. Curiously enough jazz did not much appeal to the full-time American Marxists, whose instinctive taste seemed to be for classical music and political folksong. (I still recall the disastrous evening when I took Paul Baran to hear Miles Davis at the Black Hawk in San Francisco.)

Most of my jazz contacts were men, with a few exceptions such as the tough showbiz pro who devoted her life to furthering the career of the wonderful pianist Erroll Garner, and who tried to do me a massive favour by getting me on the *Johnny Carson Show* with Garner on the assumption that I would publicize the book I had recently published on jazz. (My remoteness from the realities of

American publishing in 1960, thirty years ahead of the British scene, was such that I went through the entire four minutes of my interview slot without so much as mentioning the title of my book.) Most of them were in some ways refugees from the conventional American male life of the 1950s, decade of 'the man in the grey flannel suit', except the greatest talent-scout and promoter in the history of jazz, John Hammond Jr. No out-of-town visitor, seeing him outside, say, the Village Vanguard, would ever have asked him, as I was asked, standing with a friend outside a place in North Beach, San Francisco: 'Excuse me, but are you two gentlemen beatniks?' Of course, nobody needed to ask who he was outside the place to which he took me first, Small's Paradise in Harlem. John Hammond Jr was almost a caricature of the Ivy League White Anglo-Saxon Protestant upper class: tall, crewcut, talking in the sort of accent in which one imagines they talked in Edith Wharton novels – he was a Vanderbilt himself – and sporting an unwavering grin. As so often in the USA, this did not indicate a great sense of humour. He was not a man for informality or casual laughs, any more than his one-time brother-in-law Benny Goodman, who had the reputation of freezing his sidemen with a basilisk stare. John remained an unreconstructed and militant 1930s leftwinger to the end, even though the FBI could never tie him down as a card-carrying communist. The history of jazz in the USA before the Second World War and, since he was probably the most important single influence in launching the 'swing music' vogue of the 1930s, the history of the USA, cannot be understood without him. I asked him on his death-bed, what he was proudest of in his life. He said it was to have discovered Billie Holiday.

By the time I knew him, he was no longer at the musical centre, though no man who was about to launch Bob Dylan into the big time could be regarded entirely as yesterday's man. Another former New York jazz-lover who became my best American friend, not merely made it his business as a journalist to keep in touch with all generations within reach, old and young, but did so with a natural, good-tempered, surreal spontaneity that captured them all. This was the man who, among other things, had just discovered Lenny Bruce, and made himself election agent for the great bebop trumpeter Dizzy Gillespie's campaign for the American presidency, which neither of them regarded entirely as a joke, namely Ralph Gleason. New York

Irish, he had left the city to become showbusiness and popular music columnist for the *San Francisco Chronicle*, a paper that prided itself on not belonging to William Randolph Hearst, and on columnists who were not surprised at anything they came across in a wealthy, cool and courteously dissident city. He lived in a modest house on the upper hillside in Berkeley, full of collections of records, tapes, musical projects, print in various formats and (generally young) visitors, all kept in working order by his tough and protective wife Jeanie. I treated it as a refuge from Palo Alto, driving there in the first car I ever owned, a 1948 Kaiser, which I had bought for $100 and sold at the end of the summer quarter to a mathematical logician of world distinction for $50.

For music and showbusiness the Bay Area of San Francisco in 1960 was a hip place, a good market but on the margins. Everyone played the town, but nothing much had come out of there, except the first self-conscious wave of white Dixieland music. It was the sort of place where elderly masters such as the great jazz pianist Earl Hines settled down, secure in a good, solid club public. Even Duke Ellington accepted a club date rather than a concert there, thus providing me with the unforgettable occasion, the first since 1933, of hearing the band in the milieu for which it had been designed, namely a space with social drinkers where the real measure of a band's impact was not applause, but the sudden silence as conversations ceased at the tables.

San Francisco, though not yet established as the Gay Republic or the hinterland of Silicon Valley, had a national profile and a recognized presence on the American scene, quite apart from the sensational beauty of its bay. It was a liberal city, though less politically radical than its neighbour Berkeley became in the 1960s, proud of its dissidents (not least Harry Bridges). Even then it was relaxed about drugs. By California standards it had freightcar-loads of history, the (then) most famous Chinatown, the memory of the Maltese Falcon, and a reputation as the most prominent centre of avant-garde literature in the 1950s, the 'beat' movement, fashionable enough for Ken Tynan to congratulate me on going there. 'There' was the area around Broadway, North Beach, a sort of Pacific St-Germain-des-Prés, where I would meet Ralph at the local Flore, and Enrico's, facing the City Lights Bookstore, greeting and being greeted by the personalities of the city as they strolled past. Unlike the New York Broadway, on this Broadway people strolled. And across the Bay Bridge there was Berkeley. In the middle sixties 'the white sons of middle class America' briefly made it the quintessential scene of hippy youth and 'flower power', incidentally generating (as Gleason noted) 'the first American musicians, aside from the country and western players, who are not trying to sound black'.[5] Ralph made himself the mouthpiece for the Haight-Ashbury music, groups such as Jefferson Airplane and the Grateful Dead, although he did not by temperament belong on the drug scene. Indeed, he gave up smoking grass. He belonged to the generation of intellectuals who smoked pipes, as I then did also. Never in good health, he died in 1975 aged fifty-eight.

For three reasons he became my window on America. Living in the world of jazz, an outsider music, he caught the vibrations of coming events which escaped others – the changing *tone* of the sounds that came from the black ghetto, the white kids' avant-garde which discovered the force of the black city blues beat, the anticipations of the Berkeley student revolt which became national after 1964, global in 1968. These were not things noticed elsewhere in the summer of 1960. Nobody I knew on the faculties of Berkeley, still less the distinguished but stuffy Stanford, suggested I might be interested in going to the political camping weekend which the Berkeley leftwingers were organizing that summer, because none knew it was happening. Ralph did, who had no academic or recognizable political connections, but to whom students talked. Not that Ralph was much into organized political radicalism or moved in the circles of Bay Area leftism. The Symbionese Liberation Army was much more his style, a bizarre *reductio ad absurdum* of Bay Area millennialism, remembered (if at all) for first kidnapping and then converting the daughter of William Randolph Hearst Jr. He applauded and entertained the 1964 Berkeley Free Speech rebels, admired the mass oratory as well as the disorganized sincerity of their leader, the somewhat farouche physics student Mario Savio, and, after his expulsion, sent him and his wife/partner to me at Birkbeck where he hoped we might find something for him. (J. D. Bernal's physics department obliged, but academic life and scientific research were clearly not his bag, and he returned to life among the cafés and head-shops on Telegraph Avenue, Berkeley, within reach of his old triumphs.)

The second reason why Ralph was a marvellous introduction to post-sixties America was that, an immigrant into the most culturally utopian corner of California himself, he could understand the aspirations of its young and their cultural revolution. Besides, though the least infantile of men, he was not himself a character to grow old. He could draw on an inexhaustible reservoir of enthusiasm, which I could not share, even for rock groups. Once again, this made him wonderfully sensitive to the vibes of coming times. It was he who helped one of his young followers to start a rock magazine, he who found the title for it from a record of the Chicago blues-singer Muddy Waters, *Rolling Stone*, he, the least commercial of men, who thanks to it and to what had been a small jazz and fringe satire label Fantasy Records found himself with more money than he had been used to and in a position to send whisky and cigars to old friends.

Last, but not least, by style and temperament Ralph, himself inconceivable anywhere except the USA, made his country easier to understand, even though its civilization was in some respects stranger to Europeans than any other except the Japanese. He had what seems to outsiders the characteristic American combination of sudden loves and hates, sentimentality in feeling (but not in the spoken word). Nevertheless, he appeared to be immune to the three built-in hazards of American cultural life: self-absorption, the tendency to ponder what it means to be American and intellectual heaviness. Bullshit phrases such as 'American values' and 'the American dream' were not to be found in his dictionary, as they were not yet to be found in the private speech of the USA. He took Americans as they were. Rhetoric belonged only to their public life and the officially approved versions of love. I do not think he would have regarded even an American utopia as complete without a corrupt Chicago alderman here and there, a lecherous millionaire radio-evangelist or two, a few centres of passionate counter-cultural dissidence even from utopia, and establishments like the one I saw outside one of the main casinos in Reno, Nevada, called the Sierra Club: Horse Book and Kosher Delicatessen. On the other hand, living in the world's great cities of the plain, he would expect God to refrain from destroying this Sodom, because the ten just men required to save it were always to be found there. He was one of them.

Ralph belonged to that unique product of the US, the corps of observers, mostly journalists, the best of them probably the generation of the 1930s–50s, which was also that of the glories of American vernacular song-lyric and musical, who reported on their country with love, contempt and raised eyebrows. He steered me to others like him. I could not have had a better introduction to Chicago, a city which no lover of blues could possibly miss.

I reached Chicago by a drive from the Pacific to the east, recognized since the Beats celebrated it as the initiation rite of the true American rebel. I shared expenses with three very un-Kerouac-like students from Stanford. By European standards there is not enough variety in the vast spaces of mountain and prairie for enjoyment, at least for those not zonked out of their mind. This was difficult when four people drive round the clock in shifts, though it made me sufficiently sleepy to barely avoid crashing the car into an oncoming vehicle on the endless straight highway somewhere near Laramie, Wyoming. Chicago itself, especially when experienced in August from a small YMCA room without any form of cooling, still seems the hottest place I have ever been to. Intolerable in the heat of summer as in the cutting winter winds, it symbolizes the characteristic American belief that physical limitations are there to be overcome by technology and money if the objective – in this case trade and transportation – justifies the effort. Few great cities are less suitable for mere unassisted human living.

This effort was not enough to make Chicago more than the Second City, however hard it tried. Even in jazz, where it started out with the advantage of attracting the best musicians and singers from the Mississippi delta, it lost out to the Big Apple, and in organized crime it lost its primacy after Al Capone, though the mob was still important enough. It did remain the capital of the city blues, but unlike its globally known child rock and roll, Chicago blues, like the gospel sound, belonged to the endless, uniform, run-down black ghettos of the South and West Sides. It was still the art of poor Southern immigrants, created in neighbourhood bars, store-front churches and even the open-air street-market. It had one national chart-topper, Mayor Daley, the last and greatest of the city bosses, who could guarantee the Cook County vote to any Democratic contender, which proved lucky for Jack Kennedy, whose election it may have determined. As I write, the city is still run by his son.

And yet, just this gave it a certain sense of local community. I cannot believe that my admired Studs Terkel would have built his career in another city. It is characteristic that the first of the marvellous books which established his world reputation as the recorder of ordinary lives was *Division Street: America*,[6] a wonderfully designed oral history tapestry of Chicago in seventy voices named after one street in the Near North Side of the city – the pleasantest part in 1960 – commissioned by my friend and publisher André Schiffrin as part of a series on 'the world's villages'. In some ways I prefer it to his later, more ambitious and better-known multi-voice compositions on *Hard Times: The Oral History of the Great Depression, Work, The Good War* and the rest. When I met him he was forty-eight and as always, running a daily personal radio programme on a local station, readings, musical commentaries, anything, especially interviews. His unique gift was the capacity to make people forget that they spoke into a microphone and that anyone was listening to their voice except a little clowny guy in a bow tie, who seemed to hear what they wanted to say, and who seemed to know about good times and bad times. As indeed he did, his career as an actor and TV figure having been broken by the anti-communist witch-hunt. After a spell as publicity man for black Chicago musicians, who knew what prejudice was, he found a berth in local radio, where big money was not needed and therefore had less say. Still, thanks to the mutual self-defence pact of Chicagoans against the headline-grabbers outside, nobody raised the spectre of communism against him when he became an established personality. He was, after all, part of that small community that exists in every big city, of reporters, commentators, urban autobiographers and other bar-room philosophers and watchers which recognizes its members.

Was this the best way for the foreigner to discover the USA? The men and women I met with or through people like Ralph Gleason and Studs Terkel were not 'middle America'. They were people such as the majestic gospel singer Mahalia Jackson, one of the greatest artists of the twentieth century, whose press agent Studs had been and who trusted few men and even fewer whites. Religion

among African-Americans is both the deepest faith, a public platform, a competitive art and a profit-making industry. Mahalia, an
ample woman in her large bourgeois home, secure for the moment
from the constant need of showbiz performers to put on an act in
public, combined the quiet confidence of the soul close to Jesus with
that of the successful pro. They were people such as 'Lord Buckley',
then in the last months of his life, a plummy-voiced combination
of Victorian circus ringmaster, hipster and reciter of Bible and
Shakespeare in flawless black street-corner language, who played
the two a.m. set at the Gate of Horn. They were people such as Bill
Randle of Cleveland, who had introduced Elvis Presley to northern
audiences, disc jockey by profession, amateur scholar of radio history, Indians and other Americana by vocation. (Why Cleveland,
that endless strip along Lake Erie, has played such a large part in
the promotion of rock and roll, still puzzles me.) The least one can
say is that the America I got to know through such men and women
was not boring.

The academic America which framed my professional experience
of the USA over forty years was nothing like as good an introduction
to the country, if only because the lives of university teachers,
villagers within their small national and global villages, are pretty
much alike in most developed countries, and so are the lives of
students. American academics establish relationships with new-
comers with great ease, since geographical mobility is built into
their career structure, as, indeed, it is into the local lifestyle. The
USA remains a country of men and women who change places,
work and relationships to a far greater degree than elsewhere. Moreover, with a few notable exceptions universities were self-contained
communities attached to small and medium-sized cities not much
concerned with academic affairs, at least until the last third of the
century, when it was discovered that the information revolution had
turned universities into major generators of economic wealth and
technical progress. They were communities into which immigrants
used to university life could be easily, if superficially, integrated,
provided they spoke enough English, which by the 1970s had become
the usual international second language. An Indian physicist at
Cornell, brother of a former student at Cambridge, told me: 'If I
were to take a chair in Britain, I would always feel a foreigner. I don't

feel a foreigner here, because in a sense everyone is a foreigner.'
Permanent communities largely composed of transients develop
patterns of instant sociability, neighbourliness and everyday mutual
help, but, as communities, do not tend to throw much light on what
happens outside.

Looking back on forty years of visiting and living in the United
States, I think I learned as much about the country in the first summer
I spent there as in the course of the next decades. With one exception:
to know New York, or even Manhattan, one has to live there. For
how long? I did so for four months every year between 1984 and
1997, but even though Marlene joined me for the whole semester
only three times, it was quite enough for both of us to feel like
natives rather than visitors. I have spent a lot of time in the USA
teaching, reading in its marvellous libraries, writing or having a
good time, or all together in the Getty Center in its days in Santa
Monica, but what I learned from personal acquaintance with
America was acquired in the course of a few weeks and months.
Were I a de Tocqueville, that would have been quite enough. After
all, his *Democracy in America*, the best book ever written about the
USA, was based on a journey of not more than nine months. Alas,
I am not de Tocqueville, nor is my interest in the USA the same
as his.

III

If written today, de Tocqueville's book would certainly be attacked
as anti-American, since much of what he said about the USA was
critical. Ever since it was founded, the USA has been a subject of
attraction and fascination for the rest of the world, but also of detrac-
tion and disapproval. However, it is only since the start of the Cold
War that people's attitude to the USA has been judged essentially in
terms of approval or disapproval, and not only by the sort of inhabitants who are also likely to seek out 'un-American' behaviour in
their own fellow-citizens, but also internationally. It substituted the
question 'Are you with the USA?' for the question 'What do you
think of the USA?' What is more, no other country expects or asks
such a question about itself. Since America, having won the Cold

War against the USSR, implausibly decided on September 11 2001 that the cause of freedom was again engaged on another life-and-death struggle against another evil but this time spectacularly ill-defined enemy, any sceptical remarks about the US and its policy are, once again, likely to meet with outrage.

And yet, how irrelevant, even absurd, is this insistence on approval! Internationally speaking, the USA was by any standards the success story among twentieth-century states. Its economy became the world's largest, both pace- and pattern-setting, its capacity for technological achievement was unique, its research in both natural and social sciences, even its philosophers became increasingly dominant, and its hegemony of global consumer civilization seemed beyond challenge. It ended the century as the only surviving global power and empire. What is more, 'in some ways the United States represent the best of the twentieth century'.[7] If opinion is measured not by pollsters but by migrants, almost certainly America would be the preferred destination of most human beings who must, or decide to, move to a country other than their own, certainly of those who know some English. As one of those who chose to work in the USA, my own case illustrates the point. Admittedly working in the USA, or liking to live in the USA – and especially in New York – does not imply the wish to become American although this is still difficult for many inhabitants of the United States to understand. It no longer implies a lasting choice for most people between one's own country and another, as it did before the Second World War, or even until the air transport revolution in the 1960s, let alone the telephone and e-mail revolution of the 1990s. Binational or even multinational working and even bi- or multi-cultural lives have become common.

Nor is money the only attraction. The USA promises greater openness to talent, to energy, to novelty than other worlds. It is also the reminder of an old, if declining, tradition of free and egalitarian intellectual enquiry, as in the great New York Public Library, whose treasures are still, unlike in the other great libraries of the world, open to anyone who walks through its doors from Fifth Avenue or Forty-second Street. On the other hand, the human costs of the system for those outside it or who cannot 'make it' were equally evident in New York, at least until they were pushed out of middle-class sight, off the streets or into the unspeakable *univers concen-trationnaire* of the largest jail population, per capita, in the world. When I first went to New York the Bowery was still a vast human refuse dump or 'skid row'. In the 1980s it was more evenly distributed through the streets of Manhattan. Behind today's casual mobile phone calls on the street I still hear the soliloquies of the unwanted and crazy on the pavements of New York in one of the city's bad decades of inhumanity and brutality. Human wastage is the other face of American capitalism, in a country where 'to waste' is the common criminal slang for 'to kill'.

Yet, unlike other nations, in its national ideology the USA does not simply exist. It only achieves. It has no collective identity except as the best, the greatest country, superior to all others and the acknowledged model for the world. As the football-coach said: 'Winning is not just the most important thing, it is all there is.' That is one of the things that makes America such a very *strange* country for foreigners. Stopping for a brief holiday with the family in a small, poor, linguistically incomprehensible seaside town in Portugal, on the way back from a semester in New England, I still remember the sense of coming home to one's own civilization. Geography had nothing to do with it. When we went on a similar holiday to Portugal a few years later, en route this time from South America, there was no such feeling of a culture gap overcome. Not the least of these cultural peculiarities is the USA's own sense of its strangeness ('Only in America . . .'), or at least its curiously unfixed sense of self. The question which preoccupies so many US historians of their own country, namely 'What does it mean to be American?', is one that rarely bothered my generation of historians in European countries. Neither national nor personal identity seemed as problem-atic to visiting Brits, at all events in the 1960s, even those of complex central European cultural background, as they seemed in local aca-demic discussions. 'What is this identity crisis they are all talking about?' Marlene asked me after one of them. She had never heard the term before we arrived in Cambridge, Mass., in 1967.

Foreign academics who discovered the USA in the 1960s were probably more immediately aware of its peculiarities than they would be today, for so many of them had not yet been integrated into the omnipresent language of globalized consumer society, which fits in well with the deeply entrenched egocentricity, even solipsism, of US culture. For, whatever was the case in de Tocqueville's day, not the passion for egalitarianism but an individualist, that is anti-authoritarian, antinomian though curiously legalistic anarchism, has become the core of the value system in the USA. What survives of egalitarianism is chiefly the refusal of voluntary deference to hierarchic superiors, which may account for the – by our standards – everyday crudeness, even brutality with which power is used in and by the USA to establish who can command whom.

It seemed Americans were preoccupied with themselves and their country, in ways in which the inhabitants of other well-established states simply were not with their own. American reality was and remains the overwhelming subject of the creative arts in the USA. The dream of somehow encompassing *all* of it haunted its creators. Nobody in Europe had set out to write '*the* great English novel' or '*the* great French novel', but authors in the US still try their hand (nowadays in several volumes) at '*the* great American novel', even if they no longer use the phrase. Actually, the man who came closest to achieving such an aim was not a writer, but an apparently superficial image-maker of astonishingly durable power, of whose significance the British art critic David Sylvester persuaded me in New York in the 1970s. Where else except America could an oeuvre like Andy Warhol's have come into being, an enormously ambitious and specific, unending set of variations on the themes of living in the USA, from its soup cans and Coca-Cola bottles to its mythologies, dreams, nightmares, heroes and heroines? There is nothing like it in the visual arts tradition of the old world. But, like the other attempts by the creative spirits of the USA to seize the totality of their country, Warhol's vision is not that of the successful pursuit of happiness, 'the American dream' of American political jargon and psychobabble.

To what extent has the US changed in my lifetime, or at least in the forty-odd years since I first landed there? New York, as we are constantly told, is not America and as Auden said, even those who could never be Americans can see themselves as New Yorkers. As indeed anyone does who comes to the same apartment every year, a vast set of towers overlooking the gradual gentrification of Union Square, to be recognized by the same Albanian doorman, and to negotiate domestic help as in years past with the same Spanish lady, who in her twelve years in the city has never found it necessary to learn English. Like other New Yorkers Marlene and I would give tips to out-of-town visitors about what was new since the last time they had landed at JFK and where to eat this year, though (apart from a party or two) unlike the permanently resident friends – the Schiffrins, the Kaufmans, the Katznelsons, the Tillys, the Kramers – we would not entertain at home. Like a real New Yorker I would feel the loss of a favourite establishment like that of a relative, I would exchange gossip at the regular lunches of the New York Institute of Humanities with the mixture of writing people, publishers, show persons, professors and UN staff which makes up the local intellectual scene – for one of the major attractions of New York is that the life of the mind is not dominated by the academy. In short, there is no other place in the world like the Big Apple. Still, however untypical, New York could not possibly exist anywhere except the USA. Even its most cosmopolitan inhabitants are recognizably American, like our friend the late John Lindenbaum, haematologist in a Harlem hospital and jazz-lover, who, sent to Bangladesh for a project of medical research, had travelled there with a collection of jazz records and his ice-cream scoop. There are a lot more Jews in New York, and, unlike in large stretches of the US, more people there are aware of the existence of the rest of the world, but what I learned as a New Yorker is not fundamentally at odds with what little I know of the Midwest and California.

Curiously, the experience, what in the sixties they used to call 'the vibes', of the USA has changed much less than that of other countries I have known in the past half-century. There is no comparison between living in the Paris, the Berlin, the London of my youth and those cities in 2002; even Vienna, which deliberately hides its social and political transformation by turning itself into a theme park of a glorious past. Even physically the skyline of London as it can be seen from where I live on the slopes of Parliament Hill has changed – Parliament is now barely visible – and Paris has not been the same since Messieurs Pompidou and Mitterrand have left their marks on it. And yet, while New York has undergone the same kind of social and economic upheavals as other cities – de-industrialization, gentrification, a massive influx from the Third World – it neither feels nor even looks like it. This is surprising when, as every New Yorker knows, the city changes every year. I myself have seen the arrival of fundamental innovations in New York life such as the Korean fruit-and-vegetable store, the end of such basic New York lower-middle-class institutions as the Gimbel department stores, and the transformation of Brighton Beach into Little Russia. And yet, New York has remained New York far more than London has remained London. Even the Manhattan skyline is still essentially that of the city of the 1930s, especially now that its most ambitious postwar addition has disappeared, the World Trade Center.

Is this apparent stability an illusion? After all, the USA is part of global humanity, whose situation has changed more profoundly and rapidly since 1945 than ever before in recorded history. These changes there looked less dramatic to us because the sort of prosperous high-tech mass consumer society which did not arrive in western Europe until the 1950s, was not new in America. Whereas I knew by 1960 that a historic chasm divided the way Britons lived and thought before and after the middle fifties, for the USA the 1950s were, or at least looked like, just a bigger and better version of the kind of twentieth century its more prosperous white citizens had known for two generations, its confidence recovered after the shock of the Great Slump. Seen from the outside, it continued along the same lines as before, though some sections of its citizens – mainly the college-educated – began to think differently about it, and, as the countries of the European Union became more modernized, the furniture of life with which European tourists came into contact began to look less 'advanced', and even a bit tatty. California did not seem fundamentally different to me driving through it in the 1970s, 1980s and 1990s from what it had looked and felt like in 1960, whereas Spain and Sicily did. New York had been a cosmopolitan city of immigrants for all my lifetime; it was London which became one after the 1950s. The details in the great carpet of the USA have changed, and are constantly changing, but its basic pattern remains remarkably stable in the short run.

As a historian I know that behind this apparent shifting stability, large and long-term changes are taking place, perhaps fundamental ones. Nevertheless, they are concealed by the deliberate resistance to change of American public institutions and procedures, and the habits of American life, as well as what Pierre Bourdieu called in more general terms its *habitus* or way of doing things. Forced into the straitjacket of an eighteenth-century constitution reinforced by two centuries of talmudic exegesis by the lawyers, the theologians of the republic, the institutions of the USA are far more frozen into immobility than those of almost all other states in 2002. It has so far even postponed such minor changes as the election of an Italian, or Jew, let alone a woman, as head of government. But it has also made the government of the USA largely immune to great men, or indeed to anybody, taking great decisions, since rapid effective national decision-making, not least by the President, is almost impossible. The US, at least in its public life, is a country that is geared to operate with mediocrities, because it has to, and it has been rich and powerful enough in the twentieth century to do so. It is the only country in my political lifetime where three able Presidents (FDR, Kennedy, Nixon) have been replaced, at a moment's notice, by men neither qualified nor expected to do the job, without making any noticeable difference to the course of US and world history. Historians who believe in the supremacy of high politics and great individuals have a hard case in America. This has created the foggy mechanisms of real government in Washington, made even more opaque by the sensational resources of corporate and pressure-group money, and the inability of the electoral process to distinguish between the real and the increasingly restricted political country. So, since the end of the USSR, the USA has quietly prepared to function as the world's only superpower. The problem is that its situation has no historical precedent, that its political system is geared to the ambitions and reactions of New Hampshire primaries and provincial protectionism, that it has no idea what to do with its power, and that almost certainly the world is too large and complicated to be dominated for any length of time by any single superpower, however great its military and economic resources. Megalomania is the occupational disease of global victors, unless controlled by fear. Nobody controls the USA today. This is why, as I write this in April 2002, its enormous power can and obviously does destabilize the world.

Our problem is not that we are being Americanized. In spite of the massive impact of cultural and economic Americanization, the rest of the world, even the capitalist world, has so far been strikingly resistant to following the model of US politics and society. This is probably because America is less of a coherent and therefore exportable social and political model of a capitalist liberal democracy, based on the universal principles of individual freedom, than its patriotic ideology and constitution suggest. So far from being a clear example which the rest of the world can imitate, the USA, however powerful and influential, remains an unending process, distorted by big money and public emotion, of tinkering with institutions, public and private, to make them fit realities unforeseen in the unalterable text of a 1787 constitution. It simply does not lend itself to copying. Most of us would not want to copy it. Since puberty I have spent more of my time in the USA than in any country other than Britain. All the same, I am glad that my children did not grow up there, and that I belong to another culture. Still, it is mine also.

Our problem is rather that the US empire does not know what it wants to do or can do with its power, or its limits. It merely insists that those who are not with it are against it. That is the problem of living at the apex of the 'American Century'. As I am eighty-five years of age I am unlikely to see its solution.

23

Coda

I

Biographies end with the subject's death. Autobiographies have no such natural termination. However, this one has the advantage of ending at the moment of an undeniable and dramatic caesura in world history, in consequence of the attack of September 11 2001 on the World Trade Center and the Pentagon. Probably no other unexpected event in world history has been directly experienced by more human beings. I saw it on a London hospital television screen as it happened. For an old and sceptical historian born in the year of the Russian Revolution, it had everything that was bad about the twentieth century: massacres, high but unreliable technology, the announcements that a global struggle to the death between the causes of God and Satan was now taking place once again as real life imitated Hollywood spectaculars. Public mouths flooded the western world with froth as hacks searched for words about the unsayable and unfortunately found them.

Magnified by the worldwide images and rhetoric of the American age of media and politics, a sudden gap appeared between the way the USA and the rest of the world understood what had happened on that awful day. The world merely saw a particularly dramatic terror attack with a vast number of victims and a momentary public humiliation of the USA. Otherwise the situation was no different from what it had been since the Cold War ended, and certainly no cause for alarm for the globe's only superpower.[1] Washington announced that September 11 had changed everything, and in doing so, actually *did* change everything, by in effect declaring itself the single-handed protector of a world order and definer of threats against it. Whoever failed to accept this was a potential or actual enemy. This was not unexpected, since the strategies of US global military empire had been in preparation since the late 1980s, indeed by the people who are now applying them. Nevertheless, September 11 proved that we all live in a world with a single global hyperpower that had finally decided that, since the end of the USSR, there are no short-term limits on its strength and no limits on its willingness to use it, although the purposes of using it – except to manifest supremacy – are quite unclear. The twentieth century is over. The twenty-first opens on twilight and obscurity.

There is no better place than a hospital bed, quintessential locus of a captive victim, to reflect on the extraordinary inundation of Orwellian words and images that floods over print and screen at such a time, all of it designed to deceive, conceal and delude, including those who produce it. They ranged from simple lies to the dynamic evasiveness with which diplomats, politicians and generals – and indeed all of us today – fend off public questions that we do not want or are afraid to answer honestly. They ranged from the patently disingenuous, such as the pretence that Sadam Hussein (admittedly an inviting target) must be overthrown because of Iraq's world-threatening 'weapons of mass destruction', to the justifications of US policy by those who should know better, on the grounds that it got rid of Stalinism in the past. That the policy-makers and strategists of Washington are today talking in terms of the purest politics of power – one has only to listen to them off, and sometimes even on, the record – accentuates the sheer effrontery of presenting the establishment of a US global empire as the defensive reaction of a civilization about to be overrun by nameless barbarian horrors unless it destroys 'international terrorism'. But, of course, in the world where the borders between ENRON and the US government are hazy, believing one's own lies, at least at the moment of telling, makes them sound more convincing to others.

As I lay in bed, surrounded by sound and paper, I concluded that the world of 2002 needs historians more than ever, especially sceptical ones. Perhaps reading the perambulations of an old member of the species through his lifetime may assist the young to face the darkening prospects of the twenty-first century not only with the requisite pessimism, but with a clearer eye, a sense of historical memory and a capacity to stand away from current passions and sales pitches.

Here age helps. In itself, it makes me a statistical rarity, since in

1998 the number of human beings in the world aged eighty or above was estimated at 66 millions, which is roughly 1 per cent of the global population. Merely by virtue of long life, the history that belongs to books for others is part of the lives and memories of this tiny minority. For a potential reader just about to enter the age of higher education, that is to say born in the early or middle 1980s, most of the twentieth century belongs to a remote past from which little has survived into actual consciousness except historic costume dramas on film and videotape, and mental images of bits and pieces from the century which, for one reason or another, have become part of collective myth as episodes from the Second World War have become in Britain. Most of it belongs not to life but to the preparation of school examinations. The cold winter day when Adolf Hitler came to power in Berlin, which I remember vividly, is immeasurably distant for twenty-year-olds. The Cuban missile crisis of 1962, during which I married, can have no human meaning in their lives, nor indeed in the lives of many of their parents, since no human being aged forty or less was even born when it occurred. These things are not, as they are for those of my age, part of a chronological succession of events that defines the shape of our private life in a public world, but at best a subject for intellectual understanding, at worst part of an indiscriminate set of things that happened 'before my time'.

Historians of my age are guides to a crucial patch of the past, that other country where they did things differently, because we have lived there. We may not know more about the history of the period than younger colleagues who write about our lifetime in the light of sources not then available to us or, in practice, to anybody. Least of all can we rely on memory, even when age has not eroded it. Unaided by written documentation, it is almost certain to get the facts wrong. On the other hand, we were there, and we know what it felt like, and this gives us a natural immunity to the anachronisms of those who were not.

Living for over eighty years of the twentieth century has been a natural lesson in the mutability of political power, empires and institutions. I have seen the total disappearance of the European colonial empires, not least the greatest of all, the British Empire, never larger and more powerful than in my childhood, when it pioneered the strategy of keeping order in places like Kurdistan and

Afghanistan by aerial bombardment. I have seen great world powers relegated to the minor divisions, the end of a German Empire that expected to last for a thousand years, and of a revolutionary power that expected to last for ever. I am unlikely to see the end of the 'American century', but it is a safe bet that some readers of this book will.

What is more, those who are old have seen the fashions come and go. Since the end of the USSR it has become political orthodoxy and conventional wisdom that there is no alternative to a society of individualist capitalism, and political systems of liberal democracy, which are believed to be organically associated with it, have become the standard form of government almost everywhere. Before 1914 this was also widely believed, though not as widely as today. However, for most of the twentieth century any of these assumptions seemed quite implausible. Capitalism itself seemed on the edge of the abyss. Bizarre as it may seem today, between 1930 and 1960 level-headed observers assumed that the state-commanded economic system of the USSR under the Five-Year Plans, primitive and inefficient as even the most sympathetic visitors could see it was, represented a global alternative model to western 'free enterprise'. There were as few votes in the word 'capitalism' then as in the word 'communism' today. Level-headed observers considered it might actually outproduce it. I am not surprised to find myself once again among a generation that distrusts capitalism, though it no longer believes in our alternative to it.

For someone of my age living through the twentieth century was an absolutely unique lesson in the impact of genuine historical forces. In the thirty years after the Second World War the world and what it was like to live in it changed more rapidly and fundamentally than in any other period of comparable length in human history. Those as old as I in a few countries of the northern hemisphere are the first generation of humans to have actually lived as adults before this extraordinary launch of the spacecraft of collective humanity into orbits of unprecedented social and cultural upheaval, which the world is experiencing today. We are the first generation to have lived through the historic moment when the rules and conventions that had hitherto bound human beings together in families, communities and societies ceased to operate. If you want to know what it was like, only we can tell you. If you think you can go back, we can tell you, it can't be done.

II

Age produces one kind of historical perspective, but I hope my life has helped me to project another: distance. The crucial difference between the historiography of the Cold War – let alone the snake-oil salesmen of the 'war against terrorism' – and that of the Thirty Years' War of the seventeenth century is that (except in Belfast) we are no longer expected to take sides as Catholics or Protestants, or even to take their ideas as seriously as they did. But history needs distance, not only from the passions, emotions, ideologies and fears of our own wars of religion, but from the even more dangerous temptations of 'identity'. History needs mobility and the ability to survey and explore a large territory, that is to say the ability to move beyond one's roots. That is why we cannot be plants, unable to leave their native soil and habitat, because no single habitat or environmental niche can exhaust our subject. Our ideal cannot be the oak or redwood, however majestic, but the migrant bird, at home in arctic and tropic, overflying half the globe. Anachronism and provincialism are two of the deadly sins of history, both equally due to a sheer ignorance of what things are like elsewhere, which even limitless reading and the power of imagination can only rarely overcome. The past remains another country. Its borders can be crossed only by travellers. But (except for those whose way of life is nomadic) travellers are, by definition, people away from their community.

Fortunately, as readers who have followed me so far know, all my life I have belonged to untypical minorities, starting with the enormous advantage of a background in the old Habsburg Empire. Of all the great multi-lingual and multi-territorial empires that collapsed in the course of the twentieth century, the decline and fall of the Emperor Franz Josef's, being both long expected and observed by sophisticated minds, has left us by far the most powerful literary or narrative chronicle. Austrian minds had time to reflect on the death and disintegration of their empire, while it struck all the other empires suddenly, at least by the measure of the historical clock, even those in visibly declining health, like the Soviet Union. But perhaps the perceived and accepted multi-linguality, multi-confessionality and multi-culturality of the monarchy helped them to a more complex sense of historical perspective. Its subjects lived simultaneously in different social universes and different historical epochs. Moravia at the end of the nineteenth century was the background to Gregor Mendel's genetics, Sigmund Freud's *Interpretation of Dreams* and Leoš Janáček's *Jenufa*. I recall the occasion, some time in the 1970s, when I found myself in Mexico City at an international round table on Latin American peasant movements, and suddenly became aware of the fact that four of the five experts who made up the panel had been born in Vienna . . .

But even beyond this I recognize myself in E. M. Forster's phrase about C. P. Cavafy, the anglophone Greek poet from my native Alexandria, who 'stood at a slight angle to the universe'. For the historian, as for the photographer, this is a good way to stand.

For most of my life this has been my situation: typecast from a birth in Egypt, which has no practical bearing on my life-history, as someone from elsewhere. I have been attached to and felt at home in several countries and seen something of many others. However, in all of them, including the one into whose citizenship I was born, I have been, not necessarily an outsider, but someone who does not wholly belong to where he finds himself, whether as an Englishman among the central Europeans, a continental immigrant in Britain, a Jew everywhere – even, indeed particularly, in Israel – an anti-specialist in a world of specialists, a polyglot cosmopolitan, an intellectual whose politics and academic work were devoted to the non-intellectual, even, for much of my life, an anomaly among communists, themselves a minority of political humanity in the countries I have known. This has complicated my life as a private human being, but it has been a professional asset for the historian.

This has made it easy to resist what Pascal called 'the reasons of the heart of which reason knows nothing', namely emotional identification with some obvious or chosen group. As identity is defined against someone else, it implies not identifying with the other. It leads to disaster. That is exactly why in-group history written only for the group ('identity history') – black history for blacks, queer history for homosexuals, feminist history for women only, or any kind of in-group ethnic or nationalist history – cannot be satisfactory as history, even when it is more than a politically slanted version of an ideological sub-section of the wider identity group. No identity group, however large, is alone in the world; the world cannot be changed to suit it alone, nor can the past.

This is particularly urgent at the beginning of the new century, in the aftermath of the end of the short twentieth century. As old regimes disintegrate, old forms of politics fade away and new states multiply, the manufacture of new histories to suit new regimes, states, ethnic movements and identity groups becomes a global industry. As the human hunger for continuity with the past grows in an era designed as a continuous break with the past, the media society feeds it by inventing its versions of a box-office national history, 'heritage' and theme parks in ancient fancy dress. And even in democracies where authoritarian power no longer controls what can be said about past and present, the joint force of pressure groups, the threat of headlines, unfavourable publicity or even public hysteria impose evasion, silence and the public self-censorship of 'political correctness'. Even today (2002) there is shock when a consistently anti-Nazi German writer of notable moral courage, Günther Grass, chooses as the subject of a novel the tragedy of a sinking ship filled with German refugees fleeing from the advancing Red Army in the last stages of the Second World War.

III

The test of a historian's life is whether he or she can ask and answer questions, especially 'what if' questions, about the matters of passionate significance to themselves and the world, as though they were journalists reporting things long past – and yet, not as a stranger but as one deeply involved. These are not questions about *real* history, which is not about what we might like, but about what happened, and could perhaps have happened otherwise but did not. They are questions about the present not the past, which is why they are important to those who live at the start of the new century, old or young. The First World War was not avoided, so the question whether it could have been is academic. If we say its casualties were intolerable (as most people agree) or that the German Europe that would have emerged from the Kaiser's victory might have been a better proposition than the world of Versailles (as I hold), I am not suggesting it could have been different. And yet, I must fail the test, were I asked such a question even in theory about the Second World War. I can, with enormous effort, envisage the argument that Spain might have been better off if Franco's coup had succeeded in 1936, avoiding the Civil War. I am prepared to concede, with regret, that Lenin's Comintern was not such a good idea nor – this time without difficulty, for I was never a Zionist – Theodor Herzl's project of a Jewish nation state. He would have done better to stay with the *Neue Freie Presse* as its star columnist. But if you ask me to entertain the proposition that the defeat of National Socialism was not worth the 50 million dead and the uncounted horrors of the Second World War, I simply could not. I look forward to an American world empire, whose long-term chances are poor, with more fear and less enthusiasm than I look back on the record of the old British Empire, run by a country whose modest size protected it against megalomania. What marks have I got in the test? If they are too low, then this book will not give readers much help as they go into the new century, mostly with a longer life ahead of them than the author.

Still, let us not disarm, even in unsatisfactory times. Social injustice still needs to be denounced and fought. The world will not get better on its own.

Notes

1. Overture

1. This and the following paragraphs are based on my mother's letters to her sister during May 1915.

2. A Child in Vienna

1. I deliberately use the German names of these places since these were the ones we used, though all towns of any size in most of the empire had two or three names.
2. Nelly Hobsbaum to her sister Gretl, letter dated 23 March 1925.
3. Nelly Hobsbaum to her sister Gretl, letter dated 5 December 1928.

4. Berlin: Weimar Dies

1. James V. Bryson, *My Life with Laemmle* (Facto Books, London, 1980), pp. 56–7. Drinkwater had so little sense of Hollywood that he did the job for less than half what Laemmle's agent was authorized to offer.
2. Most of the information about the school in the following pages is based on Heinz Stallmann (ed.), *Das Prinz-Heinrichs-Gymnasium zu Schöneberg, 1890–1945. Geschichte einer Schule* (privately printed, Berlin, 1965?), my own memories and those of Fritz Lustig.
3. In 1929 the school had 388 Protestant, 48 Catholic, 35 Jewish and 6 other pupils. Stallmann, *op. cit.*, p. 47.
4. Mimi Brown to Ernestine Grün, letter dated 3 December 1931, announcing her plans to leave England – for Ragusa (Dubrovnik)? For Berlin?

5. Berlin: Brown and Red

1. Stephan Hermlin, *Abendlicht* (Leipzig, 1979), pp. 32, 35, 52.
2. Karl Corino, 'Dichtung in eigener Sache', *Die Zeit*, 4 October 1996, pp. 9–11.
3. Heinz Stallmann (ed.), *Das Prinz-Heinrichs-Gymnasium zu Schöneberg. 1890–1945. Geschichte einer Schule* (privately printed, Berlin, 1965?) provides no information, except one mention of 'Leder' in a list of fellow-pupils of 1926–35 by a contributor who graduated in 1935.
4. My information comes from Felix Krolokowski, 'Erinnerungen: Kommunistische Schülerbewegung in der Weimarer Republik', a text which I was given, possibly by the author, during a visit to Leipzig in 1996.
5. *Kommunistische Pennäler Fraktion* ('Pennäler' = secondary-school students, from the schoolboy slang 'Penne' = secondary school).
6. *Tagebuch*, 17 March 1935.

6. On the Island

1. *Tagebuch*, 8–11 November 1934. Much of this chapter is based on the material in this diary, which I kept from 10 April 1934 to 9 January 1936.
2. *Tagebuch*, 16 June 1935 and 17 August 1935.
3. See the social analysis of the British jazz-lovers in my *The Jazz Scene* (London, 1959; New York, 1993).
4. Josef Skvorecky, *The Bass Saxophone* (London, 1978).
5. Luckily for them, my first attempt to contact a Party branch, somewhere on the outskirts of Croydon, discovered from advertisements in the *Daily Worker*, had been abortive. I happened to land on a small group of critical comrades who listened with interest to my account of the last Party demonstration in Berlin, but insisted that the triumph of Hitler indicated errors by the KPD or perhaps even the Comintern. I could not answer them, but felt that being recruited to a unit criticizing the generals might not be the best way of rejoining the army of the world revolution. Not that the 5,000 or so British communists were much of an army compared to the German Communist Party of 1932.
6. *Tagebuch*, 4 June 1935: 'Today I happen to look at Mama's 1929 letters to me. She calls me "darling". I am astonished and vaguely disturbed that it is so long since anyone called me that, and try to imagine how it would be today if someone used the word.'
7. *Tagebuch*, 12 July 1935.

8. Louise London, *Whitehall and the Jews 1933–1948: British Immigration Policy and the Holocaust* (Cambridge, 2001), cited in Neal Ascherson, 'The Remains of der Tag', *New York Review of Books*, 29 March 2001, p. 44.

7. Cambridge

1. Michael Straight, *After Long Silence* (London, 1983).
2. E. Hobsbawm and T. H. Ranger (eds), *The Invention of Tradition* (Cambridge University Press, in the 'Past & Present' Series, 1983). The book has remained in print since the original publication.
3. I am quoting what I wrote in 1937 about the celebrated English don George ('Dadie') Rylands (*Granta*, 10 November 1937).
4. T. E. B. Howarth, *Cambridge Between the Wars* (London, 1978), p. 172.
5. *Financial Times*, The Business weekend magazine, 4 March 2000, p. 18.
6. I recorded this figure in 'Cambridge Cameo: Ties with the Past: Ryder and Amies' by E.J.H. and J.H.D. (my friend Jack Dodd) in *Granta*, 26 May 1937.
7. My description of a Sheppard lecture in 1937 is quoted in Howarth, *op. cit.*, p. 162.
8. E.J.H., 'Professor Trevelyan Lectures', *Granta*, 27 October 1937.
9. H. S. Ferns, *Reading from Left to Right: One Man's Political History*, Foreword by Malcolm Muggeridge (University of Toronto Press, 1983), p. 114.

8. Against Fascism and War

1. *Cambridge University Club Bulletin*, 18 October 1938.
2. 'The membership of the CUSC is still not much over 450', Weekly Bulletin of the Cambridge University Socialist Club No. 2, Autumn term 1936 (duplicated).
3. *Spain Week Bulletin No. 1*, n.d. (October 1938).
4. H. S. Ferns, *Reading from Left to Right: One Man's Political History*, Foreword by Malcolm Muggeridge (University of Toronto Press, 1983), p. 116.
5. *CUSC Weekly Bulletin*, 25 May 1937.
6. *CUSC Faculty and Study Groups Bulletin*, Lent Term, 1939.
7. Eric Hobsbawm, 'In Defence of the Thirties' in Jim Philip, John Simpson and Nicholas Snowman (eds), *The Best of Granta 1889–1966* (London, 1967), p. 119.

8. H. S. Ferns, *op.cit.*, p. 113.

9. Yuri Modin, *My Five Cambridge Friends* (London, 1994), pp. 100–101.

9. Being Communist

1. Alessandro Bellassai, 'Il Caffè Dell' Unità. Pubblico e Privato nella Famiglia Comunista degli Anni 50', *Società e Storia* XXII, No. 84, 1999, pp. 327–8.

2. Anthony Read and David Fisher, *Operation Lucy: Most Secret Spy Ring of the Second World War* (London, 1980), pp. 204–5.

3. Theodor Prager, *Zwischen London und Moskau: Bekenntnisse eines Revisionisten* (Vienna, 1975), pp. 56–7.

4. E. J. Hobsbawm, *Primitive Rebels* (Manchester, 1959), pp. 60–62.

5. Julius Braunthal, *In Search of the Millennium* (London, 1945), p. 39.

6. Agnes Heller, *Der Affe auf dem Fahrrad* (Berlin–Vienna, 1999), pp. 91–2.

7. How scarce real information in these fields was before the Cold War and how sceptically it was received by the eminent medieval numismatist who compiled it can be seen from Philip Grierson, *Books on Soviet Russia 1917–1942: A Bibliography and a Guide to Reading* (London, 1943).

8. Quoted in P. Malvezzi and G. Pirelli (eds), *Lettere di Condannati a Morte della Resistenza Europea* (Turin, 1954), p. 250. The name as transcribed in the book. 'Feuerlich' should probably be 'Feuerlicht'.

9. Zdenek Mlynař, Postscript to Leopold Spira, *Kommunismus Adieu: Eine ideologische Autobiographie* (Vienna, 1992), p. 158.

10. Fritz Klein, *Drinnen und Draussen: Ein Historiker in der DDR Erinnerungen* (Frankfurt-am-Main, 2000), pp. 169, 213.

11. Charles S. Maier, *Dissolution: The Crisis of Communism and the End of East Germany* (Princeton, 1997), p. 20.

12. Ibid., pp. 28–9.

10. War

1. Ian Kershaw, *Hitler* (London, 2001), vol. II, p. 302.

2. Ibid., p. 298.

3. Theodor Prager, *Zwischen London und Moskau: Bekenntnisse eines Revisionisten* (Vienna, 1975), p. 59.

4. Joseph R. Starobin, *American Communism in Crisis, 1943–1957* (Cambridge, MA, 1972), p. 55.

11. Cold War

1. Peter Hennessy, *The Secret State: Whitehall and the Cold War* (London, 2002), chapter 1.
2. In any case, if any such problem impinged on British politics immediately, it was not Soviet but American behaviour, namely the ruthless terms on which Washington made dependent the grant of its 1946 loan to Britain. (See R. Skidelsky, *Keynes*, vol. III.)
3. It included Bernard Floud, who was later hounded into suicide as a suspected spy or recruiter of Soviet spies by the security services. (He was found dead by his son, Roderick Floud, an economic historian who later became my colleague at Birkbeck, and is now head of the London Guildhall University.) Ironically, as he told me, the CP functionary David Springhall had once tried to recruit him as an agent, and he had told him he had no authority to do so. In any case it is unlikely that a man who attended Party branch meetings after the war was engaged in the kind of activity which usually implied breaking contact with the Party.
4. On the day in August 1947 I went there I estimated the number of travellers to the 'green frontier' at *c*. 500, of travellers back at *c*. 7–800. There were then three trains a day.
5. The words of a British prisoner of war, escaped from a camp in Poland, who fought his way back with the advancing Red Army. I owe the citation to George Barnsby of Wolverhampton.
6. Professor Reinhard Koselleck.
7. See Eric Hobsbawm, *The Age of Extremes* (paperback), p. 189.
8. Its title *For a Lasting Peace and a People's Democracy* [*sic*] was usually shortened to 'Forfor'. It disappeared from sight in 1956.
9. R. W. Johnson, 'Do they eat people here much still? Rarement. Très rarement', *London Review of Books*, 14 December 2000, pp. 30–31. Hodgkin, whose heart was in the Third World, abandoned the delegacy during his travels in Africa, whither he had gone to extend its work. He returned to Oxford in the 1960s as a Fellow of Balliol College, which also elected the dean of Marxist historians, Christopher Hill, as Master. His widow, the Nobel Laureate (Chemistry) Dorothy Hodgkin, continued the family tradition, for in 1984 I found myself with her on a visit of solidarity to Bir Zeit University, in the Israeli-occupied West Bank of Palestine.
10. 'Academic Freedom' in *University Newsletter*, Cambridge, November 1953, p. 2. I edited and wrote most of the ten issues of this Newsletter, 'published on behalf of a group of Communist graduates by the Cambridge

Communist Party' (i.e. the Graduate branch of the CP) which appeared between October 1951 and November 1954.

11. I am grateful to Nina Fishman for the relevant documents from the BBC archives, Controller, Talks to D.S.W., 20 September 1950 and G.22/48 circulated on 13 March 1948, THE TREATMENT OF COMMUNISM AND COMMUNIST SPEAKERS, NOTE BY THE DIRECTOR OF THE SPOKEN WORD. The Director appears to have regarded the famous physicist, later Nobel Laureate and President of the Royal Society, P. M. S. Blackett, as a communist, presumably because of his hostility to nuclear warfare.

12. The guinea, a notional currency unit of £1 1s, was a convenient way for shopkeepers to charge more. It disappeared with the decimalization of the currency.

13. W. C. Lubenow, *The Cambridge Apostles 1820–1914: Imagination and Friendship in British Intellectual and Professional Life* (Cambridge, 1998).

14. Alan Ryan, 'The Voice from the Hearth-Rug', *London Review of Books*, 28 October 1999, p. 19.

15. Hans-Ulrich Wehler, *Historisches Denken am Ende des 20. Jahrhunderts (1945–2000)* (Göttingen, 2001) pp. 29–30.

16. Robert Conquest's pioneering *The Great Terror* was not published until 1968.

17. See Hennessy, *op. cit.*, p. 30.

12. Stalin and After

1. Ken Coates, 'How not to Reappraise the New Left' in Ralph Miliband and John Saville (eds), *The Socialist Register* (Merlin Press, London, 1976), p. 112.

2. Thus in the rules of the British CP the right of members to take part in the 'formation of policy' had been changed into the mere right to its 'discussion'.

3. Aldo Agosti, *Palmiro Togliatti* (Milan, 1996); Felix Tchouev, *Conversations avec Molotov; 140 Entretiens avec le Bras Droit de Staline* (Paris, 1995); Robert Levy, *Anna Pauker: The Rise and Fall of a Jewish Communist* (Berkeley, 2000); K. Morgan, *Harry Pollitt* (Manchester, 1993).

4. Letter from E. J. Hobsbawm, *World News*, 26 January 1957, p. 62.

5. See Eric Hobsbawm, 'The Historians' Group of the Communist Party' in M. Cornforth (ed.), *Rebels and Their Causes: Essays in Honour of A. L. Morton* (London, 1978), p. 42.

6. Francis Becket, *Enemy Within: The Rise and Fall of the British Communist Party* (London, 1995), p. 139.

7. It may be useful to cite the main part of this document. Here it is:

> All of us have for many years advocated Marxist ideas both in our special fields and in political discussion in the Labour movement. We feel therefore that we have a responsibility to express our views as Marxists in the present crisis of international socialism.
>
> We feel that the uncritical support given by the Executive Committee of the Communist Party to the Soviet action in Hungary is the undesirable culmination of years of distortion of fact, and failure by British Communists to think out political problems for themselves. We had hoped that the revelations made at the Twentieth Congress of the Communist Party of the Soviet Union would have made our leadership and press realise that Marxist ideas will only be acceptable in the British Labour movement if they arise from the truth about the world we live in.
>
> The exposure of grave crimes and abuses in the USSR and the recent revolt of workers and intellectuals against the pseudo-Communist bureaucracies and police systems of Poland and Hungary, have shown that for the past twelve years we have based our political analyses on a false presentation of the facts – not an out-of-date theory, for we still consider the Marxist method to be correct.
>
> If the left-wing and Marxist trend in our Labour movement is to win support, as it must for the achievement of socialism, this past must be utterly repudiated. This includes the repudiation of the latest outcome of this evil past, the Executive Committee's underwriting of the current errors of Soviet policy.

Sent to *Daily Worker* on 18 November 1956; published in the *New Statesman* and *Tribune* on 1 December 1956.

8. Eric Hobsbawm, 'The Historians' Group of the Communist Party' in Cornforth, *op. cit.*, p. 41.

9. Andrew Thorpe, *The British Communist Party and Moscow 1920–1943* (Manchester, 2000), pp. 238–41.

10. Henry Pelling, *The British Communist Party: A Historical Profile* (London, 1958).

11. See chapter 1, 'Problems of Communist History', of my *Revolutionaries* (London, 1973).

12. See my Memoir of him in *Proceedings of the British Academy* 90 (1995), pp. 524–5.

13. Ibid., p. 539.

14. A recent version may be found in my book (with Antonio Pollito) *The New Century* (London, 2000), on pp. 158–61.

13. Watershed

1. Tony Gould, *Insider Outsider: The Life and Times of Colin MacInnes* (London, 1983), p. 183.
2. *Chambers Biographical Dictionary* (1974 edn), art.: Darwin.
3. Francis Newton, *The Jazz Scene* (London, 1959), Introduction, p. 1.
4. It was published in the USA in 1960 by a small left-wing publishing house, republished in an updated edition by Penguin Books in 1961, and subsequently translated into French for a series edited by Fernand Braudel, into Italian and into Czech.

14. Under Cnicht

1. Richard Haslam in *Country Life*, 21 July 1983, p. 131.
2. As I write this chapter, my son Andy tells me for the first time of the occasion, presumably in the 1970s, when, after two other Croesor boys had left them, his friend told him apologetically: 'The others told me to beat you up, but I don't want to. Could you pretend I did, when they show up?' Even so, the friendship faded as the mother made him increasingly unwelcome in the farm.

15. The Sixties

1. For my contemporary judgement of the May events, see 'May 1968', written later that year in E. J. Hobsbawm, *Revolutionaries* (London, 1999, and earlier editions), chapter 24.
2. *MAGNUM PHOTOS: 1968 Magnum Throughout the World*, texts by Eric Hobsbawm and Marc Weitzmann (Paris, 1998).
3. I did not consciously note this at the time, but the point is well taken by Yves Pagès, who has edited the complete record of the graffiti in the Sorbonne, collected and preserved by five university employees at the time. See *No Copyright. Sorbonne 1968: Graffiti* (Editions verticales, 1998), p. 11.
4. Quoted in H. Stuart Hughes, *Sophisticated Rebels* (Cambridge, MA and London, 1988), p. 6.

5. Alain Touraine, *Le Mouvement de Mai ou le Communisme Utopique* (Paris, 1968).

6. Eric J. Hobsbawm, *Les Primitifs de la Révolte dans l'Europe Moderne* (Paris, 1966).

7. This article is chapter 22 in my *Revolutionaries: Contemporary Essays* (London, 1973, and various editions since).

8. Sheila Rowbotham, *Promise of a Dream* (London, 2000), pp. 118, 203–4, 208.

9. Ibid., p. 203.

10. Ibid., p. 196.

11. Carlo Feltrinelli, *Senior Service* (Milan, 1999), p. 314.

12. Rowbotham, *op. cit.*, p. 196.

13. *New Left Review*, 1977.

16. A Watcher in Politics

1. Martin Jacques and Francis Mulhern (eds), *The Forward March of Labour Halted?* (London, 1981); Eric Hobsbawm, *Politics for a Rational Left* (London, 1989).

2. 'Labour's Lost Millions', written after the 1983 British General Election, in Hobsbawm, *Politics for a Rational Left*, p. 63.

3. Ibid., p. 65.

4. 'Out of the Wilderness' (October 1987), *Politics for a Rational Left*, p. 207.

5. *Marxism Today*, April 1985, pp. 21–36 and cover.

6. Geoff Mulgan in *Marxism Today*, November–December 1998 (Special Issue), pp. 15–16.

7. Leader in *Marxism Today*, September 1991, p. 3.

8. Eric Hobsbawm, *The Age of Extremes* (UK paperback edition), pp. 481, 484.

9. 'After the Fall' in R. Blackburn (ed.), *After the Fall, the Failure of Communism and the Future of Socialism* (London, 1991), pp. 122–3.

17. Among the Historians

1. For the substance of the following paragraphs, see also Eric Hobsbawm, '75 Years of the Economic History Society: Some Reflections' in Pat Hudson (ed.), *Living Economic and Social History: Essays to Mark the 75th Anniversary of the Economic History Society* (Glagow, 2001), pp. 136–40.

2. Information from Professor Zvi Razi, Postan's biographer, to whom, as well as to the late Isaiah Berlin and Chimen Abramsky, I also owe the data about his early life.

3. IX Congrès International des Sciences Historiques: Paris 28 Aôut–3 Septembre 1950, vol. II, Actes (Paris, 1951), p. v.

4. Professor Van Dillen of Amsterdam, in ibid., p. 142.

5. Jacques Le Goff in *Past & Present* 100, August 1983, p. 15.

6. Hans-Ulrich Wehler, *Historisches Denken am Ende des 20. Jahrhunderts: 1945–2000* (Göttingen, 2001), pp. 29, 30.

7. *Daedalus: Journal of the American Academy of Arts and Sciences* (Winter 1971), 'Historical Studies Today'. The French contributors, all linked to the Braudel empire, were Jacques Le Goff, François Furet and Pierre Goubert, the British – two of them linked to *Past & Present* – were Lawrence Stone, Moses Finley and myself, the US ones mainly had links with Princeton and included Robert Darnton and the only specialist on a non-western region, Benjamin Schwarz of Harvard.

8. Ibid., p. 24.

9. For Braudel: his obituary in *Annales*, 1986 n. 1; for my own inaugural lecture: Eric Hobsbawm, *On History* (London, 1997), p. 64.

10. In Clifford Geertz, *The Interpretation of Cultures* (New York, 1973).

11. Lawrence Stone, 'The Revival of Narrative', *Past & Present* 85, November 1979, pp. 9, 21.

12. Carlo Ginzburg, *Il formaggio ed I vermi* [The cheese and the worms] (Turin, 1976). Curiously enough, though it was reviewed (by me) in the *TLS* ten years earlier, the more interesting, in my opinion, study of a case of beneficent witches, *I Benandanti*, had not then attracted attention.

13. See chapter 21 of my *On History* (London, 1997), originally published as 'The Historian Between the Quest for the Universal and the Quest for Identity'.

14. Pierre Bourdieu, *Choses Dites* (Paris, 1987), p. 38.

18. In the Global Village

1. Noel Annan, *Our Age* (London, 1990), p. 267 n.

2. The *Estado*, the local *Times*, wrote of a 'a packed auditorium . . ., ending with enthusiastic and prolonged applause', *Estado de São Paulo*, 28 May 1975.

3. Julio Caro Baroja, quoted in E. J. Hobsbawm, *The Age of Extremes* (London, 1995), p. 1.

19. Marseillaise

1. See the biography of this remarkable figure by Annie Kriegel and S. Courtois, *Eugen Fried: Le Grand Secret du PCF* (Paris, 1997). The relative roles of Moscow and Paris in the genesis of the Popular Front have been much discussed, but it now seems clear that its real innovation, the readiness by communists to extend the so-called 'United Front' from other socialists to frankly non-socialist Liberals, and eventually to all antifascists, however opposed to communism, originated in France.

2. Hervé Hamon and Patrick Rotman, *Les Intellocrates: Expédition en Haute Intelligentsia* (Paris, 1981), p. 330.

3. On the French Revolution, see my *Echoes of the Marseillaise: Two Centuries Look Back on the French Revolution* (Rutgers, 1990) and 'Histoire et Illusion' in *Le Débat* 89, March–April 1996, pp. 128–38.

20. From Franco to Berlusconi

1. *Primitive Rebels: Studies in Archaic Forms of Social Movement in the Nineteenth and Twentieth Centuries* (Manchester University Press, 1959).

2. E. J. Hobsbawm, *Revolutionaries: Contemporary Essays* (London, 1973), 'Reflections on Anarchism', p. 84.

3. Gerald Brenan, *The Spanish Labyrinth: an Account of the Social and Political Background of the Spanish Civil War* (Cambridge, 1943), Preface. For obvious reasons the first edition, published during the Second World War, attracted little notice.

4. The results are in chapter 5 of *Primitive Rebels* and chapter 8 of *Bandits* (1968).

5. These form the basis for the present account of my first visit.

6. 'Franco in Retreat', *New Statesman and Nation*, 14 April 1951, p. 415. This article, which I wrote on my return, was described as 'some extracts from the notebook of an Englishman in Barcelona'.

7. E. J. Hobsbawm, *Primitive Rebels* (1959 edn), Preface, p. v.

8. For a biography of this lifelong militant (1900–1973), 'always one of the most esteemed leaders of the Communist Federazione of Palermo', see the article 'Sala, Michele' in Franco Andreucci and Tommaso Detti (eds), *Il movimento operaio italiano: dizionario biografico*, vol. 4 (Rome, 1978).

9. 'The vast bulk of scholarly and sensible literature about Mafia appeared

between 1890 and 1910, and the comparative dearth of modern analyses is much to be deplored', *Primitive Rebels*, p. 31, fn 3.

10. Giorgio Napolitano and Eric Hobsbawm, *Intervista sul PCI* (Bari, 1975).

21. Third World

1. E. J. Hobsbawm, 'The Revolutionary Situation in Colombia', *The World Today* (Royal Institute of International Affairs), June 1963, p. 248.

2. Andres Villaveces, 'A Comparative Statistical Note on Homicide Rates in Colombia' in Charles Bergquist, Ricardo Peñaranda and Gonzalo Sanchez G. (eds), *Violence in Colombia 1990–2000: Waging War and Negotiating Peace* (Wilmington, Delaware, 2001), pp. 275–80.

3. Monsignor G. Guzman, Orlando Fals Borda and E. Umana Luna, *La Violencia en Colombia* 2 vols (Bogotá, 1962, 1964).

4. Eduardo Pizarro Leongomez, *Las FARC (1949–1966): De la Autodefensa a la Combinación de Todas las Formas de Lucha* (Bogotá, 1991), p. 57.

5. E. J. Hobsbawm, *Rebeldes Primitivos* (Barcelona, 1968), p. 226.

6. E. J. Hobsbawm, 'Guerrillas in Latin America' in J. Saville and R. Miliband (eds), *The Socialist Register*, 1970, pp. 51–63; E. J. Hobsbawm 'Guerrillas' in Colin Harding and Christopher Roper (eds), *Latin American Review of Books I* (London, 1973), pp. 79–88.

7. See my 'What's New in Peru' and 'Peru: The Peculiar "Revolution"' in *New York Review of Books*, 21 May 1970 and 16 December 1971.

8. E. J. Hobsbawm, 'Chile: Year One' in *New York Review of Books*, 23 September 1971.

9. *International Herald Tribune* and Pew Center Poll of 'opinion leaders', *International Herald Tribune*, 20 December 2001, p. 6.

22. From FDR to Bush

1. This was close enough to the truth, but not literally correct. I am pretty sure that some of the teachers in the Graduate Faculty of the New School for Social Research in New York, where I was later to teach, continued to advertise their Marxism.

2. P. A. Baran and E. J. Hobsbawm, 'The Stages of Economic Growth' in *KYKLOS*, vol. XIV, 1961, Fasc. 2, pp. 234–42.

3. See F. Ianni and E. Reuss-Ianni, *A Family Business: Kinships and Social Control in Organized Crime* (New York, 1972).

4. E. J. Hobsbawm, 'The Economics of the Gangster' in *The Quarterly Review*, No. 604, April 1955, pp. 243–56.
5. Quoted in S. Chapple and R. Garofalo, *Rock'n'Roll is Here to Pay: The History and Politics of the Music Industry* (Chicago, 1977), p. 251.
6. Studs Terkel, *Division Street: America* (New York, 1967).
7. Eric J. Hobsbawm, *Intervista sul Nuovo Secolo a Cura di Antonio Polito* (Bari, 1999), p. 165.

23. Coda

1. See my summary of the world situation published in *The Age of Extremes* eight years earlier (paperback edition), chapter XIX, 'Towards the Millennium', especially pp. 558–62.

Index

Significant information in notes is indexed in the form 424n11:3, ie. page 424, chapter 11, note 3

433